D0908241

The Broadcast 41

The Broadcast 41

Women and the Anti-Communist Blacklist

Carol A. Stabile

Published in 2018 by Goldsmiths Press
Goldsmiths, University of London, New Cross
London SE14 6NW

Printed and bound by Sheridan, USA
Distribution by the MIT Press
Cambridge, Massachusetts, and London, England

A CIP record for this book is available from the British Library

ISBN 978 1 906897 86 4 (hbk)
ISBN 978 1 906897 87 1 (ebk)

www.gold.ac.uk/goldsmiths-press

[T]here are always those that will supply you with speeches of their own, and put them right into your mouth for you too; and that sort are like the magicians who can throw their voice, at fairs and shows, and you are just their wooden doll.

Margaret Atwood, *Alias Grace*

Fellow citizens: I am not indifferent to the claims of a generous forgetfulness, but whatever else I may forget, I shall never forget the difference between those who fought for liberty and those who fought for slavery; between those who fought to save the Republic and those who fought to destroy it.

Frederick Douglass, *The Essential Douglas*

Contents

Acknowledgments

Most of this book was written before sunrise, at my kitchen table in Eugene, Oregon. That table was held up by invisible networks of resistance, comfort, and delight. I am grateful to the many people whose hands made this work possible.

Some of the preliminary thinking and research for this book appeared in essays published elsewhere: " 'The Typhoid Marys of the Left': Gender, Race, and the Broadcast Blacklist," *Communication and Critical/Cultural Studies* 8 (Fall 2011, pp. 266–85) and " 'We Can Remember It for You Wholesale': Lessons of the Broadcast Blacklist," in *Moment of Danger: Critical Communication History*, ed. Janice Peck and Inger Stole (Milwaukee, WI: Marquette University Press, pp. 105–32).

Librarians and archivists around the United States made this book possible. At the University of Oregon's Special Collections and University Archives, Linda Long's commitment to preserving writing and other materials created by women and her assistance in navigating the university's incredible holdings on feminist science fiction gave me a new appreciation of the importance of women writers' networks with one another and of the unsung labor of those people—often women as well—who preserve these materials and make them available to scholars and students. I am grateful to Sarah M. Hutcheon, Lynda Leahy, and Caitlin Stevens at the Schlesinger Library who set me off in the right direction at an early point in my research, and to Diana Carey, who helped with access to images. The American Heritage Center staff carried more boxes back and forth for me than I could count over the course of a short but (thanks to their work) highly productive visit. Although I never visited the Wisconsin Historical Society in Madison, Wisconsin in person, they reliably delivered Vera Caspary's papers to Milwaukee, where I had time to read them and still pick my child up after school. The staff at the Nightingale Library at Syracuse University helped me access Gertrude Berg's papers. Library of Congress staff assisted with Ruth Gordon's and Garson Kanin's papers, Mary Margaret McBride's papers, Margaret Webster's papers, and the Federal Theatre Project holdings. Chamisa Redmond Nash fielded questions by email and telephone about Shirley Graham's Federal Theatre production of *Sambo* and Melissa Lindberg assisted me in locating photographs in Ruth Gordon's papers. Mary Huelsbeck at the Wisconsin Center for Film and Theater Research found a copy of Joan Scott's autobiography at the eleventh hour and helped me with images for the book as well. Laura Beth Schnitker at the University of Maryland's Special Collections and University Archives also provided generous last-minute assistance with images. Matthew S. Darby and staff at the Booth Family Center for Special Collections of the Lauinger Library at Georgetown University guided me through Lisa Sergio's holdings.

Archivists at the National Archives and Records Administration helped me with requests for dozens of FBI files over the years: thank you to Jennifer Blakslee, Rebecca Calcagno, Christina Jones, Laurel Macondray, and Noah Shankin. My chapters on the FBI and the American Business Consultants would not have been possible without the groundbreaking work of researchers who have painstakingly documented the FBI's war on dissent, including literary scholars William Maxwell and Mary Helen Washington; journalists Betty Medsger and Seth Rosenfeld; and anthropologist David Price. David in particular was unstintingly generous in sharing his vast knowledge of the inner workings of the FBI, fielding my many queries over the years with patience and humor.

Many other people helped me connect some of the dots of this complicated story. After coming across letters in archives that he had written to people listed in *Red Channels*, one of my research assistants tracked down scholar Allen Mussehl. Allen opened his personal archive to me and helped me think about *Red Channels* and its legacies. He exemplifies the fighting spirit of the people I have had the privilege to spend the last decade researching and writing about.

Margaret Bauer, actress Jean Muir's daughter, met with me on a warm spring day in Arizona to talk about a painful period in her family's history. Margaret and her brothers David and Michael Jaffe gave me access to their mother's papers. Talking to David's daughter Catherine Jaffe after the election of Donald Trump (she happened to be a senior at the University of Oregon at the time) reminded me of how relevant the stories of women like her grandmother remain and gave me new determination to finish the book.

Author Julie Phillips generously shared writer Alice Sheldon's unpublished essay about 1950s-style misogyny. Her brilliant biography of Sheldon (aka science fiction author James Tiptree, Jr.) painted a vivid picture of what it was like to be an ambitious, creative woman at the start of the Cold War. Cynthia Meyers shared research on the blacklist in advertising that changed how I thought about the relationship between advertisers and the television industry. I am also grateful to Paul Buhle and Patrick McGilligan for helping me locate a copy of Joan Scott's autobiography. Dana Polan gave me the incredibly generous gift of his time, reading and offering feedback on not one, but two drafts of this book.

Students were the lifeblood of this project. Many of them, like Ruth Kaplan, cheered me up and on. Others worked as research assistants, tracking down sources, compiling bibliographies, finding articles, and putting together materials so that I could hit the ground reading and writing during the summer months. I am grateful to Sarah Mick (University of Wisconsin-Milwaukee (UWM)) and Stephanie Schuessler and Janine Zajac (University of Pittsburgh), who worked with me as I made my way through the thicket of the Broadcast 41's lives in the early days of this project. Eric Lohman and Zach Sell, then brilliant undergraduates at the University of Wisconsin-Milwaukee, helped field my requests with enthusiasm and aplomb and then hunted down additional sources on their own. Without Mary Erickson's unflagging cheer and diligence, the book's sources would not have been half as rich as they are. Andrea Herrera was a terrific researcher and assistant at a later stage of this project, juggling the multiple strands of this project with ease and competence. Matthew Eichner, Younsong Lee, and Laura Strait provided valuable additional support. Jeremiah Favara helped me lay the groundwork for the website for this project by researching and drafting biographies for some of the Broadcast 41.

Graduate students I have had the privilege to work with in other capacities have provided vast reservoirs of intellectual companionship and uplift, long after they defended their theses and dissertations and went out into the world. Aimee-Marie Dorsten's work on forgotten women academics gave me sharp new insight into the broad spheres of cultural and intellectual activity from which women's names have been erased. Conversations with Allen Larson about female stardom and the suppression of women and queer people's work in media industries moved my thinking forward in powerful and abiding ways. Heather Fisher's dissertation on the quiz show scandal advanced my own thinking about the 1950s. Kelly Happe's, Melody Hoffmann's, and Michelle Rodino-Colocino's commitments to social change of the kind that the Broadcast 41 advocated for made me even more committed to telling the story of what happened to them. And Phoebe Bronstein, Sarah Hamid, Shehram Mokhtar, and Whitney Phillips all discussed ideas that made their way into this book. Avery Dame-Griff ably copy-edited this manuscript, talking me down off some ledges, gently pointing out many interminable sentences (the remaining are all my fault), and catching errors that had become invisible to my impatient eyes.

Presentations I gave at several universities and libraries significantly sharpened my ideas. I thank audiences of faculty members, graduate students, and undergraduates at the Ohio State University, Indiana University, the University of Oregon, Connecticut College, and the University of Maryland, as well as participants on panels at the National Women's Studies Association conference and the International Communication Association's conference. These experiences shaped my thinking about this project in significant and game-changing ways. I am grateful to Rebecca Wanzo, Lisa Nakamura, Cricket Keating, Linda Mizejewski, Cynthia Burack, Suzanna Danuta Walters, Rosemary Ndubuizu, and Ariella Rotramel. At the University of Wisconsin-Milwaukee, my colleague Elana Levine and a marvelous group of students in my television history seminar provided critical inspiration and feedback. At the University of Oregon, Daniel Pope of the History Department and Kathleen Karlyn of the English Department gave me feedback on an early draft of what became Chapter 4. The late Peggy Pascoe cautioned me not to lose sight of the agency of the women I was writing about. I hope this book shows that I took her advice to heart. The staff at the Center for the Study of Women in Society and the Department of Women's, Gender and Sexuality Studies at the University of Oregon provided deep reservoirs of everyday support. Peggy McConnell and Shirley Marc believed in this book from the beginning. Josie Mulkins and Eryn Cangi were warm and brilliant feminist co-workers. The Department of Sociology at the University of Oregon invited me to present material from Chapters 3 and 4, helping me to think about the final shape of those chapters. I am grateful to Oluwakemi Balogun for setting that session up. Audiences at libraries in Coos Bay and Portland, Oregon and at the Baker Center in Eugene shared stories about 1950s popular culture with me, as well as their enthusiasm for learning about the Broadcast 41.

The College of Arts and Sciences Dean's Office at the University of Oregon provided me the best possible environment for finishing the penultimate draft of this book. Working with people like Alicia De Gonzalez, Anna Duncan, Ellen Coughran, Cathy Soutar, Miriam Bolton, Ellen Laing, Bethany Robinson, Lisa Mick Shimitzu, Pauline Miller, Sherri Nelson, Bruce Blonigen, Hal Sadofsky, and Andrew Marcus during the beginning of a dismal period in American history—one that felt dangerously like the era I was writing about in this book—helped me keep my eyes on people who struggle to do good work, even in the midst of calamitous circumstances. To my colleague Karen Ford: like the women I've had the privilege of writing about, your dedication to institutional change awes me.

I owe a most long-standing debt to my dear friend Jonathan Sterne, who was one of three people who turned up to an 8 a.m. conference presentation I gave many years ago. "You should turn that into an article," he told me afterwards. His support for this project kept it alive, long years after the memory of the presentation itself faded.

I have benefited so much from working with other feminists in very different institutional settings. A co-worker, Pearl Smith, at the State of Rhode Island's Department of Transportation, set me off in this direction many, many years ago. Katherine Meyer, who worked with me at the Department of Transportation as well, modeled what it meant to be a creative, political woman in work spaces where the going could be tough. Robin R. Means Coleman's scholarship and her commitment to institutional change encouraged and sustained me. And thanks to the stalwarts of the Pittsburgh *Buffy* group for hours of great delight all those years ago, as I was embarking on the path that became this project: Erin Deasy, Kelly Happe, Kimberly Latta, Maria Magro, and Courtney Maloney.

My journal co-editor Radhika Gajjala unfailingly picked up the slack on that front when this book demanded my attention. I could not have wished for a kinder or more generous collaborator than her. The broader community of the Fembot Collective reminded me of the importance of feminist networks of alliance and support. Rachel Ida Buff loved this project even in its most gangly and unshapely stages. Larin McLaughlin was enthusiastic about this book as well, from the beginning to the end, and gave me an important push to finally let go of it. My dear friends Kate Mondloch and Laura Vandenburgh offered intellectual sustenance, hilarity, and abundant support. Karen Hoff read an early version of the book and convinced me that people other than academics might be interested in it. Gabriela Martinez's courage, humor, and political conviction inspire me. Linda Fuller's words of encouragement and her own determination to finish a similarly daunting project provided precious solidarity and friendship. I benefited enormously from Joan Haran's thinking about feminist science fiction as theory, which helped me see the creative work of the Broadcast 41 in a new light. Working with Alexis Lothian has deepened my appreciation of the speculative as a vital political tool. JV Sapinoso's wisdom, calm good humor and hard work allowed me to devote some portion of my brain and time to final revisions for this book. I am thankful also to Alisa Freedman, Ina Asim, Steve Beda, Debbie Green, Margaret Hallock, Ellen Herman, Cheris Kramarae, Katie King, Lisa Henderson, Lynn Stephen, Bonnie Thornton Dill, and Marsha Weisiger, as well as the late Joan Acker and Sandi Morgen, for comments and support. Although I discovered Karina Longworth's podcast *You Must Remember This* late in the writing of this book, her feminist sensibilities and commitment to telling stories of Hollywood in all their complexity pushed me over the finish line.

The extensive research this project required was possible only because of institutional support. The University of Wisconsin-Milwaukee (UWM) provided funding for travel to the Library of Congress and the Schlesinger Library. Funding from the Morris Fromkin Memorial Lecture at UWM allowed me to travel to Syracuse University and the American Heritage Center at the University of Wyoming. The University of Pittsburgh and UWM facilitated participation in undergraduate research opportunities that significantly advanced my research. The University of Oregon's School of Journalism and Communication offered support for several terms of graduate research assistance. I am especially grateful to Leslie Steeves for making that assistance possible. I was honored to receive a 2013 Farrar Award in Media and Civil Rights History and am grateful to Ron and Gayla Farrar for their generosity, as well as for the opportunity to discuss this project with faculty and students at the University of South Carolina. An American Council of Learned Societies fellowship, coupled with a sabbatical at the University of Oregon, gave me time to reconceptualize the project and make headway on the final draft.

In completing this book, I have been fortunate to work with a feminist editor, Goldsmiths Press' Sarah Kember. Sarah is visionary. I come away from each meeting with her with fresh insight and energy. Adrian Driscoll's brilliant suggestions about the shape of the book improved it. Michelle Lo's attention to every detail of production has made the process of creating this book a very different experience. I appreciated her patience with my inability to say goodbye to the Broadcast 41's stories. To the three scholars who reviewed the manuscript for Goldsmiths—your reviews were a gift I can only hope I deserve. Your sense of its contributions made me believe that I had written something of value.

A more personal thank you is owed the very dear people I consider my extended pack: Michael Stabile, Melody Hoffmann, Bryce Peake, Courtney Thorsson, Chelsea and Steve Bullock, Matt Sandler, Peter Colot Thorsson, Jen Wood, Alice Crawford, Kelly Happe, Carrie Rentschler, Andrew Adam Newman, Elayne Tobin, Jon Sterne, Jeremiah Favara, Angie Rovak, Susan Unger, Courtney Maloney, and Martin Allen. Alice (and her late mother, the remarkable Mary Ruthsdotter, a founder of the National Women's History Project) were early boosters: their passionate support for this book was exhilarating at a point in time when I most needed it. Melody drove out to Allen Mussehl's home in Wisconsin and spent a day making photocopies of his materials at a local library. Bryce, Courtney Thorsson, Carrie, Jon, and Jen waded through drafts of the manuscript at crucial junctures. I'm not sure I could have let go of these stories without them. Dearest people: I would have to write a separate book just to capture all the ways you have supported me.

I am sorry to have overlooked anyone; the journey to the end of this book has been a long one. To everyone: your support has been invaluable. I can't imagine what I have done to deserve it. I hope this book is a modest recompense for the many gifts you have shared with me.

Finally, my beloved child Tony grew up with this book into a brilliant and funny person. I hope the stories we talked about on planes and cars and over the many dinners of his childhood always remind him of the importance of standing up to bigotry and bullies.

My enduring thankfulness to my sweetheart Mrak, the best chargé d'affaires in the world. He tracked down images for the project, helped me fact check (the errors are always mine, my love), and made me many spreadsheets. He lived with these stories and the political commitments that accompanied them. For nearly three decades, he has shown up for marches, rallies, meetings, and events, and schlepped us all around. Writing this book has reminded me of the unsung role that the partners, lovers, and spouses of feminist writers, artists, and performers play in making all manner of things possible. Like Gertrude Berg, Ruth Gordon, and Joan Scott I was incredibly lucky to have found such a mensch.

Dramatis Personae

The Broadcast 41

Stella Adler: Actress, director
Edith Atwater: Actress
Vera Caspary: Writer, novelist
Mady Christians: Actress; council member, Actors' Equity Association
Louise Fitch: Actress
Ruth Gordon: Actress, writer
Shirley Graham: Musician; writer; civil rights activist
Uta Hagen: Actress, teacher
Lillian Hellman: Playwright, author
Rose Hobart: Actress; board member, Screen Actors Guild
Judy Holliday: Actress
Lena Horne: Singer, actress
Marsha Hunt: Actress
Donna Keath: Actress
Pert Kelton: Actress
Adelaide Klein: Actress
Gypsy Rose Lee: Burlesque artist; quiz show host; recording secretary, American Guild of Variety Artists
Madeline Lee (Gilford): Actress, activist
Ray Lev: Concert pianist
Ella Logan: Singer
Aline MacMahon: Actress
Margo (María Marguerita Guadalupe Teresa Estela Bolado Castilla y O'Donnell Albert): Actress, dancer
Jean Muir: Actress
Meg Mundy: Actress
Dorothy Parker: Writer; co-founder Hollywood Anti-Nazi League
Minerva Pious: Actress
Anne Revere: Actress; secretary, member of the board, Screen Actors Guild
Selena Royle: Actress; writer; co-sponsor, Actors' Dinner Club
Hazel Scott: Musician; actress
Lisa Sergio: Radio commentator; writer
Ann Shepherd: Actress
Gale Sondergaard: Actress
Hester Sondergaard: Actress

Helen Tamiris: Choreographer
Betty Todd: Director; secretary, Radio and Television Directors Guild
Hilda Vaughn: Actress
Fredi Washington: Actress; writer, *The People's Voice*; secretary, Negro Actors Guild of America
Margaret Webster: Writer, director, producer
Ireene Wicker: Radio show host
Betty Winkler: Actress
Lesley Woods: Actress

Additional Black- or Gray-listed Women

Gertrude Berg: Actress, director, producer, writer
Lee Grant: Actress
Joan LaCour Scott: Writer
Hannah Weinstein: Producer, director

Anti-Communists

Kenneth M. Bierly: Lawyer, former FBI agent, co-founder, American Business Consultants; founder Kenby Associates
Elizabeth Dilling: Journalist and founder *Patriotic Research Bureau*; writer
Vincent J. Hartnett: Writer, author of the introduction to *Red Channels* and co-founder of AWARE, Inc., an offshoot of the American Business Consultants
J. Edgar Hoover: Director, FBI
Laurence Johnson: Syracuse-based grocery chain owner, co-founder, *AWARE, Inc.*
Theodore C. Kirkpatrick: Former FBI agent, co-founder, American Business Consultants
John G. Keenan: Lawyer, former FBI agent, co-founder, American Business Consultants
Colleen McCullough: Wife of *Time* magazine picture editor, defendant in *Paul Draper and Larry Adler* v. *Hester McCullough*, one of the first libel lawsuits filed against anti-communists
Louis B. Nichols: FBI assistant director, in charge of the Bureau's records and communications

Prologue

I do not assume the right of the authors of Red Channels *to smear and defame people. Who are they to say what the American people shall read or hear or see? This is the very dictatorship which America professes to despise.*

Shirley Graham (musician, writer, civil rights activist)[1]

On August 27, 1950, American actress Jean Muir picked up a cake on her way to the premiere of the new televised version of the popular radio sitcom *The Aldrich Family* on NBC. The cake was meant to be a surprise for the cast and crew of the television series, a celebration of Muir's comeback after a decade devoted to being a wife and mother. Muir stowed the cake beneath her dressing table and joined the set for a final rehearsal before the live taping at 7.30 p.m. The rehearsal went smoothly and the seasoned cast returned to their dressing rooms for a short break. In an unexpected turn of events, they were immediately called back to the set, where a nervous young assistant producer informed them that he had an announcement to make. "There can't be any questions afterwards," he added, "I've been instructed to ask you not to talk about it." He continued, "The announcement is this: the show tonight has been cancelled."[2]

Muir was stunned and confused. As she later recalled, "Television was still a relatively new medium, but it had a long enough history, and I knew enough about it for me to be aware that the cancellation of a show, and particularly only an hour before airtime, was utterly unheard-of." Despite her growing sense of unease, Muir insisted on sharing the cake that she had had lettered, "Long Live Henry Aldrich." She then returned home, only learning much later that evening that the cancellation had "something to do with that *Red Channels* outfit." *New York Times* journalist Jack Gould told Muir's husband that anti-communists had made a handful of telephone calls and sent two telegrams: "They've whipped up some sort of protest on your appearance."[3]

According to Muir, this incident marked "the beginning of the infamous television blacklist" launched by what she described as "misguided, or foolish, or vicious people who called themselves 'patriots.' " Muir's name was among those of forty-one women identified in *Red Channels: The Report of Communist Influence in Radio and Television* as "members or sympathizers" of the Communist Party. The authors of *Red Channels* were self-described anti-communists and patriots, few in number, but—as Muir put it—making up "for their lack of numerical strength through paranoiac zeal and funds they were able to obtain first from their richer cohorts and then from the very industry they were attempting to control."[4] The only way to clear their names, those accused would learn as the blacklist in broadcasting unfolded, lay in seeking out the editors of the book and, as musician, writer, and civil rights activist Shirley Graham (also listed in the pages of *Red Channels*) put it, "groveling in the dust before them."[5]

This book recounts what happened to this small but potentially powerful group of women, many poised to move into influential positions in broadcasting in the 1950s. I refer to them in the pages that follow as the Broadcast 41 in order to draw attention to how—in a powerful backlash against progressives in media—they were excluded from the industry because of their inclusion in a blacklist engineered by Cold War anti-communists. These women had worked hard to get to where they were by the late 1940s. As we will see, they had ideas that could have transformed the medium. In 1950, they were denied the means to do so. As a similar backlash against women unfolds today, in industries that have long remained hostile to their presence, the stories of the Broadcast 41 have much to tell us about resistance, repression, and resilience.

❖ ❖ ❖

We are living in a changing world. Our teacher was talking to us about all the different cultures—new ideas are really old ones made new. You'd be surprised, Uncle David. There are many places in the world where the men stay at home and the women are the bread-winners. It's just not new with us.

Gertrude Berg (actress, director, producer, writer)[6]

American television had plenty to say about women and work in the 1950s, even if women were not allowed to say much for themselves. Late in the decade, the *Lucy-Desi Comedy Hour*—the successor to the iconic sitcom *I Love Lucy*—featured an episode titled "Lucy Wants a Career."[7] In a formula familiar to fans of the show, actress Lucille Ball pouts her frustration with the dull, daily routine of being a housewife, hatching one of her trademark, screwball schemes to shake things up. After convincing neighbor Ethel Mertz to be her housekeeper, Lucy hops the train to Manhattan to interview for a "Girl Friday" position with character actor Paul Douglas, the host of a fictional "Early Bird Show."

Lucy arrives at Douglas' office, only to be quickly surrounded by a bevy of younger, far more glamorous starlets. In a brilliant display of the physical comedy Ball was known for, she tries to shorten her hemline, lower her neckline, and primp her hair. Dissatisfied with the manic effects of these efforts, she takes another tack, whispering to each of the women in turn that Paul Douglas is a sexual harasser—or "wolf"—of such predatory proportions that even his middle-aged, bun-haired secretary has to keep him at bay with a letter-opener. Overhearing this, Douglas demands that Lucy leave his office immediately, but the sponsor of the program overrules him. "The one thing a housewife likes to look at is another housewife," the sponsor exclaims, and hires Lucy on the spot.

Naturally, Lucy soon learns that she cannot have it all. Having a career means sacrifices and Lucy finds that she "doesn't have much time to spend with her family." When son Little Ricky calls Ethel "Mommy," Lucy bursts into tears, wailing to Ethel, "things aren't working out the way I planned. I miss my family!" Desi agrees to help her get out of her contract and the couple celebrate. On her way to bed and "a pill" that will allow her "to sleep until noon," she exclaims: "Oh, and isn't it wonderful! Now I can cook the meals and do the dishes and dust the house!"

At roughly the same time that "Lucy Wants a Career" aired, blacklisted film producer and screenwriter Adrian Scott, writing under the pseudonym Richard Sanville, was shopping a more unusual script to television producers. The script, variously titled *Ellie, Pay-Day,* or *The Wayward Wife,* recounts the discontent of a young woman who suspects her emotionally distant husband Al of cheating on her. Also fed up with cooking the meals and doing the dishes and dusting the house, Ellie packs her bags and leaves Al and their two children to fend for themselves, determined to make her way in the paid economy. She stops first at the unemployment office, where she discovers that her experience as a wife and mother counts for nothing because "The government doesn't recognize housewife as a category."[8] The short-suffering Ellie chastises the unemployment office clerk, "The government better get wise, that's all! It's hard work being wife and mother! If they don't know that in Washington, someone oughta tell 'em!"[9] In the meantime, Al tries to hire someone to cover Ellie's household duties. Much to his chagrin, he discovers that the long hours, poor working conditions, and low pay are unappealing to workers with options.

After learning that Al was not having an affair, Ellie finally returns home on her own terms: 75 dollars a week (a discounted price, she tells Al, because they are her children, too) and two nights off so she can take courses at the local college. Al agrees to one additional demand: he must pay into social security so she is eligible for benefits. The couple fully reconcile after Al loses his job and, as Ellie puts it, he finally understands what it is like to be on the bottom "with somebody sittin' on you."[10]

These two conflicting stories about women's domestic roles highlight the divergent post-World War II beliefs about gender and class that are at the heart of this book (other stories described in the pages that follow more obviously foreground race and nation). These beliefs appeared in the stories postwar American culture told about curious norms of social behavior in which what was good for the gander, so to speak, was distinctly not good for the goose. In the years following the end of World War II, when relations of gender, race, and nation were in flux, political forces in the United States competed for control over the stories the new medium of television would feature. The stakes were high: the struggle involved nothing less than the ability to define and represent America and Americanism for millions of viewers. The Americanism that resulted from this conflict reflected not so much the spontaneous desires of the millions who watched the new media as it did the common sense of groups of men who had historically dominated American politics and culture. Their Americanism expressed a worldview shaped by their powerful interests and then delivered to audiences in a manner that suggested that these images were what viewers had been demanding all along.

This book does not assume that gender alone determines perspective, although it acknowledges gender as a powerful shaper of standpoint. While both were written by white men, for example, "Lucy Wants a Career" and *Ellie* reflected vastly different points of view, reflective of the very different experiences, beliefs, and values of their writers, and the political aims these writers advanced. Bob Schiller and Bob Weiskopf, the screenwriting team who shared credit for the script for "Lucy Wants a Career," established themselves during the first decade of television and continued to write scripts for sitcoms, variety shows, and prime-time dramas for decades. Writers like them mastered formulae and perspectives featuring women in subordinate relationships to men. People of color—when they wrote parts for them at all—appeared in roles subservient to white people. Writers who succeeded in television either agreed with anti-communist beliefs about race and gender, or learned not to rock any boats, instead reproducing images and stereotypes undisturbing to viewers who found anti-racist images distasteful. Men (and a few women) taught these formulae to new generations of writers, producers, and directors. As for women, these writers spoke about them, but they did not speak to them, and their scripts betrayed their lack of knowledge about women's everyday lives. What middle-class housewife with small children, after all, takes a pill that makes her sleep until noon?

The perspectives that successful television writers learned to voice in the 1950s embraced white male fantasies about family life, where women uncomplainingly raised children, managed households, and volunteered in their communities. They did all this with grace and alacrity during the day. At night, they catered to their husbands' social and sexual needs, with fresh energy and ready smiles. In the world that appeared in most family sitcoms until the 1970s, no one suspected that Margaret Anderson's obsessive cleaning might be a symptom of a problem that had no name, as Betty Friedan was to put it less than a decade later. Instead, entertainment programming on television presented a world in which white people lived in a redlined landscape populated by white people like themselves, in leafy suburbs from which all the tensions simmering around them had been deleted.

Ellie shared elements of this 1950s vision, but the script was shaped by screenwriter and film producer Adrian Scott's own experiences as a single parent, responsible for raising a son with serious mental health issues, which increased his awareness of the backbreaking nature of caring for other human beings. Scott was a member of a writing team as well, but with his wife, Joan LaCour Scott. Citing "the distant sounds of revolt ... emanating from this oppressed majority" of women, Scott understood how much perspective mattered. In a letter to his agent, Scott remarked on the importance of perspective: "I don't know whom you'll be talking to at Warner's—I assume a man—who is likely to be less sympathetic than a woman to this subject." He told his agent not to emphasize the "wildly radical aspects of this subject matter," but instead focus on the possibility that "such a program might steal audiences" from other, less intelligent programs. Scott, who had been blacklisted by anti-communists because of his political beliefs, shopped this script to producers for years, with no success. In 1960, he told gray-listed director Joseph Losey that he had withdrawn *Ellie* from the market, but would "continue to prepare projects, *Ellie* included, for some amiable change in the climate."[11] *Ellie* was never produced, although nearly thirty years later, actress and writer Roseanne Barr fought networks, advertisers, and other writers to create a sitcom that raised similar concerns.

However much *I Love Lucy* and the *Lucy-Desi Comedy Hour* were unique in co-starring an immigrant who spoke accented English, the content of these shows reflected the perspective of the era's Cold War manhood, or what this book refers to as G-Man masculinity, the form of American masculinity popularized by anti-communists in the first half of the twentieth century. Popularized by acolytes of the Federal Bureau of Investigation (FBI), an arm of the state that played a decisive role in the blacklist, G-Man masculinity advocated for the return of women to the domestic sphere, where they could devote themselves to their natural role in society: cooking the meals, doing the dishes, and dusting the house. Women who did not obey this mandate they considered unnatural, perennially conflicted, and bitterly unfulfilled. Lucy fit their bill. Ellie did not.

Why did scripted television on the new medium of American television eschew the drama and complexity of Ellie's point of view, instead embracing the universalizing point of view of G-Man masculinity? As a rule, when this question comes up, it gets answered in ways that make what appeared on American television screens seem the inevitable outcome of historical forces.[12] Whether viewed as the result of a commercial media system or the reflection of a postwar consensus about American values, the "containment culture" that appeared on American television, and its procession of prime-time nuclear families and Cold War genres like Westerns and police procedurals, is understood to have been a straightforward reflection of postwar American desires.[13] But it takes a real stretch of the imagination to believe that "Lucy Wants a Career" reflected actress and producer Lucille Ball's perspective. After all, Ball was one half of the husband-and-wife team that produced her show; she was an ambitious entrepreneur who had made *I Love Lucy* a success, despite studios' initial reluctance to gamble on it. She went on to become a high-powered studio head. Ball was not a housewife or stay-at-home mother or, for that matter, the kind of woman who wanted nothing more than to cook the meals and do the dishes and dust the house. But she knew what it took to survive within the stereotypes comprising television's Cold War narratives of American identity and she worked within those constraints.

Rather than looking at programs that, like *I Love Lucy*, were actually produced, *The Broadcast 41: Women and the Anti-Communist Blacklist* studies television's origins by directing attention to what was deliberately and strategically excluded from the new medium by the political forces converging on it in the late 1940s. Looking behind and beyond the bland homogeneity of 1950s television families, it details the repressive war over popular culture that accompanied the new medium's birth. This war was initiated by conservatives in the United States who called themselves anti-communists, but who were arch-white supremacists, defenders of segregation and sexism, vehemently opposed to immigration. In the late 1940s, these political forces set out to cleanse (their word) the airwaves of what they defined as subversive influences. The resultant struggle yoked the power of the Cold War security state to the retrenchment of racial and gender norms unsettled by World War II. The struggle over how America defines and represents itself via massively influential new media continues today as the G-Man masculinity born of the Cold War era reasserts itself amidst contemporary new-media systems.

The sets of narratives that resulted from the blacklist influenced American television content for many decades. B-movie actor and liberal turned anti-communist crusader Ronald Reagan played a key role in attacks on progressives, smearing the reputations of Hollywood rivals in order to law: civil rights, Judaism, feminism, homosexuality, socialism, peace, and equality.

This book also shows how the anti-communist perspective was generated, funded, and promoted by powerful corporate and governmental entities. What conservative billionaires like the Koch Brothers or the Mercer family are up to in the contemporary moment can be difficult to discern (although courageous and dogged journalists and historians like Jane Mayer and Nancy MacLean have done much to document the plans the radical right has for America, as well as the progress they have made on these).[19] The extent to which contemporary critics and dissenting cultural producers are being monitored by institutions like the FBI, the National Security Administration, and others is equally hard to assess, although recent reports that the FBI continues to monitor "black identity extremists" speaks to the terrible tradition of state surveillance and harassment of black progressives that began in the first decades of the twentieth century.[20]

The anti-government libertarianism of Trump's base has poisonous, twisted roots in the bigotry of the anti-communist movement. Evidence from the blacklist era helps us piece together the alliances among wealthy capitalists eager to pour billions of dollars into anti-communist causes, powerful government forces like the FBI, and the private security industry that emerged in the years after World War II. Studying this era provides grim evidence of the lengths to which white supremacists and their allies have been willing to go to maintain control over representations of race and nation.

By restoring to view the blacklist that anti-communists used to cleanse the television industry of viewpoints they found distasteful, subversive, and thus un-American, this book dwells, with much anxiety, on the possible futures of this past in a contemporary world of fake news, alternative facts, and white supremacist calls for free, hate-filled, and violent speech. Those sharing progressive dreams of social and economic equality—who wish to appeal to the best in publics rather than the worst—must make no mistake: this political regime intends nothing less than the reimposition of ideologies their role models created in the 1950s. Like the anti-communists of the blacklist era, what has been alternately described as white nationalism, the alt-right, or, simply, the Base, fears the power of an emergent progressive resistance. In the service of a similarly violent and hateful rhetoric, they intend to use the banner of Americanism to police, disparage, and ultimately suppress the views of all who disagree.

Anti-communist suppression of progressive perspectives in the 1950s, however, is only one part of the picture. *The Broadcast 41* reclaims and represents the story of a group of women who were smeared, harassed by the

FBI and the privatized security forces of the anti-communist movement, and rendered historically and politically invisible by the blacklist. But rather than narrating a story only of struggle and defeat, this book also recounts what might have been for women and people of color who worked in front of, and behind, the cameras that recorded televised entertainment programs. Their stories of resistance and resilience emphasize that television narratives that reduced white women to smiling wraiths milling around suburban homes were not inevitable in the U.S. Nor were representations that censored images of people of color, working-class people, and immigrants the only possible future for American television. As the chapters that follow reveal, there were many possible futures for television in the 1940s and 1950s, and not merely the one that won out.

How we remember the past matters, especially when those memories are based on industrial products like television programs. What happened in the television industry in 1950 is a critical moment in the history of American media, a moment when television was struggling to find its footing. It is also a textbook example of how political forces used a new medium to impose their viewpoints, in the process encouraging a country to swiftly betray its citizenry and fostering conditions that allowed restrictive and unjust images and hostile climates for women and people of color to flourish across media for decades. As a resurgent wave of G-Man masculinity sweeps American media and politics, we must listen carefully to what this past can tell us.

Chapter 1
Redacted Women

One pattern of suppression is that of omission.

Patricia Hill Collins (feminist theorist)[1]

The people want democracy, real democracy, Mr. Dies, and they look toward Hollywood to give it to them because they don't get it any more in their newspapers. And that's why you're out here, Mr. Dies—that's why you want to destroy the Hollywood progressive organizations—because you've got to control this medium if you want to bring fascism to this country.

Dorothy Parker (writer)[2]

It seemed as though the writers of the American situation comedy *Leave It to Beaver* knew from the start that the show would be on the air—without interruption—for generations to come. Its first episode, broadcast in 1957, suggested as much. "Beaver Gets Spelled" began with a voice-over by Beaver's father, Ward Cleaver. "When you were young," the omniscient male voice intoned, you had "values that nothing could change. An ice cream cone was a snow-capped mountain of sheer delight. An autographed baseball was more precious than rubies. And a note from the teacher meant only one thing: disaster."[3] Against images of a soda jerk handing an ice cream cone to an eager Beaver; Beaver and two friends marveling over an autographed baseball in a tree-filled park; and a female teacher scolding a chastened Beaver, the voice-over conjured a utopian past for the boy's present.

The person—the you—this episode both addressed and remembered was male (someone for whom an autographed baseball was more precious than a gem), American (as the iconic game of baseball), middle class (a person who could afford ice cream cones and professional ball games), and white (a child for whom school discipline was a comic episode in an otherwise idyllic childhood). In less than fifty seconds, this montage conveyed a vision of 1950s America rooted in the suburban tranquility, consumerism, and masculine order symbolizing the American family and its values. The episode merged present and future in its vision of America, as the moment when viewers "were young" combined with a past, the narrator confidently asserted, for which they would someday most assuredly yearn.

In the decades following the emergence of American television, viewers were encouraged to remember, through similarly rose-colored lenses, the medium's early period as a conflict-free era when women were happy with their domestic lot and African Americans with their subordinate place in American society. Judging from the scenes that flickered across television screens in the 1950s and 1960s, American culture mirrored a Cold War consensus. In it, the consumer was king and the new medium's content a reflecting pool for the hopes and dreams of white veterans and women eager to return to the domestic sphere and get on with the business of having babies, settling into their new suburban homes, and buying the mass-produced items being churned out by a booming postwar economy. Other sitcoms of the era celebrated these postwar American values in similarly suburban settings, in Westerns that portrayed the individualistic triumphs of white masculinity, and in police procedurals that taught viewers to fear urban areas increasingly associated with disruptive black residents. Much like the inaugural episode of *Leave It to Beaver*, mass-mediated narratives of television's rise presented images from an untroubled, halcyon epoch, full of wholesome content and broad social agreement about American "values nothing could change."

Many of those watching television in 1957, when this episode aired, or in the years that followed had no reason to suspect that these images of a nation that shared universal values and happy consensus at the end of World War II were made possible by ongoing acts of repression. Television shows did not hint at the circumstances that prevented people of color from appearing in the medium's imaginings of American life only in demeaning roles—as cooks in Westerns, like *Bonanza*'s Hop Sing, and the butts of racialized humor in the sitcom *Amos 'n' Andy*. Instead, the absence of any other images reassured white viewers that racial hierarchies were natural and just. Black people either entertained white people on variety shows or turned up as domestic servants and mammy figures in the lives of white people. In *Beulah*, a series about a black housekeeper and cook for a white family, the series' titular character was played by a succession of brilliant African American actresses—Ethel Waters, Hattie McDaniel, and Louise Beavers—unable to find roles other than maids. Women were consigned to racially stratified domestic roles: by the mid-1950s, even *The Goldbergs*' formidable Molly—a physically and emotionally large, working-class, Jewish matriarch—had been reduced to uttering clichés about the perverted, un-American desires of women who worked outside the home. No one seemed to notice when immigrants all but disappeared from small screens.

Contrary to popular beliefs, the images that appeared on American television after 1950 were not simply reflections of American culture. They were undermine their careers and work. From the early 1960s onward, Reagan used the phrase family values to attack groups that did not conform to anti-communists' preferred version of Americanism: welfare moms, people of color, immigrants, students, and his progressive critics. During his 1986 State of the Union address, Reagan told his listeners, "despite the pressures of our modern world, family and community remain the moral core of our society, guardians of our values and hopes for the future. Family and community are the costars of this great American comeback."[14] Presumably having been made unpopular during the social upheavals of the 1960s and 1970s, the traditional American family, according to conservative politicians like Reagan, was staging a comeback in the 1980s. Respect for white male authority and conformance to its directives, conservatives argued, resulted in a cornucopia of economic and social blessings. Family values would "let us make America great again." Throughout the second half of the twentieth century, American conservatives spoke reverentially about "family values" whenever they wanted to condemn those who did not agree with anti-communist values.

Curiously, when white men like Ronald Reagan, Newt Gingrich, Rush Limbaugh, Bill O'Reilly, and Donald Trump spoke about American families, or when media felt that they needed some visual example for a piece on family values, they turned not to images of their own or other actual families, since these were often hardly bastions of the family values they prescribed for the economically disadvantaged. Instead, politicians, pundits, and media used images of television families from the 1950s to anchor their words. In 1992, NPR's *Morning Edition* hinted at the fictive nature of this practice: the phrase family values "conjures up images of 'Leave it to Beaver' or 'Father Knows Best,' families featured in TV shows from the 1950s."[15] An article in *Business Week* on family values included a still from *Father Knows Best*, featuring the show's patriarch Jim Anderson in the loving embrace of wife Margaret and their progeny, Bud, Princess, and Kitten.[16]

During a segment of CBS's *The Osgood File*, commentator Charles Osgood facilely blurred the boundaries between television and reality, declaring that, "Family values are back in the United States and not just on the 1950s sitcoms running on cable TV. The number of nuclear-style families, the kind with a man, his wife, and their kids, has been growing all decade, according to the Population Reference Bureau ... But Ozzie and Harriet might not feel so at home anymore." Osgood continued, "On a typical day back in 1950s TV land, June Cleaver of 'Leave it to Beaver' and Margaret Anderson of 'Father Knows Best' would send the kids off to school and their husbands off to work and then the ladies would get down to serious housekeeping and talking on the phone."[17] In the hands of politicians and commentators, images like those invoked by Osgood functioned as yardsticks against which a dystopian present was measured: a present in which single mothers; lesbian, gay, bisexual, and transgender people; people of color; and immigrants threatened the sanctity of the family values that had once been enshrined on television screens and, presumably, in the nation.

Ronald Reagan's 1980 campaign ("Let's Make America Great Again") and Donald J. Trump's 2016 revival ("Make America Great Again") drew on sexist, isolationist, and white supremacist visions of the past rooted in the television narratives anti-communists had created in the 1950s. Decades later, journalist Seth Rosenfeld documented Reagan's intimate relationship with J. Edgar Hoover and Reagan's role as an FBI informant, a gig that began during the Hollywood blacklist. Reality show host and real estate developer Donald Trump was groomed by prominent anti-communist Joseph McCarthy's henchman, lawyer Roy Cohn. Well versed in the art of bullying and bravado wielded by anti-communists in the late 1940s and 1950s, in 2016, Trump reenergized a base that shared his devotion to projecting and protecting legacies of white supremacy and masculine domination.

As the contemporary climate once again becomes more aggressively hostile toward women, people of color, immigrants, and the poor, the links between the white supremacy and misogyny that appeared on American television in the 1950s and their contemporary manifestations have become more evident. After the 2016 election, for example, Ku Klux Klan member James Zarth mourned the betrayal of white America in a conversation with *New Yorker* journalist Charles Bethea. The terms he used to describe the moral decline of the nation underscore the enduring influence of the anti-communist narratives that originated in the 1950s and the inspiration these provide today for those following in the footsteps of G-Man masculinity. "'I noticed something was going wrong in America decades ago,' Zarth told me. He mentioned the TV shows 'Father Knows Best,' 'Andy Griffith,' 'The Brady Bunch,' and 'Little House on the Prairie.' 'Usually, those shows had a Christian moral,' he said. 'But now that the Jews own the majority of the media stations, they're showing things that are against God's law, like race-mixing and homosexuality.'"[18]

With its attacks on "race-mixing and homosexuality," and its anti-Semitism, Zarth's statement could have been lifted directly from anti-communist media of the 1950s (although the 1950s version would have blamed these on the contaminating influence of communism). His words offer an alarming reminder of how the stories shaped by the anti-communist blacklist created a tradition that for generations has nurtured the perspective of people who reviled all those things they considered to be against God's products of suppression, fear, and, eventually, self-censorship. This book is about how the values and happy consensus viewers saw on their television screens came about. It is about what seemed possible for the new medium in 1945, as progressives gathered in the broadcast capital of New York City, and how those possibilities were eliminated within a ten-year period. While what happened to the '41' shows us the limits of that rosy image of TV consensus, their efforts were not limited to TV alone: they were cultural workers across media and took advantage of all the means by which mass cultural forms could be used in the service of progressivism. Although most of the book's action takes place in the past, its resonance for the present and the future lies in the lessons this story can teach us about the impact of political struggles over new media and the consequences of allowing one set of perspectives to dominate all others.

To dislodge the notion that what appeared on television screens after 1950 resulted from some broad social agreement, this book tell two overlapping stories. One story centers on the white, native-born anti-communists who created and carried out the blacklist in television, the principal means by which anti-communists were able to impose their version of Americanism on television. Three men in particular, Kenneth Bierly, John Keenan, and Theodore Kirkpatrick, former FBI agents, founded a group that called itself the American Business Consultants in 1947. They coined an anti-communist tautology—"factual information"—to distinguish between the media they wrote and disseminated and what they described as the Communist propaganda of anti-racist progressives. Unfettered by journalistic accountability to facts, these men published the influential anti-communist newsletter *CounterAttack* and the book *Red Channels: The Report of Communist Influence in Radio and Television.* As former agents of the FBI, Bierly, Keenan, and Kirkpatrick drew on the power of the anti-communist security state in their efforts to impose stories favoring the political and economic objectives they shared with others who aspired to G-Man masculinity.

The second story documents the dramatically different perspectives of a group of progressive women who had been influencing media production in New York City in the 1930s and 1940s. In 1950, the American Business Consultants identified 41 women and 110 men as "members or sympathizers" of the Communist Party in *Red Channels,* the publication that became the central vehicle for the ensuing blacklist.[4] Although *Red Channels* listed far more men in its pages than women, anti-communists singled out women for their initial attacks. These women were engaged in oppositional cultural production: they criticized anti-communist norms of gender, race, class, and nation and resisted the imposition of these norms in their personal, professional, and political lives. Playwright Lillian Hellman's father once told Hellman that she "lived within a question mark," referring to the profound curiosity that caused her to constantly ask questions about the world that surrounded her.[5] The Broadcast 41 were all women who lived within similar question marks, asking questions and creating new ways of seeing a world that was in the midst of massive and divisive changes. Their contributions to American culture, and what happened to them in the harsh dawning of the Cold War era, show how the consensus American television presented in the 1950s existed only by virtue of anti-communists' ability to criminalize dissent, drive dissenters from media industries, and then make it all but impossible to remember that dissent had existed in the first place.

These repressed realities of resistance are far richer than most versions of American television's history allow. Sociologist Herman Gray observes that in the early days of television, "Blacks appeared primarily as maids, cooks, 'mammies,' and other servants, or as con artists and deadbeats."[6] Gray is right, but as this book shows, those stereotypes were not reproduced without a fight. Not all of those present at the birth of American television in New York City willingly acquiesced to the rigid norms imposed by the American Business Consultants or subsequent Cold War prescriptions for race and gender. Not all of those working in and around the new industry were white, male, or middle class. Indeed, in 1945, it was not pre-ordained that the content of American television would center the perspectives of Cold War masculinities rather than the chorus of heterogeneous, politically progressive voices that were in conversation with each other in media industries in New York City.

Laying bare the conflict between progressive women and the anti-communists who opposed them not only challenges the belief that what appeared on television screens reflected what was in the hearts and minds of American viewers in 1950, it shows that struggles over television's stereotypes predated the social movements of the 1960s. Indeed, accounts of the Broadcast 41's lives and work reveal the contours of another history of American television, one that has been clouded by the legacies of anti-communism. In this counterfactual version of television's history, people of principle and courage tried to present the perspectives of diverse groups of Americans to national audiences in the years following World War II. Their efforts offer a new context for understanding contemporary debates about the need for heterogeneous voices and ideas in media production and thus in media representations. The Broadcast 41's experiences remind us of the weighty cultural and political work done by the stories we hear, and the people and ideas that are permitted to enter our screens, homes, and hearts. Without this context, we undertake the struggle over complex and respectful representations of all people thinking that we are the beginning, when in reality we participate in a long line of resistance.

There is cruel irony in the fact that this book depicts the repression of the histories, to borrow a phrase from activist and scholar Angela Y. Davis, of a group of women who were themselves deeply conscious of forces in the past that had conspired to exclude dissenting perspectives from historical view.[7] The Broadcast 41 and other progressives knew that the blacklist was a mechanism for throttling dissent and preventing its dissemination and recollection. Many of them lived long enough to watch as their perspectives were erased by histories of the medium's "Golden Age," stories told from the points of view of the white men who subsequently went on to prosper in Cold War television, accounts popularized by scholars and journalists who listened to those men, affirmed their experiences, and universalized their stories.[8] We should not be surprised that when we view the history of television through lenses fashioned by anti-communism, what we see is the absence of anyone but white men and a handful of white women, most of them stars. The continued erasure of the Broadcast 41 and other progressives in media industries, as feminist theorist Patricia Hill Collins reminds us, is an ongoing process of suppression.

❖ ❖ ❖

Everything about you—your race and gender, where and how you were raised, your temperament and disposition—can influence whom you meet, what is confided to you, what you are shown, and how you interpret what you see. My identity opened some doors and closed others. In the end, we can only do the best we can with who we are, paying close attention to the ways pieces of ourselves matter to the work while never losing sight of the most important questions.

Matthew Desmond (sociologist)[9]

I was rebellious when I was four years old, I think, and a nuisance, too. All rebels are nuisances too.

Lillian Hellman (writer)[10]

Unlike later generations of writers, directors, and producers—almost exclusively white and economically privileged, mostly male—the Broadcast 41's lived experiences hinted at the diversity of American culture in urban areas like New York City in the first half of the twentieth century. Four of the Broadcast 41 were African American (Shirley Graham, Lena Horne, Hazel Scott, Fredi Washington); one was Mexican-American (María Marguerita

Guadalupe Teresa Estela Bolado Castilla y O'Donnell, a dancer and actress who performed as "Margo"). Most of the women listed in *Red Channels* in 1950 were from working-class or immigrant backgrounds (sometimes both). More than a third were Jewish women from politically progressive urban enclaves. As artists and cultural workers, they were aware that they were being represented in ways that were untrue to their lived experiences and degrading. Hollywood forced white women like Judy Holliday to play dumb blondes in order to mask their intelligence. The film industry cast African Americans strictly as maids or hypersexualized women, stereotypes that Lena Horne, Hazel Scott, and Fredi Washington fought against for the entirety of their careers.

Their experiences of being excluded encouraged the Broadcast 41 to participate in progressive social networks across media industries. Kate Mostel, wife of blacklisted actor Zero Mostel and close friend of blacklisted actress Madeline Lee, once said that living in New York City made her feel as though "there are only 200 people in the world. They all know each other."[11] Progressives like Mostel encountered each another personally, politically, and professionally across spheres of cultural production in New York City. Writers Dorothy Parker and Lillian Hellman worked together in theater, forging a friendship surprising to those who believed that independent, strong-willed women could not get along.[12] Blacklisted actresses Madeline Gilford and Jean Muir were close friends whose husbands worked together in the American Federation of Television and Radio Actors (AFTRA).

Like other women of their era who enjoyed economic advantages, Broadcast 41 members Lena Horne and Dorothy Parker attended benefits like a fundraiser for the United Negro and Allied Veterans of America, intended to help African American veterans get the cash payments they were owed when they left military service.[13] After a dinner party they both attended in Manhattan, actress Rose Hobart became fast friends with actress Selena Royle after Royle publicly reprimanded Hobart's verbally abusive (and soon-to-be former) husband.[14] Actress and journalist Fredi Washington and musician and actress Hazel Scott traveled in the same circles in Harlem: Washington's sister was politician Adam Clayton Powell, Jr.'s first wife; Hazel Scott was his second.

These women and their friends partied at Café Society, a hangout frequented by progressives founded by Communist Party member Barney Josephson because he "wanted to own a club where blacks and whites could work together as entertainers and a mixed audience could sit out front together to watch the show."[15] Years later, in her one-woman show, Lena Horne described how much it meant to her to have "her beautiful sister Billie Holliday" performing at one of Josephson's clubs, while her "other beautiful sister Hazel Scott" performed at the other.[16]

The Broadcast 41 often admired one another's work and relished opportunities to work with each other. Dorothy Parker, Lena Horne, Fredi Washington, and Shirley Graham counted blacklisted actor Paul Robeson among their circle of friends. Later, the FBI took great pains to investigate all those who moved within Robeson's international orbit. Lena Horne admired actress Ella Logan's singing and made a point to keep in touch with her in New York and Los Angeles.[17] Lillian Hellman was a fan of Judy Holliday's work with the comedy group the Revuers.[18]

Many of those listed in *Red Channels* knew one another from working on writer, director, and actor Gertrude Berg's popular radio series, *The Goldbergs*. Actress Louise Fitch's first husband was character actor Richard H. Harris, who played Jake in the radio series; actor and union leader Philip Loeb played husband Jake in the television series; Fredi Washington had a recurring role as well; Adelaide Klein was on the show; as a young man, writer Garson Kanin appeared on the radio program; blacklisted screenwriter and novelist Abraham Polonsky got his start writing for Berg; and actress Madeline Lee appeared in the television series even after her name appeared in *Red Channels*.

Obligations of citizenship also brought the Broadcast 41 into contact with one another. During the war, Margaret Webster, Selena Royle, Hester Sondergaard, and Lillian Hellman shared billing in a program sponsored by the Artists' Front to Win the War. Dozens of other progressives supported and attended a broad array of cultural and political events that would later be used by anti-communists to blacklist them.[19] Actress Anne Revere was a leader in efforts to defend the Hollywood Ten (a group of white, male writers, directors, and producers who refused to cooperate with the House Un-American Activities Committee [the HUAC] and were jailed as a result in 1950), while Lena Horne and Hazel Scott used their stardom to promote civil rights. Over the course of a life cut short by FBI surveillance and harassment, concert pianist Ray Lev lent her talent to a procession of political events, eventually running for City Council in Manhattan as an American Labor Party candidate.

The Broadcast 41 knew about one another, even when they did not know each other intimately, and they understood their work to be part of a much larger conversation about popular culture's role in a democracy. Critics and producers of popular culture themselves, the Broadcast 41 saw in mass media and popular culture new opportunities to effect social change and to influence American culture on a massive scale, ushering innovative and diverse perspectives, ideas, and representations onto the historical stage. Outsiders in a variety of media industries, the Broadcast 41 understood their perspectives were one among many views on the social worlds that surrounded them.

Alienated from mass-mediated narratives that represented women, people of color, queer people, and immigrants as inferior, abnormal, and subversive, the Broadcast 41 wanted to represent perspectives that had been hitherto unrepresented, seeking ways to break out of forms of thinking and representing that, in sociologist Pierre Bourdieu's words, reflected a "monopoly over the universal."[20] To monopolize the universal in the case of television was to assume that there was a singular perspective from which an American experience could be told, a standpoint that invisibly regulated what could be seen and represented. The anti-communist perspective that achieved dominance during the 1950s was such a monopoly, reflecting the standpoint of white, native-born, Cold War masculinity. From this vantage point, the lives of people of color, women, and immigrants were largely hidden, or reduced to stereotypes confirming their inherent inferiority.

To challenge this monopoly, progressives like the Broadcast 41 emphasized the heterogeneity of American life rather than its alleged uniformity, drawing on historical and personal reservoirs of richly varying racial, ethnic, religious, gender, and class backgrounds to do so. These perspectives were refined in the crucible of Popular Front organizations, a movement that cultural studies scholar Michael Denning describes as "the insurgent social movement forged from the labor militancy of the fledgling CIO, the anti-fascist solidarity with Spain, Ethiopia, China, and the refugees from Hitler, and the political struggles on the left wing of the New Deal."[21] Influenced by the vibrant art and popular culture that emerged from the Popular Front, the Broadcast 41's experiences of the Depression further caused them to wrestle with capitalism's systemic inequalities. Republican Spain's war against fascism moved many of the Broadcast 41 to political action. Most of these women strongly identified with the progressivism of the left wing of the New Deal, inspired by the Popular Front's constellation of communist-inspired and led anti-racist organizations. They believed in peaceful democracy, and they translated their passion into action, campaigning for the rights of African Americans, women, immigrants, and workers.

The Broadcast 41 called themselves progressives, a term that from roughly 1934 (when the Comintern announced its Popular Front strategy for fighting fascism) until the end of World War II, to borrow cultural historian Alan Wald's definition, referred to "a radical who was willing to collaborate with Communists and who looked on the Soviet Union favorably as a force for peace and anticolonialism."[22] While this definition was obvious to those on the organized left anxious to distinguish among communists, socialists, Trotskyists, anarchists, and New Dealers, in the early years of the Cold War, anti-communists increasingly identified anyone expressing opinions to the left of center as ideologically suspect and un-American. Although the term progressive was gradually redefined by the left as well as the right after World War II, throughout this book I use "progressive" as an umbrella term incorporating a range of the leftist political thought and alliances running throughout the Popular Front, before the Cold War reshaped its meaning.

While the perspectives of the Broadcast 41 bookend the following chapters, the middle section of this book describes the forces conspiring against the Broadcast 41 in the years before anti-communism became institutionalized in media. I use the verb conspire intentionally here, because as the postwar era gave way to the Cold War, anti-communists were nothing if not deliberate in their campaigns against progressives in broadcasting. Evangelical in their beliefs, the founders of the American Business Consultants viewed America from a standpoint they considered natural, uncontroversial, and unassailable because their superiority was conferred on them by God. To question the anti-democratic and often illegal behaviors of anti-communists, to challenge the belief that women and people of color were biologically inferior to white men, to have been at any point in time *infected* by the politics of the Popular Front was to be in the eyes of anti-communists forever potentially treasonous and un-American.

Anti-communists in government, industry, and the private sector (including the American Legion, a veterans' organization, and the Boy Scouts) had been monitoring progressives since before the end of World War I, creating lists of people, groups, and organizations they claimed were communists or communist sympathizers (known as "fellow-travelers" because they moved in overlapping progressive cultural and political circles). Activist and white supremacist Elizabeth Dilling created the first anti-communist political blacklist in *The Red Network* (1934).[23] The blacklist orchestrated by anti-communists built off her model, and it enveloped media along with government, education, manufacturing, and other industries considered vulnerable to communist infiltration. Anti-communists in government and the private sector shared their lists with likeminded organizations, using this information to attack, smear, defund, and otherwise undermine the reputations of progressives and the organizations and institutions with which they were associated. Anti-communists and progressives recognized that this new medium, whose audiences were anticipated to be so vast as to make all previous audiences tiny in comparison, had the potential to create what Bourdieu describes as a "single, central, dominant, in a word, quasi-divine, point of view."[24]

Anti-communists used the blacklist to create this divine point of view by eliminating progressives from the industry, forging a lasting link between criticism and controversy on one hand and communism and treason on the other. To be critical of white supremacy was to be communist; to be communist was to be a treacherous and un-American. These links imposed conditions of conformity within the television industry, generating the appearance of postwar consensus on television screens that provided cover for anti-communists' distinctly undemocratic political activities. Anti-communists made it dangerous to even remember progressive ideas or the people who had held them by repressing the history of the vibrant and contentious field of perspectives that had attended the birth of television in New York City.

To counter the forms of repression that linger many years after the events in this book took place, *The Broadcast 41: Women and the Anti-Communist Blacklist* reflects on the birth of television not from the center of the television industry, but from its margins, where progressive ideas and culture had flourished in the 1930s and 1940s. In doing so, it understands the content of American television not as the product of consensus, but as the effect of a culture war whose casualties included the perspectives of a generation of progressive women. By documenting the perspectives of these women and the blacklist that anti-communists used to suppress them, this book takes a first step toward undoing their erasure from history.

By providing a counterfactual history of what American television might have looked like had anti-communists not succeeded in eradicating the perspectives of the Broadcast 41 from the industry, this book vividly illustrates what American culture lost when anti-communists succeeded in driving all but a very narrow swath of perspectives from the new medium of television. The Broadcast 41's stories challenge us to think about what the new medium might have become had anti-communists not won this culture war. What would it have meant to create programs where women, people of color, and immigrants were neighbors and schoolmates, colleagues and supervisors, people with agency and complexity and not secondary and subservient to the lives and objectives of G-Men and their allies? What might American culture have looked like if stories about democracy and equality had dominated rather than narratives about homicide?

❖ ❖ ❖

After a hundred years of the modern struggle for women's equality Soviet women are urged in their magazines to educate themselves and grow, to fulfill their production quotas and thus add to the happiness and well-being of the nation; while judging from the number of square feet given over to the subject in every issue of the Ladies Home Journal, *the highest ideal of American womanhood is smooth, velvety, kissable hands.*

Betty Millard (writer, artist, feminist)[25]

The fad of denouncing the American woman has another effect which is more tangible and even less funny than its effect on people's feelings. There is today a real danger that resentment against women, especially against women in industry, will be promoted into an issue by professional agitators. Many know that this is becoming a serious threat.

Alice Sheldon (author)[26]

Historian Stephanie Coontz once observed that people in the United States treat sitcoms like *Leave It to Beaver* as if they were documentaries, describing the traditional family or its family values through images drawn directly from representations originating on television screens.[27] This observation has stuck with me over the years, causing me to think about why conservatives of all genders persist in endorsing values that privilege a family ideal grounded in so many exclusions. Even when their lived experiences do not match those of the idyllic American family, as was the case with politicians like Ronald Reagan, Strom Thurmond, Sarah Palin, and Donald Trump and pundits like Rush Limbaugh and Bill O'Reilly, conservatives stubbornly cling to these images. When I began researching representations of family on television, I jokingly referred to the tendency of mass media to represent the American family in terms supplied by television as the "*Leave it to Beaver* syndrome," a condition caused by years of watching reruns of family sitcoms, viewings that induced nostalgia among many white people for a form of family that was historically contingent and far from universal.

After researching this book, I am less inclined to treat this suggestion as a joke. In the second half of the 1940s, anti-communists—including powerful organizations and institutions like the FBI, the HUAC, the American Legion, the National Association of Manufacturers, the Catholic Church, Chambers of Commerce, and myriad others—initiated an apocalyptic battle over their definition of Americanism. Some of them believed that this war was reality; others were swift to recognize the political and economic utility of frightening people into giving up fundamental rights in exchange for promises of security. Arguing that the ends (stemming what anti-communists depicted as a rising tide of atheistic communism) justified the means (unconstitutional, illegal, and often brutal forms of surveillance and retaliation), anti-communists set out to make sure that the new medium of television would be free of progressive influences.

Television served as a crucial battleground over American values for a number of reasons. In the first place, anti-communists feared the intrusion of this new medium into American homes and its effects on domestic security. J. Edgar Hoover told the HUAC, "The best antidote to communism is vigorous, intelligent, old-fashioned Americanism." For anti-communists, the home was the most important front in the war over old-fashioned Americanism.[28] Hoover considered the family the first line of defense against the dangerous perspectives of his critics. Ignoring the historical variability of family forms, as well as demographic changes that had occurred during the tumultuous first half of the twentieth century, anti-communists defined the American family as "the old-fashioned loyalty of one man and one woman to each other and their children ... the basis, not only of society, but of all personal character and progress," as anti-communist Elizabeth Dilling put it.[29]

Gender and race lay at the heart of anti-communists' anxieties about a family form they diagnosed as being in crisis at the war's end. Following on the heels of the Depression, a catastrophic global economic disaster that challenged conservative notions of American identity, a successful war effort required the labor of women and men of color in industries that had previously excluded them. As women and people of color joined in wartime production, moving into positions previously reserved for white men, norms of race and gender were temporarily waived, a form of social destabilization, according to political theorist Cynthia Enloe, typical of periods of militarized conflict.[30] At the end of the war, white anti-communist men and women mobilized to restore the social hierarchies that had existed before 1941, expecting that white women would cede their freedoms to returning veterans and that African Americans who had fought a war against fascism in Europe would quietly accept the injustices of racism at home.

The anti-communist movement drew much of its strength from organizations that represented white veterans of war. These organizations encouraged white men traumatized by World War II to understand the changes that had happened in their absence as evidence of subversive, communistic influence. Veterans who had returned home to find families, homes, and communities changed in their absence were urged by anti-communist ideologues to redirect their anger, resentment, and pain toward American women and African Americans in particular, a tactic still used today. In exchange, anti-communists promised them nothing less than the restoration of their birthright as white men. According to historian Katherine Belew, "The return of [white] veterans from combat appears to correlate more closely with Klan membership than any other historical factor," highlighting the link between all-white veterans' organizations and renewed racist violence.[31] Indeed, in the years following World War II, veterans' organizations, working closely with fellow anti-communist institutions and organizations, redoubled their efforts to maintain segregation in American society and media industries, playing a key role in supporting and expanding the blacklist on television.[32]

The anti-communist movement was unified in its hatred of women who stepped out of the social roles conservatives approved for them. In their efforts to roll back changes that had begun well before the war, and as the shadow of the Cold War lengthened, images of a white Rosie the Riveter giving her patriotic all to support the war effort gave way to representations of white women whose wartime freedoms had compromised their femininity. One GI quoted in a *New York Times Magazine* article lavished praise on the infinite superiority of British girls who knew their place, "who think a man is important.... these girls over here don't want so many *things*. You get married to a girl back home and pretty soon she's got to have a fur coat and a washing machine and your car's got to be better looking than the one next door. You could bring a British girl 'some little thing' and you'd think you'd brought them a diamond bracelet."[33] Another veteran observed of his German girlfriend that, despite the fact she was "much better educated than I am and comes from a better family," she remained more subservient than her American counterpart: "when I get up in the morning I find my shoes shined and trousers pressed. Can you imagine an American woman doing that for you? Kee-rist, my own little sister wouldn't do that even for her old man!"[34]

Anti-communists held white women who defied conservative norms responsible for an ostensible decline in the American family's morals. Philip Wylie, a novelist, screenwriter, and commentator on American culture, first published his *Generation of Vipers* in 1943, but the book's popularity surged after World War II. Stimulated by new and unnatural cultural and political freedoms, American women, Wylie floridly maintained, had abandoned the only labor they were biologically suited for: "The machine has deprived her of social usefulness; time has stripped away her biological possibilities and poured her hide full of liquid soap; and man has sealed his own soul beneath the clamorous cordillera by handing her the checkbook and going to work in the service of her caprices."[35] Blaming "moms" and "momism" for the moral shortcomings of American culture, Wylie depicted mid-twentieth-century American women as grasping and physically repulsive.

Wylie was not alone in blaming all manner of social problems on American women. A cadre of emerging Cold War gender experts joined this chorus, proffering research that *proved* that American women had begun to devolve at the very moment they gained the right to vote in 1920. Wartime independence had only worsened women's moral decline. Ralph S. Banay, a professor of criminology at Columbia University, former chief psychiatrist at Sing Sing Correctional Facility and a popular anti-communist expert on juvenile delinquency, claimed that crime and juvenile delinquency resulted from the emotional childishness, cruelty, and materialism of women (the racism of the 1965 Moynihan Report criticizing black families also drew rhetorical force from vast reservoirs of Cold War misogyny).[36] Using scientific objectivity to mask his misogyny, Banay wrote, "Women's emotional development lags far behind their social-economic progress." In Banay's expert opinion, equality for women could only result in disaster: "The danger is already showing in the aggressive and uncontrolled behaviour of many women—often in outright criminal conduct, for the natural tendency of women toward infractions of law is probably greater than that of men."[37]

Anti-communists claiming to speak for all Americans dismissed progressive women who criticized their viewpoints as unnatural and unrepresentative of American womanhood. In 1950, for example, the American Legion published a newsletter, *Summary of Trends and Developments Exposing the Communist Conspiracy*. This tract declared that only a communist would object to the fact that "a woman worker carrying out the same work as a man" was paid "30 to 40 percent lower wages than the man." In fact, this kind of criticism, the writer maintained, was "nothing more than another example of the 'present Communist line.' "[38] Readers were left to infer that since communists criticized disparities in pay equity, such disparities were only a problem in the eyes of communists.

For anti-communists, sexism was just plain common sense. They unabashedly expressed their conviction that women were intellectually and politically inferior to men, a core belief that American culture shared with its wartime allies. But the violence of American racism was not as easily dismissed. During the war, civil rights activists had adopted the Double V campaign—signifying victory over the Axis powers, as well as a second victory over racism at home—to amplify the contradictions between a war fought in the name of democracy and domestic practices of violent discrimination. After the war, anti-communists' continuing expressions of racism evoked comparisons with the white supremacy of Nazism. For European countries coming to terms with the aftermath of the Nazi genocide, American white supremacy was alarmingly familiar.

Anti-communists recognized that American-style white supremacy cast them in a bad global light, even as they continued to believe that it was as natural and just as their misogyny. The FBI and other anti-communists monitored civil rights activities scrupulously but surreptitiously during World War II, increasingly uneasy about what they saw as the propaganda potential of anti-racist activism. The Soviet Union did indeed use American racism to malign capitalism. But anti-communists claimed that charges of racism had no basis in reality at all, but were fabricated by masterful Russian propagandists. They did not consider racism to be "factual information." Rather, it was their version of "fake news"—a public relations problem to be addressed through relentless attacks on those expressing anti-racist sentiments.

Still, anti-communists subtly adjusted the language they used to talk about race in New York City after the war, betraying their worry about international criticism of American white supremacy. The former FBI agents who founded the American Business Consultants were particularly circumspect around race, as Chapter 3 describes in more detail. They shared the belief that black people were racially inferior, but in order to maintain the illusion of benevolent Cold War consensus, they distanced themselves from racist fellow-travelers like anti-communist Elizabeth Dilling and Mississippi Senator John Rankin, whose bigotry was so overt as to make comparisons with Nazism unavoidable.

In their efforts to make such comparisons less obvious, anti-communists used language in their media campaigns that was less directly racist than that of their predecessors, relying on chains of racist signification rather than fervent avowals of white supremacy. Anti-communists, for example, did not object to violence against African Americans on moral grounds because largely they agreed with the use of violence to maintain the existing racial order. Instead, they objected to racist violence because it could be used by communists to *embarrass* Americans internationally, encouraging other countries to question and deride American democracy. The FBI's fear of being embarrassed by progressive women and people of color, as we will see in Chapter 3, was a recurring theme in the secret files they maintained on the Broadcast 41 and other progressives. The authoritarianism of anti-communism was such that they did not like being questioned in the first place. When the questions came from groups of people they considered their inferiors, anti-communist retaliation was swift and vicious.

By surveying the lively and dissenting perspectives on gender, race, and nation that were in the air in 1930s and 1940s New York, and then by detailing the suppression of these ideas and the people who held them, this book pieces together the events that allowed anti-communists to seize the ability to speak for all Americans, reinforce forms of storytelling favorable to white supremacy, and shape the content of televised American entertainment programming that would appear on network television. The events that transpired between 1949 and 1952 offer a textbook example of how political forces used a new medium to impose their viewpoints, in the process supporting conditions that enabled the reproduction of a narrow and restrictive formulation of tradition across decades, to be invoked repeatedly in the service of G-Man masculinity.

❖ ❖ ❖

Vera Caspary in The White Girl, *has probed closer to the heart of the almost white Negro than any writer who has thus far attempted to portray the girl who steps over—"passes" in short. She has not allowed herself to be swept into conventional mental attitudes, nor silly sentimentality. There is a delightful absence of "primitive passion," "back to Africa," "call of the blood," "Racial consciousness" "urge for service," "natural inferiority," "primitive fear."*

Alice Dunbar Nelson (poet, journalist)[39]

American culture is fond of the notion of a marketplace of ideas, but less astute when it comes to acknowledging ideas that either were prevented from making it to market in the first place or were set up to fail. Consequently, stories that never made it to market and did not become part of official histories can tell us a great deal about media production and history-making. As the following pages show, the goods that came to market in television were narrowly controlled by anti-communists determined to impose their restrictive perspective. Despite its claims to speak for all Americans, 1950s entertainment programming was told from a very specific perspective, one that shared conservative values concerning race, gender, class, and nation. Both anti-communists and communists shared a masculinist certainty in the rightness of their outlook and the wrongness of those who disagreed. This book argues that in order to evaluate the rightness of a perspective, it is vital to be able to compare and contrast it with many others.

The Broadcast 41 wanted to tell an array of stories, from many different points of view. In contrast to anti-communists' brutal efforts to quash dissent, the Broadcast 41's lives and work reflected their investment in the cultural and political importance of diverse perspectives. Although many of the Broadcast 41 did not consider gender to be the defining characteristic of their identities, I describe the Broadcast 41 as women because gender was a characteristic they all shared, in industries and political circles that were dominated by white men. Their professional work took place within the broader confines of being diverse women in professions that were reserved for white men, within industries requiring them to create demeaning and degrading representations of women and people of color. While they understood themselves to be women and progressives, the Broadcast 41 lived the heterogeneity of those categories, reminding us that people always exceed our attempts to herd them into categories.

However inadequately the term "women" captures the range of their perspectives, the Broadcast 41 knew their perspectives conflicted not only with the racism of anti-communists, but with the sexism of progressive white and black men as well. As Michael Denning remarks, "the Popular Front was more prepared for the racial realignments of the war years than for the gender realignments."[40] Consequently, progressive women like the Broadcast 41 fought for equality on multiple fronts: against the misogyny of the postwar era, against white supremacists, against xenophobic isolationism, and often with their own comrades who, like blacklisted actor Zero Mostel, expected their wives "to be home seeing that everything was nice for him, taking care of him and the boys."[41] For black women, these struggles were far more grueling. Years later, singer and actress Lena Horne recalled the strain that racism and sexism put on her first marriage. Black women, she observed, "have to be spiritual sponges, absorbing the racially inflicted hurts of their men," while at the same time giving them the courage to deal with the "humiliations and discouragements of trying to make it in the white man's world." It was not easy, she noted, "to be a sponge *and* an inspiration."[42]

For the Broadcast 41, gender did not exist in isolation from other aspects of their identities. Instead, modifiers crisscrossed the identity of women: they were working-class women, progressive women, black women, immigrant women, Jewish women. Progressive women had few illusions about women as a category, recognizing that their perspectives and the lives they led contradicted those of white conservative women who considered themselves guardians of what the FBI termed domestic security. The Broadcast 41 apprehended the social world in ways that were radically different from those of white conservative women and many men on the left and right, creating media, art, and culture that celebrated change and variety rather than despising those as harbingers of civilization's moral decline. Because of their capacious understandings of identity, the Broadcast 41's political and creative work did not reflect a single dimension of their identities as much as it did a belief that perspectives with different vantage points enhanced democracy and freedom. In contrast to anti-communists' efforts to monopolize the universal—to speak in one voice for all Americans—the Broadcast 41 cherished the notion that in the words of writer, director, and producer Gertrude Berg, gray-listed for her support of blacklisted actor Philip Loeb, "to be different then wasn't such a sin."[43]

The Broadcast 41 knew what it was like to be different. Their lived experiences defied the perspectives on Americanism favored by anti-communists. Because of the Depression, the Broadcast 41 had firsthand experience of economic hardship, understanding the determinative role that economic advantages play in people's lives. Many of them, like writer Vera Caspary, came from families that had experienced massive reversals of fortune in the 1920s and 1930s. At the same time, black middle-class women like Lena Horne recognized that wealth shifted, but did not eliminate, the oppression they experienced at the hands of white supremacy. Operating within the critical framework of the Popular Front, progressive white women working in broadcasting were more likely to agitate for civil rights and to assert their rights as workers than they were to demand equality for women, because while racial justice was part of the Communist Party's organizing platform, gender equality was not. Lesbian directors like Margaret Webster likewise remained quiet about the impact of homophobia on their lives in order to survive, but devoted substantial energies to efforts to fight racism in theater.

The lives and work of the Broadcast 41 unfolded against the dynamic backdrop of progressive cultural production in New York City, a place where many of them were born, worked, and died, a city they believed was like no other city in the world. Unlike Paris, London, and Berlin, New York City had emerged from World War II an unrivalled cultural and intellectual center, unscathed by the war's physical devastation. More international and liberal than any other major American city, the anti-racist politics of the Popular Front flourished in the fertile ground of Harlem. As literary scholar Farah Jasmine Griffin observes of Harlem during World War II, progressive black women in particular "couldn't wait to return.... Amid the noise, the rush, the thrill, and the trepidation, they came, they settled, they made homes, and they made art."[44] Blacklisted author and New Yorker Dorothy Parker shared a similar sense of the city: "New York is always hopeful. Always it believes that something good is about to come off, and it must hurry to meet it."[45] Actress Judy Holliday said that leaving New York was like " 'losing a leg,' and returning was finding that, after all, 'both legs were there and walking around.' "[46]

The Broadcast 41's attachment to New York City was especially profound during the second half of the 1940s, when progressives believed that the defeat of fascism in Europe was going to translate into the defeat of racism at home. New York City's dynamic traffic across theater, music, news, magazines, book publishing, and broadcasting drew actors, musicians, dancers, writers, and likeminded progressives into critical and creative exchanges about U.S. history, politics, and culture. Having fought against fascism, white supremacy, anti-Semitism, and xenophobia in the 1930s and 1940s, progressives working in and around broadcasting anticipated turning their talents and energies to enhancing American democracy.

Progressives in New York City recognized that televised popular culture—from sitcoms to soap operas to prime-time melodramas—was going to play an unprecedented role in disseminating new perspectives to a vastly expanded national audience. The Broadcast 41 were not naïve or uncritically utopian about the limitations of mass media. Many of them had worked in the less restrictive environment of theater and recognized that the economic imperatives of industries like film and radio made challenges to the status quo difficult. But they chose to fight over popular culture, holding fast to the belief that media might yet serve as tools for resistance. With the goal of introducing hitherto suppressed perspectives into popular culture, they produced, created, and performed in narratives that appealed to justice and democracy, agreeing that popular culture could educate people and promote compassion and understanding rather than fear and anger. Against tide and times, the Broadcast 41 appealed to the best in audiences. Anti-communists, as we will see, catered to the worst.

❖ ❖ ❖

The only conspiracy I know about in the entertainment industry is the one of blacklisting by Aware, Inc., Red Channels, *and* CounterAttack.

Madeline Lee (actress)[47]

It was known as one of those dangerous shows, because history was dangerous in those days. History is always dangerous.

Abraham Polonsky (writer)[48]

Throughout much of the twentieth century, critics and scholars dismissed television as a hopelessly lowbrow medium, inferior and common. But the FBI recognized that prime-time entertainment programming was a key battleground in the anti-communist war over American identity. The Bureau and other anti-communists were far less likely than progressives to make aesthetic distinctions between Hollywood and broadcasting, believing that Hollywood films and scripted radio and television programs alike exposed large audiences to dangerously radical social ideas and issues, by which they meant ideas not compatible with their preferred ways of seeing the world.

These concerns caused the FBI to initiate investigations of communist influence in Hollywood before World War II, but the U.S.'s wartime alliance with the Soviet Union stalled right-wing attempts to rid film of progressives. After the war ended, however, anti-communists renewed these efforts, initiating three new investigations into communists in Hollywood in September 1947, April 1951, and September 1951. The first of these investigations bore fruit when members of the group of filmmakers who came to be known as the Hollywood Ten were cited for contempt of Congress in 1947. "The long interval between the first and second investigations," according to blacklisted writer Albert Maltz, resulted from the fact "that the legal case of the Hollywood Ten was proceeding through the Courts during that time."[49] That legal case concluded in June 1950, when three separate judges sentenced nine of the Ten to pay fines and serve time in prison.

Inspired by their victory over the Hollywood Ten, anti-communists turned their attention to television. The FBI considered broadcast programming threatening enough to require continuous surveillance and intervention. Indeed the Bureau helped produce programs favorable to the FBI's point of view. Their most successful collaboration was with Phillips H. Lord on the popular reality series *Gang Busters* (1935–57), which used material drawn from the cold cases of the FBI. Not surprisingly, crime programs like *Gang Busters* and police procedurals were anti-communists' preferred form of programming, since these genres affirmed their law and order perspectives and celebrated patriarchal moral values considered to be 100 percent American, a phrase anti-communists shared with the Ku Klux Klan.[50]

In the late 1940s, a group of former FBI agents and military intelligence officers espousing these law-and-order perspectives led the charge against progressive influence in broadcasting. Financed by an unusual collaboration between Jewish anti-communist importer Alfred Kohlberg and the Catholic Church, these men established the American Business Consultants in 1946 (the definite article emphasizing their sense of self-importance). This organization published the influential anti-communist newsletter *CounterAttack* (1947–71) and their self-proclaimed bible of the blacklist, *Red Channels: The Report of Communist Influence in Radio and Television* (1950).[51] The American Business Consultants also inspired imitators who helped spread the gospel of anti-communism, including AWARE, Inc., founded by the author of *Red Channels*' "Introduction", Vincent J. Hartnett, in collaboration with anti-communist supermarket-chain owner Laurence A. Johnson.

The American Business Consultants propagated the idea that communists had infected broadcasting with their subversive virus, with the intent of spreading the disease of dissent to audiences. In his introduction to *Red Channels*, Harnett wrote, "The Communist-operated escalator system in show business has been in force for at least 12 years—since the Spanish Civil

War. Those who are 'right' are 'boosted' from one job to another, from humble beginnings in Communist-dominated night clubs or small programs that have been 'colonized,' to more important programs and finally to stardom."[52] Anti-communists argued that the "so-called 'intellectual' classes—members of the arts, the sciences, and the professions" possessed dangerous, un-American ideas and that they must be prevented from access to the airwaves by any means necessary.[53] As we will see, FBI files confirm journalist Betty Medsger's observation that for the Bureau, "to be an intellectual, like being black, was to be regarded as a potential subversive, if not an active one."[54] Progressive intellectuals (including scientists, artists, and educators), in the estimation of anti-communists, were intent on nothing less than the "increasing domination of American broadcasting and television, preparatory to the day when—the Cominform believes—the Communist Party will assume control of this nation as the result of a final upheaval and civil war."[55]

With its cultural and intellectual elites, interracial social venues, and more liberal attitudes toward gender and sexualities, New York City loomed large in the anti-communist imagination as an incubator for subversive ideas, organized dissent, and, ultimately, revolution. The only way to stop this New York-based red menace, they argued, was to detect, expose, and prosecute communists and fellow-travelers working in broadcasting.[56] To this end, the authors and publishers of *Red Channels* conducted research to "detect" threats, collaborating with the FBI, the HUAC, and other anti-communist researchers and organizations. They used publications like *CounterAttack* and *Red Channels* and a network of gossip columnists that stretched coast to coast to share information about progressives and give anti-communist organizations fodder for letter-writing campaigns and boycotts. Although anti-communists never won the legal victories they hoped for, as the following chapters demonstrate, they successfully tried and convicted those who dared to challenge them in a court of public opinion they had bullied into submission.[57]

The publication date of *Red Channels* proved auspicious: the American Business Consultants self-published it on June 22, 1950, just three days before the start of the Korean War. The book's cover featured a large, masculine red hand dramatically grasping a radio microphone, a metaphor for the impending seizure of radio and television by communists and their fellow-travelers (Figure 1.1). In *Red Channels*' "Introduction", freelance anti-communist writer Vincent J. Hartnett followed J. Edgar Hoover in defining a fellow-traveler as a person who, while not technically a member of the Communist Party, "actively supports (travels with) the Party's program for a period of time."[58] The expansiveness of this definition, and anti-communists'

Figure 1.1 Cover, *Red Channels: The Report of Communist Influence in Radio and Television*, The American Business Consultants, New York, NY: The author, 1950

liberal application of it, allowed the anti-communist movement to cast a capacious net in their hunt for communist influence.

Red Channels' pages contained an alphabetized list of 151 names, each name accompanied by an inventory of Communist and Communist "front" organizations those listed were alleged to have supported (Figure 1.2). The slender volume served as a crucial weapon in anti-communists' war on dissent. As early as 1950, social psychologist Marie Jahoda and *New York Times* journalist Jack Gould recognized that the primary function of the blacklist was, as Medsger later put it, to prevent "people from exercising their right to dissent."[59] In her study of "Anti-Communism and Employment Policies in Radio and Television," Jahoda found that "'blacklisting' procedures are met with fear, frustration, a conviction that innocent people are suspected, constriction and cynicism on the part of talent; an unresolved conflict of conscience on the part of management, with a notion that going along with the temper of the times is required if they are to serve the best interests of their clients."[60] One employee Jahoda interviewed gave the following advice to those working in broadcasting: "Don't do things that might show you in an unfavorable light. It's not wise to get involved in politics."[61] Jahoda was herself an example of the price people paid for criticizing anti-communists: she left the U.S. after she was blacklisted for her research on blacklisting.

The culture war anti-communists waged against those identified as subversive and politically impure reverberated across broad swaths of media, encompassing the liberal and literary left (poetry, novels, children's literature, and non-fiction), news (print and broadcast), and mass-mediated popular culture (animation, film, radio, and comics).[62] Conservatives attacked poetry in the 1950s, claiming that experiments with form (and thus challenges to tradition and convention) were a communist plot against American culture.[63] Literary scholars have abundantly documented the impact of the Red Scare on African American literature, since anti-communists believed that cultural production on the part of black people could only be the work of outside (read: white) agitators.[64] As literary critic William J. Maxwell put it, the FBI waged a "fifty-year crusade to bully and savor African American writing, always presumed to be a type of communist sophistry."[65] The anti-communist crusade, which eventually expanded to include all American popular culture, stifled creativity across media industries, including those from which television might have drawn for inspiration and innovation.

As a consequence of the blacklist, being involved—or having been at some point in the past been involved—in progressive politics could get you fired. Even though actual membership in the Communist Party was in steep decline

People's Radio Foundation	Member, Advisory Council. Official leaflet.
Civil Rights Congress	Sponsor, Bill of Rights Conference, Henry Hudson Hotel, New York City, 7/16, 17/49. Official bulletin.
	Signer. Telegram to Attorney General McGrath in behalf of the eleven Communist Party Leaders, 10/24/49. *Daily Worker*, 10/25/49, p. 3.

ALINE MacMAHON

Actress, Member of Equity Council

	Reported as:
Artists' Front to Win the War	Sponsor. *House Un-Am. Act. Com., Appendix 9*, p. 576.
Committee for a Democratic Far Eastern Policy	Sponsor. Letterhead, 10/46.
League of Women Shoppers	Honorary Vice-president, *House Un-Am. Act. Com., Appendix 9*, p. 1006.
National Wallace for President Committee	Member. Press release, 3/23/48.
Open Letter For Closer Cooperation with the Soviet Union	Signer. *Soviet Russia Today*, 8/39, p. 25.
National Council of the Arts, Sciences and Professions, Theatre Division	Nominee for office. Rally at Hotel Woodstock, New York City, 9/20/48. Handbill.
Stop Censorship Committee	Sponsor. Meeting, Savoy-Plaza Hotel, New York City, 2/24/48. *NY Herald-Tribune*, 2/25/48.
	Sponsor. Rally, Hotel Astor, New York City, 3/23/48. *NY Herald-Tribune*, 3/24/48.

(References to organizations listed begin page 161.)

PAUL MANN

Actor-Director—Stage, Radio

	Reported as:
Stage for Action	Member, Board of Directors. Letterhead, 5/28/46.
National Council of American-Soviet Friendship	Starred in Norman Corwin's script, "Untitled." Rally to greet Soviet Writers, 5/29/46. *Counterattack*, 8/19/49.
Scientific and Cultural Conference for World Peace	Interpreter. "The composer's (Shostakovich) 5200 word speech was read in English by Paul Mann, an interpreter." *NY Times*, 3/28/49, p. 1.
Voice of Freedom Committee	Speaker. Rally to defend Bill Sweets, Hotel Abbey, New York City, 8/11/49. Official program.
	Performer. "The Case of the Loaded Mike," Town Hall, New York City, 10/22/49. Town Hall Program, 10/22/49.
New York Council of the Arts, Sciences and Professions	Sponsor. Pre-Conference Rally for the Cultural and Scientific Conference for World Peace, Hotel Diplomat, New York City, 3/16/49. Handbill.

MARGO

Actress, Dancer

	Reported as:
American Labor Party	Speaker. Garment Rally. *Daily Worker*, 4/23/45, p. 5.
Allied Voters Against Coudert	Sponsor. *House Un-Am. Act. Com., Appendix 9*, p. 316.
American Rescue Ship Mission	Sponsor. *House Un-Am. Com., Appendix 9*, p. 493.
Artists' Front to Win the War	Sponsor. *House Un-Am. Act. Com., Appendix 9*, p. 575.
Committee for First Amendment	Sponsor. *Hollywood Reporter*, 10/24/47, p. 5; *Un-Am. Act. in California, 1948*, p. 210.

(References to organizations listed begin page 161.)

Figure 1.2 Page, *Red Channels: The Report of Communist Influence in Radio and Television*, The American Business Consultants, New York, NY: The author, 1950

during the 1950s, anti-communist estimates of the power and reach of the red network were increasing. For all their talk of greedy red hands reaching hungrily for the reins of control over media production, by the early 1950s, anti-communists controlled a far more powerful and influential anti-red network, one that combined the power of the FBI and other government branches and agencies with the reach of veterans' organizations, private anti-communist organizations, television networks, advertisers, sponsors, and professional snitches. Hoover's definition of a communist front—"an organization which the communists openly or secretly control"—equally applied to the FBI's own relationships with the publishers of anti-communist newsletters and books like *CounterAttack*, *Red Channels*, *AWARE, Inc.*, and *Confidential Notebook*, to take just a few examples.[66] The authors of *Red Channels* may have had an acrimonious and paranoid relationship with their former employer, as Chapter 4 documents, but they remained united with the Bureau in efforts to suppress challenges to their authoritarianism.

In an irony not lost on those smeared and vilified by the anti-communist web of paranoia and conspiracy, anti-communists like Hoover and Senator Joseph McCarthy lent urgency to their war on subversion by reference to the vastness of the communist propaganda machine, while at the very same time implementing their own vast propaganda machine. The machine they made, in the words of media critics Edward Herman and Noam Chomsky, allowed them to "mobilize the populace against an enemy" so amorphous that it could be strategically deployed against anyone identified as a "Public Enemy" who threatened the values of the John Birch Society, the FBI, rising politicians like Richard M. Nixon, Ronald Reagan, and others who took up the torch of anti-communists' political legacies.[67] Equating struggles for civil rights and immigrants' rights with the revolutionary overthrow of the U.S. government, anti-communists declared that challenges to their views resulted from the contaminating influence of the "Comugressive Party," a portmanteau term frequently used in the pages of *CounterAttack*.[68]

While the stated goal of anti-communists was to rid the airwaves of "parlor pinks" (a reference to East Coast intellectuals) and other subversives, the long-term effects of the blacklist proved as significant as the initial purge.[69] The blacklist shaped the foundations of the new medium of television, sending a clear message to people working in the industry: avoid anything that could be construed as progressive or risk never working in television again. In this way, anti-communists controlled definitions of America and American values by creating climates hostile to progressive viewpoints in media industries. The elimination of subversives on the basis of presumed political sensibilities and the fear that followed from their removal allowed anti-communist ideas, as Chomsky and Herman observed, to function for decades as powerful mechanisms for imposing conformity.[70]

Some years later, writer Studs Terkel put his finger on the logic that attributed any criticism of anti-communism to the dire influence of communism. If, he asked an NBC executive, communists are against cancer, does that mean we have to be for it?[71] The answer to Terkel's question was a resounding yes. To extend this logic, if communists were for civil rights, then real Americans had to oppose them. If communists supported state-subsidized child care, then child care must be a communist plot. Thus did the blacklist set well-defined limits for the ideas that could be expressed in television without fear of "controversy" (a code word for subversive content), invoking these limits for years to come in order to govern the content of entertainment programming.

Progressives' resistance to these postwar retrenchments was formidable and courageous. In the years after the war's end, progressives promoting the rights of African Americans and immigrants clashed with anti-communists, who wanted to arrogate for themselves the right to speak for a nation that viewed the world from a single perspective, based on homogeneous understandings of god, country, family, gender, race, and class. The Broadcast 41 swam against this rising postwar tide of anti-communist racism, misogyny, and xenophobia. They criticized the discriminatory nature of anti-communist beliefs and fought against these, even as opportunities for dissent began to narrow in the late 1940s, and as a powerful anti-communist backlash against progressivism began to loom on their horizons.

Anti-communists did not single out women specifically for attack, but as this book makes clear, postwar shifts in gender made women attractive targets. Even though media industries were dominated by men in occupations like producing, directing, and writing, a full 30 percent of those personnel *Red Channels* identified as communists or fellow-travelers were women. The ranks of the blacklisted included actresses like Rose Hobart, Pert Kelton, Gypsy Rose Lee, Madeline Lee, Jean Muir, Fredi Washington, and Minerva Pious who had achieved modest forms of fame; choreographer Helen Tamiris, known for dances celebrating African American culture and protest; musicians and singers like Ray Lev, Lena Horne, and Hazel Scott who fought racism; Mexican-American dancer Margo, an early celebrant of Latinx identity; anti-fascist news commentator Lisa Sergio; progressive writers like Gertrude Berg, Vera Caspary, Ruth Gordon, Shirley Graham, and others listed in this book's *Dramatis Personae*. One indication of the blacklist's success is that where actress Lucille Ball, who survived her own scrape with the blacklist in 1953, remains a household name, very few of these women's names are remembered today, even by broadcast historians.

❖ ❖ ❖

For a long while, I wouldn't talk about it at all. I do now, because there's a whole new generation that doesn't remember. And the more one knows, the more one can see, and not allow history to repeat itself.

Kim Hunter (actress)[72]

It was a cloud that never went away. It was terrible. It destroyed a lot of people, more than anybody is ever going to know. It killed them, even when they weren't dead. It struck fear into the hearts of all kinds of people.

Arthur Miller (playwright)[73]

Accounts of the blacklist and its impact on American culture remain rare in scholarship and popular culture, while images of the happy days of the 1950s abound. Because our attention has been drawn to the content that viewers ultimately saw on their screens, we have had fewer opportunities to consider who made that content and the circumstances that shaped production. And understandably so: it remains more time-consuming and difficult to document the content that was in the air before the anti-communist purge eclipsed it than content readily available on network and cable television, DVDs, and streaming services. Redirecting attention not to what we have seen on screens, but to what we were prevented from seeing is to tell a very different story about the possibilities of television as a new medium as well as the wide-ranging perspectives of those who had once dreamed of writing stories for it.

Histories are shaped by what appeared in the pages of newspapers and what appeared on screens around the nation. Because what happened during the blacklist era has been so deeply suppressed in popular culture, few histories of television recount the impact of the blacklist on the industry, despite its occurrence at such a formative moment in the new medium's development. Radio writer, director, producer, and historian Erik Barnouw described the blacklist at length in his history of broadcasting, written while events were still fresh in the minds of progressives, but many later books on television scarcely refer to it.[74] Other books have sporadically documented aspects of the blacklist—some of them mentioning its effects on broadcasting.[75] Some, like Thomas Doherty's scholarly *Cold War, Cool Medium*, have taken a more benign view of Cold War television, arguing that "During the Cold War, through television, America became a more open and tolerant place."[76] The women and men who were driven out of the industry in the early 1950s would have disagreed with this view.

Compounding the initial suppression, journalistic histories of television have been frequently told from the perspectives of cold warriors who approved of the blacklist. Freelance writer David Everitt's 2007 *A Shadow of Red: Communism and the Blacklist in Radio and Television* is a case in point. In it, Everitt concedes that anti-communists may have gone too far in violating the constitutional rights of progressives but argues that they were broadly justified by the magnitude of the Communist menace.[77]

To the extent that the blacklist does come up, it does so in regard to Hollywood and, to a lesser extent, theater. The cinematic example of the Hollywood Ten certainly helped solidify the association of the blacklist with film. Because film has long been considered a more culturally and aesthetically meaningful medium than broadcast media, anti-communist efforts to censor film were taken much more seriously by later generations raised on the belief that American television could never have been more than what it became after the blacklist made controversy (and thus innovation) synonymous with communist influence and un-Americanism.

The elitism that characterized cultural criticism in the 1950s on the right and the left has also contributed to amnesia around the blacklist. Whatever their political beliefs, male intellectuals agreed that television was the opiate of the masses, a medium so lowbrow as to scarcely merit their attention. In contrast, and as Chapter 3 emphasizes, both the Broadcast 41 and anti-communists took forms of storytelling like broadcast entertainment programming, children's literature, dance, and music—especially as these were transmitted via television—very seriously indeed. Intellectuals from the Cold War onward continued to disparage these modes of storytelling, privileging instead news and political programming, seen as rational spheres of political persuasion and muscular debate. Televised news and political programming, in their estimation, were the places where hearts and minds would be won and lost, not media made for women and children.

Consequently, despite the thousands of passionate fan letters received by programs like *The Goldbergs* that credited the radio sitcom with combatting intolerance and anti-Semitism, the persuasive dimensions of such programming were dismissed as being nothing more than feminized, mass-produced fantasies. As a result, scholars have painstakingly documented anti-communist and corporate control over news media, paying substantially less critical attention to anti-communist surveillance of, and control over, entertainment programming.[78] Not surprisingly, this preoccupation with news media—a segment of the industry that has been especially resistant to incursions by women and people of color—has resulted in a marked lack of attention to the efforts of women and people of color to intervene in broadcast entertainment programming, efforts that had begun to alarm anti-communists as early as the mid-1930s.

Regardless of subsequent recollections, at the end of World War II, progressives and anti-communists recognized that television was poised to affect not only how Americans understood American identity in the 1950s, but how they would remember the past for long decades to come. These were prescient views. Although television itself has long dramatized its own version of its genesis and subsequent role in historical events ranging from the Vietnam War to the terrorist attacks of September 11, 2001, it has had surprisingly little to say about the dramatic series of events that transformed the new medium in the late 1940s and 1950s.[79] This silence reflects the medium's own investment in a consensus version of history. In the industry's version of television's history, the medium figures as domestic hearth, a reflection of the hopes and dreams of the Cleavers, the Andersons, and other white middle-class people who conformed to anti-communist understandings of what it meant to be American. The origins of the medium in a war on dissent have been thus obscured; the story of the blacklist hard to tell because it challenges myths about television's history and its role in American culture.

While television fondly looks back on the images of domestic life it created in the 1950s, the broadcast industry has had little to say about the lively dissent that characterized the late 1940s media industry in New York City and the repressive realities of the blacklist era that followed. Every once in a while, the blacklist has come up, but when it does, it has appeared as a story in which CBS, for example, bravely televised the Army-McCarthy hearings in 1954 and nurtured the liberalism of journalist Edward R. Murrow. Of course, these accounts do not mention that by the end of 1950, CBS had begun enforcing the most stringent loyalty oath program in the industry, creating its own "spook" department to monitor and investigate employees and to ensure compliance with anti-communist definitions of Americanism.[80]

The memory of the blacklist introduces troubling contradictions into television's celebrations of the very consensus to which the industry attributed the homogeneity of its pictures of American life. Indeed, according to television history as it was shaped by anti-communism, the images that appeared on television were what postwar Americans demanded of the industry. Rather than affirming the belief that televised entertainment programming grew out of the desires of viewers, the blacklist forces us to acknowledge the repressive measures taken to ensure the dominance of this anti-communist view of America. In place of consensus, the blacklist reminds us that it took loyalty oaths, boycotts, and firings of progressive workers; the chilling of speech; the censorship of appearances by African Americans; and surveillance and retaliation by the FBI to impose these sets of stories on the new medium of television. Absent images of dissent, it was easy to dismiss the bigotry of the 1950s as though it was in fact a consensus of that era—one shared by all people who identified as Americans. Restoring the blacklist to television history shows us consensus was partial at best.

The silence surrounding the blacklist era and the suppression of the perspectives of people like the Broadcast 41 have allowed representations of family, gender, race, and class shaped by anti-communism to serve as sleeper cells, imitated by later television programs, appropriated by politicians to invoke a nostalgic, conservative past, and celebrated by media industries invested in a narrative about a sexist and racist consensus that in turn legitimizes continued industrial practices of stereotyping and exclusion. The resultant amnesia has allowed television to treat its image vaults as historical archives rather than industrial products, as reflections of reality rather than versions of reality shaped by political and economic forces. This book marks an effort to counter what literary critic Mary Helen Washington calls "the amnesia that McCarthyism, the FBI, and the CIA have promoted," but with regard to control over television and popular culture rather than literature or film.[81]

Drawing inspiration from the significant body of feminist scholarship exploring the roles that women and people of color have played in literary production and in the making of history, this book restores to view the work that people who would later be described as minorities had been doing across entertainment industries, as well as the role that they were poised to play as this work fed the hungry new medium of television. The forty-one women blacklisted in 1950 were eager to find ways to use the emerging medium to educate Americans and promote civil rights, political and economic justice, and peaceful political struggle. They were at points in their careers where they might have done so. Their accounts of what they had dreamed of creating and what happened to those dreams have long been missing from the history of television.

❖ ❖ ❖

I didn't set out to make a contribution to interracial understanding. I only tried to depict the life of a family in a background that I knew best.

Gertrude Berg (actress, director, producer, writer)[82]

Maybe tell how I nearly missed the train in Sault Ste. Marie. Is that what people mean when they say don't go on the stage, it'll ruin your health, break your heart, and you'll wish you were back in Wollaston living a normal life, loved by some good man?

Ruth Gordon (actress and writer)[83]

Documenting the perspectives of progressives like the Broadcast 41 led me through a maze of sources. Because the women listed in *Red Channels* had all been born in the first decades of the twentieth century, I was forced to resort to means other than oral history to understand their varied perspectives. Given the vagaries of human memory, reading what the Broadcast 41 had written in the 1930s, 1940s, and 1950s, as events were unfolding, probably offered a more accurate sense of events than what they remembered many decades later, filtered as memories are by time and trauma.

The sources I consulted to address considerable gaps in historical records were varied and numerous. Certain members of the Broadcast 41, as well as other blacklisted women, left papers in institutional archives, some like Joan La Cour Scott because of their better-known husbands; others such as Gertrude Berg, Vera Caspary, and Shirley Graham because they understood that their lives had historical value. In the case of Jean Muir, my website provided a point of contact with Muir's daughter, Margaret Bauer, who subsequently donated her mother's papers to the University of Oregon's Special Collections and University Archives. Archival materials like these proved to be a precious, if partial, antidote to the historical amnesia that resulted from the blacklist, particularly insofar as they provided empirical evidence of content that never made it onto the air, evidence that allowed me to assemble the counterfactual history of television programming that appears in Chapter 6.

To supplement the materials in official archives, I read published novels, plays, poems, newspaper and magazine articles, scripts, autobiographies, and letters written by members of the Broadcast 41, as well as the memoirs and biographies of people who were close to them. I also listened to radio broadcasts and watched performances and fragments of performances. I watched Hollywood films and television broadcasts. I read media accounts of the work of these women in the black and mainstream press, as well as reviews of their performances, plays, novels, and other work that appeared at the time of publication, performance, or release. I read much of what was said about these women in the New York City press of their time, as well as what was said years later, by people who either admired or despised them.

As progressive media workers' perspectives on gender, race, and nation came into focus, I realized that I needed to better understand the perspectives of those who charged the Broadcast 41 as being threats to American identity in the late 1940s. To do so, I focused on the perspectives of the FBI and its privatized spin-off, the American Business Consultants, publishers of *CounterAttack* and *Red Channels.* Relying on the work of scholars like David Price and Matthew Cecil, I learned of the FBI's highly successful, largely covert public relations operation known as the Crime Records Division. This division allowed Hoover and Bureau agents to function as expert consultants for film, radio, and television industries, as well as to produce media favorable to their point of view.[84]

According to Betty Medsger, "Under Hoover's byline, his staff and freelance ghostwriters penned dozens of books and hundreds of articles for magazines and newspaper columns where he expressed his views on countless subjects."[85] Their list of friendly contacts and informants included many journalists working for conservative William Randolph Hearst's newspaper empire: gossip columnist Igor Cassini, Howard Rushmore of the anti-communist newspaper the *New York Journal-American* and later the *Police Gazette,* and syndicated journalist Westbrook Pegler. The list of FBI friendlies also included Hollywood gossip columnist Hedda Hopper; George Sokolsky (a radio broadcaster for the National Association of Manufacturers and a newspaper columnist for a number of anti-communist papers); columnist Walter Winchell; photographer Ernest Withers; and many others. In his exhaustive study of the FBI's war on student radicals in the 1960s, journalist Seth Rosenfeld shows how the FBI "sought to change the course of history by secretly interceding in events, manipulating public opinion, and taking sides in partisan politics."[86] The Bureau's role in the television blacklist is without a doubt one of its most successful efforts to intercede not only in historical events, but to influence how those events were remembered by subsequent generations as well.

To document FBI surveillance of the Broadcast 41, as well as how agents of the Cold War surveillance state regarded progressives, I requested FBI files for all forty-one of the Broadcast 41, as well as for Henry Jaffe (Jean Muir's husband), Gertrude Berg, Philip Loeb, and the authors of *CounterAttack* and *Red Channels.*[87] As Chapters 3 and 4 demonstrate, access to these files—even as heavily redacted as many of them were—allowed me to describe for the first time the role the FBI played in making the television blacklist successful. It also forced me to reconsider my own thinking about the forces that control media industries. Although, as we will see, the commercial nature of U.S. media helped the Red Scare flourish, my research on the FBI and its former agents made me consider what happens when the primary obstacle to dissent is not economic in nature, but political—the result of friction between the ideological needs of the surveillance state and media industries' own practices.

As I researched the blacklist, I came to think about the story of the blacklist not as a tale of individuals who were in one way or other remarkable, but rather as a story about groups of people whose perspectives about gender, race, and nation collided in the turbulent waters of the post-World War II era and how one of those groups worked out compromises with powerful institutions that effectively undermined basic democratic processes. Media production in the 1930s and 1940s was full of far richer, more varied, and complex perspectives than what ensued as a result of anti-communist efforts. The effect of the Red Scare was to shrink the field of perspectives to such a narrow band of opinion that even the most liberal of viewpoints would appear dangerously leftwing. In the telling of this story, specific individuals on the left and right come in and out of focus. I have endeavored to tell the story of the Broadcast 41 and the forces opposing them as perspectives and positions that were contentious and full of tension and disagreement.

This book is divided into six chapters. Building on the themes introduced in the prologue and Chapter 1, the second chapter, "A Field of Many Perspectives," describes the circumstances that encouraged members of the Broadcast 41 to develop and cherish perspectives that reflected anti-racist, internationalist points of view. This chapter explores the experiences that led these women to perceive the world so differently from anti-communists, captains of industry, and even other progressives. These personal and professional experiences as women (albeit women of different class and racial backgrounds, whose sexualities were often at odds with the morals of their day) equipped them to pursue careers in media at a point in time when the obstacles to doing so were immense.

Chapter 3, "G-Man Nation," shifts gears to examine the standpoints of the anti-communists who found the presence and ideas of the Broadcast 41 so threatening. The blacklist resulted from decades of collaborative efforts among anti-communists to convey a powerful myth of the supremacy of white, male Americans. This chapter unravels the making of this myth, as well as the hidden realities and massive state power of G-Man masculinity that allowed anti-communists to retaliate against and punish those who dared to question their vision.

Where Chapter 3 sketches out the contours of G-Man masculinity as it was created and practiced by the FBI and other anti-communists, Chapter 4, "Cashing in on the Cold War," shows how three former FBI agents picked up the banner of G-Man masculinity, turning the Bureau's media practices into a private business capable of bullying mighty capitalist industries into submission. In just a few short years, this group of former G-Men went from being considered ridiculous by progressives and reviled as "persona non grata" by the Bureau to a formidable privatized security force that could coerce television networks into firing people the American Business Consultants had labeled politically impure. This chapter tells the story of how struggles among G-Men for control over the television industry were resolved, laying the groundwork for the successful campaign against the Broadcast 41 in 1950.

Chapter 5, "Cleaning the House of Broadcasting," recounts the series of attacks that initiated the blacklist. These first attacks on progressives in television during the summer of 1950 were aimed at women: Ireene Wicker, the host of a popular children's television show; trade unionist, burlesque artist, writer, and quiz show host Gypsy Rose Lee; actress and labor activist Jean Muir; and musician and civil rights activist Hazel Scott, the first black woman to host her own television show. This chapter explains the anti-communist attack that transformed the perspectives of the Broadcast 41 into offenses costing them their jobs, engendering a climate in the new industry hostile to perspectives defined by anti-communists as controversial, subversive, and inherently treasonous.

The book's final chapter, "Red *Lassie*: A Counterfactual History of Television" (several blacklisted writers found work after the blacklist on the children's program *Lassie*), takes up what historian Ellen Schrecker describes as the real cost of the Red Scare in media industries—the scripts that were never written, the ideas that were never aired, and the innovations that would be prevented from taking place for decades.[88] Based on the evidence left by this group of left and left-leaning women, the chapter offers a counterfactual history grounded in archival research, analyses of the work these women had accomplished prior to the blacklist, and the work they continued to conduct before they were erased from the history of the medium. Just as so many of the Broadcast 41 sought inspiration in the lives of those who had struggled before them, so this book concludes by restoring to view women's struggles to change the storytelling practices of a new medium, struggles that remain very much alive today. Unlike popular and inherently conservative alternative histories that ask us to consider what would happen if fascists proved victorious during the Civil War or World War II, this history challenges us to consider what might have happened if the voices of this generation of progressive women had been allowed to air instead.

Suppressing the memory of these women and those who shared their views allowed anti-communists to conjure consensus by erasing dissent. As feminist sociologist Patricia Hill Collins writes, "Suppressing the knowledge produced by any oppressed group makes it easier for dominant groups to rule because the seeming absence of dissent suggests that subordinate groups willingly collaborate in their own victimization."[89] While this book mainly focuses on television, the story of the Broadcast 41 also reorients our understanding of the history of women's activism in media industries as well. Black left feminists wrestled with issues of race, class, and gender in popular and literary cultures throughout the twentieth century, as had their predecessors in previous social movements. Women like Shirley Graham, Lena Horne, Hazel Scott, and Fredi Washington provided leadership on these issues in entertainment industries, influencing progressives across divides of race and class. What a later generation of feminists would call intersectionality was not something invented by a second, third, or even fourth wave of feminism, however much the anti-communist elision of black left feminism made this appear to be the case.[90] Chronicling the lives and work of the Broadcast 41, who labored in industries and against political foes who were dead set against their doing so, this book returns us to a moment in the 1940s when what media studies scholar Kristen Warner describes as complicated and historically accurate representations of people of color and women seemed both desirable and within reach.[91]

The omission in scholarship and popular culture alike of the Broadcast 41 and those who shared their perspectives has forced successive generations to reinvent wheels in the ruts of historical memory. By looking to writers, directors, producers, and artists like Shirley Graham, Lena Horne, Dorothy Parker, Vera Caspary, and other blacklisted women, we can identify vital precedents for contemporary efforts to make media industries less hostile to the presence of women and people of color. The struggles of Horne, Jean Muir, Hazel Scott, Fredi Washington, and others to dismantle stereotypes in film show that people of color and anti-racist whites were bluntly critical of racism in media industries from the start. Recognizing that what came to be known as intersectionality, and struggles to represent ideas like this in media and popular culture, were not inventions of the waning years of the twentieth century, but a vital part of the field of cultural production in the years before the blacklist deepens our understanding of contemporary struggles over new media, providing context and insight for forms of full cultural and political representation that remain unfinished.

Although the stories of the Broadcast 41 involve tremendous collective and personal suffering, this book is not a defeatist narrative about the impossibility of social change or the triumph of capitalism. One part of this story does recount the jubilant misogyny of 1950s television and the stereotypes and silences around people of color and immigrants. Nevertheless, it is also a story about the existence of irrepressible alternatives to the white supremacist masculinity central to anti-communist beliefs and practices. Just as the introduction of new media and technologies at the end of the twentieth century allowed groups of people to create and share ideas and media outside the more established fields of cultural production that remain closed to them, so the introduction of television in the 1940s encouraged similarly marginalized groups to make inroads into radio and television.[92] Documenting the struggles of people of color and women to gain access to the airwaves in the 1930s and 1940s offers an important context for contemporary efforts to make media accessible and inclusive.

The Broadcast 41 were strong, outspoken women, whose lives and points of view were limited by the crosswinds of their era. Because they were so uncommon, they were often labeled "difficult" or "tough" by contemporaries using a language of discrimination that persists today. They may have been difficult in the eyes of those intent on protecting Jim Crow, or tough from the perspective of the men whose control they challenged in media industries, but they were not motivated by the fear of difference and change that caused anti-communists to reinvest in white supremacy, misogyny, and xenophobia at the end of World War II. This book shows that unlike anti-communists, people like the Broadcast 41 were inspired by the belief in a world that if not perfect, was at the very least more expansive, forgiving, and less violent.

The contrast between the lives and work of the Broadcast 41, who wanted to create art and culture that reflected their belief in democracy and equality, and the beliefs of anti-communists intent on protecting bigotry and the advantages it conferred on them, allows for fresh and timely insight into what the new medium of television might have offered viewers in the 1950s. Television might well have represented significant differences of opinion rather than the illusion of a Cold War consensus achieved covertly and underhandedly through the suppression of dissent. The relevance of this book for the contemporary moment lies in what the history of this culture war can tell us about how white, masculine supremacy and its institutions maintain power and reproduce oppressive representations of people of color, women, and immigrants through subterfuge, manipulation, and suppression.

Today, the forces of white supremacy and misogyny reassemble and unite around online cultures, nurtured and goaded on by a president who daily enacts the worst excesses of G-Man masculinity. That conservatives conjured the Soviet Union as the bogeyman to anti-communist white knights in the 1950s, while downplaying the repressive nature of Vladimir Putin's regime in the second decade of the twenty-first century, hints at a point made throughout the book: the real stakes all along involved white male control over domestic security and a domestic sphere over which men feared they were losing control. It will take decades to assess the disastrous consequences of this ongoing culture war. The Broadcast 41 initially viewed the creators of *Red Channels* as buffoons full of bluster and bravado. Like them, we must recognize this political regime, with its attack on all media that dare to criticize it, for the deadly serious threat that it is. The story of the Broadcast 41's struggle may help those who continue to persevere during an era of similarly considerable anxiety and uncertainty.

Chapter 2

A Field of Many Perspectives

Cohn saw us to the door of his office and as we were leaving, he decided to cap the hour gaily by telling a joke. "Say, listen," he said, "Did you hear this one? Jessel told it to me. You'll get a belly out of it. Listen. These two little Jews get into a rowboat, see—" That was as far as he got. My wife turned away abruptly and disappeared. "What's a matter with her?" asked Cohn. "Nothing," I said. "She just doesn't like that kind of comedy." "What kind of comedy? Jew comedy?" "That's right." "I don't get it," said Cohn. "She's not even Jewish." "That's right." "So why should she care?"

Garson Kanin (writer)[1]

Sometime in the mid-1940s, the Broadcast 41's Ruth Gordon (Figure 2.1) walked out of a meeting with Columbia Pictures' president Harry Cohn, refusing to listen to his joke. Cohn's question—"why should she care?"—gives a sense of how puzzling Gordon's response was to purveyors of anti-Semitic, racist, and sexist humor. Gordon left a meeting with a powerful Hollywood mogul to discuss a script because she understood that a joke that began with the words "These two little Jews" could only end in the disparagement and disrespect of Jewish people, regardless of whether the listeners and tellers were themselves Jewish. With Hitler's genocide of Jews very much on the minds of progressives, Gordon simply could not bear to listen. Since she was not going to change Cohn's mind—the man was notorious for such slurs—she did the one thing she could do: she left.

The Broadcast 41 shared similar forms of refusal and resistance when it came to media images that denigrated groups of people. Anti-communists, in contrast, maintained a narrow notion of what they called Americanism, one rooted in an unshakeable conviction of their superiority. For them, Americans were white and conventionally male or female. Americans were born in the U.S. and if they had ever been poor in the past, they no longer were because they had seized hold of the American Dream. In opposition to these forms of thinking, the Broadcast 41 refused to accept the belief that whiteness, masculinity, and Christianity meant that some groups of people were biologically superior to others, and thus that others could be blamed by virtue of race, ethnicity, gender, or economic class for being disadvantaged. Instead of an Americanism that saw in all those considered other to it cause for hostility and fear, the Broadcast 41's sensibilities were shaped by what blacklisted actress

Figure 2.1 Ruth Gordon
Source: Courtesy Library of Congress, Washington, DC

Gale Sondergaard described as a love of "the complexity of our people, their complex freedoms."[2]

They were complex people themselves, this generation of women who lived in question marks and scrutinized the values and norms of the worlds around them. How they were drawn to complexity rather than the white supremacist certainties of anti-communists is key to understanding the threat they posed to the new medium of television in the middle of the twentieth century. It would be easy to say that they looked at the world differently because they were women who came of age in a society that made certain that they knew their subordinate place in it. But gender, as we will see, was only one part of their stories. Being assigned the gender identity of female at birth did not automatically lead to respecting a range of perspectives other than one's own and advocating for these. After all, conservative white women like Elizabeth Dilling, Hester McCullough, Ayn Rand, and others who followed in their footsteps wholeheartedly embraced the racist and nativist logic of anti-communism, serving as foot soldiers in Cold War conflicts over gender, race, and migration.

Of course, the Broadcast 41 had either experienced discrimination in their personal histories or were members of racial, ethnic, or economic groups that had suffered at the hands of white supremacy. Progressive women often had direct experiences of multiple forms of discrimination: as workers, women of color, Jewish women, immigrants, lesbians, and people who loved and worked alongside members of these groups. These experiences shaped their perspectives, causing them to be alienated from the stories anti-communists told about America, because those stories so pointedly excluded people like them, as well as people they loved.

Perhaps the sense of simply *not appearing* in any meaningful way in either American political life or the stories that American culture was telling about real Americans was what drew the Broadcast 41 and other women to media industries in the years between the wars. They recognized the vast divide between their everyday lives and what they were allowed to write and perform about those lives. They realized that changing the narrator of a story changes what that story tells us. Tell the story from the point of view of the dog and perhaps carrying the master's slippers around in their mouth did not look so appealing. Tell the story of domestic service from the point of view of the maid and not the woman who paid her and white family life was far less idyllic than sitcoms like *Beulah* and *Hazel* let on.[3] Tell the story of the FBI from the perspective of deportees and African Americans, and the G-Man looked more like a predator than a protector.

This chapter describes the forces that led the Broadcast 41 to question the totalitarian belief that the story of America had a single narrator, perched godlike above the messy business of living, and that there were simple solutions (be they capitalist or communist) for the world's complex problems. They questioned and dissented, even within their own progressive circles. There was much that progressive women did not agree on in the uncertain days of the 1930s and 1940s. Many enjoyed advantages unavailable to others and took these for granted. Although private and public histories of exclusion disposed them to identify not with the centers of power but with those who were excluded from them, their experiences of the world were not interchangeable.

In order to get to where they were in media industries, the Broadcast 41 had to be immensely competitive survivors. In the creative ferment of the early days of television, these survivors saw new and potent opportunities to speak for themselves and thus to defy misrepresentations and stereotypes. The forces that impelled them toward defiance rather than capitulation—the forces that shaped their perspectives and the stories they wanted to tell through literature, radio, film, dance, music, and television—were intensely personal, professional, and political.

❖ ❖ ❖

"No son, those cabs won't carry colored folks. We got to go outside and wait till a colored cab comes." That was my introduction to Washington.

Lena Horne (singer, actress)[4]

My grandfather said [Frederick] Douglass had a superb voice and stage presence, but small humor.... [He] cited a Republican rally, in the seventies perhaps, where a white orator, after the fashion of the time, told several very humorous "darky stories." When he was finished, the tall Douglass, with his leonine mane, was introduced. He said, "Those stories were funny, very funny, but I felt each of them to be a foot pressing upon my mother's grave."

Lloyd Lewis (biographer, in a review of Shirley Graham's There Once Was a Slave*)*[5]

The Broadcast 41 knew that they were living in singular times. Most were born in the first two turbulent decades of the twentieth century. A few outliers like Mady Christians and Hilda Vaughn (both born in 1892) and Madeline Lee Gilford (born in 1923) bookended the group. Despite some differences in age, they shared sensibilities born of a crisis-prone era that had called into question many conventional convictions about American identity.

Progressive women realized that they were living through historic changes, particularly in terms of gender and race. The Nineteenth Amendment to the U.S. Constitution gave women the right to vote in 1920. Their generation of women remembered what it was like to be prevented from voting. They were daughters and granddaughters of women who had mobilized for women's right to vote, like Lena Horne's grandmother. Despite the suffrage, the black women among them continued to live in a country where African Americans were still prevented from voting. Disenfranchisement was fresh in the minds of all these women; the right to vote new and far from universal. All shared the sense, as author Vera Caspary put it in an interview toward the end of her life, that "This has been the century of the woman, and I know myself to have been a part of the revolution."[6]

But the right to vote was only one of the many changes in women's lives, less influential perhaps than others. Birth rates had declined precipitously between 1910 and 1945; the average age of marriage for women increased; and women's educational levels were on the rise. These changes made women's lives markedly better than those of the generation that had preceded them. Because of these changes, the Broadcast 41 could see how very different their lives were from those of their mothers' generation. Gertrude Berg described the ceaseless labor that characterized her mother's life in her autobiography:

> My mother was divided into three parts. Or, even worse, she was three people—a wife, a worker, and a mother. I'm a wife, I'm a mother, and I'm also a worker but at least I have washing machines—one for the dishes and one for the clothes. To be a wife and a mother is a pleasure—to be a worker around the house I can do without. You want to know why? Because it never stops! If it's not the dishes, it's the beds, after the beds it's the floors, and then the windows, then the furniture, then the clothes. And when you stop it's only to rest up so you can start all over again in the morning. If that sounds like complaining, it is.[7]

Actress Madeline Lee said that her mother was "an early feminist" who was determined that her daughters would "have an education and careers so they wouldn't end up as housewives whose only life was in the kitchen," with its endless drudgery.[8]

But as Berg's description of her mother's labors emphasizes, the Broadcast 41's thinking about gender was profoundly influenced by the class-consciousness of their era. For some, this consciousness stemmed from personal experiences of deprivation and class struggle. Many grew up in poor families, finding work in entertainment industries as child laborers to supplement meager family incomes. Madeline Lee (years later listed in *Red Channels* along with musician Hazel Scott) recalled that when she took voice lessons, the rehearsal pianist was none other than the eleven-year-old Scott.[9] Gypsy Rose Lee (née Rose Louise Hovick) began performing with her sister June in vaudeville at the age of four; actress Pert Kelton (the first actress to play the role of Alice Kramden in *The Honeymooners* before being fired because of the blacklist) worked steadily from the age of three. Like Ruth Gordon, they came "from hard-working people" and it never occurred to them not to work.[10]

Because of the disastrous consequences of the 1929 stock market crash, even the most privileged among the Broadcast 41 were aware of the country's pervasive economic inequalities. Writer Dorothy Parker, raised in affluence on the upper West Side of Manhattan, attributed the origins of her class-consciousness to an exchange with her "rich aunt—a horrible woman": "I remember going to the window and seeing the street with the men shoveling snow; their hands were purple on their shovels, and their feet were wrapped with burlap. And my aunt, looking over my shoulder, said, 'Now isn't it nice there's this blizzard. All those men have work.' And I knew then that it was not nice that men could work for their lives only in desperate weather, that there was no work for them when it was fair."[11]

Vera Caspary began her life in similarly affluent circumstances, but when her father's attempt to establish a department store ended in bankruptcy, her family's economic status changed overnight. She spent her adolescence torn between poles of despair. On one hand, her mother and sister indulged in "self-pity and subterfuge" as a result of their diminished circumstances but thought that work was beneath them. On the other hand, her father experienced considerable guilt "because he could not provide the luxuries to which his women were entitled."[12]

Experiences like these imbued this generation of progressive women with a class-consciousness that anti-communism helped eliminate from popular culture. Throughout her long career, Caspary remained a trenchant critic of romances because the genre treated women as "golden" creatures, "heaped about with costly and useless things that prove a woman has captured a man and he is willing to give his life to her adornment." Capitalism, Caspary maintained, sold these fantasies to women "every day, on celluloid and airwaves and coated paper, and it makes wealthier the procurers of permanent wave lotions, furs and silks, percale sheets, nylon, motor cars, cleaning tissues, moving pictures and laundry soap."[13]

Where anti-communists' strain of populism viewed education as the playground of elites, most of the Broadcast 41 grew up in communities that valued culture and education. Anti-communists regarded education with equal measures of misgiving and contempt. Intellectuals were elitists, in their minds, who did not know the value of a day's work. Worse still, education corrupted the purity of American youth, causing them to question authority and disrespect their elders, who unquestionably knew better about everything. Anti-communist crusader Elizabeth Dilling left the University of Chicago, resentful for the remainder of her life that "Red" educators had caused her to question her certainties about American culture and history. Fearful of losing control over their children and young adults, insecure in the belief that their ideas could stand up to questioning, and defensive in the face of challenges to their authority, anti-communists had good reason to worry that exposure to progressive ideas might make people question anti-communists' version of Americanism.

In contrast to anti-communists' homespun anti-intellectualism, many of the Broadcast 41 were raised in communities of artists and intellectuals. Actress Meg Mundy's mother was Australian opera singer Clytie Hyne and her father, British cellist John Mundy. Actress Uta Hagen's father founded the Department of Art History at the University of Wisconsin, while Gale and Hester Sondergaard's father was a professor of agriculture at the University of Minnesota.[14] Judy Holliday's uncle was noted Jewish-American writer Joseph Gollomb, her mother taught piano in New York City, and her father was a journalist for the Yiddish-language press. Actress Aline MacMahon's father edited *Munsey's Magazine*.[15] Their communities embraced culture and learning as essential elements of citizenship, rather than despising them.

Even households that enjoyed substantially less privilege valued education. Education was the means by which their children could avoid being "condemned to work in the needle trades and sweatshops," as Madeline Lee's parents put it.[16] The Reverend David Graham's household prized literacy: he read the novels of Charles Dickens and *The Crisis*, the magazine of the National Association for the Advancement of Colored People (NAACP), aloud to his children. The young Shirley Graham encountered some of the country's most prominent intellectuals in her childhood home.

Encouraged by their communities of origin, those of the Broadcast 41 who could afford to do so eagerly took advantage of new educational opportunities for women. Graham graduated from Oberlin and later took graduate courses at Yale and New York University, writing part of a dissertation on the Gullah people (descendants of West Africans who settled in the low-country region of South Carolina and Georgia). Radio children's show host Ireene Wicker attended the University of Illinois, patrician actress and labor activist Anne Revere (a descendant of American patriot Paul Revere) went to

Wellesley, actress Aline MacMahon graduated from Barnard, Hellman from New York University, and Hilda Vaughn from Vassar. Betty Todd studied for three years at the University of North Carolina at Chapel Hill and later at Columbia University.

Despite often ambivalent experiences of an educational system in which institutionalized racism and sexism abounded, the Broadcast 41 passionately believed in the ideals of public education, sharing utopian beliefs about its democratic potential and devoting considerable energies throughout their lives to expanding access to education. Shirley Graham was educated in "mixed schools" in segregated cities like Colorado Springs and Seattle (where black history was suppressed) and "separate schools" in the south (where black teachers taught black history).[17] That contrast instilled in her a lifelong commitment to literacy and education. In addition to her biographical fiction for young adults, Graham and her husband W.E.B. Du Bois supported the Communist Party's Jefferson School of Social Science before it was forced by the U.S. government to close its doors in 1956. After the blacklist, dancer Maria Margarita Guadalupe Teresa Estella Castilla Bolado y O'Donnell (or Margo, as she was known on stage) co-founded and built Plaza de la Raza (Place of the People), a cultural center for arts and education in East Los Angeles.

The Broadcast 41's perspectives were further shaped by one of the worst anti-immigrant backlashes in U.S. history, a legacy which subsequent anti-communists periodically revived. They were immigrants and the children of immigrants, whose experiences of migration and the backlash against immigrants that led to the restrictive Immigration Act of 1924 gave them unique insights into what anti-communists really meant by Americanism. Fredi Washington fled the violence of the American South during the Great Migration, an experience as formative as those of people who migrated across oceans. News commentator and writer Lisa Sergio was forced to leave her native Italy in 1937 because of fascism. Mady Christians (Austria), Uta Hagen (Germany), concert pianist Ray Lev (Russia), Margo (Mexico), actress Meg Mundy (England), actress Minerva Pious (Russia), musician Hazel Scott (Trinidad), and Margaret Webster (England) understood historical events and politics through international lenses. Others grew up in immigrant or diasporic communities, maintaining long-lasting attachments to war-torn countries of origin. Stella Adler, Vera Caspary, Judy Holliday, and Madeline Lee were children and grandchildren of immigrants and participants in ethnic cultures that kept memories of migration alive through vaudeville and the Yiddish theater and press.

Their experiences of dislocation and nativist hostility showed them that the language of the melting pot was a ruse of power, extended when immigrants provided cheap labor but revoked during times of crisis, when nativism proved politically expedient and anti-communists required scapegoats for broader structural problems. These experiences further disposed the Broadcast 41 to sympathize with and respect the experiences of other outcasts, recognizing that the language of 100 percent Americanism was meant to exclude them all.

Given their backgrounds, it made sense that the Broadcast 41 were perhaps most passionate in their commitment to civil rights. Many of them were raised in families and communities where discussions of civil rights were part of the air children breathed. Lena Horne's grandmother, Cora Calhoun, was her political role model. Calhoun had been "active in the Urban League and the NAACP, the Suffragette movement, and all kinds of social-work activity."[18] Horne's first media appearance was as a two-year-old in the pages of the NAACP's *Branch Bulletin.*[19] "The part of me," Horne wrote, "that responds to causes or to injustices, or issues fighting statements on all kinds of issues, that part of me is the creation of my proud, activist grandmother, who never seemed to be afraid of anything."[20]

Vera Caspary inherited her anti-racist politics from a family member as well. Her father had been raised in an abolitionist family in Wisconsin. During her childhood in Chicago, anti-lynching activist and journalist Ida B. Wells-Barnett and her husband, Judge Ferdinand Barnett, moved into the second unit of their double house, the first African Americans to move into their Chicago neighborhood.[21] Caspary's father stood up to his white neighbors when they tried to force the Barnetts to move. Nearly fifty years later, his daughter Vera followed in his footsteps, resisting racist neighbors who tried to drive Lena Horne and her children from their neighborhood on Sunset Boulevard in Los Angeles.[22]

The work of anti-racist resistance was rough and inconsistent on the part of white women, then as now. On one hand, the Popular Front's trenchant analysis of capitalism's failures as an economic system and the links between economic exploitation and white supremacy in the U.S. provided a powerful lens through which white women and men began to understand racism. Progressive writers frequently voiced this connection, as Vera Caspary put it, in the context of "the rise of Hitler in Germany, the stories of concentration camps, persecution of Jews, the aggressions of Mussolini, starvation persisting in the United States, union organizers thrown into prison, radicals manhandled by sheriffs' deputies, [and] poor people and Negroes deprived of justice."[23]

Still, Jewish women like Caspary sometimes conflated their struggles with those of African Americans, not fully cognizant of the advantages they enjoyed by virtue of their own whiteness. In order to succeed professionally, they were able to conceal their ethnic origins in workplaces that valued whiteness and Christianity. They often adopted, or were forced to adopt, pseudonyms to do just this: Eli Strouse's daughter became Hilda Vaughn, Hilda Vaughn, ironically naming herself after a New Orleans claiming race in which all the horses were for sale; Shaindel Kalish took the stage name of Ann Shepherd; Judith Tuvim became Judy Holliday; and Louise Riekes disguised her Orthodox roots by taking the name Louise Fitch.[24] These were terrible and humiliating experiences, but they did not prevent these women from escaping other, even more destructive forms of discrimination.

In the families they grew up in, the schools they attended, and the theaters, stages, and studio lots where they performed, the Broadcast 41 participated in vibrant conversations about class, race, national identity, and—to a lesser degree—gender. But one aspect of their lives was not up for discussion: their sexualities. Few of them spoke openly about their sexualities, even in letters and memoirs, a silence that reflects American culture's toxic blend of homophobic and sexist attitudes toward women who desired other women or did not understand themselves to be women in the first place. The Communist Party criticized racism and capitalism, but sexism and homophobia were rampant in the movements associated with the Popular Front. Feminist scholar Bettina Aptheker, for example, remembered "an older comrade" who years later confided in her that in the early 1950s, "she had been instructed by the Party leadership to question women in the Party about their sexuality." Those who admitted to having had "a homosexual liaison" were asked to resign from the Party or face expulsion.[25] While anti-communism may have forced gay male New Yorkers into hiding, as historian George Chauncey says, for lesbians and those who may have identified outside the gender binary, the combined forces of misogyny, homophobia, and heteronormativity meant that being open about their sexualities was never an option in the first place.[26]

Despite the widespread condemnation of gay, queer, and non-conforming lives across the political spectrum and the tremendous risks queer women incurred, the perspectives of lesbian, bisexual, and other women who did not conform to the sexual and gender identities of their day shaped the Broadcast 41's work in subtle and coded ways. Hellman's play *The Children's Hour* recounted the fatal consequences of acknowledging same-sex desire. Theater owner Lee Shubert acknowledged the very real danger of even writing about lesbianism, warning Hellman when the play opened in 1934 that its content "could land us all in jail."[27] Vera Caspary's disdain for heteronormative expectations was a constant theme in the dozens of novels she wrote, many of which recounted intimate relationships among "girls who had read Freud and Havelock Ellis" and who were, in her words, "the end of the explorer generation, a decade or so after the discovery that sex was also for women."[28] Caspary's scathing depictions of heterosexuality and her contempt for romance (combined with the fact that she did not marry until she was in her forties) fueled rumors that she was a lesbian.

Despite the dangers, the Broadcast 41 moved in communities that tolerated (even if they did not accept) a broader range of sexual identities and practices than other spheres of American society. Many progressives dwelt in "a very bohemian, eclectic atmosphere," in which, as Gertrude Berg's daughter recalled, "Jews, non-Jews, Blacks, Whites, gays, non-gays—all kinds of people were in and out."[29] Judy Holliday had a relationship with a woman in the late 1930s when she was working in theater because "there was no stigma attached to homosexual or bisexual behavior" and, as Holliday's biographer observes, "a goodly portion of the first ladies and gentlemen of the American and English stage were known to be (in the slang of the period) 'double-gaited.' "[30] In the more liberal environs of theater, lesbians, bisexuals, and progressives who—a generation or two later—might identify as queer or transgender found small but vital communities of support and resistance.

Lesbian and bisexual women built yet-to-be-documented support networks in broadcasting, of which influential radio show host Mary Margaret McBride was a main hub. McBride, who was targeted by the blacklisting publication *CounterAttack* but not listed in *Red Channels*, lived with her business manager and longtime companion, Stella Karn.[31] McBride was close friends with Ann Batchelder, *Good Housekeeping*'s food editor.[32] Although the FBI spread rumors that radio news host and Broadcast 41 member Lisa Sergio had been Benito Mussolini's mistress, Sergio was intimately involved with Batchelder. Batchelder adopted Sergio in 1944, a strategy that gay men and lesbians used in the decades before marriage equality to gain access to some of the legal protections enjoyed by married heterosexuals.[33]

Just as McBride was central to lesbian communities in broadcasting, so blacklisted director Margaret (Peggy) Webster participated in queer networks in theater. In 1933, Webster cast actress Mady Christians—whom she described as "blonde, distinguished, and opulent"—as Queen Gertrude in her production of *Hamlet*, and the two became close friends and likely lovers.[34] Webster co-founded the American Repertory Theater in 1946 with another former lover, Eva Le Gallienne, and lesbian producer Cheryl Crawford.

Working-class, middle-class, black, white, Latina, Jewish, and queer progressive women working in the whirling occupations that later coalesced into television in the 1950s tried to reflect the complexities of American identities in their work. Unlike Communists, the Broadcast 41 were not concerned with class or economic exploitation alone, although unlike the generations that followed, even the most privileged among them found economic oppression impossible to ignore. Nor did they consider economic oppression in isolation from race. Black left feminists like Shirley Graham, Fredi Washington (who had spent part of her childhood in a convent school for orphaned black and Native American children in Pennsylvania), and Claudia Jones, author of "An End to the Neglect of the Problems of the Negro Woman!", imprisoned and then deported in 1955 for her political beliefs, powerfully articulated the relationship between race and class in their social criticism and creative work alike.[35] Indeed, black women pushed all progressives to recognize that the experiences of black women under capitalism were singular in intensity, governed by forces of white supremacy and misogyny.[36]

At the same time, black women remained more attuned to the nuances of identity categories. They were suspicious of being lumped into a single category of class or race, understanding how these categories were used to stereotype and scapegoat them. Shirley Graham's membership in the Communist Party and criticism of the black middle class distanced her from other African Americans of her era. Lena Horne credited Trinidadian-born Hazel Scott with teaching her "a new sense of pride" in her race and told *Ebony* magazine that she was "fighting for a better world ... where her daughter Gail will never be called 'N----r' and where all races can live in dignity."[37] But Horne also observed that Scott had "a superiority that can be infuriating to an American Negro," because she came from a place where "no one ever taught the Negroes they were inferior."[38]

Light-skinned women of color like Horne, Scott, and Fredi Washington were caught between rocks and hard places when it came to their work in entertainment. On one hand, media industries eroticized them because their skin color allowed white audiences to understand them "in ways that upheld the racial status quo." On the other hand, they faced criticism from African American communities critical of Hollywood's fascination with "white mulattoes" and the black actresses who played them.[39] Literary scholar Shane Vogel describes how early in her career, Horne fought against this bind, seeking "to transcend the obligations of racial representation—imposed by both white audiences and black uplift elites—even as she actively fought for civil rights."[40] For years after playing the character of Peola (a light-skinned woman who passed as white) in *Imitation of Life* (1934), Washington had to defend herself against charges that she had also tried to pass as a white woman in her everyday life.[41]

In 1945, the Broadcast 41's embrace of the multifaceted lives of Americans formed part of a great river of resistance that threatened to erode the narrow channels of anti-communist Americanism. Anti-communists bitterly fought progressive attempts to expand rights and democracy for groups they considered naturally subordinate to them, fearing the changes that would follow. The Broadcast 41 embraced the possibilities of postwar social change. Without the changes that had happened during the years between the two World Wars, they would not have achieved their still-precarious positions within media industries. Additional social changes held out the promise of advances in equality they wholeheartedly believed in. Their personal histories had shown them the importance and value of progressive struggles. Their struggles to represent the presence, values, and desires of diverse Americans as workers in those industries deepened their commitment to initiating and leading change.

❖ ❖ ❖

In short, the modern woman, if she wants both marriage and a career, must compromise a bit with the one to preserve the other. But compromise, heaven knows, is nothing new to her. For generations she has had to practise it, and surely she hasn't forgotten how, even though she travels new paths and engages in battles of her own.

Mary Margaret McBride (radio show host, writer)[42]

Marilyn [Monroe] would have been a terrible problem, though I am crazy about her. The studio is beginning to view her as Marat must have regarded the lethally-poised Charlotte Corday. Of course, Marilyn can't help her behavior. She is always in terror. Not so different from you and me, only much prettier!

Dorothy Parker (writer)[43]

Of the generation of women that came of age in the 1930s and 1940s, literary scholar Lisa Yaszek wrote, they "were living the dream that first-wave feminists had worked so hard to secure for themselves and their daughters." In return for this hard work, they "expected the same rights and privileges as American men."[44] After the end of World War II, these daughters became more insistent in demanding rights due to them as citizens and workers. An FBI informant reported that at a luncheon to celebrate the twenty-fifth anniversary of women's suffrage in 1946, Uta Hagen gave what the Bureau deemed a subversive talk from "the viewpoint of the professional woman, stressing that they are not living in a world of their own but rather are more than unusually interested in what is going on in the world." Hagen then proceeded to cite "instances of the great work which the women of the theater have done toward a liberal and more progressive attitude in public thinking."[45]

This great work that women were doing, as Hagen put it, came at a cost. Even before the blacklist took hold of the industry, the Broadcast 41 had all encountered glass ceilings of varying heights. Veterans of stage and screen, experience had shown them that successful careers in theater, music, and film demanded sacrifices of women workers that were not expected of men, while at the same time presenting uniquely dangerous obstacles. As single parents and primary caregivers to their children, Ruth Gordon, Lena Horne, Gypsy Rose Lee, and others understood all too well the nature of these sacrifices. Life on stage and in the studio alike was not easily combined with raising children. The industry, moreover, viewed women with children as nuisances and financial liabilities. For those who wanted to raise their children outside the glare of Hollywood, commuting to New York City from Los Angeles was disruptive and exhausting.

Women who did not wish to have children, or who wanted to limit the number they had, faced risks associated with newfound sexual and economic freedoms, particularly in an era when birth control and abortion were illegal. Ruth Gordon recalled that it was hard to figure out what to do when a woman got pregnant.[46] Gordon, Lillian Hellman, and others had illegal abortions. Some who became pregnant and wished to have children, but avoid scandals that could ruin careers, gave birth in secrecy or got married in a hurry. Ruth Gordon chose to conceal her pregnancy, leaving New York in 1929 to give birth secretly to her son in France, while the child's father, theater producer Jed Harris, continued to work—professionally unaffected by scandal—in New York City. When actress Rose Hobart became pregnant in the 1940s, she quickly wed the father of her child.

Those who chose not to (or could not) have children were treated as deviants in sexist cultures that continued to see women's role as Americans in strictly reproductive terms. More than half of the Broadcast 41 did not conform to the procreative mandates of Cold War culture and never had or raised children. As Americanism became equated with fecundity, women like these were thought un-American, for what woman would not want to fulfill her biological destiny? A studio head rebuked the childfree Vera Caspary when she wrote a scene in which a teen mother refused to look at the baby she was giving up for adoption.[47] Such an act was, in his eyes, "unnatural."

Working women's economic independence was also viewed as unnatural, making men in the industry alternately fretful and indignant. For many men, independent women who were not "crazy about men," or did not wish to devote their lives to husbands and families, as Caspary put it in one of her trademark critiques of romance, had "got too far from the harem. You earn your living and enjoy it. I have an income and live quite adequately alone.

Men aren't our lords and masters. And they resent us."[48] In entertainment industries, this resentment intensified abundant workplace dangers. Women who worked in entertainment were considered vulgar and promiscuous, stereotypes that men used to justify predatory behaviors. When Ruth Gordon announced her decision to go into acting, her family responded in terms shared by many in American culture: "'For Ruth to go to be an actress is like being a harlot.'"[49] Lena Horne was also raised to believe that being on the stage was only slightly more respectable than being a prostitute.[50]

These stereotypes gave men license to behave as if their female co-workers formed a vast preserve of sexually available dames and broads. Far from being a metaphor, the casting couch was a way of life.[51] The Broadcast 41 regularly experienced sexual violence—unrelenting, traumatic reminders that they were subordinate in all ways to men. Gordon recalled one audition in which the director told her to read from a script he had specifically prepared for her: "'We'll read from this. Stand here.' He pointed to a space beyond his desk. 'It's with your husband in Act One.' He gently put his lips to mine. I had to have the part. 'You're sweet. Shall we begin?' He leaned over and covered my mouth with his lips. His tongue went slowly in, out, in."[52] In her autobiography, actress Jean Muir remembered working on a film in which "Two prominent actors in the cast, Ned and the before-mentioned Martin, tried to make love to me, using whatever place was available, taxis, for instance, and odd corners.... both Martin and Ned were persistent. Week by week I repulsed their advances, as first one, then the other attacked."[53] Darryl Zanuck, head of Twentieth Century Fox, "had the reputation of exercising *droits de seigneur* over his indentured lady players," as Judy Holliday's biographer put it, meaning that he expected new starlets to have sex with him.[54]

The risk of sexual violence was worse for women working in music, theater, or on location, since travel made them particularly vulnerable. Life on the road required erratic working hours and a combustible mix of alcohol and unpredictable lodgings. Women were isolated from networks of protection and support. Managers intent on cutting costs often booked the cheapest and least reputable hotels available. Rose Hobart recalled being "kept awake all night" in Atlantic City, "crouched behind all the furniture which I had piled in front of the door—I didn't trust the key—while drunken guys kept banging on the door telling me to 'come on out and have a little drink.'"[55]

The combination of sexual and racial violence made life on the road especially perilous for black women and the performers and musicians who accompanied them. As music historian Sherrie Tucker documents in her history of 1940s all-girl bands, black bands had limited employment opportunities in the North, leaving them no choice but to tour the South to make ends meet. Unless touring companies and bands owned their own buses, musicians and performers were forced to rely on public transportation that put black bands and integrated bands, whose presence threatened Jim Crow laws, at grave risk of violence.[56]

In 1941, producer, director, and actress Eva Le Gallienne, who was not one of the Broadcast 41 but shared their sympathies and worked closely with many of them, toured thirty-eight states, covering over 30,000 miles in a six-month period. During the time the company spent in the South, their black co-workers were forced to "live in rooming houses for Negroes, under conditions that no human being should be asked to tolerate" and were refused service in "even the cheapest and dirtiest lunchrooms." Although she had been warned that traveling with an integrated company would mean that they would "have a difficult time," with the limited perspective of even the best-intentioned anti-racist white people, Le Gallienne admitted, "we none of us believed it could be as bad as it turned out to be."[57]

Not all women had the resources to cope with these climates. Some women internalized this culture's norms, encouraging one another to use sex as a bargaining chip. "Make 'em think you'd go to bed with them, *but!* You will, *but!* And don't lay down on the desk when the stenog goes home," Gordon was advised, "unless they sign a ten-year starring contract at umpteen dollars!"[58] Others (including many who had already experienced sexual violence) did what they thought they had to in order to succeed. In the postwar era, aspiring actresses eager to make it big hit the Hollywood party circuit—"a brutal, degrading, sometimes dangerous business"—where women "in exchange for dinner and the chance to meet some of Hollywood's most important players ... were expected to make themselves available" to rich and powerful film industry executives and their guests.[59] Some, like Marilyn Monroe, did not survive the systematic sexual violence that still flourishes in Hollywood in the twenty-first century, as high-profile allegations of rape and sexual harassment against prominent producers, actors, and journalists have demonstrated.[60]

In addition to endemic sexual violence, women also had to perform their debasement onscreen, in roles that provided justification for their subordination in the workplace. Harassed and degraded as workers, they were forced to write and perform in roles that reaffirmed the stereotypes used to justify sexual violence against them. If progressive women were keen critics of stereotypes in film and television, it was because they understood all too well that their experiences of discrimination as workers in media industries were linked to the images and ideas that appeared in media content. In 1953, writer Sylvia Jarrico (wife of blacklisted screenwriter and producer Paul Jarrico) wrote, "When women of independence and purpose are consistently presented not only as subject to anguish and neurosis (as in the past), but as degraded and murderous, the complacent theme that submission is the natural state of women has given way to the aggressive theme that submission is the *necessary* state of women."[61]

Still, white female neurosis was an improvement over the degradation awaiting black women in Hollywood. Considered too "controversial" by studio heads and moneymen harboring white supremacist viewpoints, black women found little in the way of work in film or radio. When they did, they were relegated to stereotypical roles as domestic servants, exotic natives, and hypersexualized entertainers.[62] This made some actresses even long for the less restrictive stereotypes applied to white women. Actress Dorothy Dandridge described how stereotypes shaped cultural understandings of black women. "America," she observed, "was not geared to make me into a Liz Taylor, Monroe, or a Gardner.... My sex symbolism was as a wanton, a prostitute, not as a woman seeking love and a husband, like other women."[63] Lena Horne worried that her MGM contract "would force me to play roles as a maid or maybe even as some jungle type," roles "that most Negroes were forced to play in the movies at that time."[64] "From *Birth of a Nation*," Hazel Scott wrote, "to *Gone with the Wind*, from *Tennessee Johnson's* to *My Old Kentucky Home*; from my beloved friend Bill Robinson to Butterfly McQueen; from bad to worse and from degradation to dishonor—so went the story of the Black American in Hollywood."[65] Brilliant actresses like Hattie McDaniel and Butterfly McQueen had to play racist caricatures in *Gone with the Wind*, a film celebrating the white supremacist myth of the Lost Cause of the Confederacy.

Black women were further caught between the racism of producers and the racism attributed to white audiences. Producers used the bottom line to justify their racism. White audiences, they maintained, would boycott films featuring African Americans in roles that defied racist stereotypes. When Garson Kanin refused to accept an advance on a script, studio head Harry Cohn admonished him, "Listen, I know if you take my hundred thousand, you're going to write me somethin' good, somethin' I can use and nothin' controversial, like *n-----s* or *God*!"[66] An RKO executive told Orson Welles that his proposed "mixing of the blacks and the whites" in *The Story of Jazz* "cannot be accepted by Iowa, Missouri, not to mention all the people on the other side of the Mason/Dixon line."[67]

Even when African Americans were cast in film or television, their roles were strictly policed. "MGM didn't want blackness in those days, except in the role of being some native in the jungle or a loving, confidential maid," Lena Horne told a reporter, "Mississippi wanted its movies without me."[68] Black performers frequently had the humiliating experience of performing in musical numbers meant to be easily cut from films when local distributors decided audiences in their towns would object to seeing black performers on screen.[69] When Lena Horne appeared on the *Charlie McCarthy Show* for twelve weeks in 1945, the scripts were written so she "did not figure in a single conversation with any of the principals. The idea was to avoid addressing me by full name, and having me speak to other people—white people—as an equal."[70]

Of course, very few actresses had much say over the lines they spoke and the narratives in which they figured. Even white women found few opportunities to include their perspectives in scripts.[71] A handful, like Vera Caspary, Lillian Hellman, Anita Loos, and Dorothy Parker, muscled their way into screenwriting, but once there, they quickly discovered that their ideas were at loggerheads with the film industry's jaundiced views of female audiences. Caspary, for example, was dropped from consulting on the adaptation of her novel *Laura* because she and director Otto Preminger disagreed about having the storyline focus on the title character. Preminger thought that the focus on a female character was misguided. For her part, Caspary considered Preminger unable to represent women as full and complex characters. Because Preminger (a philanderer with a reputation for sleeping with his leading ladies) knew so "little about women," in Caspary's estimation, he reduced her complex title character to "the Hollywood version of a cute career girl."[72]

Caspary also repeatedly fought with studio head Harry Cohn over scripts: "He always denigrated you, trying to get you to feel low, so you knew he was a big shot," she said. According to Caspary, Cohn once "called together all the creative people on the studio payroll. In a fighting mood, he made a brief address. Things weren't going well, and it was time to get down to basics. 'Lemme tell you what this business is about. It's about *cunt and horses*! ... Oh, excuse *me*, Miss Caspary' ".[73] By calling attention to her presence first by reducing women to "cunt," and then condescendingly emphasizing her singular presence in a room full of men, men like Cohn ensured that women would never forget their position as sexualized objects of desire, as marginalized workers, and as audience members often not even considered worth addressing.[74]

Although work in Hollywood was more lucrative than work in most other media industries, the writers among the Broadcast 41 (Caspary, Gordon, Hellman, and Parker) resented working in an industry whose representations of women were demeaning and whose treatment of them as workers was even worse. Progressive women made money when they could in Hollywood, but they fled the film industry for New York City as soon as possible. One actress complained that when she "went out to Hollywood, the first thing they did was fit me with falsies that went out to here." In New York, in contrast, she said, "there was always a sense that what was important was the work and the performance."[75] Actress Ethel Waters turned down two film roles in Hollywood in order to star in the play *Mamba's Daughters* in New York City, alongside a cast of actors of color that included several others who would later be blacklisted (José Ferrer, Canada Lee, and Fredi Washington).[76] When Washington left Hollywood for good during World War II, she began working for Adam Clayton Powell, Jr. at his Harlem newspaper, *The People's Voice*, where she wrote her own theatrical column, "Headlines/Footlights," which later became "Fredi Says."[77]

For her part, Jean Muir quit film because she had grown "very tired of learning and saying awful lines of dialogue, written mostly by cynics or idiots or hacks" and because, as she grew older, "the quality that had made me a star in the beginning was disappearing."[78] The best that Lillian Hellman had to say of Los Angeles was, "it's unbearable to any civilized person as a mere visitor, but with something to do it's no worse than being in jail."[79] Dorothy Parker was characteristically blunter. "I can't talk about Hollywood," she wrote, "It was a horror to me when I was there and it's a horror to look back on. I can't imagine how I did it. When I got away from it I couldn't even refer to the place by name. Out there, I called it."[80]

The Broadcast 41's experiences in media industries confirmed that to be a woman who wanted to change the treatment of women on and off screen in the 1930s and 1940s was to struggle constantly against incredibly rigid and powerful institutional norms. Along with Dorothy Parker, the Broadcast 41 "dreamed by day of never again putting on tight shoes, of never having to laugh and listen and admire, of never more being a good sport. Never."[81] They resented having to be good sports when confronted with sexism and racism. They complained that when they lobbied "for an acknowledgment of black humanity," as did Fredi Washington, they were ostracized and censored.[82] Because of their increasingly public criticisms of the entertainment industry, they gained reputations for being intractable, difficult, or vicious. In the words of Lillian Hellman (one of the most famously difficult of the Broadcast 41), "You're always difficult, I suppose, if you don't do what other people want."[83] Where stubbornness and iconoclasm were praised in male colleagues, the personal, professional, and political experiences of the Broadcast 41 reminded them time and again that traits considered virtues in men were fatal character flaws in women.

In spite of the many hardships they endured, the Broadcast 41 loved their work. Years later, Vera Caspary wrote "work made my life what it has been.... everything came through working ... independence to live and love and travel; joy in work; heartbreak in work; survival through work."[84] But they were candid about the challenges. When asked what two characteristics a woman had to have to succeed in show business, Ruth Gordon replied, "imagination and indestructibility."[85] In order to survive work in media, women needed to be indestructible, in Ruth Gordon's estimation, or, in the words of one of Gordon's twenty-first-century descendants, "unbreakable," like producer, writer, and actress Tina Fey's sitcom character Kimmy Schmidt. Lena Horne could have been speaking for all of them when, years later, she modestly told the audience for her one-woman show, "I'm just a survivor."[86]

Survivors they were, in an industry that destroyed many talented, independent, creative, and supposedly difficult women. In the years before the blacklist, the Broadcast 41 not only managed to survive, they developed resources, support networks, and strategies of resistance. At the end of World War II, they looked forward to enjoying some of the fruits of these labors, recognizing that their struggles to be included in media industries—in workplaces and on screens alike—were part of wider efforts to achieve full democracy and social justice. They had no intention of backing down from those fights.

❖ ❖ ❖

Now, I was determined not to be a symbol. I wanted my responses to be determined not by the symbolic me—and the protection of the same—but by the real me. Unconsciously I think I wanted to act now as I knew my grandmother would have acted. I wanted, at last, to be my own woman, to be as sure of my motives, my place in society, my rights and privileges, as she had been.

Lena Horne (singer, actress)[87]

Should an actress or actor become politically involved? I have never found a good reason for anyone who has eyes to see with and a brain to think with to blind himself or herself to the realities of the world we live in. I lived in a period when hate was made manifest by such as Father Coughlin, with his dimly veiled anti-Semitism and fascistic ideas, when the Nazi Bund *freely functioned, in uniform no less, on the streets of cities, when the horrible crimes of Nazism made Europe a stinking heap of corpses.... I refused to wear blinkers.*

Jean Muir (actress)[88]

When questioned by the FBI about her political activities, the Broadcast 41's Uta Hagen told the special agent who was interviewing her that "she had always considered herself a liberal and progressive American and the activity of these organizations appealed to her because they appeared to operate for the benefit of the people of the United States."[89] By "organizations," Hagen was referring to the array of progressive political organizations that had sprung up from the dusty and resistant earth of the Great Depression, organizations that claimed to operate for the benefit of all Americans.

A vibrant and energized labor movement was part of the array of progressive social movements that proliferated in the 1930s and 1940s. Many of the Broadcast 41 came of age as workers after the National Labor Relations Act of 1935 (also known as the Wagner Act) made it possible for private-sector workers to organize. Poor working conditions in media industries encouraged them to join the struggle to remedy abuses. Gypsy Rose Lee took up the cause of child laborers in entertainment, recalling the abuse she and her sister suffered at the hands of their cruel stage mother.[90]

For actress Rose Hobart, working conditions in Hollywood transformed her into an ardent supporter of the eight-hour day:

> On my first three pictures, they worked me 18 hours a day and then complained because I was losing so much weight that they had to put stuff in my evening dress.... When I did *East of Borneo* (1931), that schlocky horror I did, we shot all night long. They started at 6 o'clock at night and finished at 5 in the morning. For two solid weeks, I was working with alligators, jaguars and pythons out on the back lot. I thought, "This is acting?" It was ridiculous. We were militant about the working conditions. We wanted an eight-hour day like everybody else.[91]

Jean Muir took a job as an "organizer for the newly legal vaudeville and night-club performers union, AGVA" in 1939, acting on her conviction that "whether she was a girl working the bar-rail as well as the floor-show, or whether she was a top-name performer earning thousands a week, my job was to make sure she belonged to her union."[92]

Progressive women like Hobart, Lee, and Muir found leadership opportunities in the labor movement, especially during World War II, when the scarcity of men forced reluctant unions to open up these positions of power to women. Hobart, Muir, and Anne Revere took advantage of these opportunities, directing progressive efforts in the Screen Actors Guild until anti-communists (led by Ronald Reagan) forced them out after the war. Radio director Betty Todd ran for secretary of the Radio and Television Directors' Guild (RTDG) in 1949, before being fired for her communist ties.[93] Several members of the Broadcast 41, including Mady Christians, Rose Hobart, Lena Horne, Gypsy Rose Lee, Madeline Lee, Anne Revere, Selena Royle, Betty Todd, and Margaret Webster, actively participated in unions representing workers from the many professions and occupations that comprised the television industry.

Most of these trade unions had historically excluded African Americans. As the leftwing *Hollywood Review* put it, "There is an older and larger blacklist that also has a significant influence on the pictures Hollywood makes—the blacklist of Negro artists and film craftsmen."[94] In order to counter this exclusion, African American performers and musicians had been organizing their own guilds and unions. In response to their exclusion from these organizations, Fredi Washington, along with tap dancer and actor Bill Robinson and bandleader Noble Sissle, helped found the Negro Actors Guild in 1937.[95] By 1945, the situation seemed ripe for change. Progressive members of Actors Equity and the American Federation of Radio and Television Artists began mobilizing to protect the rights of African American workers in the entertainment industry.

A groundswell of related anti-racist activity in New York City media during and after World War II enveloped progressives. Nearly all of the Broadcast 41 supported the rights of African Americans as workers and as citizens, lending their often-substantial star power to the advancement of civil rights. Black women like Fredi Washington, Lena Horne, and Hazel Scott led the fight against racism in entertainment industries. During the war, Washington was active in the Double V campaign that lobbied for victory overseas and victory over racism at home. Horne and Scott used their contracts to fight segregated performance venues by including provisions that stipulated that they would not perform before audiences that were segregated by race.[96] Scott's refusal to perform before such an audience in Austin, Texas resulted in her being escorted from town by Texas Rangers. She used the resulting publicity to ask a *Time* magazine reporter, "Why would anyone come to hear me, a Negro, and refuse to sit beside someone just like me?"[97]

African American performers further used their fame to draw attention to racism in American society. Horne filed a complaint with the NAACP when she performed for soldiers at Fort Reilly, Kansas, only to discover that German prisoners of war were seated in front of black soldiers.[98] In 1950, Scott brought a successful lawsuit against a restaurant near Spokane, Washington, where she and a traveling companion had been denied service, the waitress told them, "because they were Negroes."[99] Historian Dwayne Mack says that Scott's victory not only helped African Americans challenge racial discrimination in Spokane, but that it inspired civil rights organizations "to pressure the Washington state legislature to enact the Public Accommodations Act" in 1953.[100]

White progressives followed the lead of black progressives. Reflecting shared concerns about the impact of racist propaganda in media industries, Jean Muir joined Fredi Washington in campaigning throughout the early 1940s to compel "the movie industry to abandon its old stereotypes of Negro caricature."[101] From the 1930s until her career was curtailed by the blacklist, producer, director, and actress Margaret Webster cast black actors as leads in theater productions.[102] In 1947, actress Selena Royle told her peers in the Hollywood Council of the Arts, Sciences, and Professions that they had the choice of being "good citizens or bad citizens," the last defined as people who could "overlook racial intolerance" and "forgive lynchings in the South."[103]

Stella Adler, Uta Hagen, Judy Holliday, Ray Lev, Dorothy Parker, Minerva Pious, Hazel Scott, Lisa Sergio, Gale and Hester Sondergaard, and Fredi Washington were identified as communists because of their support for the Civil Rights Congress, an organization that campaigned internationally to defend African Americans convicted of crimes, especially in cases involving the death penalty. Hagen was repeatedly cited by the FBI for supporting efforts to enforce voting rights in the South and ensure a fair trial for the Trenton Six (six young black men who were convicted of killing a white shopkeeper and sentenced to death by an all-white jury), and her public opposition to deportation (especially attempts to deport African American communist Claudia Jones). Ruth Gordon was investigated by the FBI merely for signing a pledge to boycott Washington theatres that barred African Americans from attending performances.[104] One FBI report condemned Lena Horne's columns in *The People's Voice* for "glorifying Negro womanhood."[105]

The Broadcast 41's support for civil rights at home was shaped by social movements and political conversations that in the first place understood domestic racism to be connected to Nazism and, in the second, saw global capitalism as the source of exploitation. More than a quarter of the 41 (Stella Adler, Edith Atwater, Mady Christians, Ruth Gordon, Uta Hagen, Lena Horne, Dorothy Parker, Hazel Scott, Lisa Sergio, Helen Tamiris, Margaret Webster) worked on behalf of the American Committee for the Protection of the Foreign Born, recognizing that the resurgence of the Ku Klux Klan and the backlash against immigrants were part of a larger mobilization of white supremacists.[106] Even in the face of considerable censure and attack, the Broadcast 41 remained united in defending the rights of immigrants and refugees, believing that struggles for racial justice and for the rights of the foreign-born were parts of a broader battle against injustice.

The Broadcast 41's experiences and political beliefs led them to be forceful critics of the media's role in fomenting bigotry and discrimination. As fledgling artists and workers in the 1930s, most of the Broadcast 41 did not yet fully understand how media industries worked. Nor did they have the confidence or power to criticize and rebel. But by the 1940s, things had changed. They were veterans of stage, studio, and screen, savvy, powerful, and far less likely to suffer indignities in silence. Lena Horne delivered a fierce critique of broadcasting in her short-lived *People's Voice* column: "Radio in the US is afflicted with racism in a bad way. It is time for us to start a campaign to clean racial discrimination out of the radio industry. Radio is now super-big business, employs thousands, and reaches millions. But the Negro is all but left out in the cold by this gigantic industry which, as a medium of public information and entertainment, has a legal as well as moral responsibility to practice the principles of democracy."[107] As the 1940s wore on, women like Horne became even more outspoken in their disapproval of how media treated women, people of color, and immigrants.

In these efforts, the Broadcast 41 were motivated not by personal gain—to the contrary, their political activities cost them dearly—but by the belief that their visibility gave them an ethical responsibility to serve as role models for American citizenship. In the years between the wars, they embraced their responsibilities as global citizens, agreeing with Horne that "Anyone who is a performer ... does have a power that is more than that of a private citizen."[108] Although this is hardly an exhaustive inventory of the political activities of these women, the examples above show that in the years before the blacklist proved that progressive political activism could be used to destroy careers and lives, the Broadcast 41 idealistically and passionately worked to change the world.

The range of their political work confused and angered anti-communists who believed that all Americans were motivated by narrow self-interest. The Broadcast 41 provided living proof that anti-communists were dead wrong when they said that people only cared about the rights of their own kind, whether their kind was defined by race, class, or ethnicity. Jean Muir lent her star power primarily to the fight against racial stereotypes in Hollywood, but as a trade unionist, she supported the rights of the economically diverse groups of women, men, and children working in vaudeville. Shirley Graham fought against the execution of Ethel and Julius Rosenberg and served as a trustee for their two young children, while at the same time fearlessly participating in the civil rights organization Sojourners for Truth and Justice, opposing a criminal justice system that meted out death sentences to black people, while allowing white murderers to escape punishment.

Despite the diversity of progressives' backgrounds and beliefs, anti-communists painted them as robotic Stalinist minions who mindlessly repeated the Party line. But the Broadcast 41's political commitments were far more diverse than the politics of those who destroyed their careers. The majority of the Broadcast 41 cared more about economic and civil rights than they did about building the Party and working toward proletarian revolution (a phrase that was probably not in many of their vocabularies). Although few of them had qualms about working with the Party until such a time as it became clear that they would be persecuted for this work, only a small minority were members. As actress Anne Revere later explained, "I had always refused to accept a Party card ... because of the reservations that abraded me when I joined. In fact ... I considered myself a liberal reformer who had joined the Communist Party in order to bring about desirable social ends that would make this the best of all possible worlds."[109] Of those who had joined the Party in the 1930s, many held private reservations but overcame them because, like Revere, they considered the Communist Party to be the only political party fighting against racism and economic exploitation. For African Americans, the Party, unlike trade unions, other political parties, or the U.S. government, offered them dignity and respect they rarely received from either Democrats or Republicans.

Vera Caspary, Revere, Betty Todd, and Shirley Graham were part of a small group of documented Communist Party members among the Broadcast 41. Caspary's sympathies for the Party's anti-racist politics were evident as early as 1932, when she penned an article for the African American newspaper the *Chicago Defender* about the nine young men accused of raping two white women in Scottsboro, Alabama.[110] But in *The Rosecrest Cell*, a novel she later described as "a confession disguised as a novel about my two and a half years in the Party," Caspary complained angrily about the Party's abysmal treatment of female members, especially lesbians.[111] She left the Party along with a wave of other people in media industries in 1939, when Stalin signed the German-Soviet Nonaggression Pact, pledging not to take military action against Hitler.

Like Caspary and Revere, radio director Betty Todd's relationship with the Communist Party began in the late 1920s, when she was working at the J. Walter Thompson Advertising Company.[112] Todd was a trade union organizer, married to a member of the Communist Party. The FBI never confirmed her membership in the Party (meaning that they had found neither a signed membership card nor a witness willing to attest that she was a member). Todd too had drifted away from the Party by the mid-1940s, although that did not prevent her from being subpoenaed by the HUAC in June 1950, where she pled the Fifth Amendment forty-six times during her interrogation.[113]

Shirley Graham's involvement with the Communist Party was unique among the Broadcast 41. She joined the Party after membership was in steep decline around 1945, in the wake of "the greatest tragedy" of her life, the 1944 death of her son Robert, denied medical treatment at a segregated hospital.[114] Graham remained a member even after the Soviet Union invaded Hungary in 1956, a point in time when the Party's decline became terminal. Despite her commitment to the Communist Party, Graham balked at the idea that the

Party exercised a form of total mind control over members, bristling when another writer suggested that she had written a positive review of a novel at the behest of the Communist Party. "I can't be either for or against his last BOOK," Graham wrote to T.O. Thackeray, editor of the leftwing *Daily Compass*, "I am, however, for a writer writing what he dam [sic] pleases. Maybe he'll do it well, or maybe he won't. That's up to him."[115]

By the late 1940s, Communist Party membership hardly mattered. The Communist Party of the United States of America was no longer a threat to the American political system, if indeed it ever had been. But communism remained a compelling trigger for white Americans' fears about the challenges to white supremacy that were coalescing in the postwar era. It was clear that anti-communists wanted, in Paul Robeson's words, to shut up "every Negro who has the courage to stand up for the rights of his people, for the rights of workers."[116] To do that, anti-communists, like the ideologues who would follow them into the twenty-first century, wanted to unsettle and undermine Americans' belief in government, education, and culture. They did so by discrediting political positions they deemed "synonymous with radical liberals, bleeding-heart leftism, New Deal-Fair Deal-New Frontier programs, and Democratic politics in general," as actor Robert Vaughn (ironically best known for his starring role in the Cold War TV thriller, *The Man from U.N.C.L.E.*) put it in a doctoral dissertation he wrote about the blacklist.[117] Regardless of whether they were members of the Communist Party or could even remotely be considered threats to security, women, people of color, and immigrants posed a threat to anti-communists' goal of imposing representations that recentered and celebrated white masculinity.

❖ ❖ ❖

They cut out my favorite character, Patty, and all the nice mother-daughter scenes because (Siegel told me long before Lana Turner was thought of for it) the mother of a sixteen year old daughter would not seem sexy and appealing enough to the younger generation of picture goers. At that time they were waiting for Cary Grant and it would be impossible, they said, to have him in love with a woman in her thirties.

Vera Caspary (writer, novelist)[118]

She should be the kind of a girl who is so in love with her husband she continually does the wrong thing.... She should be small town all the way through and always struggling to please the man she loves, and yet always fumbling the ball.

Darryl Zanuck (producer)[119]

Having been denied freedoms themselves, the Broadcast 41 had little patience for people who would deny freedom to others, especially the freedom to represent dissenting standpoints and perspectives. In all their work in the years before anti-communists made progressive politics synonymous with treason, the Broadcast 41 worked to expand the category of American, redefining it to represent and value the beliefs and traditions of diverse groups of people. In the late 1940s, the Broadcast 41 thought that the emerging medium of television would provide rich openings for this work, hoping to do nothing less than change the way Americans thought about the world at a moment when the prospects for full democracy had never seemed brighter.

Of course, television was no newcomer to the cultural scene. The medium had been on the horizon since the 1930s, developing in fits and starts, but its ascendance was interrupted first by the Depression and then by World War II. By the mid-1940s, it was ready to take off. Both anti-communists and progressives realized that television was going to be the most influential mass medium in history. The new medium's content was going to have widespread and unpredictable effects on U.S. culture and politics. Television, Shirley Graham observed, was "the newest, the most powerful, the most direct means of communication devised by Man. Its potentialities for Good or for Evil are boundless."[120] Jean Muir, whose husband Henry Jaffe was general counsel for the American Federation of Radio Actors (AFRA), noted with some irritation: "I hardly needed to be told by Henry that 'nothing bigger has ever happened to this country,' and that its benefits and opportunities for the entertainer were incalculable."[121]

The question of whether television would reproduce existing ideas about gender, race, and nation or transform them had been the subject of debate among progressives for years. As early as 1939, the *Chicago Defender* speculated about the new possibilities television might provide for "sepia actors" (African American performers) and artists alike: "Though television is going through its experimental stages the Race is playing quite a big part as seen by the broadcasts of several groups of Race entertainers." Understanding the rhetorical power of the specter of "southern whites" who might not "want to see them brought into their homes," the *Defender* was concerned about how the new medium would portray African Americans: "Will he be made to cut up and act like a fool or shall he portray himself as he is in every day life?"[122] Will television provide "a new day for the Race," the *Defender* asked, or will "the fate of the colored artist be the same in television as it is now in radio"?

The Broadcast 41 and other progressives fervently hoped the new medium would foster better conditions for artists of color. In New York City, the center of broadcast production, these hopes were buoyed by the Popular Front's optimism about creating culture belonging to all people. Art and popular culture, progressives were convinced, could hold a mirror up to society and expose social inequalities, ultimately giving people powerful tools for social change.[123] Harry Belafonte, who shared progressive politics, followed actor Paul Robeson's lead in believing, "If art was not political, to me it wasn't even art. It was Paul Robeson who once said to me, 'The purpose of art is not just to show life as it is but to show life as it should be.' "[124]

The contrast between the lives of the Broadcast 41 and those of their mothers had proved that political transformations—or life as it should be—were possible. That women like them had achieved successes in media industries held out the promise of further social change. And the creative ferment surrounding the new industry was another beacon for progressives like the Broadcast 41. According to historian Erik Barnouw, many in the industry felt that "something new was developing; many an artist had an exhilarating sense of finding and sharpening new tools."[125] As television drew on the creative energies of literature, theater, and radio while at the same time opening up new horizons, the future seemed full of possibility. Gertrude Berg recalled the enormous excitement people in the industry experienced at the prospect of inventing this new medium: "Television was still a baby. The studio was being built around us as we rehearsed and there were no experts who knew what some other experts told them a survey said the public wanted."[126]

Television held out the hope that in an era following so much devastation, uncertainty, and violence, Americans might learn from the past and create art and culture that promoted understanding, liberal forms of tolerance, and a renewed commitment to democracy for everyone. The Broadcast 41 identified with economically and symbolically dominated populations and wanted to represent their perspectives. Like Shirley Graham, they wrote plays and novels about the struggles of people of color in the Americas, slavery, and the genocide of indigenous peoples. Like Graham, Hagen, Lev, and many others, they cheerfully raised money at hundreds of events for the unemployed, for children, refugees, and victims of an unjust criminal justice system. They were citizens of their communities and the world, imperfect in their own ways, who loved their country and dreamed of democracy. Actress Gale Sondergaard spoke to the contrast between the perspectives of those who were blacklisted and those who conducted the blacklist in her testimony before the HUAC in Washington, DC in 1951. She had been criticized, she told them, for being "a Jew-loving, Negro-loving, Red-loving, culture-loving, peace-loving, un-American woman." It was, she added, "incredible to be hated for loving so much and so many and so well."[127]

However much the Broadcast 41 suffered from their own forms of myopia, they sincerely believed that seeing the world from different standpoints was vital to raising consciousness of bigotry and hate. Lena Horne's description of how perspective affected perception during her courtship with her white husband, Jewish pianist, conductor, and composer Lennie Hayton, offers a compelling instance of this. As they traveled together, Horne wrote, Lennie "just quietly began to learn ... to think as I did." In order to adopt her standpoint, Hayton had to "efface a certain amount of himself"—to view the world instead from the standpoint of the person he loved, whose position in society and experiences were dramatically different from his own: "He just quietly began to think as a Negro. He had to become aware of everything I was aware of." Changing his optics meant, in turn, that the way Horne "saw the world became the way we both saw the world. It had to be so, because my problems were the hard ones to solve"[128] (Figure 2.2).

Anti-communists built worlds of fiction, policy, and law in which a whole host of others threatened the purity of their conceptualization of identity, which bore more than a passing resemblance to the fascism they claimed to despise. It was small wonder that anti-communists favored genres—like the Western and the police procedural—that allowed them to create worlds in which they protected their own privilege under the guise of protecting women, children, and the nation, endlessly producing stories about their own mastery and control. Anti-communists did not want to change the way they saw the world. In fact, they saw efforts to see the world through different lenses as evidence of communist contamination. Dead-set on protecting the industry and audiences from content defying their bigoted worldviews, they had good reason in the postwar era to fear progressive perspectives' capacity to undermine their authority.

Against the fear-mongering and paranoia of anti-communists, in the late 1940s, the Broadcast 41 tried to claim Americanism for purposes of full democracy. As Shirley Graham wrote: "I am an American, proud that our Declaration of Independence lifts itself like a beacon for all mankind, proud that our Constitution is conceived as a living instrument, capable of growing and expanding, proud that to our shores has come the oppressed and persecuted, believing that in spite of all our short comings we are moving

Figure 2.2 Lena Horne
Source: Carl Van Vechten, Courtesy Carl Van Vechten Photographs Collection, Library of Congress, Washington, DC

forward toward ideals and aspiration worthy of great sacrifice."[129] Likewise, on a road trip from Los Angeles to New York, Jean Muir surveyed Oklahoma's "immense dustbowl and all its human tragedy," expressing the hope that "the promise" of America would "not be betrayed, that the greatness be made manifest."[130] Gertrude Berg embraced a more sentimental if nonetheless genuine faith in an American Dream in which immigrants "crossed strange oceans and vent vhere a strange lengwidge is talking; because dey know vhatever de lengwidge, dere is only vone longing, vone lengwidge of de human heart, and dat is—liberty and justice!"[131]

Few of them knew that their presence in an industry that despised them and their individual and collective acts of resistance to white supremacy, xenophobia, and misogyny had set them on a collision course with anti-communists intent on reasserting their power to determine who would count as an American. Appalled by the changes progressives promoted in the postwar era, anti-communists marshaled their resources, activated their extensive national networks, and set about the work of forcibly imposing a monopoly over Americanism that would deny the plural perspectives of progressives like the Broadcast 41 had ever existed.

Chapter 3

G-Man Nation

The [House Un-American Activities] Committee's role was to storm the citadels of reason with fear and unreason, to make the public believe that the menace was terrifyingly alive and monstrously evil.

Adrian Scott (screenwriter and film producer)[1]

For a full decade thereafter the hunt raged at blood heat, roving wherever its masters wished, summoning whomever it pleased, demanding answers to questions never before heard in chambers that displayed the American flag—not, as some may have hoped, only in Hollywood (where over two hundred decent American citizens, including forty-four returned veterans, were humiliated, bankrupted, and driven from their professions), but in every area of American life that dealt with ideas and their dissemination.

Dalton Trumbo (writer)[2]

The daughter of Polish Jewish immigrants, Madeline Lee (born Madeline Lederman) learned about being ostracized for her political beliefs at an early age. She was expelled from her Bronx high school for organizing a chapter of the socialist National Student Union. As a young, socially conscious actress, she met her second husband, character actor Jack Gilford, at a political meeting in 1947. By 1950, the Gilfords had three small children, two under the age of five, and like most actors, they mainly struggled to make ends meet. Those struggles became much harder that year when choreographer Jerome Robbins told the HUAC that the Gilfords were members of the Communist Party.[3]

Three years later, the unemployed mother of three was subpoenaed (or "commanded to appear," as the language of her subpoena read) before the HUAC. Stubbornly idealistic, committed to the belief that the HUAC had no business asking her about her political affiliations, Lee refused to cooperate. When the committee demanded to know whether she was, or had ever been, a member of the Communist Party, she pled the First and Fifth Amendments. Asked if she had marched in a May Day parade in 1942, Lee retorted, "Look, I'm a comedian, not Joan of Arc. The words 'recant,' 'confess,' 'you're a heretic' are not exactly my dish."[4]

Beyond the testimony of Robbin, the FBI had no evidence that Lee was a member of the Communist Party. Nor did they have evidence the unemployed actress was in a position to jeopardize national security. But her "defiance," as subsequent Bureau reports put it, infuriated FBI director J. Edgar Hoover, and put Lee squarely in the sights of the Cold War security state. Agents (who learned swiftly, as we will see, to cater to Hoover's biases) remarked on "her truculent attitude towards the House Committee and her effort to denounce it," and observed that Lee had "received complimentary notoriety in CP press for her uncooperative attitude before hearings of [the] House Un-American Activities."[5] The words "complimentary notoriety" were all Hoover needed to hear. He placed Lee on the FBI's Security Index, a secret list of dissidents Hoover hoped to be able to arrest in the event of a communist takeover of the U.S. government. Although the Security Index was aspirational insofar as Hoover could not yet round up communists and put them in detention camps, it had a more practical dimension as well. Until a person was removed from the list, those included on it were subjected to aggressive surveillance and harassment campaigns.[6]

For members of the Broadcast 41, this surveillance went on for years, long after their careers were ruined, in some cases ending only when they died. For Madeline Lee, this meant that for months FBI agents sat in cars across the street from the Gilfords' Greenwich Village apartment to spy on the family's comings and goings. Agents rifled through their trash and mail, questioning neighbors and friends about activities proving they were communists. This surveillance was far from subtle. Years later, Lee told the *New York Times* that the superintendent of her building "had a son in jail for armed robbery and she hated the F.B.I. So she considered us in trouble the same way she was. She would tell us that they would come on the first Tuesday: 'They've been here. They wanted to look in your garbage. They wanted to look at the mail that has been thrown out.' "[7] This surveillance did not yield much. Agents reported that the dangerous dissident Madeline Lee, best known for making "baby sounds" for radio and television programs, "spends much of her time caring for her two young children and seldom leaves the apartment house without them."[8]

Of course, the point of this surveillance was not merely to turn up evidence of membership in the Communist Party or treasonous activities on the part of the Gilfords. Rather, it was to intimidate and silence people like them. In Lee's case, this strategy backfired. Delores Scotti, a Bureau investigator, ambushed Lee and her children as she was picking up mail outside the family's vacation home on Fire Island in order to serve a second subpoena to appear before the New York City Un-American Activities Committee. "Cooperate with us," Scotti reportedly told the actress, "or we will tell your employers that you are a Communist. We've got plenty on you. Look what you're doing to your children."[9] Scotti alleged that Gilford "struck" her "with magazines she was carrying," although the charge was later dismissed.[10]

Irate, Lee went to the press, charging that the committee had tried to coerce her into giving false testimony. In the words of an article that appeared in the Communist Party paper the *Daily Worker*, "The un-American invasion of Broadway got a staggering repulse last week in its moth-eaten thought-control hearings ... when Madeline Lee, TV actress, revealed in a tumultuous, gavel-banging session that two committee agents came to her home and tried to browbeat her into giving false testimony."[11] This unflattering press coverage was Hoover's worst nightmare. A woman—a TV actress, no less—had publicly charged the Bureau with intimidation and harassment, thereby generating the very embarrassment that, as the following pages show, the Bureau struggled to repress while waging their war on dissidents.[12]

The form of masculinity that underlay these behaviors—with its bullying, subterfuge, and refusal to brook disagreement—defined the anti-communist movement. Robert Vaughn may have been right when he pointed out that the totalitarian impulses of Soviet-style communism mirrored those of anti-communists, but the crucial difference in the U.S. was this: anti-communists had the power to impose their perspective.[13] Moreover, progressives like the Broadcast 41—whatever their political affiliations—believed that a plurality of points of view was essential to democracy.[14] As we saw in the previous chapter, they also considered learning a means for transformation. To live in "question marks" like Lillian Hellman, to be curious about the world around them and vantage points other than their own, to learn from past mistakes, were positive character traits rather than mortal vulnerabilities.[15]

The worldview of anti-communists, on the other hand, was rooted in the experiences of the dominant, who sought to make their domination appear natural and eternal. Their struggle to take a perspective based on the experiences of the dominant and turn it into a populist mandate using the new medium of television was the culmination of years of collaborative efforts among anti-communists, first to produce and popularize a powerful myth of white American manhood and to teach its agents and audiences to read like a G-Man, whose primary, altruistic objective was to protect America. Supported by the FBI, these anti-communists gained the power to retaliate against, and punish, those like Lee who dared to defy their authoritarianism.

❖ ❖ ❖

Mr. Robeson: You are the authors of the bills that are going to keep all kinds of decent people out of the country.
The Chairman: No, only your kind.
Mr. Robeson: Colored people like myself. And just the Teutonic Anglo-Saxon stock you would let come in.
The Chairman: We are trying to make it easier to get rid of your kind, too!
Mr. Robeson: You don't want any colored people to come in?
Pause.

Paul Robeson (actor, testimony to the House Un-American Activities Committee)[16]

As I took a closer look at my classmates, I started to notice a certain sameness about the fifty of us. Although we came from every type of background, there were no Jews, blacks, or Hispanics in the class. I was later to learn that this was Hoover's policy.
William C. Sullivan (former head of the FBI intelligence operations)[17]

In his memoir, written after he had been forced into retirement by Hoover, former FBI intelligence head William Sullivan described the homogeneity of the FBI he had joined at the start of World War II, noticing for perhaps the first time the whiteness of his cohort. Even years after the Bureau had been forced in the early 1970s to hire women as special agents, Sullivan failed to notice that his class was made up only of men.

The Bureau's racism and misogyny were products of the standpoint of the man who built the institution from the ground up: J. Edgar Hoover. Hoover presided over the FBI from its origins in attacks on progressives after World War I, through the upheavals of the Great Depression and a second World War, through six different presidents, and into the Vietnam War era. To maintain power, Hoover popularized a mythic masculinity. This form of manhood romanticized a federal police force that received its mandate not from the government, but as historian Richard Gid Powers puts it, "directly from the public, a force responsible only to the public, free from any effective political supervision."[18] The first modern government agency to be explicitly opposed to government itself, the Bureau's manly populism preceded the assault on big government launched by Ronald Reagan by several decades.

Hoover knew that managing mass media was central to his institution-building efforts. He had learned this lesson the hard way, through his nearly disastrous involvement in the Palmer Raids during the first Red Scare in 1919 and 1920. Under the direction of attorney general Mitchell Palmer, a then twenty-four-year-old Hoover was given the task of identifying, investigating, and punishing "subversives," mainly anarchists and members of the Industrial

Workers of the World (IWW). More than 500 were eventually deported. As public awareness of the brutality and unconstitutionality of the raids mounted, Hoover displayed what would be a lifelong knack for evading accountability for his actions. Public opinion turned against Palmer instead of Hoover, ending the former's career. The resultant scandal bore Palmer's name rather than Hoover's, just as nearly thirty years later, the Red Scare would be named after Senator Joseph McCarthy, rather than its primary author, J. Edgar Hoover.

The Palmer Raids showed Hoover that manipulating public opinion was vital to building a federal police force. In order to conjure threats that could justify repressive responses by the state, the Bureau needed to create shadowy, secretive enemies of diabolical proportions. These enemies, in turn, legitimized actions on the part of the Bureau and its allies that were themselves shadowy and secretive. To set the national stage for the manufacture of these threats, the FBI borrowed from the advertising and public relations industries to create a problem for which they could then provide the solution. Just as Listerine proposed to cure the condition of halitosis which the company had invented for that purpose, or antiperspirant treated the newly defined problem of underarm odor that manufacturers said prevented young women from finding romance, so the Bureau proposed their brand of masculinity as the solution to forms of deviance they defined as threats to America. Only the Bureau could combat the "public enemies" they had identified because only masterful minds like theirs could fight these "masters of deceit," or, for that matter, even detect them. The success of this formula, and partly the key to Hoover's forty-eight-year reign as FBI director, owed much to the Bureau's effective deployment of what Powers describes as the "action-detective formula," or the genre of the police procedural that was popularized during Depression-era America.[19]

Although the FBI and like-minded producers and writers in media industries did not always agree completely on the details of the myths they were creating, they agreed on the broad outlines of the police procedural they were inventing. This formula required arch-villains (criminals and commies), powerless victims, and, of course, the Bureau's legion of superheroes, who used the objective and unbiased science of detection (fingerprinting, data collection, research) to restore law and order. G-Man masculinity, the mainstay of this genre, was as much a fantasy of manhood as the superheroes emerging in American comic books at the same time. Both were antidotes to economic and political uncertainty during a period in which the patriarchal foundations of the country were being shaken to their core. G-Men and superheroes alike shared magical powers bestowed on them to fight crime and corruption, and they protected feminized, speechless victims (although comics provided more creative and entertaining fare). Hoover's language of Americanism made the gender of the nation clear. Under communism, he wrote, "The soul of America would be entombed; her body disemboweled."[20] His mute, feminized victims proved eternally vulnerable. On Hoover's watch, rates of crime and evidence of subversion never declined, but instead multiplied, creating an endless and politically useful procession of threats.

For all its rhetoric of protecting women, children, and a feminized nation state, for G-Man masculinity, femininity was always a problem, and women were regarded with scorn and suspicion. On one hand, it was the very weakness inherent in femininity that necessitated the need for the G-Man's protection. Women's natural inclination to care for other people, anti-communists maintained, made them susceptible to deception since they were easily misled by their identification with the downtrodden. Angels in the house could sometimes open the door to the devil, a misogynistic storyline drawn straight from the Bible.

Because they were not as smart as white men, women were also easily "hoodwinked"—a verb anti-communists frequently applied to women who supported progressive causes. As Elizabeth Dilling put it, progressive women eagerly consumed the "Communist bait of offering women sex equality with men through free love, state orphanages and collectivized factory kitchens" as truth, when it was actually nothing more than an exploitative ruse.[21] Hoover shared this reasoning. "The sole purpose of the new Party line" about democracy and civil rights, he wrote in one of the many magazine articles that appeared under his byline, "is to hoodwink" unsuspecting women and children.[22] The House Un-American Activities Committee described the leftwing Congress of American Women as "just another Communist hoax specifically designed to ensnare idealistically minded but politically gullible women."[23] Commenting on actress Judy Holliday's support for progressive causes, the American Legion told the Bureau, "We won't assume that Judy Holliday pretends to know a lot about Spain, peace, Africa, the Russian theater, or intellectualism," but she was nevertheless willing "to sign statements, lead picket lines, etc., for organizations cited as subversive by competent government agencies."[24] In the eyes of anti-communists, women were not equipped to think reasonably or rationally.

This belief that women could not think for themselves extended to African American women and men as well. Nazism, as sociologist Troy Duster points out, forced homegrown American white supremacists to be more cautious in their use of overtly racist language, if not in their practices.[25] Hindered in their ability to use openly racist tropes in their more public forms of address (their classified correspondence was another matter altogether), anti-communists instead argued that calls for civil rights were actually the work of communists. Anti-communists maintained that African Americans had been perfectly pleased with their status in American culture until communists created racial tensions for their own, selfish purposes. As Hoover put it in the *American Legion Magazine*: "The red hand of communism intensifies racial division while pretending to strive for equality. The Party's sole interest is to hoodwink the Negro, to exploit him and use him as a tool to build a communist America."[26] Resistant to any perspective but their own, anti-communists characterized African Americans in much the same way they did women: as feminized dupes, easily hoodwinked by the Communist Party.

The weakness attributed to these supposedly gullible populations inculcated in G-Men contempt toward those people they believed required protective services. Borrowing from the misogyny of Freudian psychoanalysis, anti-communist men saw women as overbearing maternal figures and hysterics, purveyors of "Momism," a debilitating condition that writer Philip Wylie identified in *Generation of Vipers*. Writers often cited by anti-communists, like Ralph Banay, Ferdinand Lundberg, and Marynia F. Farnham, shared Wylie's belief that women suffered from the "general affliction" of "penis-envy," which caused them to dominate their sons, engendering epidemics of juvenile delinquency. According to these experts, "The spawning ground of most neurosis in Western civilization is the home," where it was caused by the behavior of mothers.[27]

From the G-Man's standpoint, politically uninvolved women—whether easily hoodwinked or domineering, penis-envying matriarchs—were bad enough. But progressive women personified anti-communists' worst fears about female nature. Far from being grateful for the G-Man's protection, women like Madeline Lee dared to question his motives. As actress and writer Mae West quipped in *My Little Chickadee* (1940), a film she wrote, "Every man I meet wants to protect me. I can't figure out what from."[28] Whether women refused protection or poked fun at it, anti-communists responded by vilifying these critics. Women who challenged male authority became unnatural, manipulative viragos and agents of communism, with the Soviet Union figuring as the mother of all these evils, in Elizabeth Dilling's words as "The Mother of harlots and abominations of the earth."[29]

In anti-communist correspondence and media, progressive women appeared along these lines as well, as confidential informants and communist seductresses, snitches and whores, confirmation of anti-communists' belief in the duplicity of female nature. Anti-communists used tropes like the "blonde 'Communist Party Girl' " to cast progressive women as gold diggers who exchanged sexual favors for men's acquiescence to "Stalinist interpretations of current events," habitually seducing unsuspecting lovers and husbands.[30] In his testimony before the HUAC, Marc Lawrence said that fellow actor Lionel Stander recruited him into a Communist Party cell in Hollywood by saying, "Get to know this stuff [Marxist literature] and you will make out more with the dames!"[31] FBI informant Angela Calomiris repeated allegations of women trading sexual favors for Party loyalty in her bestselling account of her experiences spying on the New York Photo League, a leftist cooperative of socially conscious photographers.[32]

Progressive women, the FBI maintained, used their sexuality to advance their own selfish interests and the Communist Party's revolutionary project. FBI special agent Milton Jones reported that Broadcast 41 member Louise Fitch, "played the field and pushed [future husband and scriptwriter for *This is Your FBI*] Jerry Lewis aside. Later on, she started going with Lewis again when it appeared that he was the best bet of the group she was running around with."[33] Of actress Judy Holliday, another FBI agent reported, "Despite the recent build-up given her by *Life* Magazine (and incidently [sic] *Life* seems to have a bad shot of virus infection, having boosted recently two fellow travelers with long records in recent issues), Judy Holliday has been a great solace to the Moscow-tied lads and lassies who look for big names as sucker bait for their front operations."[34] The FBI accused other stars of being "sucker bait" as well. Lena Horne, the Bureau wrote, was "an asset to our Russian Firsters" who "consider her a great 'find'; destined to lure many celebrity-worshippers into siding with Comintern's program."[35]

Gender factored into anti-communist representations of progressive white men as well. Unlike women and people of color, progressive white men threatened to usurp anti-communist men's right to protect the nation and those considered vulnerable within it. In order to undermine such challenges, anti-communists made concerted efforts to distinguish their brand of real, American masculinity from the masculinity of progressive white men. Where G-Man masculinity was virile, individualistic, and Christian, white male communists and fellow-travelers were effeminate, intellectual, furtive, and either atheistic or Jewish. Claims that progressive men were by nature effeminate were frequently accompanied by anti-Semitic tirades against the intellectualism of men considered "socialists, misfits, and perverts" and invectives against Stalin's "little minions," or men they deemed unnaturally servile.[36]

G-Man masculinity introduced a virulent, aggressive strain of homophobia to aid in these endeavors. The protection they offered was "machine gun" rather than the "cream puff" crime-fighting typical of progressive men.[37] Anti-communist journalist Westbrook Pegler described blacklisted dancer Paul Draper as "the pretty pirouetician [sic] who stamps a dainty foot with hand on hip," "this mincing twirp," "a pink and mincing dancer, rather on the elfin side." Pegler described Draper's style of performance in terms meant to leave no doubt about Draper's proclivities: "Affecting skin-tight pants, he puts his hands daintily on his hips, tosses his head, makes a saucy mouth and whirls and flounces madly."[38] When Illinois governor Adlai Stevenson ran for president in 1952, on a platform anti-communists considered dangerously progressive, his FBI file included "a report from a New York police detective who said that the governor not only was one of the best-known homosexuals in the state of Illinois but used the drag name 'Adeline.' "[39]

But G-Man masculinity was not just rhetoric anti-communists used in their correspondence or public relations materials. It was also a set of practices embedded in the work culture in which FBI agents were groomed and socialized. Hoover did nothing less than build a world within the Bureau that reflected his fantasies about white masculinity, creating what historian Matthew Cecil describes as an "alternative reality" through public relations.[40] In the Bureau, J. Edgar Hoover had the power to project his vision of American masculinity onto his employees, who then carried those beliefs outward into American society.

The previous chapter hinted at some of the ways in which work cultures in media industries were hostile places for women and people of color. But where some women had gained a modicum of power in broadcasting during the 1930s and 1940s, only white men were allowed to even apply to be Bureau agents, those icons of American masculinity. Under Hoover's watchful eyes, the FBI's hiring practices resembled a casting call for the police procedurals that soon proliferated on television. FBI job application forms called for men of "unblemished character and reputation," with specific (if indeterminate) "physical and educational requirements."[41] Applicants were asked not only to identify their "color" (a rhetorical question, since only white men were hired as agents), but to disclose "physical defects" like baldness or near-sightedness that might detract from the virile image the Bureau wished to project.[42] Performance evaluations of agents reinforced this emphasis on image, praising those who made "a very good appearance" and rewarding "general" and "clean-cut" appearances, shorthand for white, middle-class masculinity.[43]

The FBI, like the HUAC, employed men who came from the American South, descendants of English, Scottish, and Irish stock, preferably lawyers, who shared Hoover's commitment to what historian Thomas Borstelmann describes as a social order "grounded in segregation and white domination of people of color."[44] "Dark-complected" men, like FBI public relations director Louis B. Nichols, who was of Greek descent, opted to wear "pale blue shirts" rather than the standard issue white, anxious that they might appear to be less than racially pure.[45] Everyday life in the Bureau also reinforced the G-Man's foundational white supremacy: one agent's idea of "fun" to help "break the tension" at FBI headquarters involved dressing up in Ku Klux Klan robes and running through hallways the Bureau shared with lawyers in the Civil Rights Division.[46]

Regardless of differences in their cultural and economic backgrounds—and there were some in terms of class—men who applied to the Bureau were already inclined to share Hoover's outlooks on Americanism and the dangerous nature of dissent. They joined an organization dedicated to protecting Hoover's authority, an organization that reinforced agents' convictions about their superiority at every step. Agents interacted with white women and people of color only as social inferiors. White women were assigned to more intimate domestic roles, as mothers, wives, and secretaries (the last category serving as the pool for the second), while people of color worked as chauffeurs, butlers, gardeners, housekeepers, and other servants whom agents deemed "very faithful" and content with their lot.[47] Neither women nor African Americans would serve as special agents until after Hoover's death in 1972.[48]

Thus insulated from encountering perspectives that might challenge their own, these G-Men resided in an intensely homosocial world, shielded from emotion and femininity, regulated by objective, scientific, rational manliness. Ironically, many years later, those who sought to rationalize the Bureau's violent actions against its own citizens tried to turn G-Man masculinity on its head. Hoover, according to this revisionist history (based mainly on Hoover's notorious dislike of women), was a homosexual, who for years lived with his "wife" and second-in-command, Clyde Tolson, flagrantly defying the normativity of anti-communist family values. Hoover's alleged queer identity became the explanation for Hoover's racism and, to a lesser degree, his misogyny, as if his bigotry had been caused not by the toxic values that underlay this form of white masculinity, but by sexual practices anti-communists continued to consider perverted and un-American.

❖ ❖ ❖

Do they think they'll protect the younger generation with this kind of smirking dishonesty?

Vera Caspary (writer, novelist)[49]

If we fail—if we allow ourselves to be duped by communist cunning and the "new look"—we shall, with a casualness that is indecent, toss into discard one immortal heritage of freedom.

J. Edgar Hoover[50]

The Bureau had an unprecedented ability to popularize its version of American masculinity and to define the many threats it claimed to face in its efforts to protect America. Although the phrase "G-Man"—short for government man—first appeared in Chicago rewrite man Fred D. Pasley's 1930 book on gangster Al Capone, the phrase really took off in 1934, after FBI agents shot and killed Chicago crime boss John Dillinger. According to lore, Hoover was annoyed that national attention following the Dillinger killing focused on agent Melvin Purvis rather than him and the professional, scientific organization he led. Journalist Neil "Rex" Collier wrote a six-part article for the *Washington Star* that remedied this, centering the action on Hoover, and establishing him as the mastermind behind the FBI's success in apprehending Dillinger.[51]

Collier's celebration of the Bureau gave it some powerful positive press, expanding the G-Man's reach beyond print media. The FBI initiated a collaboration with Hollywood that resulted in the making of Warner Brothers' *G-Men* (1935). *G-Men* featured James Cagney as "Brick" Davis, whose nickname emphasized his masculinity. In the film, Davis' best friend, Eddie Buchanan, tries to persuade him to join the FBI. Davis—a law-abiding lawyer seeking to create an honest practice amidst a sea of corruption—initially rebuffs these efforts. Only after Buchanan is murdered by a gangster does Davis feel compelled to join the FBI in order to avenge his friend's death. Intended to glorify the values and virtues of men who joined the FBI to wage war on public enemies, *G-Men* was a hit, becoming one of the top-grossing films of 1935.

The FBI soon got into the business of radio as well, teaming up with successful radio producer Phillips H. Lord and NBC on the production of the radio series *G-Men*. Renamed *Gang Busters* in 1936, the long-running, popular crime reality program's opening lines touted it as the only radio program produced "in cooperation with police and federal police departments throughout the United States." The FBI and Lord did not always agree on how best to represent the G-Man. Hoover, who refused to allow Lord to say that the Bureau was the official source of the content, thought that *Gang Busters* "was a very unsatisfactory and rather cheap presentation." Lord—a self-described "loyal rooter of the Federal Bureau of Investigation"—offered to incorporate a "little propaganda" for the FBI into the show, but Hoover remained noncommittal, at least in the pages of FBI correspondence.[52]

Originating in the conspiratorial, masculinist perspective and practices of the FBI, G-Man masculinity had an often-tense relationship with what producers like Lord thought they could sell to advertisers. As historian Matthew Cecil documents, Hoover fought to exercise white-knuckle control over how his preferred version of American manhood would appear in popular culture. The compromise looked something like this: audiences were drawn to the theater because of the genre's conflict between the G-Man and the public enemy *du jour*. Then, as Powers puts it, "once they sat down to enjoy their G-Man adventures they also got a full dose of the J. Edgar Hoover gospel: documentary-like tours of the F.B.I. labs and classrooms, peeks at the fingerprint files and ballistic microscopes, and the message that the 'F.B.I. method' developed by J. Edgar Hoover was the secret weapon that would rip up 'the roots of crime.' "[53]

Refusing to compromise, and seeking more control over mass media than producers were willing to grant, the Bureau established its own production unit, the Publications Section, in 1935.[54] Hoover hired PR man Louis B. Nichols to spread their message: "the Bureau was doing great work and that the public should know the accomplishments."[55] In 1938, under Nichols' direction, the Publications Section evolved into the FBI's Crime Records Section, whose name concealed the division's real mission, which would have proved troublesome for the FBI, since government agencies were not supposed to be in the business of creating their own public relations.[56] And personnel in Crime Records did just that, writing articles, reports, speeches, and publications that appeared under Hoover's byline in *Parade* magazine, *Popular Mechanics*, the *Harvard Business Review*, and an impressive array of other publications.[57] Crime Records staff writers wrote anti-communist classics, such as Hoover's *Masters of Deceit*, and helped author Don Whitehead with his nonfiction best-seller *The FBI Story*, as well as the 1959 film version starring Jimmy Stewart. Crime Records staff also consulted on radio and television programs like *The FBI in Peace and War* (1944–48) and *This is Your FBI* (1945–53).

In addition to producing all manner of media, Crime Records cultivated and managed relationships with journalists and organizations who shared the G-Man's perspective. The FBI's so-called friendly journalists (a nomenclature Republican president Richard M. Nixon would learn from friend and mentor J. Edgar Hoover) were those who had ingratiated themselves with Hoover by publicly praising the work of the Bureau, writing adulatory letters to Hoover, or providing information about suspected communists and fellow-travelers in media, government, education, and industry.

Many of these friendly journalists were gossip columnists like Igor Cassini, Hedda Hopper, and George Sokolosky, or journalists with reputations for being disagreeable toward their colleagues, like Westbrook Pegler, Howard Rushmore, and Walter Winchell. Conveniently, these writers were not subject to the constraints of fact checking or, for that matter, journalistic ethics. Because they were not highly respected by their peers, the validation they received from the Bureau was enormously meaningful to them.[58] Those who glorified the work of the FBI, as the American Business Consultants'

John Keenan did in a letter he wrote to the director, received praise in return from Hoover for "advising your readers on the merits of the movie ['The FBI Story']." In return for their loyalty, anti-communist journalists were added to the Bureau's "special correspondents' list," enjoying all the benefits that came with this, such as exclusive interviews, scoops, and leaked information from the FBI's files. Friendly reporters and editors, such as Allen Dibble of *Time* magazine, had powerful direct lines to Hoover and Tolson.[59]

The feedback loops the special correspondents' list forged between the FBI and friendly journalists were extraordinarily powerful ones for the Bureau. They created a shared vocabulary (G-Men, public enemies, war on crime) that in turn reinforced the terms of the Bureau's protection racket. And they helped to mask the connections between the Bureau and its public relations efforts, disseminating anti-communist images with no obvious links to the Bureau itself. Finally, they allowed the Bureau to treat its own creations as if these were historical facts. When *G-Men* was rereleased in 1949, a date that happily coincided with the Bureau's twenty-fifth anniversary, many of the prints included a prologue featuring a senior agent screening the film to new FBI recruits in order to teach them about the Bureau's history.

However much the identities of its public enemies varied, the formula the FBI created remained constant in its celebration of G-Man masculinity, distinguishing the G-Man, as Powers puts it, "from the other detective heroes because he spent less time with his girl and more time in the classroom, the laboratory, and on the phone to Washington."[60] This formula was not addressed to female viewers—it was instead a form of self-affirmation for anti-communist men. If relationships with women appeared in it, those were largely beside the point, frequently relegated to death or final scenes that pointed in the direction of some off-camera domestic sphere without having to waste screen time representing it.

In its focus on a masculine world of criminals and white crime fighters, the G-Man concept proved an effective marketing tool for ideas about anti-communist masculinity and law and order pitched specifically to young white boys, influencing a generation of them in the process. These stories about "brave agents and dangerous criminals" resonated with an eager, young, white male audience, receptive to stories celebrating their identity.[61] Hoover frequently acknowledged this: "The value of this sort of thing to the growing boy cannot be overestimated. He is taught that the policeman can be and is his friend, and he learns to see crime in its true light—as something far from glamorous, something sordid and evil that must be stamped out."[62] Obedience to law and order, these narratives taught boys, was the most important virtue white men possessed, and threats to tradition were always threats to America.

As a result of the Bureau's efforts, narratives of G-Man masculinity became pervasive in American culture. As historian Claire Bond Potter notes, the G-Man franchise "eventually embraced all forms of consumable culture available to a depression-era audience: movies, prime-time radio shows, comic strips, magazines, and most important, toys, books, and other items produced for a children's market."[63] *Gang Busters* spawned a DC Comics version as well as a series of Little Blue Books. With the aid of friendly journalist Rex Collier, Hoover endorsed an FBI comic strip called "War on Crime" that claimed to be "True Stories of G-Men Activities."[64] The FBI's unofficial involvement in *Gang Busters* paved the way for its official control over *The FBI in Peace and War*.

These stories took hold in the imaginations of Depression-era white men and boys. FBI files contain numerous fan letters to Hoover, from men and boys alike, who commended Hoover's hard-on-crime attitude and unequivocally endorsed G-Man masculinity. Vinton Hayworth, actress Rita Hayworth's uncle and an anti-communist crusader, said that he could not close his letter to Hoover "without a personal word to you: as citizens, we are most grateful to you for the magnificent job you have done in what is probably one of the most difficult posts in the world." Hayworth was further moved to praise Hoover's positive influence on their teenaged son.[65] Many of those who later joined the Bureau cited stories they had listened to, read, or seen as having motivated them to pursue a career at the Bureau. FBI agent James R. Healy attributed his "interest in law enforcement" to "the exploits of G-men" that he read about as a child. FBI director Louis Nichols "cited dramatic, action-packed FBI radio programs as having influenced his decision to join the Bureau."[66] For those already inclined to accept the G-Man's views on Americanism, the G-Man brand gave them license to never doubt their own judgement.

❖ ❖ ❖

Books aren't intended to give Communist propaganda plainly ... for the most part they just set a mental tone, to lead the children on by degrees.

CounterAttack[67]

As a government patron of the arts, there have been few rivals to J. Edgar Hoover.

Richard Gid Powers (historian)[68]

The Bureau's carefully cultivated façade of neutrality and confidentiality helped hide its role in creating G-Man masculinity. But media production alone was insufficient to sustain G-Man masculinity, particularly in a

Depression-era America where people had many reasons to regard government and capitalist institutions with grave mistrust. The Bureau countered the progressive potential of populism by encouraging white suspicion of government assistance programs and those who supported them. Because, the FBI contended, communists were so adept at distorting the language of democracy and justice, the Bureau's anti-communist allies and the American public had to be trained to read the hidden truths behind what seemed to be democratic messages. In the decades before the blacklist, unable to completely suppress progressive criticism of racism and economic oppression, the Bureau worked diligently to teach its agents and publics alike how to read for the subtleties of subversive influence. In essence, the Bureau set out to teach Americans to regard messages calling for equality of all kinds with grave suspicion and to attribute these messages to the un-American hand of international Communism.

Literary critic William Maxwell says we should see FBI files not just as government correspondence or institutional records, but rather as works of literary and cultural criticism, "of collectively authored textual analysis and cultural history."[69] Maxwell, Mary Helen Washington, and other literary scholars have shown the impact of the FBI's criticism as it related to African American literary production in New York City during the first half of the twentieth century. The Bureau wrote racially motivated criticism in order to diminish and destroy the literary and political reputations of African American authors and their allies in publishing and the press.[70] The FBI was equally concerned about progressive influence over such elements of popular culture as film and broadcasting. The Bureau knew that mass media mattered to ever-increasing numbers of people, and that such pervasive forms of popular culture could move and inspire many people to outrage and action. Because they did not discriminate between literature and popular culture when it came to reading for subversive influence, poems by writers like Langston Hughes and Claude McKay were scrutinized with the same intensity as films like *Born Yesterday* and *Crossfire* (Hollywood Ten member Adrian Scott's searing critique of anti-Semitism), broadcast shows like Mary Margaret McBride's radio programs and Berg's *The Goldbergs*, journalist Charles Collingwood's news commentary, and Dorothy Parker's verse.

According to the Bureau, communists used chains of meaning to conceal the totalitarian purpose of their messages. Like the New Criticism of the era's literary establishment (a movement heavily influenced by white Southerners), the Bureau (an institution also dominated by white Southerners) emphasized dramatic, close readings of texts that peeled away layers of deception to demonstrate the concealed intent of progressive media. The FBI had little interest in what authors said about their work. Nor did they pay much attention to historical or biographical contexts or facts that might detract from their own interpretive virtuosity. Instead, they described a breadcrumb trail that invariably, if convolutedly, led back to the Kremlin.

Of course, only trained experts like Hoover, his second-in-command Clyde Tolson, and other FBI agents could fully detect the web of allusions and references hidden within progressive messages. As the American Business Consultants put it in their founding business plan, "To tear the mask from seditious fifth columnists requires pain-staking investigation, evaluation, and application of the facts by trained personnel of proved integrity and high intelligence."[71] In Hoover's estimation, "non-critical minds" (like those of women or people of color) were easily hoodwinked by Communist propaganda, while "The trained mind, the man benefiting by the processes of democratic education, can, through the glitter of what appears to be gold, find what is gold."[72] Only trained anti-communist minds—those that had been educated by the Bureau—could see that behind the glitter of progressives' red, white, and blue messages, Reds were pulling their strings.

Hoover hired men with training in textual analysis and public relations to conduct this work, like Crime Records Division director Nichols, a former religious works director for the Washington office of the YMCA. Nichols in turn handpicked "former newspaper reporters, radio announcers" and others with "experience in writing, English majors, journalism majors, and public relations types."[73] The pages of FBI correspondence show how Hoover served as editor and teacher, adding glosses to texts, and correcting his agents' interpretations to bring them into better alignment with his vision. He scrawled commentary in the margins of Bureau correspondence, rebuking his agents, correcting wrongheaded interpretations, and frequently exhorting them to be more aggressive in reading for subversives' secret intent. On one occasion, after visiting CBS headquarters, an agent new to the New York field office made the mistake of telling Hoover he had received a warm welcome from a network that Hoover was notorious for disliking, concluding that he saw no evidence of subversive behavior during his visit. Hoover reprimanded the agent in no uncertain terms, warning him that "the taffy" CBS had handed out to him and others was meant to distract anti-communists from the network's real subversive objectives.[74] CBS, Hoover added, had "Just recently put out a television program which was vicious in its presentation of [the] FBI," proof subversive influence was afoot.

Throughout the 1940s and 1950s, anti-communists followed in Hoover's footsteps, seeking to undermine their critics by suggesting criticism was red in nature, hysterical, and unfounded. As *CounterAttack* put it in a critique of a novel about the impact of the blacklist on one person's life:

> As connoisseurs of the distraught view know, *So Help Me God*, a novel by the TV producer (*Studio One*) Felix Jackson, is a high example. Its reasoned thesis is that a mere scrawled anonymous note of accusation can set the FBI and legislative committees off on a wild and woolly Walpurgis Nacht of persecutions, accusations, probings and general excess. Nevertheless, enough people have accepted this altogether incredible performance as worthy enough to have it serialized in *McCall's* magazine for women, published as a book by the Viking publishing company and now reprinted as a paperbound edition by Bantam Books.[75]

Reducing criticism to melodrama and ridiculing those who complained about blacklisting, anti-communists condemned those in publishing responsible for curating such a "wild and woolly Walpurgis Nacht."

Much of the material published under Hoover's name was ghostwritten by journalists like Courtney Ryley Cooper (*10,000 Public Enemies*) or FBI agents like Dr. Fern Stukenbroeker, a historian who was "the main author of *Masters of Deceit*." Hoover was "the final authority" when it came to content.[76] After a draft had been submitted to a committee assigned to work on a project, for example, Hoover would review all materials, editing, providing comments, and demanding revisions. Hoover's own rhetorical flourishes provided a model for agents and anti-communist allies. This melodramatic style dripped with rhetorical sarcasm. Hoover's frequent use of sneer quotes emphasized his unique ability to pierce the veiled assertions of progressives to discern what lay behind. In this vein, Hoover wrote that communists "grow in 'families': father, mother, children, even in-laws. The Party is proud of its 'Communist genealogy.' It may boast one day of 'three generations of Socialist fighters,' next day it may pay tribute to a 'worthy mother' who has raised her sons and daughters to be Communists."[77] Hoover taught agents and audiences to see through seemingly innocent language about mothers, families, and community to the "dread danger" progressives posed to American children and the future of the American family.[78]

Following in the steps of a G-Man masculinity that cautioned, in Hoover's words, that "decency and adherence to law and order are the only way," anti-communist criticism also taught white people to read social change not only as a threat to their whiteness and social standing, but a threat to the future of the world as well.[79] To reinforce the link they made between civil rights and communism, anti-communists repeatedly equated civil rights with subversion. Hoover's racist pedagogy had a lengthy history. As Maxwell recalls, "the FBI's first major work of literary criticism was the 1919 essay-pamphlet *Radicalism and Sedition among the Negroes as Reflected in Their Publications*."[80]

To persuade white audiences that civil rights demands did not originate in African Americans' demands for rights they were constitutionally guaranteed, but in the machinations of the Kremlin, G-Man masculinity insisted that civil rights organizing was nothing more than a communist conspiracy. "When a Communist front agitates on behalf of Negroes," anti-communist writer Vincent J. Hartnett wrote, "its real purpose is not to help them, but to create conflict between Negroes and whites."[81] African Americans had been happy with their lot in the U.S., so the G-Man story went, until Communist Party operatives (those whites who supported civil rights) began to "agitate" them. White supremacist Elizabeth Dilling made the condescending distinction between "well-meaning Negroes" who have never "stood for racial inter-marriage and social intermixture," and those who had been artificially agitated by the Communist Party.[82]

This reasoning often extended to other racial and ethnic racial groups as well. According to the FBI, the blacklisted film *Salt of the Earth*, depicting the struggles of Mexican American women and men, was "a propaganda attempt by Communist elements in Hollywood to fan the racial and minority problem in the United States and discredit the United States abroad."[83] "Stalin's international propaganda machine," anti-communists maintained, divided people by suggesting the Korean War was "a US capitalist, racist drive against the colored peoples of Asia."[84] Without communism, anti-communists insisted, there would be no racial problems in the U.S. Anyone who believed otherwise had, in Hoover's estimation, imbibed "the poisonous pills of communist propaganda."[85]

To manage the multiplying contradictions of their racial reasoning, anti-communists often diverted readers' attention from white supremacist violence to what they alleged were "the efforts of the Communist Party to utilize the American Negro for propaganda purposes.[86] When Harry and Harriette Moore, founders of the first NAACP chapter in Brevard, Florida, were murdered by the Ku Klux Klan on December 25, 1951, *CounterAttack* professed outrage not at this abhorrent killing, but at a possibility they considered far direr: that Soviets might "distort" this publicity and use it in their war against Americanism. According to *CounterAttack*, "Stalin relishes news of incidents such as this in the US. His propaganda and agitational machine immediately goes into effect."[87] Implying that the Moores had been murdered for the purpose of creating Stalinist propaganda, *CounterAttack* concluded that the public should be skeptical about the incident as a whole, demanding that the media "tell the WHOLE story: that the incident has aroused nationwide protest, that the Govt is doing everything it can to apprehend the murderers and bring them to justice."[88]

But try as he might, Hoover's G-Man myth was insufficient to stem the tide of resistance. Neither public relations nor pedagogical efforts to prevent Americans from learning new ways of seeing could silence progressives' perspectives and prevent them from taking advantage of television's new storytelling opportunities. In order to eradicate dissenting perspectives, anti-communists undertook a clandestine and aggressive campaign to suppress dissenting viewpoints.

❖ ❖ ❖

Never once did I hear anybody, including myself, raise the question, "Is this course of action which we have agreed upon lawful, is it legal, is it ethical or moral?" We never gave any thought to this line of reasoning, because we were just naturally pragmatic.

William C. Sullivan (former assistant director, FBI intelligence operations)[89]

The fact is that the FBI was asking me to violate the Constitution of the United States in order to, paradoxically, protect the Constitution from the alien traditions we in the FBI defined as "un-American," "subversive," and "communistic." I was not sure what this rationale meant, but it sounded good to me. At the age of twenty-five, I was all for my country, right or wrong.

Wesley Swearingen (former FBI agent)[90]

The FBI's public relations practices combined with their critical pedagogy to convey a picture of a nation on the brink of collapse, beset by powerful agents of subversion and defended by manly yet beleaguered G-Men. But the harassment of Madeline Lee and other members of the Broadcast 41 showed the tyrannical side of the G-Man's protection racket. As historian Ellen Schrecker observed, the FBI's efforts to silence dissent went far beyond propaganda: "During the 1940s and 1950s the FBI engaged in a massive cover-up that ranged from simple lies to a formidable campaign to smear and ultimately destroy the political legitimacy of its few remaining critics."[91]

At the center of the Bureau's campaign against its critics were the massive files the FBI had begun accumulating at the end of World War I under Hoover's supervision. This information came from sources across a wide network of loyal anti-communist allies, including individuals like white supremacist Elizabeth Dilling and the many "concerned" Americans who wrote to the

Bureau to inform on their fellow citizens. Veterans' organizations like the American Legion, the Veterans of Foreign Wars, and Catholic War Veterans provided information to the FBI as well, along with civic organizations like the Chamber of Commerce; legislative bodies like the Dies Committee and the Tenney Committee; anti-communist religious organizations (most importantly the Catholic Church); and rightwing women's organizations, including the Daughters of the American Revolution and a furtive and shadowy operation called the Minute Women of America.[92]

Members of anti-communist organizations were mobilized quickly in the service of the Bureau. American Legion members compiled lists of subversives based on reading Communist Party publications like the *Daily Worker*, listening to radio and television programs for traces of subversive content, cross-referencing their extensive newspaper and magazine clipping files with what they heard on the air, and sharing information with the FBI and with other anti-communist organizations.[93] The FBI exchanged information about communists in Hollywood and New York City with the HUAC, a collaboration whose cross-fertilizations helped publicize lists of subversives and disseminate the names of the blacklisted to anti-communists throughout the country.[94]

Although the FBI described its vast holdings of memoranda, reports, letters, and interviews as classified information of the highest caliber, the reliance on sources who told them what they wanted to hear (either for personal gain or because of intimidation) and the absence of fact-checking meant that the Bureau relied heavily on gossip and innuendo, Hoover's stock in trade. Much of the Bureau's information came from confidential informants, people who infiltrated progressive organizations in media industries or informed on co-workers, family members, and friends. The Bureau's own method for determining the reliability of these informants was typically inscrutable, although reports confidently described these sources in the pages of FBI correspondence in terms of "known reliability." The identities of those who provided this information moreover remain shrouded in mystery: nearly seventy years after the events described in this book occurred, the government continues to redact the names of confidential informants in broadcasting for reasons of national security.

In addition to its massive records-keeping operation, the Bureau subjected actors, directors, and producers (particularly those active in the labor movement) to heightened surveillance and harassment. As in the case of Madeline Lee, the Bureau assigned agents to follow people and badger them. In addition to this surveillance of families, homes, and workplaces, Bureau agents made repeated pretext telephone calls to suspected subversives' residences, purportedly to confirm that they resided there. For example, for years after she had been determined not to be a threat to America, Hoover insisted that actress Anne Revere be subjected to a ceaseless flow of these pretext telephone calls in order to verify that she resided at an address they were already monitoring. The Bureau further tampered with Revere's mail (which they described as "mail covers") and periodically went through her garbage (trash covers) in order to collect additional information.[95]

The FBI wiretapped the telephones of other persons of interest (such as Shirley Graham and W.E.B. Du Bois), although they tended to be more circumspect in describing this in the pages of their correspondence. In the case of singer Ella Logan, apropos of no evidence beyond her performance of a left-leaning song, Hoover requested "authorization of a technical surveillance on Ella Logan at the above address and wherever she may reside in the United States prior to leaving for Europe for the purpose of determining the extent of her activities on behalf of the Comintern apparatus and for the purpose of identifying espionage agents."[96] Far from being aimed at detecting dangerous communist agents, these forms of surveillance were meant to harass and intimidate progressives. The carelessness of surveillance and the obviousness of pretext telephone calls, trash covers, and mail covers intimidated and silenced many of those whom the FBI suspected of harboring ill will toward the Bureau.

The Bureau, as we have seen, considered individuals who were neither Christian nor white to have dangerous tendencies toward atheistic communism, whether because they were diabolical or especially gullible. The Bureau's anti-Semitism was a constant undercurrent in its aggressive monitoring of politically outspoken Jewish women like Vera Caspary, Lillian Hellman, and Dorothy Parker, or women married to Jewish men, like Anne Revere (married to Sam Rosen), Gayle Sondergaard (married to Herbert Biberman), and Jean Muir (married to Henry Jaffe). Of Hellman, one agent wrote, "She is, of course, of Jewish extraction. Hellman grew up in considerable wealth and luxury and having, according to her own statement, 'wasted and literally threw money away.'" Projecting his own anti-Semitism onto Hellman, the agent continued, "She acquired an extreme dislike for her mother's people because they were so greedy, grasping for money and financial gains, even to the extent of taking undue advantage of others and depriving them of an equal opportunity in a business transaction."[97]

FBI harassment of African Americans was part of its institutional DNA. From the early 1920s until his death in 1972, there was no moment in the FBI's history where African Americans were free of violent intimidation by Hoover's national police force. Broadcast 41 member Shirley Graham's career offers a textbook example of the impact and persistence of anti-communist crusades against African Americans in media industries. In 1936, Graham took a job at the Federal Theatre Project, hired by director Hallie Flanagan "as Supervisor of the Negro Unit of the Chicago Federal Theatre."[98] Three years later, anti-communists shut the project down. Next, the Phillis Wheatley YWCA in Indianapolis hired Graham to direct their adult activities. Here, she again became the target of anti-communist harassment, this time by Elizabeth Dilling.[99] In 1943, Graham was offered the position of YWCA-USO director of Negro work at Fort Huachuca in Arizona, the base of the 93rd Division, the largest African American Division in the U.S. Army. Two years after taking the position, Graham was abruptly "re-assigned" to a much smaller post in Oklahoma, sacrificed by the YWCA leadership to appease anti-communist critics. Graham was well aware of the conditions surrounding her reassignment. She was forced to leave, she wrote in a letter, because "in the final analysis white supremacy has us by [the] throat because the white man has the money."[100] White anti-communist men had more than money: they held the reins to the most powerful police force in American history.

While the Bureau's retaliation against black artists and activists has been well documented by scholars and journalists in the decades since Hoover's death, the misogyny of his police force has garnered much less attention.[101] This misogyny often took the shape of attacks on women that were out of proportion to the threats the Bureau claimed they represented. These attacks were aggressively retaliatory, as surveillance of Madeline Lee shows, aimed specifically at actresses and writers who publicly criticized the FBI or defied the Bureau's close ally, the HUAC. In 1951, Anne Revere (who had been informed on by fellow Screen Actors Guild member Ronald Reagan and then-wife Jane Wyman) refused to answer questions about possible membership in the Communist Party when subpoenaed by HUAC, a refusal that the Bureau documented and denounced in the pages of its correspondence.[102] Revere continued to speak out against the blacklist, in 1956 appearing as one of the plaintiffs in a case brought against the studios for their part in blacklisting.[103] Like Madeline Lee, Revere's status as an "uncooperative witness" and her outspoken criticisms of the HUAC earned her a spot on the FBI's Security Index.[104] For years after the blacklist had made certain, in the words of the FBI, that "agents and managers will not do business with Ann [sic] Revere," the Bureau continued to monitor her closely.[105]

The Bureau suspected all manner of deviance from outspoken women like these, who had the chutzpah to disagree with the mandates and practices of G-Man masculinity. In worlds where women were supposed to serve men and not mouth off to them (in the parlance of the day), women who raised issues of gender equality in the workplace were doubly suspect. In 1944, writer Vera Caspary requested access for a visit to childcare centers that had been established by the Navy in San Francisco to help women participate in wartime production.[106] The purpose of this visit was to produce an Office of War Information film "dealing with state child care centers, to be shown in neutral countries after the war as an example of democracy at work."[107]

This link between childcare and democracy was literally a red flag to anti-communists who understood women's work in the waged economy and subsidized childcare as communist conspiracies to undermine American family values and patriarchal control, harbingers of today's conservative notion of the nanny state. In a memorandum instructing the military to deny her request, Hoover wrote that entry to the Richmond Shipyards childcare center would put Caspary in "a position to obtain vital information concerning this nation's war effort which might be detrimental to the best interests of the United States should it be passed on to a foreign power with which Vera Caspary was sympathetic." "The Caspary woman's activities," Hoover concluded, "should be given immediate, thorough, and discreet investigative attention."[108] In a matter of days, FBI agents initiated mail covers, trash covers, and monitored Caspary's bank accounts. This surveillance continued for several months.

Hoover's reference to the "Caspary woman's activities" underscores his attitude toward women. This was a formulation Bureau and other anti-communist writers frequently used to disparagingly emphasize the gender of suspected subversives. FBI director Louis B. Nichols described actress Judy Holliday as "the Holliday woman" who "had been connected with numerous front organizations."[109] These rhetorical gestures drew attention to subjects' gender, while simultaneously stripping them of an identity beyond the dismissive conjoining of their last name and their gender. The language anti-communists used to describe the Broadcast 41 and other progressive women was meant to demean and diminish them. Judy Holliday was often referred to as a "dumb blonde" in the pages of Bureau correspondence and the anti-communist press alike, while, as we have seen, Madeline Lee was both ridiculed and feared as the woman who made "baby noises" on radio.

The FBI also made their disapproval of women's independence clear when it came to women who continued to use their own names rather than taking their husbands' names. The Bureau described their given names as "aliases" and insisted on including their husbands' names on reports even in cases where couples had been long divorced, referring to Lillian Hellman as Mrs. Arthur Krober, many years after the two had split up.[110] In one memorandum concerning Madeline Lee, Hoover corrected the special agent who had written the report: "If the subject is still married to Jacob Gelman you should in your next report carry her married name as the true and correct title" (he also insisted on referring to actor Jack Gilford as Jacob Gelman).[111] Agents quickly internalized these practices: a more obedient agent described Mrs. Herbert Biberman as "one Gale Sondergaard (it is to be noted the subject's maiden name is Gale Sondergaard)."[112]

For all the confidence the Bureau expressed in its private correspondence, where their communications were subject to neither criticism nor restraint, Hoover feared that the Broadcast 41 had the power to influence public opinion. While calling for an investigation of Lillian Hellman, Hoover advised the Special Agent in Charge of the New York Field Office to use caution when spying on her: "You are reminded that this subject has a national reputation through her writings in which she has opposed Nazism and Fascism. Under no circumstances should it be known that this Bureau is conducting an investigation of her."[113] Another FBI agent worried that defiant women like Lee might cause "unfavorable publicity to the Bureau."[114] FBI Agent Donald White of the New York Field Office told Hoover that they were considering interviewing Anne Revere. However, he added, "since subject's appearance before the HCUA in 1951 when she invoked the 5th Amendment, she has frequently castigated the HCUA in speeches and in print. Subject has referred to the HCUA inquiry as 'infringement of the Bill of Rights,' and it is believed probable that she would similarly regard the FBI interview."[115] A report from the FBI's New York City Field Office warned agents to approach Shirley Graham with great care, because "the subject is an Editor of a Communist Publication and she is a lecturer and writer of Communist propaganda having access to publication in both Domestic and Foreign Communist publications."[116]

Because of the FBI's dependence on perceptions of widespread public support to justify its use of economic and political resources and Hoover's authoritarianism (which increased each year he remained in office), the Bureau constantly fretted about people like the Broadcast 41, who were "in a position to possibly embarrass the Bureau."[117] Although the files sometimes refer to vaguely defined concerns about security, as in the case of Caspary's access to the Richmond shipyards, more typically Hoover and his directors expressed concern about the Broadcast 41 because of their potential to embarrass the Bureau by contradicting or criticizing them. The G-Man's power lay in his indisputable authority and the resources he had to punish those who questioned the terms of his protection. It is easy to see why Madeline Lee's moxie in the face of surveillance, harassment, and repression would have rankled so much—a Jewish mother of three, a woman who made baby noises for a living, someone G-Man masculinity considered beneath contempt—was publicly thumbing her nose at the Bureau and its allies. In Hoover's opinion, it did not get much worse than that.

Anti-communists were willing to go to extraordinarily repressive lengths to silence these women and avoid embarrassment. Like many conservative masculinities, G-Man masculinity occupied a paranoid, vengeful, and violent social world. The successful reproduction of this world required stifling dissenting or challenging perspectives in order to justify its practices and secure its futures. Not surprisingly, the everyday lives of many of those professing G-Man masculinity were full of unstable, abusive, and often lethal personal and professional relationships, poisoned by the suspicion they projected onto the world around them.

Like subsequent generations of anti-communists, white anti-communist men and women preached family values but did not practice them. Friendly journalist Howard Rushmore's history of domestic violence ended in the backseat of a Manhattan cab when he shot his wife in the head before killing himself.[118] The American Business Consultants' John Keenan, questioned by the police on at least one occasion because of a domestic "disturbance" involving his wife, was arrested in 1949 for driving erratically on Lake Shore Drive in Chicago. He was accompanied by "Socialite Mary Jane Mertes," who was herself put in jail overnight for becoming "very abusive" when their car was stopped.[119] Elizabeth Dilling was involved in a drive-by shooting at her serially unfaithful husband's mistress' home.[120] Joseph McCarthy abused prostitutes. Gossip columnist Westbrook Pegler condoned violence against gay men and others he suspected of subversion. After she testified before the HUAC, a pregnant Judy Holliday received letters from conservative women and men "cursing her with the malevolent wish that her child be born dead or deformed."[121]

Despite anti-communists' violent public and private behaviors toward those they considered their inferiors, they held that it was communists, as the HUAC observed in their pamphlet, *100 Things You Should Know About Communism in the U.S.A.*, who possessed a "natural lust to dominate everybody else."[122] Small wonder that anti-communists saw media promoting education and understanding as sinister, since these and other progressive values held the key to their undoing. The progressive writers of the animated film *The Brotherhood of Man* (1945)—who would all be blacklisted by the end of the 1940s—regarded the postwar period as an opportunity for men (the double patriarchal of "brotherhood" and "man" left women in another category altogether) to "get used to each other's ways and learn to work together peacefully. All we need is a little real understanding."[123] Understanding was anathema to a G-Man masculinity reliant on fear, hatred, and divisiveness to further its agenda.

The G-Man's ability to reproduce himself as the premiere symbol of paternalistic American manhood, and the acquiescence of subsequent generations of media producers to this version of masculinity, helped keep the Bureau's more disturbing and repressive behaviors in the background of public consciousness. In the 1940s, hints of these forms of toxic masculinity threatened to surface in media: in books and articles that criticized the FBI; in journalistic articles like those penned by *New York Times* entertainment reporter Jack Gould questioning the constitutionality of the blacklist; in Adrian Scott's film *Crossfire*, which sided with the murdered victim of a hate crime and refused to represent militarized masculinity in an unambiguously positive light; in speeches given by actors or actresses who compared the state repression they faced with fascism; in Madeline Lee's testimony before the HUAC. Like cornered animals, the FBI attacked these critics with all the repressive resources at its disposal. When the *New York Post* ran a series of articles critical of the Bureau, agent Milton Jones advised that a former agent be encouraged "to take on" the newspaper.[124]

Although the FBI did not directly create the blacklist, the Bureau's former agents did. These were men steeped in G-Man masculinity, trained by the FBI to hunt and punish those they had identified as subversive. As many of the G-Men hired during the wartime boom began to leave the Bureau at the end of World War II in search of more lucrative opportunities, they quickly found jobs in organizations like the American Legion (whose magazine editor was a former FBI agent) and as entrepreneurs in the growing surveillance and clearance industries of the Cold War. To transform dissent into treason, to render standpoints that had been perfectly legitimate in the years between the wars as "un-American," and to create a climate hostile to these ideas in the new industry of television was the work of the small, dedicated group of former FBI agents who founded the American Business Consultants. As they left the Bureau at the end of World War II, they joined forces with veterans' organizations, the HUAC, the Catholic Church, and powerful anti-communist industrialists to wage a domestic war on dissent.

Chapter 4
Cashing In on the Cold War

Communism is not a political party. It is a way of life—a malignant and evil way of life. It reveals a condition akin to disease that spreads like an epidemic, and like an epidemic, a quarantine is necessary to keep it from infecting the nation.

J. Edgar Hoover[1]

In the years that followed, from the early 1940s through the late 1960s, wherever I went in this country, I met thousands of men and women in every profession who shared this starry-eyed impression of the FBI.

William C. Sullivan (former assistant director, FBI intelligence operations)[2]

Many years later, actress Kate Mostel recalled that "[the] TV blacklist" began "with a small, badly printed book called *Red Channels: The Report of Communist Influence in Radio and Television*, which looked like nothing anyone would ever take seriously." Her close friend "Madeline [Lee] and her friends at CBS sat around in a restaurant laughing about how ridiculous it was that radio's earliest and best stars were listed."[3] Within a few short months, progressives had stopped laughing. By autumn 1950, just a few months after the book's publication, newspaper columnist John Crosby posed the question that was on everyone's lips: "To get to the heart of the matter: how come a huge corporation like General Foods ever allowed itself to be intimidated by anything as small and utterly unofficial as this publication?"[4]

The meteoric rise of the organization that published *Red Channels*, the American Business Consultants, began at the end of World War II, as the workforce at the FBI contracted, and veterans of the Bureau and other intelligence agencies turned their eyes to private industry, looking to make their mark and their millions. The men who founded the American Business Consultants and created the blacklist in television were former FBI agents, veterans of military intelligence operations, disciples of G-Man masculinity, and entrepreneurs who saw in the rise of the Cold War opportunities to make money on fear-induced needs for security in industry and government alike. And why shouldn't they turn a dollar from the many entrepreneurial opportunities the Cold War provided them? After all, they had seen how the Bureau turned fear into profit in the day-to-day workings of the security state. Why couldn't they do that as well, using patriotism as the brand for paranoia-induced purges of progressives in retail, manufacturing, education, government, and entertainment?

Kenneth Bierly, John Keenan, and Theodore Kirkpatrick, the founders of the American Business Consultants, publisher of the weekly newsletter *CounterAttack* beginning in 1947 and *Red Channels* in 1950, met one another while working for the FBI in New York City. Keenan and Bierly were lawyers, a professional background favored by the FBI. Kirkpatrick had a degree in economics and business administration and worked for the Beneficial Industrial Loan Corporation, "investigating credit and locating delinquent accounts before joining the Bureau."[5] As agents, these men built on their previous work experience in order to spy on suspected communists in department stores, manufacturing, education, government, and media industries, chronicling their activities in the pages of FBI files. All three distinguished themselves by their skills at conducting surveillance. As the FBI later observed of Keenan, he had participated in "highly confidential surveillances above and beyond the line of duty which had resulted in the obtaining of information inaccessible to ordinary confidential informants."[6]

By 1946, these men were former federal agents, trying to get past receptionists and turn a buck in postwar New York City. As we will see, they had left the Bureau not on the most amicable of terms. Their former boss (J. Edgar Hoover)—one of the most powerful men in the country—regarded them with suspicion and dislike. New York City industries had little interest in doing business with them. So how did this small and unofficial group of former G-Men go from being considered ridiculous by progressives and as "personae non gratae" by the Bureau to an organization that could force networks to fire people that historian Eric Barnouw described as "the most talented and admired people in the industry.... people who had helped make radio an honored medium and who were becoming active in television"?[7] The following pages show how, with the aid of the FBI, the American Business Consultants created a short-lived publishing empire that turned the G-Man's media practices into a business capable of bullying powerful industries into line with their political agenda in just a few short years.

❖ ❖ ❖

The relevant aspects of the climate of opinion in the country ... tend to be less concerned with security considerations than with ideological purity; and this concern, reflecting the diversity of motivations, is confused and confounded by the absence of generally accepted criteria for identifying the impure.

Marie Jahoda (social psychologist)[8]

After leaving the FBI, Bierly, Keenan, and Kirkpatrick joined forces with erstwhile Hearst journalist Isaac Don Levine to found the anti-communist magazine *Plain Talk*. From the beginning, there were tensions among the men. By their own account, *Plain Talk*'s circulation was low and Levine's approach to the journal was far too conventional for the former G-Men's tastes.[9] Dissatisfied with Levine's adherence to journalistic ethics, Bierly, Keenan, and Kirkpatrick quit *Plain Talk* to found a business they originally called John Quincy Adams Associates, one that billed itself as having "a ringside seat from which to monitor 'red' movements, plans, organizations, and fronts and to learn the identity of party members and sympathizers."[10]

Almost immediately, the men changed the organization's name to the American Business Consultants, commencing publication of the anti-communist newsletter *CounterAttack* in 1947 and settling into a partnership that took advantage of the skills they had developed as special agents. As president, Keenan administered the organization, soliciting subscriptions for *CounterAttack* (after private donations, the 24-dollar-per-year subscription fee was the organization's primary source of revenue); Kirkpatrick served as the American Business Consultants' secretary/treasurer and managing editor of *CounterAttack*; and vice president Bierly supervised research on suspected subversives and their activities.[11]

The American Business Consultants' partner, Catholic priest Father John Cronin, estimated that the mailing lists he supplied provided the business with 50,000 subscribers, including 10,000 priests, as well as names acquired from the American Legion, trade unions, and what the Bureau described as "'hyphenated' American groups, such as Slovak-American, Czech-American, etc."[12] Subscribers to *CounterAttack* (1947–70) included the FBI, E.I. du Pont de Nemours and Company, General Motors Corporation, Metropolitan Life Insurance Company, R.J. Reynolds Tobacco Company, Bendix Aviation Corporation, and Liggett & Myers.[13]

Bierly, Keenan, and Kirkpatrick celebrated their G-Man credentials in all their writing, paying homage to their FBI teachers. They described themselves as "A group of FBI agents charged with internal security during the war," who "became so concerned with the workings of subversive groups in this country that they resigned their posts when hostilities ceased in order to put their know-how to work in the public interest."[14] As friendly journalist Bill Cunningham put it, repeating nearly verbatim the group's public relations materials: "*Counter-Attack* is published by former F.B.I. counter-espionage agents who specialized in Communism. They resigned from the federal service and went into the same line of work on their own because, they said, they felt they could fight Red-ism better and warn the public against its deadly and devious dangers more freely, if they were unhampered by the restrictions and the necessary secrecy of the Department of Justice."[15] As *former* FBI agents, Bierly, Keenan, and Kirkpatrick contended, they could communicate openly and directly with the American public to educate and inform them about the communist menace. In one of the convoluted forms of reasoning so typical of the anti-communist movement, it was only by virtue of not being public servants that they could most effectively serve the public good.

The American Business Consultants corresponded frequently with the Bureau from the start, writing cordial letters and passing along information about suspected communists they believed the FBI would find useful. In February 1947, for example, Kirkpatrick cautioned the New York Field Office that communists were "entering the United States from Mexico as a result of becoming married to employees in the U.S. Embassy in Mexico."[16] The men offered additional services to the Bureau: "We want to assure you at this time that if, at any time, you think we could be of assistance or that our files might possibly have any information that would be helpful to you, we would be very happy to cooperate in any way we possibly can."[17]

Despite the collegial tone of the American Business Consultants' letters to the FBI, between 1946 and 1949, the relationship between the business and the Bureau was paranoid and tense. Hoover made no secret of the fact that he neither liked nor trusted Bierly, Keenan, and Kirkpatrick. For their part, the three men made it clear that they had every intention of using their FBI training and credentials for their own profit and defying Hoover.

The bad blood between the Bureau and the founders of the American Business Consultants began when the men were still working for the Bureau. In Hoover's eyes, these men kept the wrong company, associating with Lawrence E. Kerley, a fellow agent who was fired in 1945 for leaking information the Bureau considered embarrassing to friendly journalist Howard Rushmore. Hoover's suspicions appeared to be confirmed when Bierly, Keenan, and Kirkpatrick resigned from the FBI, and the Bureau's New York Field Office reported that at least ten reports were missing from the files of the New York Division on communist infiltration in labor union cases.[18] Hoover suspected that the three men had stolen these reports in order to use them to establish their new business. As one of the agents charged with investigating the three men reported to Hoover, the information they were suspected of stealing "would prove invaluable as a background for a service organization such as is apparently being set up by these former Special Agents."[19] This would not be the last time charges of stealing would follow them: when they quit *Plain Talk*, Levine complained that they had made off with some of his files, and when Bierly left the American Business Consultants in 1951, Keenan accused him of stealing files as well.

For Hoover, the purloined files were bad enough, but worse was still to come. When they set up their offices at 35 West 42nd Street, the American Business Consultants raided the Bureau's New York City Field Office for personnel, luring away experienced administrative staff with higher wages. The three men then poached the Bureau's confidential informants, offering to pay them for information in order to create their own network of industrial and political spies.[20] The FBI tersely summed this up, years later: "During the 1940's the Bureau had considerable difficulties with American Business Consultants, Inc., inasmuch as many serials dealing with communist activities were missing from New York files. It was believed they were utilizing information in publications which came to their attention as Bureau Agents, and they were guilty of trying to proselyte Bureau informants."[21]

Perhaps most galling, from Hoover's point of view, these former agents used their G-Man credentials to legitimize their business enterprise and to pry open the stubborn doors of New York City businesses. Their FBI experience appeared prominently in all their communications with potential donors and clients: "The FBI background of the officers of the American Business Consultants and the extensive files and research organization they have established have made the American Business Consultants the leading non-governmental authority in the field of Communist activities in the United States."[22] But they did more than merely reference their background: they also gave prospective clients "the impression that they had some connection with the FBI."[23] When confronted with their behavior, Kirkpatrick told the FBI that they needed these credentials "in order to get past receptionists at concerns where they may call and further that it is necessary to identify the solicitor by some type of letter of introduction because there are so many phonies running around capitalizing on anti-Communist sentiments."[24] "It certainly is distressing," Hoover scrawled angrily in the margins of one memorandum about the American Business Consultants, "that our name can be so promiscuously used by ex-Agents."[25]

In the wake of a flurry of 1946 complaints about the American Business Consultants' activities, Hoover directed the New York Field Office to investigate the former agents by wiretapping their office and monitoring their mail and trash.[26] Because of this surveillance, the FBI knew that their former agents were engaged in illegal activities of their own as early as 1946, when a Bureau agent reported that Kirkpatrick was involved in activities that were "undoubtedly for the purpose of a black bag job" (burglarizing offices or homes), to acquire information for the American Business Consultants' purposes[27]

(Figure 4.1). FBI agents reported that the new business was using mail covers, trash covers, and wiretapping the telephones of persons of interest to them. At one point, Kirkpatrick even bragged to the Bureau that the American Business Consultants had extensive experience conducting "bag jobs," urging the Bureau to use them as subcontractors for burglaries as well as for "trash covers" because they "could get information in places which were not available to the FBI and also that they would be willing to take more chances than the FBI would take."[28]

The Bureau's New York Field Office condemned the American Business Consultants in its correspondence: "These former agents have been guilty of proselyting Bureau informants and using knowledge obtained in their employment with the Bureau to their personal advantage." Their purpose—"exposing the ramifications of the Communist Party"—was "laudable, [but] the end does not justify the means and in this particular case the means are considered highly unethical, irresponsible and should not be countenanced."[29]

The Bureau knew that the American Business Consultants were thoroughly unscrupulous: an agent concluded that they "are loyal only to themselves, and expediency."[30] They knew that the business was illegally spying on Americans, lying in the pages of its publications about progressives' membership in the Communist Party and other allegations they stated as facts, and illegally impersonating federal agents. The Bureau also acknowledged that the American Business Consultants had created a blacklist of progressives in broadcasting. Where the evidence the Bureau used to convict and retaliate against so-called subversives was often extremely flimsy, the Bureau had proof the American Business Consultants were engaged in illegal activities. Agents in the New York Field Office repeatedly warned Hoover that allowing the group to continue operations would be "to the further detriment of the Bureau which is charged with the responsibility of protecting the internal security of the United States."[31]

Beyond fuming in reports and letters, Hoover took no action against the organization. Instead, in the years leading up to the publication of *Red Channels*, the FBI and the American Business Consultants played a game of cat and mouse. The FBI sat on the sidelines even when they knew—as in the cases of actors Paul Robeson and Philip Loeb—that *CounterAttack* was wrongly identifying these and other progressives as communists. Against the advice of his agents, Hoover chose to watch and wait: "There appears to be a growing tide of resentment against the tactics of these ex-agents. It will be interesting to see if this trend continues."[32]

There are a number of possible explanations for the Bureau's non-interventionist attitude toward the American Business Consultants. Possibly, the

about their relationship to the Bureau. These letters of inquiry came from advertisers, magazine editors, and staff at organizations like the Kiwanis Club, who emphasized that they were inclined to take *CounterAttack* and the business seriously, but only if the FBI vouched for the American Business Consultants. Miss M.R. Bonnell, for example, wrote to the FBI, "I have been interested in some of the alleged disclosures and charges made in the paper called *CounterAttack*. I am told that the proprietors of this paper were formerly on the staff of the FBI, which would of course make their disclosures more important."[33]

Hoover refused to confirm or deny such a relationship when asked by people like Miss Bonnell. The Bureau's reputation for protecting classified information in the interest of national security encouraged people to make what they would of the FBI's responses. For example, when pressed by Merle Miller, author of a book commissioned by the American Civil Liberties Union to investigate the blacklist, *The Judges and the Judged*, FBI assistant director Louis Nichols merely said, "We are aware of the activities of the publishers of *Red Channels* and *CounterAttack*, but since they are private citizens, we have no legal control over their practices. Individuals who have severed their relations with the FBI in no way possess our indorsement [sic] or stamp of approval. Certainly, all the information in the FBI is confidential, available only to those Government officials authorized to examine it."[34] This was their boilerplate response to such queries: they had no "legal control" over the behaviors of "private citizens." Of course, there is plenty of evidence showing that the Bureau often did exercise all manner of legal and illegal controls over private citizens when they chose to do so. In the case of the American Business Consultants, they simply chose not to.

Still, the Bureau's correspondence shows much hostility between the FBI and its former agents, making the case for deliberate collaboration unlikely. A more plausible explanation for the Bureau's laissez-faire attitude toward its former agents was that whatever their disagreements, the FBI approved of the American Business Consultants' efforts to rid media industries of progressives.

To add to this, the American Business Consultants had Hoover over a barrel. Bierly, Keenan, and Kirkpatrick knew that their former boss was spying on them: they leaked this information to the Society of Former Special Agents of the FBI, knowing that it would make its way back to Hoover. And Bierly, Keenan, and Kirkpatrick knew far too much about the FBI's covert intelligence-gathering activities, not to mention its web of intimate relationships with the Dies Committee, the HUAC, the Catholic Church, and the American Legion, among others. Were the FBI to retaliate against the American Business

Consultants, or charge them with illegal and unconstitutional activities the former agents had damning evidence of the Bureau's own unconstitutional and illegal forms of surveillance and harassment.[35]

Whatever the actual arrangement between the American Business Consultants and the Bureau, by 1949, the two groups had "straighten[ed] out" any conflicts. After an interview with agents from the New York Field Office in July 1949, Theodore Kirkpatrick was advised by telephone "that the Bureau does not desire to approve or make any further suggestions regarding this situation" and that if they received any additional complaints from businesses, they would refer these directly back to the American Business Consultants for resolution. Indeed, Kirkpatrick's "attitude toward our complaint" was considered so favorable that the FBI agent decided not to even issue an additional threat: "the possibility of the Bureau issuing a national press release regarding the *CounterAttack* situation."[36] And after all, the only rights being violated were those of progressives, who might as well be communists for all the Bureau and their allies cared. In anti-communists' view, progressives" un-American beliefs and activities meant that these traitors were getting nothing more than what they deserved.

❖ ❖ ❖

And then the CP uses the stars in fronts ... it writes speeches for them ... it gets their signatures to statements. And the prestige of the stars has a wide influence in Los Angeles and elsewhere in Calif.

CounterAttack[37]

The movie Communist and the radio Communist are working together in their campaign to smear all anti-Communist measures as "Thought Control," as "Witch Hunts," as anti-liberal—and thus to protect the Communist Party.

George K. Johnson, CounterAttack *associate*[38]

The perception that the business was operating with the approval of the FBI allowed the American Business Consultants a great degree of freedom in practicing the media strategies they had learned from their G-Man tutors and in persuading broadcast producers to concede to their demands. As we saw in the previous chapter, media producers often found the G-Man version of paranoid male melodrama formulaic and unsexy, with its tiresome talk of fingerprinting and the science of detection. And although the mainstream media reveled in gossip and rumor, the G-Man's obsession with communists and fellow-travelers was not particularly compelling, especially when it focused on manufacturers, government workers, and schoolteachers. Much anti-communist melodrama was thus confined to the pages of the *Congressional Record* (the official publication of proceedings and debates of the U.S. Congress) and the transcripts of testimony before the HUAC and other anti-communist legislative bodies. Some of the former FBI agents involved with the blacklist aspired to Hollywood fame, like Vincent J. Hartnett (author of *Red Channels*' "Introduction") and Kenneth Bierly, but they lacked talent for it and, in Hartnett's case, blamed their inability to find work writing for broadcasting on communists rather than their own creative shortcomings.

Excluded from writing for mainstream media because they lacked experience, talent, or both, the men behind the American Business Consultants developed other strategies for getting their message out. Their experiences in the Bureau had taught them how to create the perception of public concern about a problem they had identified—first to use state power to generate the belief that crime or communism was the number-one problem in the U.S. and then to claim a public mandate for this belief. The American Business Consultants used *CounterAttack* to create the perception of a problem—communist penetration of American industries, including media—and to record the names of individuals and organizations responsible for that problem. They then offered to sell a solution: information and clearance. In the process, they created what came to be known in progressive circles and the industry as the "smear and clear" business. Of course, media insiders knew what was really going on. As broadcast director and producer Ira Skutch put it, "The guys who came to see us said if we subscribed to their service, they'd clear everybody we called, so this whole business of clearing people was a blackmail scheme."[39] Progressives knew, as George Seldes put it in the muckraking progressive newsletter *In Fact*, that the authors and publishers of *Red Channels* were "a group of enterprising ex G-Men" who had "set out to cash in on the cold war and the unpopularity of communists and communism."[40]

Like the Bureau, in *CounterAttack* and later *Red Channels*, the American Business Consultants created their own media while at the same time planting interviews and stories that played up their power and influence, using their network of anti-communist journalists to plant rumors and celebrate the accomplishments of these heroic and selfless communist-fighting G-Men. To combat "American Communism," which "penetrates and uses every possible device for molding public opinion," they educated readers in how to detect red presence.[41] Like the FBI, the American Business Consultants schooled their readers in the art of connecting dots that, to take one example, equated civil rights with the Stalinist "strategy of using national minorities as a means of tearing countries apart and wrecking governments."[42] Their

COUNTERATTACK

REG. U. S. PAT. OFF.

FACTS TO COMBAT COMMUNISM

55 WEST 42ND STREET, NEW YORK 18, N. Y. LOngacre 4-1458

Figure 4.2 Masthead, *CounterAttack*, The American Business Consultants
Source: *CounterAttack*, March 19, 1948, FBI #130-8773-0, National Archives and Records Administration, College Park, MD

aim was straightforward in its masculine purpose: to "expose and render impotent" communists and fellow-travelers in all areas of political and cultural life.[43] The American Business Consultants promised potential clients and readers that they would deliver nothing less than the truth by providing readers with "facts to combat communism," as *CounterAttack*'s masthead boldly stated[44] (Figure 4.2).

The pages of *CounterAttack* reproduced the Bureau's brand of cultural criticism, with G-Men experts unpacking the hidden, communist meanings of texts for less astute readers. One issue of the newsletter offered an analysis of poet Aaron Kramer's poem "Warning," which advised those seeking freedom in the U.S. to be mindful of the legacies of slavery. Kramer, *CounterAttack* wrote, acknowledged that America was "a rich, beautiful country," only to undermine that message: America, Kramer wrote, was a land of "no justice," where "criminals are crowned, the victim sentenced, liars applauded, true words shouted down, idlers royally paid, toilers expelled." "Toiler," the newsletter explained for its readers, was a code word for "Communist labor leaders who're arrested for deportation (unfortunately the cases drag on for years and they don't get deported)." Kramer, *CounterAttack* concluded, falsely and dangerously portrayed the U.S. as remaining "enslaved. And, incredible as it seems, he can make a lot of people even in this country believe it. Such is the power of words."[45]

In its analysis of Kramer's poetry and other literary and media texts, *CounterAttack* insisted that even the most apparently patriotic texts could conceal hidden communist messages. On its surface, for example, screenwriter Garson Kanin's 1950 film *Born Yesterday* told the story of Paul Verrall, a journalist (played by William Holden) who introduces gangster's moll Billie Dawn (played by Judy Holliday, one of the Broadcast 41) to American history, in the process transforming her politics and morals. "Nobody's born smart,"

Verrall tells Billie, urging her to study. "Do you know what the stupidest thing on Earth is? An infant!" According to *CounterAttack, Born Yesterday* was a communist propaganda film. Its emphasis on change and reform, its contrast between the intellectual, nebbish journalist and the corrupt, macho man of business, and its belief in the power of education amounted to a form of "'diabolical' Marxist satire," made all the more insidious for being cloaked in apparent worship of the American Constitution.[46]

The American Business Consultants shared the broader anti-communist movement's goal of sowing suspicion and distrust of government, especially Roosevelt's New Deal. Their modus operandi, which continued to function well into the twenty-first century, was simple. Progressives in media, government, and public life alike only appeared to be earnest do-gooders. This was the gist of all anti-communist communications practices: do not trust the role of the government when it came to any of its caring functions (social welfare, education, health, etc.); do not trust progressives' talk of democracy and peace; do not trust those who would call for the rights of African Americans, immigrants, workers, or women. Behind all those demands for political, cultural, and economic rights, anti-communists insisted, loomed communist puppet masters. Only anti-communist protectors were trustworthy; only the repressive dimensions of government (police, military, etc.) could be counted on to act in the interests of Americanism.

The Bureau's skill at sowing seeds of paranoia and discord among Americans was prodigious, and the founders of the American Business Consultants had been eager and apt students of these repressive arts. Still, like the Bureau's own public relations machine, what made the American Business Consultants so incredibly powerful and finally unstoppable, was the specter of state power. Without the perception that the business was being backed by the state, the private anti-communist organization would have been unable to bully the new industry of television into submission. Media owners and producers were used to doing pretty much what they wanted, as long as it made their shareholders money. But, like several generations of politicians, government officials, and corporate executives, they feared the power J. Edgar Hoover wielded to ruin reputations and lives.

Without interference from the FBI, the American Business Consultants leveraged the perception that they too had access to state power in their efforts to control broadcasting. Expert at intimidating people with his G-Man credentials, Kirkpatrick visited businesses with a list of employees he identified as communists or fellow-travelers. He then demanded that they take two steps in order to combat communism. In the first step, businesses were told that they should buy subscriptions to *CounterAttack* not only to be better informed about the communists the American Business Consultants had identified in their organizations, but also to demonstrate their commitment to fighting communism. In the second, less public step, businesses were urged to hire the American Business Consultants to clear all their employees of suspicion and ensure that their department stores, shop floors, and studios were purified from the contaminating presence of communists and fellow-travelers.[47] Using their extensive network of spies in manufacturing and the information they had purloined from the Bureau, the American Business Consultants had some early successes. But the broadcast industry proved reluctant to take the bait, recognizing the con at the heart of Kirkpatrick's openly self-interested pitch. In order to secure the cooperation of broadcasting, the American Business Consultants had to bring additional pressures to bear.

❖ ❖ ❖

The chances that a thorough housecleaning will take place, with the rights of all persons involved respected, is better now than ever before.

CounterAttack[48]

Sponsors, even if they lose money by doing so, should adopt strict ethical standards in hiring radio and TV personnel at such a time ... there should be NO TOTALITARIANS of any kind. It is the only decent thing they can do! Money should not be a factor. Sponsors who adopt this policy will avoid embarrassing situations.

CounterAttack[49]

By 1949, the American Business Consultants were confident enough in their growing influence and their immunity from FBI censure to test the political waters in entertainment industries by drawing attention to the ostensible problem of communist influence in entertainment. Neither of these first test cases featured household names. Evidence suggests that these first attacks were born of opportunity, facilitated by the American Business Consultants' wide array of media contacts and their growing ability to use allegations published in *CounterAttack* as cudgels against progressives in entertainment.

The first attack came in the shape of the blacklisting of harmonica-player Larry Adler and dancer Paul Draper. *CounterAttack* had been monitoring Paul Draper's performances for a year, as well as reporting on his mother's allegedly communistic activities (Muriel Draper was a prominent figure on the literary and cultural left in New York City, whose famous cocktail parties often included Paul Robeson, Langston Hughes, Carl Van Vechten, and a host of other progressive artists and luminaries). *CounterAttack* was particularly outraged by the Drapers' friendship with Paul Robeson. In its December 1948 newsletter, *CounterAttack* reported that Draper had performed at a benefit in the company of "Paul Robeson," erroneously identified as "a Communist Party member ... [who] doesn't admit it yet."[50] In light of *CounterAttack* and the FBI's obsession with Robeson and his circle of friends and supporters, it seems likely that Draper was the main target of the attack, and Adler was collateral damage.

The official story of the case goes like this. Greenwich, Connecticut housewife Hester McCullough had read about Adler and Draper's left-leaning backgrounds in the pages of *CounterAttack*. Adler and Draper were scheduled to perform at a "musical evening" in McCullough's hometown in January, sponsored by the Greenwich Community Concert Association. Her sympathetic husband advised her to call anti-communist gossip columnist Igor Cassini to voice her concerns. She obliged. What, McCullough asked Cassini, did he know about Adler's and Draper's communist connections? Cassini referred McCullough to controversial anti-communist J.B. Matthews, former chief investigator for the HUAC and a person with close ties to the American Business Consultants.

Just over a week after the article on Draper appeared in *CounterAttack*, McCullough published a letter in her local newspaper, the *Greenwich Time*, protesting the concert. Adler and Draper, the letter read, were "pro-Communist in sympathy" and "exponents of a line of thinking directly opposed to every democratic principle upon which our great country has been founded." Those who bought tickets for their performance, she continued, "indirectly make cash contributions to Moscow."[51] Igor Cassini's columns in the *Journal American* helped disseminate these concerns to a much broader audience.[52] Although the Greenwich Community Concert Association prevented McCullough from censoring the performers, the damage to their reputation was done: in the months that followed, Adler's and Draper's bookings dropped by nearly 50 percent.[53] In fall 1949, they sued McCullough for libel, asking for 200,000 dollars in damages.

During the course of the trial, Cassini and *CounterAttack* played up McCullough's worthy femininity, using the G-Man's distinction between virtuous anti-communist women like McCullough and deceitful communists like Muriel Draper, a "Secret member of Communist Party. Exec V-P of Congress of American Women, US section of Stalin's international women's front."[54] Although she was not on trial, *CounterAttack* repeatedly dragged Muriel Draper into the fray to emphasize the main thrust of the defense's argument about the contaminating effects of communism and guilt by association. Muriel Draper illustrated the "Communist capture" of children that Hoover would write about a few years later, and "the depths of their degradation as parents" that helped create "a corps of young, fanatical, highly disciplined devotés ... boys and girls [who] are, in fact, 'germ carriers,' " including her son, Paul.[55]

McCullough figured in stark and populist contrast to the controlling, cultured Draper: she was "the young Greenwich, Conn. woman, who had the courage and energy to oppose their appearance in a concert there."[56] She was a paragon of American womanhood—"the greatest female patriot since Molly Pitcher"—reluctantly forced to act by the magnitude of the communist threat to her family, home, and nation.[57]

CounterAttack emphasized McCullough's heroic selflessness in leading the charge against Adler and Draper, writing that the "strain of the suit has affected her health." According to the newsletter, she had spent 11,000 dollars on legal fees. *CounterAttack* urged its readers to take a page from the Communist Party's playbook by sending money directly to McCullough to help defray costs.[58] Cassini joined this crew of would-be manly protectors, suggesting that the Greenwich Community Concert Association needed "a crack on the head" to wake them up to the communist threat posed by Adler's harmonica-playing and Draper's dancing. As if this manly display was not enough, Cassini also informed his readers that McCullough's husband "had to restrain himself from punching Mr. Adler on the nose."[59]

The trial ended in a hung jury in late May, when "the eight housewives and four businessmen" who had heard the case were unable to reach a verdict.[60] But anti-communists declared it a victory anyway: according to them, the hung jury was confirmation of McCullough's charges. Adler was a communist propagandist and mastermind. Draper—of the skin-tight pants and domineering communist mother—was an un-American communist fronter. Although she took care not to say the men were members of the Communist Party, McCullough insisted that Adler and Draper were traitors.[61] As far as anti-communists were concerned, the case against them was closed.

Or at least that was the story the American Business Consultants told the press. As was typical in cases involving G-Men and their protection rackets, the actual sequence of events was more complicated.

Far from being a mere housewife, Hester McCullough was a member of an anti-communist women's group "interested in politics," organized by conservative Clare Boothe Luce, wife of *Time* magazine editor Henry Luce.[62] McCullough's connections to *Time* magazine also included her husband, John T. McCullough, who was a picture editor for the periodical. And if *CounterAttack* treated McCullough like an old friend in its pages, it was because she probably was: McCullough and her husband lived less than five miles away from the American Business Consultants' Kenneth Bierly and his wife in Greenwich.

As far as McCullough's initial outreach to Cassini is concerned, it is difficult to prove that the American Business Consultants had a hand in writing her letter, although her embeddedness in anti-communist political circles in the New York City metropolitan area suggests that was a possibility. After Adler and Draper sued McCullough, the collaborative nature of the relationship between McCullough and the American Business Consultants came into clearer view. Bierly and Keenan, both lawyers, rallied to her defense, working closely with the powerful Manhattan firm of DeWitt, Diskin, and Nast to defend McCullough.[63] *CounterAttack* also provided financial support for McCullough's defense. After the trial, McCullough sent a note "to *CounterAttack* asking that her thanks be extended to all subscribers and other loyal Americans who gave her financial or moral support in her recent libel suit," which *CounterAttack* claimed amounted to "$29,203.50 (most in small donations)." She was, she added, grateful "to *CounterAttack* for coming to her aid and being 'among the very first supporters' she had."[64]

Despite *CounterAttack*'s claims that the lawsuit had caused her so much hardship, McCullough delighted in the attention it offered her. She and her husband visited Hollywood in order "to gather additional evidence for the Draper-Adler case," where gossip columnist and FBI intimate Hedda Hopper took them for lunch. When she was interviewed for Merle Miller's *The Judges and the Judged*, McCullough told her interviewer that she was "just somebody who lives in Greenwich." But, she added significantly, "I guess you might say I was always on the lookout for Them [Communists]."[65] When asked by Adler and Draper's lawyer "Did she hate liberals?" McCullough responded, "I certainly do."[66] Apparently undeterred by the failure of this lawsuit, McCullough used the skills and contacts she had acquired during the course of the trial to force CBS to fire Jean Muir in 1950, as we will see in Chapter 5.

As for Adler and Draper, the negative publicity proved disastrous for their careers. In light of continued bad press, they decided not to pursue a retrial. Adler moved to London because he could no longer find work in the U.S., spending the remainder of his life in England.[67] Draper kept trying to find work in American television, even as anti-communists continued to protest his appearances. When he was scheduled to appear on Ed Sullivan's *The Toast of the Town* in January 1950, Hearst journalists Cassini, Westbrook Pegler, and George Sokolosky, working with their allies at *CounterAttack*, threatened to boycott Ford Motor Company, the program's sponsor, if Sullivan did not cancel the booking. Although Draper appeared on the show, Sullivan wrote to William B. Lewis, president of Ford's advertising agency, to assure him that "every step was being taken" to make sure that such a booking "did not happen again."[68]

The American Business Consultants played a similarly discreet but critical role in the second case foretelling the rise of the blacklist. In 1950, director William M. Sweets—president of the Radio Directors Guild (RDG)—was forced to resign from the newly acquired CBS program, *Gang Busters*. Sweets was a veteran director of popular police procedurals. Like many of the Broadcast 41, he had a history of progressive trade union and civic activism. As president of the RDG, Sweets—along with actor Philip Loeb from Actors' Equity and attorney Henry Jaffe, husband of Jean Muir, from the American Federation of Radio Actors (AFRA)—was involved in the struggle within AFRA between anti-communists and their opponents, as well as growing opposition to anti-communist blacklists on the part of unions including AFRA, the American Guild of Variety Artists, Actors' Equity, and the American Guild of Musical Artists.[69] Sweets had also publicly supported the reelection of Communist Party candidate Benjamin J. Davis, Jr. for City Council.

Because of his leadership in the RDG, the FBI and other anti-communists had been keeping an eye on Sweets since 1945. In 1949, Vincent J. Hartnett (the former naval intelligence officer soon to gain notoriety as the author of *Red Channels*' "Introduction") was a freelance writer who had recently begun working on *Gang Busters*. Hartnett communicated extensively with both the FBI and the American Business Consultants, working closely with the anti-communist faction within the AFRA that supported loyalty oaths and the dismissal of employees identified as subversive. Hartnett officially became an FBI informant in 1950, but he had already been sending the Bureau information about Reds in radio before that. In addition to writing for *Gang Busters*, Hartnett had been selling his services as a self-styled expert on "How the Communist Conspiracy against the United States has affected the entertainment field."[70]

With *CounterAttack*'s support, Hartnett accused Sweets of refusing to hire anti-communist members of AFRA.[71] Hartnett said that he had told the show's producers about this anti-anti-communist blacklist, but other accounts suggest that he first alerted *CounterAttack* to the supposed existence of such a list. *CounterAttack*'s "three former Agents, Theodore Fitzpatrick [sic], John Keen [sic] and Kenneth Bierly" then notified the show's producer, Phillips H. Lord.[72] Behind the scenes, the FBI signed the death warrant for Sweets' career. In a memo to FBI public relations head Nichols, the FBI wrote that producer Jerry Devine had used Sweets to direct the radio crime drama, *This is Your FBI* (ABC, 1945–53). "Sweets was used a few times in the early days of the program" (before Hartnett's charges against him had been publicized in *CounterAttack*). At that time, the FBI "had no derogatory information concerning him," but had in the meantime been made aware of his subversive tendencies. As a result, Hoover advised the show's producer "that for personal reasons, should it be necessary for him to get another director," he should "get someone other than Sweets."[73]

The American Business Consultants told sponsors that if Sweets directed the program, conservative consumers would boycott their products.[74] As pressure mounted in the pages of *CounterAttack* and from the FBI, Sweets was forced to resign.[75] In a public statement Sweets advised, "I was told that pressure—a campaign of letter-writing complaining of my political views—had led the advertising agencies and sponsors [Pepsi-Cola and General Foods] to decide to renew their contracts only if someone else directed the shows."[76] Sweets made it clear that he had been fired as a result of the pressure *CounterAttack* had brought to bear on *Gang Busters*' sponsors Pepsi-Cola and General Foods. Fearful that the FBI was actually behind these threats, other advertisers, networks, and sponsors began to cave to anti-communist demands.

Sweets never worked in radio again, instead moving to Manchester, New Hampshire, where he ran an antique store until his death in 1968. The network also fired Hartnett, viewing him as the source of a controversy that had cost them a commercially successful director. Still, Hartnett went on to cash in on the Cold War until a libel suit brought against him by broadcast star John Henry Faulk put an end to his clearance business. But throughout the 1950s, Hartnett promoted his services as a "talent consultant" to advertising agencies and sponsors, claiming that he could clear potential employees for fees ranging from 5 dollars for the first report on an individual (and additional fees for further background checks) to more than 20 dollars for "special circumstances."[77]

For anti-communists, the Sweets case was widely acknowledged as "a test. If they [progressives] can force reinstatement of Sweets, they expect to be able to prevent the dropping of any party-liners. Anti-communists should accept the challenge of the Sweets case and should get busy at once to fight the Communist boycott."[78] As writer Merle Miller later observed, the significance of the Sweets case was twofold. Unlike the McCullough case, the Sweets controversy began and ended with broadcasting, subjecting broadcast media to increasing public scrutiny as sites of potential communist infiltration. More importantly, insofar "as the industry would surrender to pressure in 1949, then as the Cold War intensified (and the pressure intensified), it was only a matter of time until systematic political screening would become an institution."[79]

These two cases allowed the American Business Consultants to show that those who were smeared would have a hard time defending themselves in courtrooms and courts of public opinion alike. Taken together, the cases were a warning to the new industry of television that it could be forced into the waiting embrace of the only people who could protect them against anti-communist attacks: those generating these charges of subversion against progressives, who not coincidentally happened to be the same people promising to clear their names. As evidence of their mounting influence, on the day before the publication of *Red Channels*, and shortly after the firing of Sweets and Todd, a chastened Ed Sullivan boasted about his close relationship to the American Business Consultants' Theodore Kirkpatrick in his *New York Daily News* column. *CounterAttack*, Sullivan wrote, was carrying out "a magnificent American job" and he had personally hired Kirkpatrick, who "has sat in my living room on several occasions" to listen to performers "eager to secure a certification of loyalty," and to ensure that the broadcast industry remained clear of subversive influence.[80]

❖ ❖ ❖

It was immaterial whether they were Communists or not, entirely immaterial to what we were trying to do.

Kenneth Bierly (co-founder, the American Business Consultants)[81]

Mady Christian was always in her life a preventer of strife, never the cause of it. I do not think she would have wanted the position to be reversed now. Her death was unquestionably precipitated by the horrible fear of being denied the means of earning her living and by the shock consequent upon the recent and brutal evidence of this which she had suffered. She was never accused of anything. Those responsible never, I am sure, thought about her as a person. She was "on a list" and that was enough; she was accordingly refused employment.

Margaret Webster (writer, director, producer)[82]

The month of June 1950 brought with it a set of circumstances that could not have been more propitious for those intent on eliminating progressives from the industry. *Red Channels* was published a mere three days before North Korea invaded South Korea. Anti-communists used the Korean War to demand that extreme measures be taken to prevent the spread of global communism to the West. *CounterAttack*'s calls for citizens to inform on one another, which had been escalating since the beginning of 1950, took on an added urgency that the American Business Consultants quickly capitalized on. Suddenly, *CounterAttack* had become prophetic in its urging that anti-communists needed "to supply information concerning Communist activities to the public."[83]

Red Channels itself was unassuming, save for its cover, which featured the preferred anti-communist visual trope of a hairy communist hand grabbing some icon of American freedom, in this case a microphone (the American Business Consultants had earlier experimented with a similar hand seizing the Statue of Liberty). It was 213 pages long, with a seven-page introduction by Vincent J. Hartnett. The remainder of the book was devoted to an alphabetical list of the impure alongside the names of the organizations they had been associated with, as evidence of their communist tendencies. The American Business Consultants were careful not to say that those listed were members of the Communist Party. After all, Bierly and Keenan were lawyers who understood that their inability to prove those charges would lead to libel lawsuits. Instead, the juxtaposition of names and organizations encouraged readers to make those connections themselves. The intent of the volume was evident to anti-communists and communists alike, even if the former insisted that it was not: it was a blacklist to rid the industry of progressives.[84]

Riding the wave of anti-communist sentiment that followed the outbreak of the Korean War, *CounterAttack* distributed *Red Channels* free of charge to over 4,000 people in the industry, urging other advertisers, networks, and sponsors to buy it because "Newspaper reports" (which the American Business Consultants had planted) "have stated that *Red Channels* is now the 'bible' of Madison Ave."[85] The effects of this slender volume rocked the industry to its core. Its first targets were performers, all women, whose names appeared in *Red Channels* in June 1950. By October 1950, their careers would be over.

Chapter 5

Cleaning the House of Broadcasting

Naturally, men scared to make pictures about the American Negro, men who have only in the last year allowed the word Jew to be spoken in a picture, men who took more than ten years to make an anti-Fascist picture, those are frightened men and you pick frightened men to frighten first. Judas goats; they'll lead the others, maybe, to the slaughter for you.

Lillian Hellman (playwright, author)[1]

The reason no one would hire me was because my name was in Red Channels. *No one whose name was in* Red Channels *was hired, for, as everyone now knew, that little booklet was "the bible of Madison Avenue." Soon there were others beside me hit and hit hard: Philip Loeb, J. Edward Bromberg, Madie [sic] Christians. Madie Christians had avoided Hitler's concentration camps by sheer blind fortune, had come to America, where people were free, and here was persecuted, for she could find no job at all, not even in the theatre. She died a broken woman, of a heart attack.*

Jean Muir (actress)[2]

As the 1940s ended, burlesque artist and author Gypsy Rose Lee, actress Jean Muir, musician and actress Hazel Scott, and radio show host Ireene Wicker were optimistic about their future in television. Lee's quick wit made her a popular guest on radio and television quiz shows. Her success had translated into a more permanent gig as host of *What Makes You Tick?*, a program scheduled to expand from 15 to 30 minutes when she took over in fall 1950.[3] At the beginning of 1950, encouraged by Hazel Scott's critical and commercial success on a sponsored program on WABD-TV, the upstart DuMont television network signed her to star in a new series, slated to be broadcast during prime time beginning in July 1950. *The Hazel Scott Show* would be the first television show to star an African American.[4] Like Gypsy Rose Lee, Muir had been building a reputation in television after a career in film, appearing in anthologies like the *Philco Television Playhouse*, *Boris Karloff Presents*, and the *Actor's Studio*. When she was cast in spring 1950 as Henry Aldrich's mother in the televised version of radio's popular sitcom about an awkward teen, *The Aldrich Family*, Muir considered her career in television secure. As for Wicker, the Kellogg Company, sponsor of her children's radio show for nearly twenty years, had just signed a contract for the televised version of the show.

With three new contracts in broadcasting and a starring role in a popular sitcom to their credit, Lee, Muir, Scott, and Wicker had every reason to imagine that their futures in television would be bright. They had overcome numerous obstacles in order to build careers in male-dominated media industries. Television was about to take off, and new opportunities for creativity and employment seemed boundless.

Unbeknownst to most progressives in the industry, however, a storm was brewing. In early July 1950, fresh from their successes in the McCullough and Sweets case and with the wind of the Korean War at their backs, the American Business Consultants laid the groundwork for a series of attacks on "coddled" progressive personnel in broadcasting.[5] Unlike *CounterAttack*, which cast a wide net to catch those "who have aided Stalin by supporting his US fronts," *Red Channels* focused on broadcasting alone, listing progressives whom the book had identified as Communists or, more often, the many "dupes or innocents who, for one reason or another, will support" the Communist Party's fronts.[6] Not all of those listed in *Red Channels* had ever worked in broadcasting, although all had participated in the progressive cultural and political life of New York City.

Gypsy Rose Lee, Jean Muir, Hazel Scott, and Ireene Wicker were seasoned performers in 1950, who had enjoyed significant successes in media industries over the course of long careers. Lee had performed in a few films in the 1930s and 1940s, but was better known as a self-identified exotic dancer. In 1950, she was single mother to a young son (Erik, born in 1944), and she found the settled routines of television more appealing than life on the road.

Jean Muir had enjoyed some Hollywood fame. Discovered by a Warner Brothers scout while starring in the Broadway play *Saint Wench* in 1933, the tall, blonde Muir went on to make over twenty films for Warner Brothers. She was best known for playing ingénues in films like *Desirable* (1934), *A Midsummer Night's Dream* (1935), and *The Constant Nymph* (1943). In 1950, Muir was living in White Plains, raising three young children with her husband, labor lawyer Henry Jaffe.

Hazel Scott lived outside Manhattan as well, in Mount Vernon, New York, with husband Adam Clayton Powell, Jr., minister and U.S. Congressman, whom she had married in 1945. They had a young child, Adam Clayton Powell III, born in 1946. Despite the fact that she was the youngest of these four women, Scott already had the longest career in broadcasting. When she was aged fifteen, Mutual Insurance had signed her for six months of sustaining programs, and by the late 1940s, she was a frequent guest on variety shows like Ed Sullivan's *The Talk of the Town*.[7]

Ireene Wicker was the oldest and least politically active of the first four targets. Wicker got her break in radio soap operas in the 1930s. She later gained fame as "Kellogg's Singing Lady," telling stories and singing songs on the popular children's radio show that bore her name. After divorcing her first husband, Wicker married painter and sculptor Victor Hammer, brother of industrialist Armand Hammer, and the couple settled in New York City.

In 1950, the FBI was already maintaining classified files on Muir and Scott. Muir had a file because she had been identified by ex-communist John Leech as a member of the Communist Party in 1940 (a false charge, as the FBI later noted in its correspondence). Scott's file originated in a report she made to the FBI about a telegram she had received in 1944 from someone impersonating J. Edgar Hoover. The subsequent investigation turned up her association with the integrated nightclub Café Society and Scott too became a person of interest. Lee and Wicker only became subjects of FBI investigation after they were listed in *Red Channels*.

Although neither the American Business Consultants nor the Bureau ever stated that they singled out these four women because of their gender, it was no coincidence that their first targets were women. The former G-Men had been trained to exploit people's vulnerabilities for political gain by the master of that brutal art, J. Edgar Hoover. When it came to cultivating informants, for example, G-Men used a word that referred to the conversion of gentiles to Judaism: they "proselyted" informants, seeking to win them to the anti-communist cause. But theirs was more of a stick than a carrot approach. To convert people, they used information about people's private lives—their sexualities, sexual practices, and intimate relationships—to threaten ruin if they did not comply. Certainly, Kenneth Bierly—who "proselyted" FBI informant Angela Calomiris and many other informants—used Calomiris' sexuality to pressure her to inform on progressives. And, as former television star and scholar Eric Bentley showed in *Are You Now or Have You Ever Been: The Investigation of Show Business by the Un-American Activities Committee, 1947–1958*, anti-communists had no reservations when it came to coercing those they identified as fellow-travelers into giving up the names of others.[8] G-Men had reason to believe that women would be more easily converted and persuaded than men.

❖ ❖ ❖

What are you going to do about your girl, she's in the book, you know?

Advertising agency executive[9]

While she [Dorothy Parker] was living in Bucks County she was considered by the people there to be the "queen of the Communists."

FBI Special Agent in Charge (Philadelphia Field Office)[10]

The first instances of blacklisting followed swiftly on the heels of the publication of *Red Channels* in June 1950. In July, when network ABC announced that Gypsy Rose Lee had been signed to appear as the "regular femsee" on their game show *What Makes You Tick?*, the American Business Consultants and the American Legion launched a campaign to protest her appearance.[11] Brandishing *Red Channels* as evidence of Lee's subversive record, the American Legion labeled her "a dear and close associate of the traitors of our country" and demanded that she be immediately removed from the airwaves.[12]

Wicker's troubles began soon after. In early August, less than six months after it had renewed her contract, the Kellogg Company reversed course and fired her with no explanation. Wicker was left to assume that she was terminated because *Red Channels* had made her a "controversial" person. By the time the DuMont television network cancelled *The Hazel Scott Show* in September, just a week after Scott had appeared before the HUAC, the network did not bother to use a consumer boycott as justification, as they had in the other cases. Instead, the network fired Scott in *anticipation* of a protest, explaining, "It was just that we felt we could more easily sell the time if somebody else was in that spot."[13] But the case that signaled the end for progressives was yet to come. The blacklist really took hold in late August, with the campaign against Muir signaling the beginning of the industry's capitulation to anti-communist activists.

Following the pattern favored by G-Man masculinity, anti-communists asserted a public mandate for campaigns of their own devising. Muir's firing from *The Aldrich Family* did not result from a spontaneous viewer protest. Just as they had in the McCullough libel trial and the firing of William Sweets, the American Business Consultants initiated the sequence of events that led to Muir's dismissal. The day before *The Aldrich Family*'s final taping, Theodore Kirkpatrick called anti-communist stalwarts Bill Cunningham at the *Boston Herald*, Hester McCullough, and Rabbi Benjamin Schultz (the last two members of a new anti-communist organization called the Joint Committee Against Communism in New York).

Would they "organize a protest" against suspected communist Jean Muir's appearance on *The Aldrich Family*, Kirkpatrick asked.[14] McCullough launched into action. She quickly called one of the regional leaders of the Catholic War Veterans (another member of the Joint Committee Against Communism). Then she called NBC and Young & Rubicam (the advertising agency representing sponsor General Foods) to alert them to what she described as a groundswell of public sentiment against Muir's appearance (Figure 5.1).

When the unsuspecting Muir drove to what she thought would be the last rehearsal before the show was taped on Sunday afternoon, August 27, 1950—with her celebratory cake—she discovered that the sitcom's final rehearsal had been cancelled.[15] The next day, program sponsor General Foods Corporation issued a formal statement to the press. They had fired Jean Muir, the statement read, because she was " 'a controversial personality' whose presence on the show might adversely affect the sale of the advertiser's product" and "provoke unfavorable criticism and even antagonism among sizable groups of consumers."[16]

Figure 5.1 Jean Muir
Source: Permission of the University of Oregon Libraries, Special Collections and University Archives, Eugene, OR

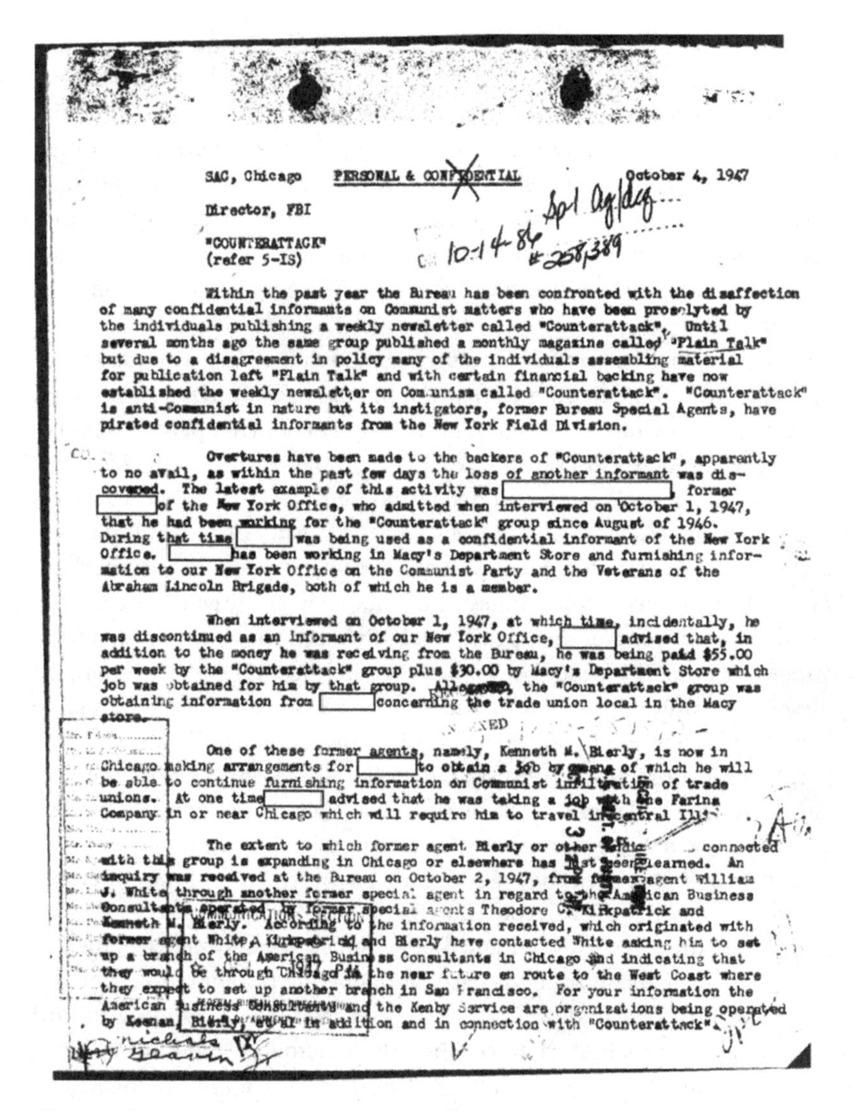

SAC, Chicago PERSONAL & CONFIDENTIAL October 4, 1947

Director, FBI

"COUNTERATTACK"
(refer 5-IS)

10-14-86 Spl Ag/dcg
#258,389

Within the past year the Bureau has been confronted with the disaffection of many confidential informants on Communist matters who have been proselyted by the individuals publishing a weekly newsletter called "Counterattack". Until several months ago the same group published a monthly magazine called "Plain Talk" but due to a disagreement in policy many of the individuals assembling material for publication left "Plain Talk" and with certain financial backing have now established the weekly newsletter on Communism called "Counterattack". "Counterattack" is anti-Communist in nature but its instigators, former Bureau Special Agents, have pirated confidential informants from the New York Field Division.

Overtures have been made to the backers of "Counterattack", apparently to no avail, as within the past few days the loss of another informant was discovered. The latest example of this activity was [redacted], former [redacted] of the New York Office, who admitted when interviewed on October 1, 1947, that he had been working for the "Counterattack" group since August of 1946. During that time [redacted] was being used as a confidential informant of the New York Office. [redacted] has been working in Macy's Department Store and furnishing information to our New York Office on the Communist Party and the Veterans of the Abraham Lincoln Brigade, both of which he is a member.

When interviewed on October 1, 1947, at which time, incidentally, he was discontinued as an informant of our New York Office, [redacted] advised that, in addition to the money he was receiving from the Bureau, he was being paid $55.00 per week by the "Counterattack" group plus $30.00 by Macy's Department Store which job was obtained for him by that group. Allegedly, the "Counterattack" group was obtaining information from [redacted] concerning the trade union local in the Macy store.

One of these former agents, namely, Kenneth M. Bierly, is now in Chicago making arrangements for [redacted] to obtain a job by means of which he will be able to continue furnishing information on Communist infiltration of trade unions. At one time [redacted] advised that he was taking a job with the Farina Company in or near Chicago which will require him to travel in central Illinois.

The extent to which former agent Bierly or other [illegible] connected with this group is expanding in Chicago or elsewhere has not been learned. An inquiry was received at the Bureau on October 2, 1947, from former agent William J. White through another former special agent in regard to the American Business Consultants operated by former special agents Theodore C. Kirkpatrick and Kenneth M. Bierly. According to the information received, which originated with former agent White, Kirkpatrick and Bierly have contacted White asking him to set up a branch of the American Business Consultants in Chicago and indicating that they would be through Chicago in the near future en route to the West Coast where they expect to set up another branch in San Francisco. For your information the American Business Consultants and the Kenby Service are organizations being operated by Keenan, Bierly, et al in addition and in connection with "Counterattack".

Nichols
Gleavin

Figure 4.1 FBI Correspondence about the American Business Consultants
Source: National Archives and Records Administration, College Park, MD

former agents were in fact working with the approval of the Bureau. If that was true, then Hoover's antipathy toward them was part of an elaborate scheme to conceal their collaboration. This would explain why Hoover refused to criticize the American Business Consultants in response to the many inquiries from business owners who had been approached by them and were confused

Muir's prior Hollywood fame helped the American Business Consultants boost attention to the alleged problem of communist influence in broadcasting. Although the American Legion's campaign against Lee and the cancellation of Wicker's contract had begun a month before Muir was fired, the attack on Muir galvanized the Joint Committee Against Communism, whose Rabbi Schultz made a statement to the press, claiming "the support of 2,000,000 members of various patriotic and anti-Communist organizations" for a possible Muir boycott and threatening that his organization had "a full-scale program" worked out "to 'police' the radio and television networks, producers and entertainers trying to 'sell' Communist ideas." The firing of Muir, he added ominously, was "Only the beginning."[17]

The "thorough housecleaning" *Counter Attack* promised anti-communists thus began in the summer of 1950 by singling out these four women for attack. How did these women improbably become the lightning rods for a campaign that purported to eliminate threats to Americanism in the broadcast industry? Unlike the Hollywood Ten, a group that included influential directors, producers, and writers, these women exercised little control over the content they performed. As one contemporary journalist observed, Muir's upcoming role as "Mother Aldrich" would have given her "no opportunity to say anything but the innocuous lines put in that harassed lady's mouth by the program's author."[18] Lee was an exotic dancer, moreover, with an already tenuous position in the industry. Wicker was a children's show host, who sang songs about pussy cats and owls, firemen and rabbits, hardly the stuff of anti-communist conspiracy theories. Scott enjoyed the very limited fame available to black women working at the intersections of music and broadcasting who refused to portray mammies, maids, or hypersexualized objects of white male desire.

Moreover, none of the women had ever been a member of the Communist Party.[19] In the pages of *Red Channels*, the evidence for Muir's and Scott's Red record rested on their membership in the nine organizations listed next to each of their names. *Red Channels*' cases against Lee and Wicker were flimsy, even by the American Business Consultants' dubious standards for identifying fellow-travelers. Where Lee had four organizations associated with her name, Wicker had only one. She was listed in *Red Channels* solely because she was alleged to have signed a petition to reelect African American Communist Party Councilman Benjamin J. Davis.

Anti-communists found these women more attractive public targets than the men who were listed in *Red Channels* for a number of reasons. To begin with, professional women were sitting ducks for anti-communists.

Because they were successful in male-dominated professions, they were immediately considered subversive. The ever-more-conservative political and cultural climate ensured that women who had enjoyed new forms of independence in the 1930s and 1940s would be politically suspicious to the men and women policing gendered behaviors during the first years of the Cold War. Earlier that fateful year, Senator Edwin C. Johnson (a Democrat from Colorado) denounced Ingrid Bergman on the Senate floor, describing her as "a powerful influence for evil," because the out-of-wedlock birth of her son "had perpetrated an assault upon the institution of marriage."[20]

By anti-communist standards, Lee, Muir, Scott, and Wicker were similarly powerful and evil influences. Lee and Wicker were divorcees. Lee and Scott had had extramarital relationships. In addition to the reputation that came along with being an exotic dancer, Lee had given birth to a son, whose father (director Otto Preminger) was married to someone else at the time. Scott's husband had divorced Isabel Washington in order to marry her.

None of these women represented proper American womanhood in the eyes of anti-communists. Where men in media industries continue to be allowed to sexually harass women with few repercussions, for women, the slightest transgression has always had the power to ruin careers. As women who depended on respectable public images, the Broadcast 41 were ideal targets for what Hazel Scott described as "the smear artist with a spray gun."[21]

In addition to personal lives that transgressed anti-communist norms of gender and race, Lee, Muir, and Scott's records of progressive civic engagement showed that these women were politically as well as morally impure. All three were active members of unions seen as nests of communist activity.[22] In 1950, Lee was the newsletter editor for the American Guild of Variety Actors (AGVA), an organization that had just announced plans to establish a national wage agreement for its members, as well as a campaign to fight bias against black entertainers.[23] She was also AGVA's representative on the board of the newly formed Television Authority (TvA), the group assigned to sort out existing unions' jurisdictional claims over television.[24] Like AGVA, TvA had recently adopted an "Industry Statement of Policy" that sought to "secure representation of Negroes on television matching their role in everyday life and providing opportunities for the employment of the many qualified Negro artists," a statement at odds with anti-communists' goals of keeping African Americans off-screen and economically and politically disenfranchised.[25]

Like many of the Broadcast 41, Muir had been criticizing Hollywood's racism publicly since the late 1930s, appearing at public events around the country and, on at least one occasion, sharing the stage with Eleanor Roosevelt.[26] Like Lee, Muir actively participated in Actors' Equity, the union in which actor Philip Loeb (also listed in *Red Channels*) had long been a leader.[27]

Scott's record of outspoken political engagement had garnered headlines and anti-communist attention throughout the 1940s. In October 1945, Scott was barred by the Daughters of the American Revolution from performing in Constitution Hall, as singer Marian Anderson had been just six years before.[28] Later that year, Scott refused to play for the all-white National Press Club.[29] And in early 1950, Scott filed her landmark civil rights lawsuit against the Spokane restaurant that refused to serve her and her companion.

Of the four women, Ireene Wicker had the most tenuous link to politics, progressive or otherwise. Wicker—a talented voice actor, dialectician, and writer—worked with a pianist, acting and singing songs to audiences estimated in the millions.[30] A recent transplant from Chicago, "the Lady with a Thousand Voices" was much loved, but left no record of political activism. *Red Channels*' allegation that she had once signed a progressive petition was all the evidence anti-communists provided for blacklisting her.

Regardless of their politics, the four women were attractive targets for anti-communists for an additional reason: they were married to well-known men who had their own reputations and careers to worry about. Muir's husband, Henry Jaffe, was general counsel for the American Federation of Television and Radio Actors (AFTRA) and a key player in the TvA. Adam Clayton Powell, Jr., Scott's husband, was the first African American to represent New York in the U.S. House of Representatives. Lee was married to visual artist Julio de Diego, while Wicker was married to businessman and philanthropist Victor Hammer, whose art and business dealings with the Soviet Union made him a person of interest to anti-communists as well. Jaffe and Hammer were Jewish, Julio de Diego was an immigrant who opposed Spanish dictator Francisco Franco, and Powell was African American. None of these husbands conformed to the G-Man's narrow racial formula.

The American Business Consultants hoped to use their spray guns, to borrow Hazel Scott's turn of phrase, to cast aspersion not only on the women listed in the pages of *Red Channels*, but on the men to whom they were married as well. Their time in the FBI had taught Bierly, Keenan, and Kirkpatrick invaluable lessons about how people's intimate relationships could be used to coerce them. Historian David K. Phillips writes about how the Bureau recruited gay men and lesbians as informants because they viewed them as being already alienated from their families and communities and thus free of emotional ties that could be used to blackmail them (except, ironically, of the fact that they were gay, which the Bureau used to coerce them). FBI informant Angela Calomiris recalled that at their first meeting, agents Kenneth Bierly and William South "doggedly" and repeatedly asked her, "Miss Calomiris ... do you have any marriage plans?"[31]

The FBI had taught the American Business Consultants' founders how to use family ties to coerce reluctant informants. The FBI files of the Broadcast 41 contain extensive evidence of the Bureau's acts of retaliation against the families of progressives they were targeting. For example, not only did the Bureau surveil Madeline Lee's home, they also admonished her to think about what she was doing to her children. In actress Louise Fitch's case, the Bureau used her husband Jerry D. Lewis—a writer for the radio program *This is Your FBI*—as a wedge to force her to name names. Alerted by his contacts in the HUAC that they might subpoena Fitch, FBI public relations head Louis B. Nichols wrote to Clyde Tolson, "I had a rumble the House Committee might check into Louise Fitch, and I had learned that her name had appeared in *Red Channels*. (I used this as a basis to open the discussion.)" Producer-director Jerry Devine, Nichols added, "was very much concerned about the matter and he suggested that a good way to bring this thing to a head would be for him to tell Jerry Lewis that he had had a tip from ABC about his wife's name appearing in *Red Channels* and that the House Committee might be checking on her."[32]

When Academy Award-winning actress Judy Holliday proved reluctant to cooperate with the Bureau (instead providing a sworn statement that she had never been a member of the Communist Party), Hoover initiated a "security investigation ... of Judy Holliday's mother and uncle, Helen Gollomb Tuvim, aka Mary Tuvim, and Joseph Gollomb."[33] Anne Revere's defiance of the HUAC and her support for the Hollywood Ten earned her husband his own FBI file. Louise Fitch's listing in *Red Channels* caused the FBI to initiate a file on her brother, Vernon.

Consequently, the blacklist placed unimaginable pressures on intimate relationships. Not all of the Broadcast 41 were married to supportive, progressive men. Some of the Broadcast 41 were married to men who were ambivalent about their wives' careers to begin with but were willing to tolerate them as long as they were making money. In addition to dealing with storms of negative publicity, these women had to manage the impact of anticommunist attacks on their relationships.

In fairness, the husbands of the Broadcast 41 had reason to be concerned. As Jerry D. Lewis discovered, their own careers suffered because of their relationships with women who had been blacklisted. He and wife Louise Fitch had three young children in 1952. Fitch had been unemployed since the blacklist began, two years earlier. In an effort to save her husband's career, Fitch agreed to be interviewed by the FBI, providing the names of more than two dozen other progressives (six of them members of the Broadcast 41). In a separate interview, Lewis told the FBI agent assigned to interview him "that had he known she was a member of the party he would never have married her."[34] These rituals of humiliation did not succeed in protecting Lewis' job: he was fired from *This is Your FBI* in 1952.

As Joanna Rapf, daughter of blacklisted screenwriter Maurice Rapf, put it, those who had been blacklisted in media "risked a great deal, including their families' security, to stand up for what they believed was right."[35] The FBI and the American Business Consultants knew how to use family ties to intimidate progressives into compliance. For progressive women already juggling careers and family in an era where this appeared not just wrongheaded, but downright un-American, the cost of these risks was considerable.

❖ ❖ ❖

She [Uta Hagen] then analyzed her own position and realized this publicity would also hurt her career which, she said it has. She cited the example that in 1951, she was offered an acting commitment on a nation-wide television program from which the company later tried to relieve her. When the rest of the cast refused to appear without her, she was reluctantly allowed to appear. Since that time she has not been asked to appear on television. As a result of this experience in 1951, subject stated she ceased all such activity and proceeded on the premise that an actor should confine his activity to the arts and not politics.

FBI Special Agent in Charge (New York City Field Office)[36]

You think you're going to be brave and noble. Then you walk in there and there are the microphones, and all those senators looking at you..., it scares the shit out of you. But I'm not ashamed of myself because I didn't name names. That much I preserved.

Judy Holliday (actress)[37]

Lee, Muir, Scott, and Wicker fought back against the blacklist as best they could. But their options for defense were few and rapidly narrowing as a hostile Cold War climate closed in around them. Anti-communists promised those who were blacklisted clearance and industrial redemption if they fully cooperated with the FBI and anti-communist organizations in answering questions about their political affiliations. In a pamphlet later published by the blacklisting organization AWARE, Inc., *The Road Back*, anti-communists summarized the road to redemption. Those who had helped or appeared to help the communist cause in the past, but had broken with the "party line," could "perform deeds indicative of this change and thus clear themselves of suspicion and return to normal employability."[38]

The only way to effectively do this, according to the FBI, the American Business Consultants, the American Legion, and AWARE, Inc. was to appear before the HUAC, answer questions about any involvement with the communist movement and its front organizations, and—most importantly—provide the names of others who had been involved as well. Actress Anne Revere summarized these options as follows. A person could choose "To deny membership and face a charge of perjury (for which of us did not belong to some of these organizations?); to refuse to answer and face a contempt citation with a fine and a year in jail; or finally to admit membership and inform upon all others that we might have known as members, thus subjecting them to the degradation of being summoned before the committee with the consequent loss of livelihood." And if you admitted that you had been a member of the Communist Party or a front organization, but refused to inform on others (which many considered morally appropriate), Revere added, you could still be cited for contempt.[39]

Progressive women did not want to name names and subject friends and colleagues to the danger and degradation of being blacklisted.[40] Some, like Lillian Hellman and Judy Holliday, took an approach known as a "diminished Fifth," and refused to answer questions about anyone but themselves.[41] Others simply refused to cooperate. Caspary was advised that unless she "wrote a letter to Mr. Nicholas Schenck, then head of the company, humbly asking forgiveness and confessing that I was not and never had been a Communist," she would be fired.[42] "I wrote a letter," Caspary later noted, "minus the confession." Progressives who wanted to avoid the fate of the Hollywood Ten, whose refusal to answer questions earned them contempt charges and jail time, pled the Fifth, like radio director Betty Todd, even as they understood that, in historian Milly Barranger's words, this was "tantamount to an admission of guilt."[43]

Few of the Broadcast 41 had the stomach to publicly disavow their political beliefs. They understood that those who had smeared them were extortionists—men who were "on the take."[44] They resented being bullied into hiring the services of unsavory anti-communist clearance officers and columnists like Kenneth Bierly, J.B. Matthews, Victor Riesel, Howard Rushmore, and George Sokolsky or having to curry favor with gossip columnists like Hedda Hopper. For women who had overcome so many obstacles in their efforts to succeed in media industries, the abject penitence demanded by anti-communists—and the concessions to racism this required—were pills too bitter to swallow.

In the face of the adverse publicity that followed their listing in *Red Channels*, Lee, Muir, Scott, and Wicker tried to get their side of the story out to the press, issuing public statements that told the truth: they had never been members of the Communist Party. Lee denied the charges the American Legion had leveled against her. She was, she said, "the victim of accusations and every one of them is a lie."[45] Wicker gave a public statement that proclaimed: "The fundamental doctrine of Communism is abhorrent to me. It is in direct opposition to the American principles I have always held and advocated."[46] Counter to claims the network could not sell air time for her show, Hazel Scott told the press, "her DuMont TV show had been building steadily, had attracted considerable sponsor interest, was right on the verge of being sold, until *Red Channels* became the book of the industry."[47] Muir's statements after her firing played up her role as wife and mother, downplaying the political commitments she had publicly supported throughout the 1940s and projecting a star image that hewed closely to dominant tropes about middle-class, middle-aged, white femininity. Ultimately, the blacklist also gave networks justification for firing people who—however bankable—had histories of challenging the industry's racism, misogyny, and treatment of workers.

When conventional public relations efforts proved unsuccessful, Lee, Muir, Scott, and Wicker turned to social connections to try to clear their names. Muir asked NAACP head and family friend Walter White to set up a meeting with the FBI, where on two separate occasions she presented the case for her loyalty. Often unaware that the FBI had been monitoring them for years, other members of the Broadcast 41 sought the assistance of the very institution that was helping to ruin their reputations. Singer Ella Logan, for example, whose activities had been carefully monitored since 1945, wrote to her friend "John" Edgar Hoover, asking for assistance in clearing her name and inquiring after the health of "Clyde T." Unbeknownst to her, Hoover harbored suspicions about Logan's loyalties, adding the following comment to her FBI report: "I fear she has brought upon herself any form of communist stigma by her certainly indiscreet actions."[48]

Because progressives knew that the Catholic Church was a powerful backer of anti-communist activities in New York City, some turned to Catholic leaders in their efforts to clear their names. Wicker contacted prominent anti-communist Cardinal Francis Spellman to plead her case. When that proved futile, she and her husband visited the Pope in Rome.[49] Gertrude Berg also unsuccessfully sought the aid of Spellman in her efforts to defend blacklisted actor Philip Loeb.

For her part, Wicker directly confronted the American Business Consultants, telling *CounterAttack*, "I emphatically declare that I am not, never have been, could never be a Communist or Communist sympathizer, in any sense of these terms."[50] She then paid a personal visit to the American Business Consultants' office on West 42nd Street, where she told Theodore Kirkpatrick that the single listing next to her name in *Red Channels* was a lie. She could not have sponsored the Committee for the Re-Election of Benjamin Davis in 1945 because she had not even been in New York City when the petition for Davis' campaign was circulating.

Redirecting the conversation—a tactic anti-communists frequently used when held accountable to the inconvenient nature of facts—Kirkpatrick demanded that she show evidence of public opposition to communism. Wicker told him that in 1940, she had permitted her son to join the Royal Air Force to fight Hitler, at a moment in time when the Communist Party opposed the war. Her son was subsequently killed in action.[51] Kirkpatrick was unmoved. When Wicker's lawyer later showed that her signature had never appeared on any of the petitions supporting Davis, Kirkpatrick blamed the error on the source he had used, the Communist Party's newspaper the *Daily Worker*.[52] *CounterAttack* eventually printed a retraction. But by then, it was too late. The damage to Wicker's reputation could not be undone.

A few among the Broadcast 41 hired the services of those who had smeared them in order to clear their names. When William Randolph Hearst's *Journal-American* tried to prevent Ed Sullivan and the Ford Motor Company from hiring Lena Horne, the singer and actress took a two-pronged approach to the problem. Her longtime manager, Ralph Harris, verified "reports that the Negro singer has 'made her peace' with Theodore Kirkpatrick, the ex-FBI agent who puts out the anti-communist gossip sheet, 'CounterAttack,' and published 'Red Channels,' the compendium of alleged 'subversives' in the entertainment industry." According to Harris, Horne met with Kirkpatrick in order to "clean up once and for all the propaganda emanating from *CounterAttack* charging her with having been associated with 'subversive' causes." Kirkpatrick gave Horne a "clean bill of health," although Harris emphasized that this clearance would "not change Miss Horne's outspoken opposition to Jim Crow and oppression, even though it was this antipathy which led her into disfavor with Hearst and Kirkpatrick."[53] Horne also threatened to sue the newspaper if her contract was breached, warning them that she intended to "sue for the limit," which may have helped convince the *Journal-American* to back down.[54]

Across the country, in Hollywood, Columbia Pictures hired the services of Kenby Associates to clear blacklisted actress Judy Holliday. Kenby Associates had been founded by Kenneth Bierly after he quit the American Business Consultants in 1951 in order to clear film "actors and actresses who have been previously charged by 'CounterAttack' with being involved with subversive organizations." Although Bierly's report to Columbia was preoccupied with Holliday's potentially "subversive or unpatriotic" friendship with lesbian police officer Yetta Cohn, his advice to the brilliant actress reflected his recognition of the narrowing constraints within which progressive women now had to maneuver to preserve what was left of their careers.[55] Having fought being typecast as a dumb blonde throughout her career, Holliday was told to play the dumb blonde for all it was worth. Still, as writer Garson Kanin observed, "Of all those who were harassed in the ugly days of *Red Channels* and blacklisting, no one was more steadfast or less craven than Judy. Her behavior under pressure was a poem of grace."[56]

Alone among the first four targets, Hazel Scott directly approached "the House Un-American Activities Committee ... to ask for the opportunity of appearing and stating her case."[57] Scott would have known that the members of the HUAC, which included future President Richard M. Nixon and John S. Wood—a senator from Virginia and chairman of the HUAC, who was rumored to be a member of the Ku Klux Klan—were unlikely to be sympathetic.[58] But Scott wanted to ensure that her version of events was written into the historical record. Over the objections of committee members, Scott insisted on reading her prepared speech in its entirety, fervently denying that she was "ever knowingly connected with the Communist Party or any of its front organizations." Scott also criticized *Red Channels*' strategies and anti-communists' integrity, describing herself as "one of the victims" of *Red Channels*' "technique of half-truth and guilt-by-listing"[59] (Figure 5.2).

But nothing those accused could say mattered in the topsy-turvy universe of Cold War anti-communism, where the facts could always be made to conform to anti-communists' version of "factual information." Although Dorothy Parker denied ever having been a member of the Communist Party during an FBI interrogation, the agent observed that she "appeared to be a very nervous person" and thus unreliable.[60] As one FBI informant later said of blacklisted actor Philip Loeb, "During the interview Fillmore [Clyde Fillmore of the Hollywood Athletic Club] recalled that he had accused Loeb of being a Communist once and Loeb vehemently denied it, although Fillmore stated

Figure 5.2 Hazel Scott
Source: Permission of the Oregon Historical Society, Salem, OR

from his experience that it is just what he had expected him to do."[61] Often damned for political actions they had not engaged in and then damned again when they denied the false charges made against them, those who were blacklisted found it all but impossible to clear their names.

As for their allies, to defend someone who had been accused of being a fellow-traveler, to challenge these techniques of half-truth and guilt-by-listing, was almost certainly to become a target oneself. Few individuals and institutions, even those charged with defending civil liberties, proved willing to risk their necks in defense of those who had been blacklisted. After all, the American Civil Liberties Union (ACLU), for example, under the leadership of lawyer and co-founder Morris Ernst, had purged communists from its own membership rolls in 1940.[62]

Male-dominated unions also refused to go out on a limb for women like Gypsy Rose Lee, Madeline Lee, and Muir, regardless of the many contributions these women had made to their unions during World War II. In September 1950, the *New York Times* reported that the New York local of the AFTRA adopted a motion "asking for reinstatement of Jean Muir," but the motion had no force behind it.[63] Fighting their own battles with anti-communists in their ranks, unions were loath indeed to risk being associated with women who had been smeared. Some of the men involved in trade unionism at the time hoped to continue to work in the lucrative new television industry; crossing the FBI was not the way to achieve their career goals. In Muir's case, her husband—AFTRA counsel Henry Jaffe—(who was also giving her legal advice) had his own promising career prospects in television to worry about.[64] These men were not likely to risk their professional necks to defend progressive women. By 1955, AFTRA considered a ballot measure, specifying that if an AFTRA member refused to answer Senate or House questions about Communist Party membership, "said member shall be subject to the charge that he is guilty of conduct prejudicial to the welfare of AFTRA."[65]

As for the press, anti-communism turned many of these proverbial watchdogs into Hoover's lapdogs. Fearful of being blacklisted themselves, few journalists were brave enough to challenge anti-communists' claims. A rare few did, however. The *New York Times* television critic Jack Gould and John Crosby of the *New York Herald Tribune* penned articles protesting the firing of Lee and Wicker and objecting to General Foods' treatment of Muir. Both noted the threat to civil liberties these cases posed, as well as the ludicrous nature of the charges that had been leveled against these women. Like other progressives across media industries, journalists had reason to fear anti-communist retaliation. In response to their criticism, the Bureau began to monitor the activities of both Crosby and Gould, seeking ways to ruin their careers as well.[66]

❖ ❖ ❖

Obviously, no advertising agency wants its clients to become targets of the barrage of public-opinion dead cats to which General Foods has been subjected since. And their answer will be simple: No controversial figures will be hired for any job.

Business Week[67]

Real Americans like their country. They are proud of it. They think it is a good place to live.... There are those who would chip away our confidence so that their special brand of tyranny might creep into America. They must not succeed.

Sigurd S. Larmon (Chairman, Young & Rubicam)[68]

Behind the scenes, the television industry was confused and panicked about how to respond to the first cases of blacklisting. Many disliked the blacklist; some as we have seen because it was costing them money, others because it was ethically and legally unjust. But to oppose the blacklist was surely to get caught in its web. As television producer Bob Bendick candidly put it, "Management's line was, if you're in *Red Channels*, you're a communist. It was a terrible wrong, and I suppose I considered saying, 'If he goes I go,' but I was not that dedicated to valor."[69] Harvey Matusow (communist turned anti-communist turned anti-anti-communist) was blunter in his assessment: "Madison Avenue people are cowardly."[70]

Advertisers like Liggett & Myers and agencies like Young & Rubicam broadly shared anti-communist beliefs, but they did not want to lose talented and lucrative writers, producers, and actors. According to a CBS executive, networks were concerned that *Red Channels* would wind up costing "the industry fifty, maybe a hundred million dollars and God knows how many ulcers and gray hairs and broken hearts and shattered careers and suicides. Plus, a lot of public respect—and good shows."[71] In the early days of the blacklist, they had additional concerns about its impact on creativity in the industry: "The trouble with people who've never joined anything and therefore are 'safe' for us to use," this executive added, "is that they usually aren't very good writers or actors or producers or, hell, human beings."[72]

Despite the forces arrayed against them, industry opposition to the blacklist seemed both possible and imminent in early fall 1950. As cultural historian Cynthia B. Meyers points out, sponsors and advertising agencies in New York City "were for the most part corporate liberals" who were by no means unified in how to respond to anti-communist charges of subversion.[73] There were powerful instances of resistance. Network ABC, for example, defended Gypsy Rose Lee (Figure 5.3) throughout the summer and fall of 1950, maintaining that Lee had demonstrated her loyalty by signing both a loyalty oath and "an affidavit denying any Red ties."[74] Facing down the American Legion's threats of consumer boycotts, ABC president Robert E. Kintner demanded that the American Legion provide evidence to prove their allegations or cease their otherwise libelous accusations against Lee. Edward Clamage, chairman of the Illinois American Legion's anti-subversive commission, quickly backed down. Clamage "had based his statements on the inclusion of Miss Lee's

Figure 5.3 Gypsy Rose Lee
Source: New York World-Telegram and Sun Collection, Library of Congress, Washington, DC

name in 'Red Channels,'" he told the press, adding that the "entire matter could be easily clarified and the answer should come from the publishers of 'Red Channels.'" The American Business Consultants responded by saying that they were merely reporting "facts ... based on public documents." Once again, anti-communists dodged accountability by blaming their sources for lies they continued to promote as truth.[75]

Although ABC's refusal to give in to the American Legion's boycott of Gypsy Rose Lee won Kintner a Peabody Award three years later, the network was an outlier. CBS' actions in the wake of the blacklist set the standard for industry responses, sending a clear message to the entire industry: organizations that did not toe the G-Man line would be punished.

The FBI's hostility toward CBS predated the blacklist. The network had a reputation for independence of thought, intellectualism, and criticism, characteristics Hoover disliked. CBS also criticized anti-communist practices, further adding fire to Hoover's antipathy and causing him to irritably complain about the network in the pages of the FBI's correspondence. In 1950, Hoover directed agents in the Bureau's New York City Field Office to conduct a pretext interview with CBS officials to document CBS's purportedly un-American attitudes toward the Bureau. Pretext interviews referred to an interview technique the Bureau "used when it is necessary to accomplish an investigative end without disclosing the Bureau's interest in a matter and/or the true purpose of the inquiry."[76] Pretext interviews were, in short, fishing expeditions. Hoover resented the comparative independent-mindedness of CBS's cosmopolitan news division and its refusal to concede to his demand that media conform to the Bureau's perspectives. And he was a man who harbored a grudge.

The American Business Consultants shared Hoover's negative view of CBS. Indeed, more CBS employees were listed in *Red Channels* than those from any other network. "CBS," *CounterAttack* declared with typical lack of evidence, "is the most satisfying network for Communists.... it's plain that NBC and Mutual are LEAST satisfactory to Communists [and] ... that American Broadcasting Co is about at halfway point between most satisfactory and least satisfactory."[77] The pages of *CounterAttack* were full of diatribes against reporters like William Shirer and Howard K. Smith, writers and producers Himan Brown, Norman Corwin, Leo Hurwitz, and William N. Robson (producer of the 1943 documentary *Open Letter on Race Hatred*), all of whom, the newsletter warned its readers, were traitorous fellow-travelers.[78]

In the case of Muir, the American Business Consultants had a more personal axe to grind with both CBS and longtime sponsor General Foods. Both had rejected the American Business Consultants' business overtures in no uncertain terms. In 1949, the American Business Consultants contacted "a representative of the General Foods Company in connection with the General Foods Company radio programs, and advised this representative that Philip

Loeb was a member of the Communist Party and that they had written about him in 'CounterAttack' magazine."[79] Theodore Kirkpatrick took the additional step of contacting a General Foods representative. Loeb "was a member of the Communist Party" and "they had written about him in 'CounterAttack' magazine," Kirkpatrick said, threatening General Foods with a boycott if the corporation did not immediately discontinue sponsorship of *The Goldbergs* (the show Loeb starred in with Gertrude Berg).

In response, General Foods not only refused to hire the American Business Consultants, but an indignant advertising executive also complained to the Bureau about these attempts at extortion. After Kirkpatrick's visit to their offices, David Jacobson of Young & Rubicam told the FBI that "he regarded Kirkpatrick's conversation as a mild threat as his statements could be considered an intimidation in that he said they should subscribe to *CounterAttack*, and that possibly if they didn't subscribe, Kirkpatrick had in mind running a story on Phil Loeb and General Foods." The company, he continued, "was very much irked at the approach of Kirkpatrick and has, in effect, told Kirkpatrick and *CounterAttack* to go to [sic]."[80] General Foods' peremptory rejection of the American Business Consultants' services, and the company's subsequent appeal to the Bureau, added to the former G-Men's hostility toward the sponsor and the network.

After the publication of *Red Channels*, the American Business Consultants were in a position to retaliate against CBS. For its part, the FBI also made it clear that the Bureau would not interfere with the American Business Consultants' red-hunting business, as an incident from 1951 shows. E.H. "Dutch" Ellis of Newell-Emmett Advertising, who represented General Foods, reached out through the networks that connected media industries to the FBI to complain about the American Business Consultants' activities. During a telephone conversation with the Bureau's New York City Field Office, he told a special agent that he was "having a great deal of difficulty in regard to people scheduled to appear on programs" because of the American Business Consultants' campaigns against personnel.

Ellis summed up his quandary. While he agreed with anti-communists in principle, he did not like the American Business Consultants' approach. Specifically, he resented being forced to "subscribe to the services of 'Counterattack' in self-defense." By way of an alternative, and in a display of anti-communist solidarity, he asked the Bureau if there were other "organizations or individuals in New York which the Bureau could recommend to him for employment so that investigations could be made of all persons they planned to have on television or radio in order to determine definitely whether or not they were Communists or Communist sympathizers?"[81] The special agent told Ellis in no uncertain terms that the FBI could not help him with this problem.

Frustrated by this response, Ellis appealed to a higher power, in this case, his friend, assistant FBI director and public relations head Louis B. Nichols.[82] During a visit to Nichols' home in Virginia, "Dutch" Ellis told Nichols that Liggett & Myers' president, Benjamin Few, was "exercised" about the communist presence he had read about in *CounterAttack*, but he did not want to hire the services of the American Business Consultants to address the problem.[83] Nichols reported these concerns to associate FBI director Clyde Tolson, Hoover's second-in-command.[84] He offered "Dutch" the following advice about how the industry should handle the presence of these "questionable persons" on television: "I told Dutch he might try giving some thought to trying to find a spot in each program where a message on Americanism of a minute or two might be used; that [variety host Arthur] Godfrey was a master at such and I mentioned how Godfrey in years gone by has defended the FBI vs. Communist smears and attacks. He thought this was a good idea and would try to work out something."[85]

Nowhere did the Bureau disavow a relationship with the American Business Consultants. Nor did Nichols comment on Ellis' original concern: that the blacklisting of talent in television was costing him money. Instead, Nichols suggested that Liggett & Myers might promote Americanism and, by defending the reputation of the FBI, ensure the Bureau's continued support and respect.

This anecdote sums up what the FBI described as the "gentlemanly approach" they ultimately forged with their former agents, an approach that they reached in fall 1950.[86] This approach required that in response to questions about the American Business Consultants' relationship to the FBI, the Bureau would refuse to comment. Sometimes they said just that; on many other occasions, they told those inquiring that they had no control over former employees. This gentleman's agreement among white anticommunist men gave the American Business Consultants an extraordinarily powerful tactical advantage over progressives in media industries. From the perspective of those in the industry, it was clear that the American Business Consultants were actively collaborating with the Bureau and with the HUAC as well.[87]

Whatever the truth of the relationship between the Bureau and its former agents, the publication of *Red Channels* marked a turning point in the anticommunist campaign against progressives in broadcasting. Although the

American Business Consultants denied that they were in the blacklisting business, claiming instead that communists were discriminating against them on political grounds, the FBI knew that the American Business Consultants were creating a blacklist. "The book 'Red Channels,'" an FBI report concluded, "is very controversial as it is a blacklisting of persons with leftist backgrounds in the entertainment field."[88] Publicly, and despite the additional fact that the Bureau knew *CounterAttack* and *Red Channels* were publishing false information, the Bureau eagerly capitalized on the "facts" included in both texts. However unethical and illegal the American Business Consultants' behaviors may have been, the organization was very useful indeed to J. Edgar Hoover.

With the blacklist appearing to have the full approval of the FBI, television networks, advertisers, and sponsors capitulated to its terms. Worried about angering Hoover, understanding themselves as vulnerable to the damage that anti-communist campaigns backed by one of the most powerful men in the country could inflict, sponsors chose to fire people whose names had been touched by the blacklist.[89] With the blacklist thus institutionalized, people in the industry quickly fell into line. By 1951, Ellis had turned informant himself, writing to the FBI that "the producer of the Bob Hope show had signed a contract with Judy Holliday but that Liggett & Myers is taking a firm stand that they do not want her on their program even though she issued a statement denying that she had ever been a member of the Communist Party." In a move no doubt intended to mollify the Bureau and to affirm his commitment to the anti-communist cause, Ellis told the Bureau that he had "taken this stand on the basis of a recent House Committee report linking her with the Peace Crusade program."[90]

Networks, advertisers, and sponsors knew how dangerous it was to criticize the FBI, Hoover having proved more than willing to use the resources at his disposal to retaliate against his critics and ruin reputations and lives. For their part, the men who created *Red Channels* understood that once progressives had been linked to communism, however specious the charges or however far into the past that association stretched, the damage would prove difficult to undo. After Muir was listed in *Red Channels*, for example, one advertising executive remarked that he just could not "sell her. At the agencies they say all people will remember is that she's been in some kind of trouble and the trouble had something to do with communism. That's enough."[91] As another television executive put it, a performer who had been charged with communism was like "a bruised apple ... the brown spot remains."[92] At the outset of the Cold War, networks felt they could ill-afford to protect damaged goods.

The industry also needed to conceal the extent to which their fear of powerful anti-communists in government was guiding their decisions.

They knew that the blacklist targeted individuals as a means to control the stories the new medium of television would tell, but they had to generate a plausible scenario to account for their concessions to a private anti-communist group like the American Business Consultants without revealing Hoover's reach into media industries. To do so, they invoked the specter of pitchfork-wielding audiences enraged by the presence of progressives on the new medium, and the damage these audiences could inflict on their businesses.

Consequently, the networks blamed their concessions to anti-communism on audiences, even as they knew no populist backlash against humanitarian themes was imminent. When Wicker appeared on an ABC show from 1953 to 1954, the network received only one letter of protest.[93] Musicians who performed in Europe and the United States found their popularity—and their bookings—outside American mass media industries largely unaffected. In some cases, they even continued, like Hazel Scott, to appear sporadically on television variety shows like *Cavalcade of Stars*.

General Foods said they had fired Muir in response to protests by angry anti-communist consumers, even though the company knew the American Business Consultants' Theodore Kirkpatrick orchestrated the telephone calls that got Muir fired.[94] When General Foods commissioned a survey in 1952 to assess the impact of the Muir case, 40 percent of those surveyed had never heard of the incident. Of those who had heard of Muir's firing, less than 3 percent could link General Foods or the product involved (Jell-O) to Muir's name. When surveyors followed up with sales offices across the country to ask how "the Muir publicity affected our sales" the answer they repeatedly received was, "Muir? Who's Muir?"[95]

By the end of 1950, the elimination of Lee, Muir, Scott, and Wicker showed that progressives were not going to be able to mount significant opposition to anti-communism in television. CBS was forced to go even further in demonstrating their submission to the anti-communist agenda. In addition to the "loyalty questionnaire which is the same as that signed by Federal Civil Service employees" that CBS implemented in December 1950, the network hired its own former FBI Special Agent (Alfred Berry) to screen employees.[96] Berry provided the "clearance" necessary to convince anti-communists the network's efforts to cleanse the airwaves of communists and fellow-travelers were sincere and not merely 'taffy' meant to placate the Bureau.[97] Berry's unmarked office on the eighth floor came to be known as "CBS's spook department," where networks sent employees suspected of being reds to visit a mysterious "former FBI guy."[98] Advertising agencies soon followed suit. As Meyers observes, by 1954, advertising agency J. Walter Thompson compiled a

"Master List" of over 1,000 names to be checked before individuals would be hired for any of Thompson's programs.[99]

Although the blacklist was unprofitable and illegal—an insidious violation of progressives' constitutional rights—none of the first four targets of *Red Channels* pursued legal action. Actress Pert Kelton, her husband Ralph Bell, and Selena Royle—all listed in *Red Channels*—unsuccessfully sued the American Business Consultants for more than 2 million dollars for libel.[100] Writer Joe Julian sued *Red Channels* as well, but the suit was dismissed by notorious anti-communist judge Irving Saypol in 1956. Only radio personality and AFTRA member John Henry Faulk proved successful. In 1957, he sued anti-communists Vincent J. Hartnett (then working as a "talent consultant," based on his association with *Red Channels*) and Laurence Johnson of AWARE, Inc. for libel in the only victory progressives won over the television blacklist (awarding Faulk what was then the largest libel settlement in history).[101]

But Faulk's suit, filed in 1957, dragged on until 1962, mainly through the stalling tactics of AWARE's lawyer, anti-communist attorney Roy Cohn, a man who later schooled reality show host and U.S. President Donald Trump in the finer points of G-Man masculinity. Lawsuits merely drew people even deeper into the mud of anti-communist publicity, solidifying the connection between their names and un-American activities. As journalist Oliver Pilat put it in an article from 1953, lawsuits constituted "A special category of 'slow death' " for those who were blacklisted: "It takes years for such suits to reach trial, and meanwhile the noose tightens from month to month around the neck of the person seeking vindication in the courts."[102]

By 1952, blacklist critic John Cogley observed, "blacklisting was generally accepted in the industry. The frantic days of the Sweets case, the headlines of the Muir affair, the editorials written about Ireene Wicker were a thing of the past. The industry's solution to the problem was firmly institutionalized: don't hire controversial performers and you won't have to fire them."[103] In courtrooms and courts of public opinion alike, those who were blacklisted found little justice.

❖ ❖ ❖

In many fields of American life people who have aided Stalin by supporting his US fronts are coddled and publicized. The radio and moving pictures are used to spread Communist propaganda. Fellow travelers are defended and appeased.

CounterAttack[104]

Philip Loeb died of a sickness called "the blacklist." So did Mady Christians and John Garfield and other well-loved members of the theatre calling. The direst and obvious effects of this disease, the blacking out of employment in the entertainment industries, are well-known. But this is not the whole of it, nor in Phil's case, I think, the worst of it. He was submerged by a wave of fear and mistrust which swept most all of us. His motives and public actions were rendered suspect. Even in Equity, which he had so belligerently and passionately served, he was besmirched and maligned.

Margaret Webster (writer, director, producer)[105]

For the Broadcast 41, the blacklist closed doors to opportunities, ended most of their careers, and, in some cases, contributed to early deaths. As we have seen, being listed in *Red Channels* intensified already ongoing harassment and surveillance by the Bureau. At least seven of the Broadcast 41 were placed on the Bureau's Security Index.[106] In the wake of *Red Channels*, for example, the Bureau ramped up its existing investigation of Dorothy Parker in order to determine whether this "queen of the communists" should remain on the Security Index.[107]

While the FBI had been monitoring the activities of a handful of the Broadcast 41 for years, for most of them being listed in *Red Channels* brought them, for the first time, to the attention of the Bureau, facilitating the Cold War security state's intrusion into their lives. Louise Fitch, Judy Holliday, Lena Horne, Jean Muir, and many others had no FBI files until after they were listed in *Red Channels*, a listing the Bureau used as rationale for initiating investigations. The effects of Bureau surveillance were substantial. Years later, the indomitable Madeline Lee told a reporter, "You have no idea of the impact on personal lives, on families. Divorces, suicides, illnesses, heart attacks."[108] Lee had in mind the effects of anti-communist bullying on actress Mady Christians. In the fall of 1951, the FBI ramped up their surveillance of Christians in order to extract additional names and information about communist activities in theater, interviewing her twice at her home, where they questioned her political allegiance to the United States. Christians died after suffering a stroke in late October that her friends attributed to constant worries about employment, exacerbated by the FBI's aggressive pursuit of her.[109]

The toxic effects of the blacklist extended to other members of the Broadcast 41. Depressed and out of work, Jean Muir struggled with alcoholism throughout the 1950s. Hazel Scott suffered a nervous breakdown in 1951 and again in 1957.[110] For Muir and Scott, the blacklist combined with their husbands' infidelities in devastating ways. They both divorced their husbands in 1960. Muir went on to play a handful of roles on television and stage in the early 1960s, before pursuing a career teaching drama at Loyola Marymount, the University of New Mexico at Albuquerque, the University of North Carolina at Charlotte, and the University of Missouri, and, finally, at a more permanent teaching position at Stephens College.

Anti-communist retaliation against African Americans was deeply entrenched in media industries; its intent, as we have seen, was to halt the progress of civil rights in political, cultural, and economic life. In media industries, those who challenged the industry's racism became lightning rods for controversy. Shirley Graham lost jobs in theater and government because of anti-communist attacks on the Federal Theatre Project and the YWCA. *Red Channels* cut short her burgeoning career as a novelist, resulting in demands "that my books be withdrawn from the schools and libraries" of Scarsdale, New York.[111] Other calls to ban Graham's books soon followed—from upstate New York, a hotbed of anti-communist activism, as well as Wheeling, West Virginia, where Joseph McCarthy had made his infamous speech about communist infiltration of the U.S. government just six months before *Red Channels* was published.

Suddenly, publicity appearances for Graham's award-winning novel *Your Most Humble Servant* were cancelled with no explanation, never to be rescheduled.[112] The manuscript Graham had completed in the late 1940s—about the life of early American journalist Anne Newport Royall (another repressed figure in American history)—was rejected by multiple publishers. As Graham told a lawyer investigating the blacklist, "*No publisher has criticized the manuscript as a piece of writing.* This we could understand and accept. Novels are always worked on after being accepted by some publisher. But these refusals have each time been vague and in certain cases *obviously reluctant*."[113]

The FBI's harassment campaign against Shirley Graham and her husband intensified during the 1950s, a collaboration that included the Immigration and Naturalization Service (INS), and the State Department. Du Bois was listed in the Security Index. Shirley Graham's son David was denied a passport, and Graham later received a subpoena from the HUAC signed by Joseph McCarthy for her to appear on July 15, 1953.[114] To heighten fear and paranoia, the FBI cultivated the couple's friends and employees as potential confidential informants. Some, like Harry Belafonte, refused to cooperate. According to FBI records, many other friends and employees did. Unemployable, their movements and activities scrutinized by the FBI, their mail constantly tampered with, suspicious of even those close to them, and with the elderly Du Bois in failing health, they moved to Ghana in 1961 after Du Bois was finally issued a passport.

Other traumas inflicted by the blacklist remained hidden within the files of the FBI. Classical pianist Ray Lev, for example, was not a subject of Bureau investigation until after her name appeared in the pages of *Red Channels*. The FBI's subsequent surveillance (mainly preoccupied with Lev's support for the American Committee for the Foreign Born) landed Lev on the Bureau's Security Index. Around the time the FBI started monitoring her movements, performances began to dry up. The FBI worked with the State Department to prevent Lev from traveling to Europe, where she could still find work. Lev turned to teaching to eke out a living, while the FBI continued to spy on her, eventually compiling a file that amounted to over 400 pages of information about her life and activities. Lev was finally removed from the Security Index in 1968. The last entry in her FBI file cryptically reported her suicide: she had been found dead in her New York City hotel room, the agent wrote, "by means of asphyxia by smothering with plastic bag over her head."[115]

For those who survived, the pain of the blacklist era persisted for decades. In 1997, nearly fifty years after the publication of *Red Channels*, blacklisted writer Abraham Polonsky shared the stage at then-Museum of Television and Radio with blacklisted writer Joan LaCour Scott, widow of the Hollywood Ten's Adrian Scott. In response to a discussion about Walter Bernstein's humorous treatment of the blacklist in the film *The Front* (1976), Scott said, "It wasn't funny. Lives were broken. You know, hideous stuff.... We lived in almost perpetual fear." At the end of the broadcast, Polonsky reached across to clasp Scott's hand in his own. "And I am very sorry about your husband, who was a sweet friend of mine." "That was really terrible," he told her. "You have a right to be angry at the others."[116]

The impact of the blacklist was everything anti-communists had hoped for. In the new industry of television, fear of being linked to those considered controversial and thus ideologically impure changed the industry. The events of the early 1950s communicated a clear message to those who continued to work in television, a message that would be taught to those who entered it in the years to come: avoid even casual references to themes, ideas, and images that might be construed as controversial by anti-communists. If performers who had little control over content could be so easily ruined, writers and producers were left to imagine what would happen to those who wrote content celebrating black and immigrant lives; or series that grappled with the contradictions women experienced between work and family; or raised any of a range of liberal to left-leaning issues anti-communists had decided were off limits.

Consequently, the blacklist taught those who wished to continue working in television to self-censor content that might raise anti-communist hackles.

When writer Rod Serling was working on a script based on the lynching of teenager Emmett Till, he understood that a black victim would not be acceptable to sponsors. He "dropped the idea of a Negro victim and changed it to an old pawnbroker." But this change was not enough: "The southern location had to be changed. An unspecified location was not good enough; it had to be New England."[117] In a similar incident, writer Reginald Rose was told the black family in his *Thunder on Sycamore Street*, a drama based on the real-life attempts of a black family to move into suburban Cicero, Illinois, "Would have to be changed to 'something else.' A Negro as beleaguered protagonist of a television drama was declared unthinkable. It would, they said, appall southern viewers."[118] Of the impact of the blacklist on Hollywood, one studio executive observed that film was experiencing a new sort of self-censorship. "It's automatic, like shifting gears," a writer told him. He now "read scripts through the eyes of the D.A.R. ... Why, I suddenly find myself beating my breast and proclaiming my patriotism and exclaiming that I love my wife and kids, of which I have four, with a fifth on the way. I'm all loused up. I'm scared to death, and nobody can tell me it isn't because I'm afraid of being investigated."[119]

In television, in a last-ditch attempt to save *The Goldbergs* from the axe, Gertrude Berg finally agreed to a move she had been resisting for years: she moved the Goldbergs to a suburban enclave called "Haverville," where Molly became an outcast, ashamed about her size and her working-class ways.[120] In an episode that aired shortly before the television series was cancelled, Molly visits a "fat farm" in order to lose weight. In one of the saddest moments in sitcom history, the episode concludes with a shot of the previously loquacious Molly standing alone in her suburban kitchen, furtively shoveling spaghetti into her mouth from a pot on the stove.

Writers who survived the purge either quickly internalized the need to avoid subjects that might be considered "controversial" or quietly left an industry that was becoming ever more hostile to progressive ideas. In an interview published nearly twenty years after the events of 1950, Lena Horne avoided naming the problem, instead saying, "Sure, I'm politically aware, but you know what happens. They find something wrong about you, they make a scandal and you're finished."[121] The need to avoid "controversy"—that amorphous, "something wrong" shorthand for content anti-communists found politically distasteful—made progressive depictions of race and immigration too Red-hot for networks to handle. With content critical of segregation, or sympathetic to the struggles of immigrants ineluctably linked to communist influence, on one hand, and, on the other, Southern-style white supremacy too evocative of Nazi white supremacy for a postwar prime time priding itself on democracy, the solution was to avoid featuring African Americans or immigrants on television at all. Representations of American cultural life were thus limited to the most bland, homogeneous ones possible, as producers and writers trod on eggshells in order to avoid even a whisper of controversy. The industry, as historian Ellen Schrecker puts it, became "so timid that ... virtually everything from pregnancy to freedom of religion is considered a controversial subject, leaving almost nothing except homicide as a fit topic to enter our houses."[122]

More than anything else, anti-communists wanted to ensure their perspectives would flourish, unchallenged by criticism, questions, or alternative points of view. The now familiar conservative refrain about "liberal media" had its origins in the blacklist, as anti-communists attacked the politics of progressives, casting them as threats for attending meetings where, according to actress Louise Fitch, they discussed "how to rid radio programs of racial caricatures—the tightwad Scotchman, the razor-toting Negro, the Italian gangster, etc."[123] Maintaining that progressives were diabolical communist masterminds, intent on nothing less than undoing America and all it stood for, anti-communists represented themselves as white cowboys in white hats, intent not on personal or ideological gain, but patriotic protection of the American family that was the foundation for their vision of the nation.

By the end of 1950, advertisers, networks, and sponsors had persuaded themselves to adopt rhetoric suggesting that suppression of progressive viewpoints was in the public interest. In December, CBS—the network long reviled by the FBI as a hotbed of communist organizing—adopted a stringent loyalty act that required each of their employees to answer the infamous question "Are you now, or have you ever been, a member of the Communist party, U.S.A., or any Communist organization?" They had done so, according to executive vice president Joseph Ream, "to make certain that Columbia enjoyed the continuing confidence of both radio listeners and television viewers."[124] Despite anti-communists' claims that their actions were in the country's best interests and, contradictorily, that they were merely doing the public's bidding, people in the industry knew these claims were not true.

What happened to the Broadcast 41 and other progressives in the wake of the blacklist shows that women—and men—were driven from television in the 1950s not because of some populist revolt, as anti-communists argued, but because of concerted efforts by the anti-communist right to establish control over television. Far from being traitors to their country, those who were blacklisted had worked diligently on behalf of civil rights and economic justice. Opposed to anti-communist racism and misogyny, they wanted to ensure that television included representations of the heterogeneity they considered the unique strength of the country they loved. Progressives in broadcasting hoped to use television to convey the message that—as Gertrude Berg put it—"to be different ... wasn't such a sin."[125] As Stefan Kanfer observed in his chronicle of the blacklist, writers like Berg claimed for themselves something "the right could not—abiding humanity and tolerance."[126]

Anti-communists, in contrast, insisted on conformance to their rigid norms of race, gender, nation, and sexuality. To be different in the eyes of the American Business Consultants and the Bureau alike was a sin against American identity. The loathing they directed at those who disagreed with them was violent and unshakeable. Anti-communist journalist Westbrook Pegler (notorious for his invectives against Eleanor Roosevelt), for example, in a moment of rare self-reflection, observed, "My hates [have] always occupied my mind much more actively than my friendships."[127] When anti-communists attacked actress Lucille Ball in 1953, Pegler's invective against communists like her reveals much about the racialized sentiments that motivated anti-communists: "I hate Communists. I wish it were possible to round up all those who are reasonably known to be Communists, including all who have invoked the 5th Amendment and put them into concentration camps as austere as the Arizona state prison, or the Louisiana state horror camp at Angola, where a lot of wretches cut their heel tendons to disable themselves for work and advertise their condition to the outside world."[128]

Voices like Pegler's were by no means the most extreme of this intolerant choir—he was, after all, a syndicated newspaper columnist. Joined as Pegler's voice was with the American Business Consultants, the HUAC, the FBI, the American Legion, and other anti-communist forces, this chorus created an intensely hostile climate in the broadcast industry, one in which discrimination based on sex, race, national origin, and sexuality thrived.

This climate reduced the memory of the events that culminated in the blacklist to a mere footnote to television history, if these events were mentioned at all. Even more than a decade after the publication of *Red Channels*, the industry was reluctant to permit discussions of the blacklist on television. When Jean Muir was interviewed on television in 1968, for example, the names of the advertisers, sponsor, and network responsible for firing her were "blooped" out of her account.[129]

By first eliminating those likely to have perspectives incompatible with the authoritarianism of anti-communism, and then ensuring that progressive content would be censored as being insubordinate and politically pink (if not thoroughly red), anti-communists won what turned out to be the unprecedented ability to control the stories the powerful new medium of television would tell about American identity. Had they not, the content of television might have looked very different. Indeed, the medium might have become a source of creativity, inspiration, and inclusion based on representing a variety of perspectives decades before themes and topics considered "controversial" by anti-communists began to resurface in the "quality" television of the final years of the twentieth century. The presence of women, people of color, immigrants, and progressive writers might also have made media industries—over the years it would have taken for change to occur—less horrible places for women and people of color to work. The work the Broadcast 41 had done, and dreamt of doing, before the blacklist ended those hopes, the types of stories that might have emerged from that work, and the climate they might have ushered in, are the subjects of the next chapter.

Chapter 6

Red *Lassie*: A Counterfactual History of Television

The anti-Communist crusade and the blacklist that it imposed ended Hollywood's brief flirtation with the real world and ensured that the fledgling television industry would never begin one.

Ellen Schrecker (historian)[1]

In her talk [Anne Revere] she said that ... in Hollywood there is a group of organized writers, artists, musicians, actors and actresses and which group is working toward a better world, a modern world for tomorrow, but that the result of their efforts has branded them as disloyal. She said that she and all of the ten people from Hollywood who went to Washington are American citizens but are endangered.

Rodney Stewart (FBI Agent, Los Angeles)[2]

"The year of the melting pot" was the catchphrase that American magazine *TV Guide* used to describe the 1960 fall prime-time television line-up. Although media critics like Jean Muir and Fredi Washington thought that roles for more mature actresses were still in short supply, there was no denying that prime-time television had never been so widely representative of the experiences of the many people who lived in the U.S. In response to thousands of fan letters from television viewers, Molly Goldberg was on the air and back in school, finishing a law degree so that she could defend the rights of refugees and the foreign-born. New head of the CBS documentary unit, Shirley Graham, had produced a line-up of investigative segments with a focus on civil rights cold cases. The first episode focused on the unsolved murder of teenager Emmet Till by white supremacists. Lena Horne was starring in her own variety show, with network NBC promising that she would bring her elegant brand of style and feminist humor to the small screen. Fredi Washington headlined in a drama written by Vera Caspary based on the life of investigative journalist and anti-lynching activist Ida Wells Barnett. And the producers of the popular Western *Bonanza* announced plans for a spin-off in which Berkeley-educated actor Victor Sen Yung (who played cook Hop Sing on the series) fought anti-Chinese exclusion laws to reunite with his physician wife and children.

Of course, *TV Guide* never used such a catchphrase. And no such programs appeared on American television, the people who might have written, produced, or performed in them having been fired or silenced by the blacklist. Instead, in the years between 1949 and 1952, anti-communists used the blacklist to determine which stories would be told on television and other media and, subsequently, in schools, workplaces, and homes for years to come. This unprecedented ability, only partly realized with radio, gave them the power to determine whose experiences of America would be visible, validated, and valorized, and whose would be belittled or redacted.

Instead of these imaginary programs, the blacklist transformed Lena Horne's democratic desire for "the Negro to be portrayed as a normal person ... as a worker at a union meeting, as a voter at the polls, as a civil service worker or an elected official" into a dangerous form of subversion.[3] Because she refused to downplay her Jewishness, Judy Holliday was typecast in ways that were "patently false and vaguely insulting." Biographer Gary Carey reflected that there was something unsettlingly "distasteful about watching Judy play women who were always so much cruder and less intelligent than herself."[4] Even those who successfully resisted stereotyping found, like Lena Horne, that "they didn't make me into a maid. But they didn't make me into anything else either. I became a butterfly pinned to a column singing away in Movieland."[5] By rendering progressive perspectives on America disgraceful and un-American, anti-communists built racism and misogyny into the storytelling machinery of the industry. It also built these into the industry's workplace practices and cultures, the treatment of women and people of color on screen, as we have seen, directly reflecting how the men who ran the industry thought about women and people of color and justified continued discrimination.

Literary scholar Courtney Thorsson says of a later era of black feminist literary critics that they were inspired by the knowledge that they were "unearthing, creating, and practicing an African American archive" that had been hitherto concealed from view.[6] The account of progressive women's oppositional work in and around the new medium of television is a first step in excavating a similar archive. Viewed from the perspective of this archive of oppositional work, located across unexpected places and sources, my fictional account of 1960s television shows is not as farfetched as it might initially appear. Many of the Broadcast 41 devoted their professional lives to narrating and performing stories about American experiences that defied the G-Man's formula, leaving evidence of these efforts before, during, and after the blacklist. However much their work may have been redacted from television history and cultural memory, the Broadcast 41 were far more than casualties of the blacklist. By actively opposing the views of anti-communists, they were powerful precursors of ideas and perspectives that would not appear on television with any regularity until the turn of the twenty-first century.

This chapter is only the beginning of a larger, ongoing effort to recover the work that the forty-one women listed in *Red Channels*, and others like them, were prevented from contributing to the new medium of television. This is no speculative history. It exists in various places for those seeking to uncover it. The novels and other published work of the Broadcast 41 are concrete evidence of the themes and ideas they were exploring. The criticism that they published in newspapers and magazines highlights their opposition to the mainstream of media production. Some left the U.S. and worked in other, less restrictive national media industries, leaving additional traces of oppositional work. Performers continued to work in theater, where they challenged writers to create more complex portrayals of those who were marginalized within mainstream cultures and gave performances that moved audiences to listen and respect these. The thousands of fan letters written to people like the Broadcast 41 prove that audiences valued programming appealing to intellect and understanding rather than white defensiveness and rage. The archived papers of the Broadcast 41 provide other clues about work that was prevented from appearing. And generations of scholars—most of them women, many of them women of color—have written theses and dissertations on these women that explore in detail many of the themes and ideas this book could only hint at.[7]

What the Broadcast 41 had made, what they were making when the blacklist occurred, and what they only dreamed of making as reflected in materials like the above add up to a counterfactual history of television, based on a massive alternative archive, a dreamscape of the powerful anti-racist, proto-feminist voices and content that existed before the G-Man's fantasies became television's reality. This history points to the evolution of ideas that might have taken place in television long years ago, if it had continued to respond to the work of progressive women and people of color and their powerful criticisms of media industries' treatment of them, on-screen and off. This archive of resistance and opposition offers new ways of thinking about audiences as well, minus the power of anti-communists to render women, people of color, and immigrants either unworthy of the industry's respect or beneath its vision.

❖ ❖ ❖

I decided many years ago to invent myself. I had obviously been invented by someone else—by a whole society—and I didn't like their invention.

Maya Angelou (poet, memoirist, civil rights activist)[8]

She did not go along with the crowd. Not because she was a Negro. She was not; she was White. Not because she was an Indian, but because a Southern White woman said that slavery was a cancer eating into our national life, and that it will in the end destroy us if we do not wipe it out; because she talked about the churches who sent missionaries to Africa and yet held slaves in their own backyard ... that woman's name has been wiped out of history!

Shirley Graham (musician, writer, civil rights activist)[9]

Throughout a life and career tragically cut short by the blacklist, actor Canada Lee powerfully called for a new set of storytelling practices, one that might center the experiences of African Americans. Where, he asked,

> is the story of our lives in terms of the ghetto slums in which we must live? Where is the story of our lives in terms of the fact that in walking from our houses to the corner store we may be attacked and beaten? Where is the story of our lives in terms of the jobs not available, the very years of life guaranteed to a white man which are denied to us? Where is the story of how a Negro baby born at the same time in the same city as a white baby can be expected to die 10 years sooner? Where is the story of the lives of our people? Who would know us if he had to know us by listening to *Amos 'n' Andy*, to *Beulah*, to *Rochester*, to the minstrel show?[10]

Although largely excluded from making mass-produced popular culture like film and television, African American writers and performers like Canada Lee, Shirley Graham, Lena Horne, Paul Robeson, Hazel Scott, and Fredi Washington created popular culture that made visible the long history of struggles against white supremacy.

As historian Milly Barranger has documented, in the years before the blacklist, New York City theater generated attention to race and class that would be prevented from energizing and transforming television in the 1950s and 1960s. Fredi Washington's career took off with a role in one of the first Broadway shows to be written and directed by African Americans, *Shuffle Along* (1921); she co-starred with Ethel Waters in *Mamba's Daughters*; she shared the billing with Bill Robinson in *One Mile from Heaven*; and she starred in *Emperor Jones* with Paul Robeson.

Although many of these plays remain boxed into what Horne criticized as "cliché presentations of Negro life ... folksy things," they offered an improvement over the minstrelsy of vaudeville and the stereotypes of Hollywood.[11] In 1943, Margaret Webster went a step further, directing a production of *Othello* with Paul Robeson in the title role, José Ferrer as Iago, and Uta Hagen as Desdemona (all of whom would be listed along with Webster in *Red Channels* less than a decade later). In the mid-1940s, Fredi Washington starred in a remarkable (if very short-lived) black-cast production of Aristophanes' *Lysistrata,* some sixty years before filmmaker Spike Lee's retelling of that story in his 2015 film, *Chi-Raq.*[12] In 1947, Washington, Robeson, Webster, and other progressives helped form the Committee on the Negro in the Arts, whose stated objectives, as literary scholar Kathlene McDonald notes, were to eradicate racial stereotyping and generate employment for African Americans in the arts.[13]

In the decades before the postwar rise of television, Shirley Graham explored experiences that had been suppressed from American history. Working first in music and theater, as a musician, playwright, critic, and later novelist, Graham told stories to mainstream audiences from a perspective distinctly her own. Her first major work—the opera *Tom-Tom: An Epic of Music and the Negro* (1932)—grew out of her childhood experiences watching pageants like W.E.B. Du Bois' 1913 *The Star of Ethiopia* celebrating the history of black people in America.[14] The first opera written by a black woman, *Tom-Tom* honored and expanded on the work of a previous generation of African American cultural producers, narrating the historical arc of a community, from its kidnapping by slavers through a revolution set against the backdrop of 1920s Harlem.

Less than a decade later, Graham was the first woman to direct one of the Federal Theatre Program Negro Units, where she took the controversial step of adapting white supremacist popular culture for anti-racist purposes. In 1938, Graham produced a reimagining of Helen Bannerman's *The Story of Little Black Sambo.* Bannerman's story about a Tamil child had been popular across regional and local theater in the U.S., the white supremacy of the South Indian Sambo finding a racist counterpart in the minstrelsy of American popular culture.[15] Recognizing that the popularity of *Little Black Sambo* would draw people to theaters, Graham attempted to reinterpret the narrative so that it focused on the inventiveness and creativity of African culture rather than the stereotypes characteristic of minstrelsy.

Where other Federal Theatre Project productions of *Little Black Sambo* in places like Cincinnati, Ohio; Miami, Florida; and Newark, New Jersey featured white actors in blackface or puppets with the exaggerated racist features characteristic of minstrelsy, Graham's Pan-African version cast black actors, costumed them in African attire, and created dialogue written in lyric prose rather than dialect.[16] She portrayed the child as a trickster figure—intelligent, resourceful, and resilient. Although it is difficult to know what audiences made of the performance, the popularity of the production exposed theatergoers to radically different images and ideas about race. Anti-communists were threatened enough by anti-racist efforts like this that they shut down the Federal Theatre Project in 1939.

In the 1940s, Graham turned to writing novels for young people about racism and resistance, the achievements of women, and histories about the struggles of immigrants and poor people. Like her Federal Theatre Project productions, her novels about abolitionist Frederick Douglass; almanac writer, surveyor, mathematician, and farmer Benjamin Banneker; city of Chicago founder Jean-Baptiste Pointe de Sable; and poet Phillis Wheatley participated in a much larger conversation among those who wished to present "the case of the Negro in the making of American history," as Graham described it.[17] Her novels worked against traditions that, as feminist critic Barbara Smith put it decades later, considered the historical and cultural contributions of black people as "beneath consideration, invisible, unknown" to "white and/or male consciousness."[18] Graham herself participated in this suppressed tradition of writers and critics who wrote about African American historical figures because, like her, they "felt that Negroes were misunderstood, and were not known, and were outside of history." In 1948, CBS broadcast a teleplay of Shirley Graham's novel *The Story of Phillis Wheatley*, evidence of the growing popularity of her work.

Inspired by the work of black progressives, other progressive women joined the project of chronicling African Americans' contributions to American history and their struggles against white supremacy. Blacklisted dancer and choreographer Helen Tamiris, considered one of the founders of modern dance, believed that "no artist can achieve full maturity unless he recognizes his role as a citizen, taking responsibility, not only to think, but to act." She put her beliefs into practice in her work with the Federal Theatre Project in New York City.[19] In 1937, she created "How Long, Brethren?" a dance that performed African American protest songs in order to use those traditions to issue "a call for direct action" in the present.[20] While the work of white women like Tamiris was by no means free of the limitations of their own racialized points of view, they were significant challenges to white supremacist popular culture.

Rather than appropriating black culture, Dorothy Parker turned critical eyes on the ugliness and hypocrisy of white supremacy in her short story "Arrangement in Black and White." In it, Parker offered a spare and trenchant critique of gendered white supremacy, recounting the dinner party interactions of a white "woman with the pink velvet poppies twined round the assorted gold of her hair," a woman who visually embodies all the time-honored traits of white femininity. She asks her host to introduce her to the party's guest of honor, a black singer named Walter Williams. This icon of white femininity voices the racism of her absent husband, who, she confides to her host, is "really awfully fond of colored people.... as long as they keep their place." The story concludes as the woman observes that she and her husband will share a laugh about the fact that she addressed Williams as "mister" in their brief exchange of words, demonstrating that this awful fondness was merely a cover for the foulest kind of racism.[21]

In the 1930s and 1940s, progressive-era women also made popular culture that combatted anti-immigrant and anti-Semitic prejudices (Figure 6.1). Gertrude Berg, who earned a place on the gray list because of her defense of blacklisted co-star Philip Loeb, wrote about the worsening situation

Figure 6.1 Gertrude Berg
Source: Permission of Getty Images

of European Jews in the 1930s, at a time when both film and broadcasting were loath to do so.[22] *The Goldbergs* showcased Berg's desire to show Jews "as they really are," trying to chart a course between "the broken dialect and smutty wise-cracks of the Jewish comedians" and "the gushing, sugar-coated sentimentalities of many of the 'good-willers.' "[23]

For more than twenty years, *The Goldbergs* presented a very different understanding of what it meant to be American from the anti-communists who later put an end to *The Goldbergs*' long broadcast run. Berg said that the sitcom was based on "all the immigrant families I knew in New York City."[24] In contrast to stereotypical representations of Jewish people in popular culture, Berg showed immigrant family life in richer complexity. Judging from the volume of fan mail the program received, *The Goldbergs* resonated with other immigrant groups, capturing the generational tensions between first-generation Americans and their assimilationist children, who often had to teach parents "how to become Americans."[25]

Berg's version of Americanism celebrated a New Deal ethos of solidarity and mutual support. In this and other regards, her distinctly working-class and ethnic sense of community could not have been more dissimilar from that of anti-communists like Ayn Rand, who exhorted people instead to "Remember that all the great thinkers, artists, scientists were single, individual, independent men who stood alone, and discovered new directions of achievement—alone."[26] In contrast to the dog-eat-dog individualism of anti-communists like Rand, when Molly's husband Jake complained about helping to subsidize their relatives' emigration to America, Molly chided him: "No matter vhat anybody is got, dey got trough de help of somebody else. By ourselves ve couldn't make notting. You know dat, Jake."[27]

The Broadcast 41 also told stories about experiences of gender that did not conform to the G-Man's formula for domesticity. Vera Caspary wrote novels, short stories, and screenplays about women who worked for their living and relished their reproductive and economic independence (Figure 6.2). Caspary's mysteries were celebrated for her use of multiple points of view to explore what one reviewer described as "realistic and moving portraits of young female wage earners."[28] Unlike Helen Gurley Brown's later portraits of young women workers pursuing well-off husbands so they could leave the workforce, or women who went to college to get what was described in 1950s America as an "MRS degree" (meaning they were in college to land an upwardly mobile spouse), Caspary's girls pursued work as a means to independence. As we have seen, Caspary struggled mightily against the objections of executives and directors in her efforts to represent these female wage earners with dignity and respect.[29]

Figure 6.2 Vera Caspary
Source: Permission of the Wisconsin Historical Society, Madison, WI

Caspary's novels and screen plays also criticized the genre of romance and its reliance on an economic system that caused women to invest in miserable and sometimes lethal relationships with men. In *Laura* (1943), Caspary held romance accountable for women's ruin. Laura had been trapped by "the dream [that] still held her, the hero she could love forever immaturely."[30] Caspary's narrator in *Thelma* (1952) listens unhappily to the common sense of her era, as her childhood friend advises her, "You intelligent girls can have your careers, she told me one day and her voice made of intelligence a disability, 'but for me it's enough to be a wife.' "[31] Throughout her career, Caspary resisted the sexist conventions of romance. "You'll be happy to know," she wrote in 1962 to her editor at Dell Publishing, that her manuscript "won't be called *Happily Ever After*."[32]

Progressive women's work in radio in the 1930s and 1940s offers additional clues to the narratives about gender that they might have contributed to television. Naturally, their own shifting experiences as women were sources of inspiration. Berg's first series, *Effie and Laura* (1927), drew on themes related to the changing roles of white women in U.S. society, based on the lives of two female salesclerks from the Bronx, who discussed "everything from men to politics."[33] Reflecting ongoing conflicts between conservative industrial forces and the perspectives of women producers, *Effie and Laura* was cancelled by CBS after the first episode aired because network executives apparently disapproved when Laura observed, "marriages are never made in heaven."[34]

In the decades before the blacklist, women even made inroads into the male-dominated realm of radio news programming. Mary Margaret McBride moved from print journalism to radio in 1934, creating a long-running talk show that, as broadcast historian Donna Halper puts it, "was as much about interesting people in the news as it was about the domestic arts."[35] Where McBride worked in the more feminized domain of human interest, Lisa Sergio's WQXR program, *Lisa Sergio's Column of the Air* (1936–46), encroached on broadcast journalism, a profession almost wholly dominated by men. In it, Sergio used her own experiences of fascism to analyze its migration to South America, to criticize the support that neutral countries were providing fascists through trade, and to convey an international perspective on the war and its aftermath.[36]

Other women participated in this interwar groundswell of creativity in broadcasting through their work in soap operas, a genre G-Men considered frivolous and largely unworthy of their attention. Irna Phillips, who would later become known as the queen of the soaps, helped create some of the first radio programs that addressed female audiences, programs that were also preoccupied with the changing roles of white women, such as *Painted Dreams* (1930–43) and *Joyce Jordan, Girl Intern* (1938–52), the latter of which became *Joyce Jordan, MD* and featured the first female doctor on radio.[37] Writer Elaine Sterne Carrington created content that reflected new career and educational options for young women in the first half of the twentieth century, including popular serials like *Pepper Young's Family* and *Rosemary* (starring Broadcast 41 actress Betty Winkler).

On occasion, the successes of progressive theater productions persuaded Hollywood to take a chance on adapting content for film. In 1946, Ruth Gordon's husband, Garson Kanin, made his first foray into play writing with the surprise hit *Born Yesterday*. According to scholar Judith Smith, "Kanin wrote the part of Billie Dawn, the streetwise and brazen 'dumb blonde' mistress of a crooked junk dealer, for Jean Arthur, based, he commented retrospectively, 'on a stripper he once knew who read Karl Marx between shows.' "[38] Judy Holliday took over the role at the last minute and helped make the show a hit: it ran on Broadway for three years. The film version was released in 1950 to box office success and critical acclaim, despite attacks by anti-communists.

In addition to *Born Yesterday*, Garson Kanin co-wrote with Ruth Gordon a series of successful romantic comedies starring Spencer Tracy and Katherine Hepburn. These films reflected what happened when progressives wrote about gender, their scripts featuring white women on more equal footing with men, as lawyers in *Adam's Rib* (1949) and as athletes in *Pat and Mike* (1952).[39] Both films are in many ways witty and self-reflexive meditations on Gordon and Kanin's own exasperating professional relationship. In a scene in *Adam's Rib*, lawyer for the defense Amanda Bonner (played by Katherine Hepburn) encourages her witness (a female bodybuilder) to hoist prosecuting attorney and husband Adam Bonner above her head in a wry commentary on the physical supremacy of men. *Pat and Mike*'s Pat Pemberton (played by Hepburn), an athlete unable to compete in the presence of her domineering fiancé, finds reassurance and love in the shape of a man who supports her aspirations rather than feeling threatened by them.

These examples allude to original narratives about race, gender, class, and nation that would be glimpsed only sporadically on television in the years that followed the blacklist. The blacklist caused viewers to be treated to a far more lackluster diet of G-Man-approved fare in 1960 than the one imagined at the beginning of this chapter. Molly Goldberg would indeed go to college in 1961, but as "Mrs. G." and not an advocate for civil rights. Westerns like *The Rifleman, Maverick, The Lawman, Tales of Wells Fargo, The Texan* (its hero a Confederate captain), and *The Life and Legend of Wyatt Earp* emphasized the virtues of male autonomy and individualism. Although in 1965 *The Big Valley* featured Barbara Stanwyck as the tough and resilient matriarch of the Barkley Ranch, for the most part Westerns excluded women altogether. *Bonanza, The Rifleman,* and *The Lawman* showcased men whose wives or love interests had died or whose narratives did not feature women as recurring characters. Women were relegated to comedies like *The Adventures of Ozzie and Harriet, The Donna Reed Show, The Betty Hutton Show,* and *Father Knows Best* or soaps, while white men appeared as guardians of law and order in a world apparently populated mainly by them.

❖ ❖ ❖

PALADIN: Tell me, Sandy. What does it take to turn a young woman into an outlaw?

SANDY: Men.

Paladin blinks.

SANDY (continued): Men decide what women want—and what they need. But they never bother to ask a woman if she's happy with that.
PALADIN: I gather you weren't happy.
SANDY: Would you be? Staying home and doing the same dull things every day of your life? Everything that's interesting or exciting in this world is reserved for men.

Adrian and Joan LaCour Scott
(writers, scene cut from script of Have Gun, Will Travel)[40]

The Broadcast 41's perspectives were not as easily eliminated as female characters in television Westerns or pesky scenes that hinted at women's dissatisfaction with a world where everything that was interesting or exciting was reserved for men. Progressives who could afford to left the U.S. for work in Europe or Mexico, some were driven to the margins of television or other media industries in their quest for work, or to other professions altogether. The spectral traces of their presence in places outside prime-time television give us additional ideas about what television might have looked like in a parallel universe where networks stood up to anti-communist bullies and advertisers and sponsors supported programs on the basis of creativity and audience enthusiasm rather than conformity to a formulaic Americanism.

Blacklisted women like Ruth Gordon, Madeline Lee Gilford, Revere, Royle, Webster, and Winkler continued to work in theater because the stage remained "the last refuge for people who could no longer work in film or television or radio."[41] As *New York Times* theater critic Brooks Atkinson put it, "Broadway is not susceptible to domination by rational businessmen. Broadway showmanship is a local foible rather than a national exploit."[42] In 1950, actresses Marsha Hunt and Hilda Vaughn starred in Margaret Webster's production of George Bernard Shaw's *The Devil's Disciple.*[43] As late as 1959, Berg starred in *A Majority of One*, an interracial love story about a Japanese widower and a Brooklyn widow, for which she won a Tony Award for best actress. Although minus the exposure afforded by appearances in film and television, it remained "hard to get the few well-paying jobs in the New York theater," as Kate Mostel put it; a very few even managed to return to Hollywood in the late 1960s, like Ruth Gordon, who starred in *Rosemary's Baby* (1968) and *Harold and Maude* (1971).[44]

At the height of the blacklist some progressive women writers found work in Europe, such as Vera Caspary and Norma Barzman, wife of blacklisted journalist, screenwriter, and novelist Ben Barzman. The post-blacklist career of their colleague, producer Hannah Weinstein, provides a compelling

"General Johnson asked to see me. He said, 'Why are we sponsoring that commie show?' "[53]

Some blacklisted writers used pseudonyms or fronts (people who would be the front person for scripts written by blacklisted authors) to continue writing for television, mainly in work they completed in the medium's margins, in time slots and genres considered less valuable and culturally important, and thus less likely to attract the attention of anti-communists.[54] According to Adrian Scott, "when things were bad for me I did not, as most did, look for the best programs on the air—which everybody hoped to write for. I looked for the worst."[55] Progressives like Scott and his wife Joan left evidence of their perspectives not in what were considered the best programs on the air (those that ran during prime-time viewing hours before the advent of home recording technologies: 7–8 through 11 p.m.), but in programming deemed less valuable.

Science fiction writer Judith Merril later observed that for women writing fiction in the 1950s, science fiction was "virtually the only vehicle of dissent available to socially conscious authors working in a historical moment marked by political paranoia and cultural conservatism."[56] In television, children's programs and soap operas proved to be similar havens for women writers and performers affected by the blacklist. Soap opera writers Irna Phillips and Agnes Nixon had been telling progressive stories in the devalued regions of daytime television and soap operas well before the blacklist. Unlike the Broadcast 41, these women continued to work in soaps for decades to come. Like Gertrude Berg, Phillips created, wrote, and starred in episodes of her first program, *Painted Dreams*, a show that explored shifting gender roles in the context of intergenerational conflict. Phillips' protégée, Agnes Nixon, went on to write her own brand of distinctive storylines about class, race, ethnicity, and national identity. Doris Hursley (daughter of Milwaukee, Wisconsin's socialist mayor, Victor Berger), who along with her husband, Frank, created the soap opera *General Hospital*, was known for tackling the kind of controversial topics that attracted anti-communist attention in prime time. After the blacklist, women like Phillips, Nixon, and Hursley hired actresses who had been made otherwise unemployable by anti-communist campaigns against them. Anne Revere starred in *The Edge of Night* and *Search for Tomorrow*; Selena Royle in *As the World Turns*; Meg Mundy in *The Guiding Light*; and Louise Fitch in *Paradise Bay* and *General Hospital*.[57]

Like soaps, children's programs also hired progressive writers who could not find work in prime-time television. For blacklisted writers Joan and Adrian Scott, the children's show *Lassie* (1954–73) became the couple's most reliable source of income.[58] Wryly acknowledging the limitations of this work, Adrian Scott told a friend, "For several years Joan and I, individually, wrote programs for the LASSIE series. At one point we were considered the best LASSIE writers they had! Because, as Joan says, we are house broken and barked well."[59]

Nonetheless, as Joan Scott observed in her unpublished autobiography, they appreciated the show's emphasis on "humane, caring values—not the violence and shallowness characteristic of so many of the TV programs on the air."[60] And *Lassie*'s wagging tail concealed a rebellious streak. *Lassie* often referred to humanitarian work recognizable as progressive, like an episode where a priest adopted an orphaned boy whose martyred parents had worked with him in South America "to improve crop yield among peasants."[61] The show departed from the 1950s suburban ideal in significant ways, evoking the lost world of the New Deal rather than the shimmering consumerist settings of the 1950s. Originally, it featured a widowed mother, who lived with her elderly father on a farm. Over the years, *Lassie*'s families frequently refused to conform to the suburban norm, expanding to include a series of young adopted boys, forestry workers, and finally the inmates of a home for troubled children. In an early episode of the series, Lassie tried to prevent Timmy's mother Ruth from replacing their old icebox with a refrigerator because the dog feared that friendly iceman Mr. Cuppy would lose his job.[62] Although adoptive dad Paul Miller chided Lassie for being "a reactionary" because of her attachment to tradition, in this case (as in many others), Lassie's empathy was the lesson of the day.

Where Cold War programming used the non-human world to defend patriarchal nuclear families and the subjugation of the natural world, *Lassie* offered a different perspective, hinting at an incipient animal rights attitude. *Mutual of Omaha's Wild Kingdom* presented a vision of the non-human world where lions, crocodiles, and hippos were each in their turn cast as rulers and kings in a natural order of domination. But *Lassie* and *Daktari* (another children's program the Scotts wrote for) referenced a different natural order of things, one that echoed with the cadences of progressives' political vocabulary, refusing to see man's domination of the non-human world natural or just. Forestry rangers in an episode of *Lassie* eschewed the competitive language of Cold War representations of nature, instead commenting approvingly on eagles' collaborative approach to parenting:

RON: Papa does the hatching ...?

KEITH: In the case of eagles, it's Mama *and* Papa ... each taking their turn. A division of labor, so to speak.[63]

To the extent that scripted children's programming featured values like sharing, peace, and respect, it may have been because of writers like the Scotts, the ubiquitous Ruth and Rita Church (credited for writing several episodes of *Lassie* between 1958 and 1960), the Hursleys, and other progressives who wrote for shows like these, and whose perspectives remain to be excavated. Similarly, the evolution of ideas on soap operas—and the fact that soaps historically addressed controversial social ideas in many cases decades before other television genres did—suggest how people like the Broadcast 41 might have influenced the stories television told about American ways of life. Because of the blacklist ideas like theirs were relegated to the margins and, as Adrian Scott put it, "ideas, new, good, provocative, daring ideas, the very lifeblood of the industry have been denied to creators."[64] Writer Eileen Heckart poignantly expressed the frustration of having to write within the grooves of acceptability established by the blacklist. "Honey," she asked an executive, "can't you get me out of the kitchen? I'm so sick of making the cocoa for Mama and the eggs for Dad."[65]

❖ ❖ ❖

You will ask me one day how I came to write about this. The answer is for two years I took care of my son as both father <u>and</u> mother. I was nag, shrew, housekeeper, shopper, and unsuccessful writer. Prior to this I'd had the usual exposure of a progressive to the woman question. But it was all very unreal until I was forced by circumstances into the role of a woman in the house. My abstractions became concrete. From fellow traveler, I became hardcore militant associate of the movement. I came away with a healthy respect for what women are forced to endure in this society. I concluded that real equality as in every other movement toward equality will be won by the oppressed with very little help from the outside. I only hope when the revolution takes place and when the inevitable excesses follow that, as I am led to the guillotine, one woman will remember I wrote Ellie.

Adrian Scott (screenwriter and film producer)[66]

I felt you do not have to be white to be good. I've spent most of my life trying to prove that to people who thought otherwise. Yes, it was pointed out that I might be useful to the group by passing. But to pass, for economic or other advantages, would have meant that I swallowed, whole hog, the idea of Black inferiority. I did not think up this system, and I was not responsible for how I looked. So I said to myself: I'm a Black woman and proud of it.

Fredi Washington (actress, journalist)[67]

Figure 6.3 Shirley Graham
Source: Courtesy of the Schlesinger Library, Radcliffe Institute, Harvard University, Cambridge, MA

Despite the blacklist, what Adrian Scott described as "ideas, new, good, and provocative ideas," the result of the rich perspectives the Broadcast 41 brought to their work, persisted in the nooks and crannies of historical memory. In archives, interviews, letters, and other autobiographical writings those who were blacklisted left concrete evidence of their ideas. This book began with such an example: Adrian Scott's *Ellie*, a story based on his perspectives as caregiver to a son with significant mental health challenges and the ways in which his experiences transformed him into a "hardcore militant associate" of the movement for women's liberation.

Ellie is just one example of programs that progressive cultural producers with feminist sensibilities had hoped to create in the years after war's end. Shirley Graham envisioned a whole range of transformative projects (Figure 6.3). In the late 1940s, she was hard at work on a new novel, a book about white journalist Anne Newport Royall, a woman who was, by some accounts, the first woman journalist in the U.S., an abolitionist who published a newspaper about political corruption in Washington, DC from 1832 to 1854. Occupying Royall's perspective, Graham used the experiences of people of color to contextualize Royall's life and explore the relationships among race, class, and gender that shaped it. Describing Royall's adoption by Native Americans after the burning of the settlers' stockade in western Pennsylvania, Graham contrasted Royall's childhood and adolescence spent among Native

Americans with the barbaric sexism and racism she encountered when she reentered white society:

> And there had been men—soft, flabby men who stretched out pudgy hands in her direction. Anne knew her body was beautiful; she and Pelo and the other Indian boys and girls had swum the Mushingum many times, in her growing-up summers, naked and free. She had known a lot about birth and death and mating, but she ... had never been pursued for her body until she came to Sweet Springs.[68]

The contrast between the matter-of-fact sexuality that she had experienced among Native Americans and the predatory white men who pursued her sexually challenged the conventional tropes of barbarism and savagery.[69]

Instead of looking to the past for inspiration, Vera Caspary was preoccupied with a century that had witnessed huge changes for many women. Reflecting this, she proposed a television series in the 1950s about a family in the midst of similar social changes, creating stories distinct from the bland domestic intrigues of family sitcoms and the heroic frontier protection scenarios of Westerns. Titled *The Private World of the Morleys,* Caspary's proposal for the series revolved around what Caspary described as "an acute inspection of the most urgent questions of our time." These questions included what happens to the family's matriarch once the children have grown up; how the family's patriarch ages and experiences the loss of male power in "a world that has gone past him"; and the youngest daughter's struggles to enter the sexist profession of surgery.[70] A woman entering the male-dominated world of surgery had appeared on radio in *Joyce Jordan, Girl Intern* and *Joyce Jordan, MD,* but many of the issues raised in Caspary's proposal for *The Private World of the Morleys* did not air again on prime time until the series *Family* premiered in 1976.[71]

Progressive performers expressed their frustration at the limited roles available to women and people of color through their criticism of stereotypes. They hoped someday to play the kind of roles that writers like Berg, Caspary, Graham, Hellman, and Parker wrote about women and people of color as makers of history and political agents. In 1945, when asked by a writer from *Ebony* magazine what roles she dreamed of playing, Lena Horne responded, "I could play some of the Negro characters of history, like Sojourner Truth, the Civil War abolitionist, or maybe I could play the part of the Negro WAC of today."[72] Actress and writer Fredi Washington kept copies of film scripts that presented African Americans as heroes rather than as servants or comics, like Dorothy Heyward's script about Denmark Vesey (who led a rebellion against white supremacy in Charleston, South Carolina in 1822) and a script by Paul Peters about Nat Turner's 1831 rebellion.[73]

Denied opportunities to appear in programs that featured African Americans as full citizens and multi-dimensional human beings, African American performers mainly landed guest appearances on variety shows hosted by white men and women. Performance studies scholar Shane Vogel maintains that performances by women like Horne on these shows actively resisted "the circumscribed roles available to black women on the Jim Crow stage."[74] Horne, Scott, and Washington fought for better roles for African Americans until the end of their lives, but these efforts were stalled by the blacklist. Subsequent generations of performing artists thus had limited abilities to shape television's representations of race and racism.

When it comes to television, it can be easy to overlook actors' power not only to incorporate defiance and resistance into their performances, as critics argue Louise Beavers did in her performance in *Imitation of Life* (1934), but to influence writing as well. Fredi Washington, Beavers' co-star in *Imitation of Life*, recalled that she had "to fight the writers on lines like: 'If only I had been born white.' They didn't seem to realize that a decent life, not white skin, was the issue."[75] Performers too could affect what appeared on screens, which perhaps also explains the G-Man's determination to remove progressive actors from television and movie screens.

❖ ❖ ❖

I did a good deal of radio work from time to time—I always enjoy this, providing the material is worthwhile. If I were not so insistent on that point I should undoubtedly have worked a great deal in this medium, but unfortunately, the good programs are few and far between, and I have a foolish distaste for entering people's homes bearing unworthy gifts.

Eva Le Gallienne (theater producer, actress, director, author)[76]

There are all-girl stations on which everything is done by what once used to be called the weaker sex—even the technical jobs of operating cameras and light.... The first metropolitan station to go all-girl was WNEW-FM, New York, which celebrated the Fourth of July, 1966, by announcing that four beautiful and intelligent-sounding young women would divide the station's broadcast hours—10 a.m. until midnight.

Robert St. John (broadcaster and journalist)[77]

The Broadcast 41 made art and culture that criticized racism and sexism. But progressive content was not the only casualty of anti-communism in television: progressive media criticism was as well. Criticism plays an often unsung role in improving media content. New and innovative content generates criticism and discussion. Criticism and discussion, in turn, can shape and change creative ideas. As Farah Jasmine Griffin points out in relation to black feminist literary criticism, criticism played a vital role in providing a context for, and directing attention to, African American women's writing.[78] In the case of theater and literature, progressive media criticism—by producers, actors, writers, and journalists—educated readers about stereotypes, pushing one another and the industry to change and innovate. Criticism served as midwife for progressive content, facilitating progressive media production. Without criticism, traditions do not get invented, representations do not change or become more inclusive.

The Broadcast 41 were born critics. As people who had never experienced being at the centers of industrial, political, or cultural power, the Broadcast 41 were inclined to be critical of media that demeaned and excluded them. Fredi Washington used her entertainment column in *The People's Voice* to criticize Hollywood's representations of African Americans, as well as the exclusion of African Americans from jobs on film and broadcast crews. In her column, she pledged to fight so that "the Motion Picture Industry and the radio shall become more conscious of the tremendous revenue paid by Negroes for their products and be made to handle with regard and respect, all material dealing with and pertaining to Negroes."[79] Lena Horne similarly used her own *People's Voice* column to criticize the radio industry for discrimination against African Americans in representations and hiring practices alike. Drawing on her experiences, Horne described how radio programs were written so as to prevent her "from having a conversation with any of the principals."[80]

Anti-communists knew that criticism had the power to shape and change representations, which explains why anti-communists were so defensive about Margaret Mitchell's novel *Gone with the Wind* and its film adaptation. Just as the FBI and the American Business Consultants connected progressive literary and political criticism—especially of white supremacy—with communist influence, so they attacked those who dared criticize the novel and film versions of Mitchell's tribute to the Confederacy, describing such critics as communist operatives. Anti-communist journalist and star HUAC witness Howard Rushmore, in fact, said that he left the Communist Party in 1939 because members demanded he address *Gone with the Wind*'s racist sentimentality in his review.[81]

The best of progressive criticism and research contains within itself a utopian germ: it wants what it criticizes to be better, it seeks to use the results of critical analysis to improve and expand content and to shift perspective. Shirley Graham described how her own research caused her perspective to change. As she researched her novels on Jean-Baptiste Pointe de Sable, the Haitian founder of Chicago, Pocahontas, and Anne Newport Royall, Graham wrote that she "became aware that this was not as narrow a problem as I had thought. It wasn't only the Negro. I began to realize that as I was trying to widen the horizon of other people, my own horizon was widening."[82] By suppressing progressive criticism, the blacklist denied producers and television the means to grow and evolve, especially when it came to long repressed issues of race, gender, and nation.

❖ ❖ ❖

My method is perhaps an old-fashioned one, based perhaps upon an old-fashioned belief ... that the American people do not need "protection." I have an immense respect for the intelligence of the American people. I believe it to be at least as great as mine, and at least as great as that of any official whom we may elect to carry out the arduous tasks of government.... I believe that you cannot really believe in democracy without trusting the intelligence and integrity of our fellow-citizens.

Anne Revere (actress, trade unionist)[83]

"There Was Once a Slave" not only told me the heroic story of Frederick Douglass but it told me something about America that I will never forget. America is a great country, but if we are to build from the foundation our forefathers laid, and set an example for the rest of the world, we must have complete freedom within our own boundaries. Your book strengthened that foundation and gave me something to remember and live by through this time of hatred and war. Thank you Miss Graham, thank you very much.

Susan Welch (7th Grader)[84]

The blacklist further affected the future of American television by reinforcing racist and sexist stereotypes about audiences said to object to the content preferred by anti-communist masculinity. As the FBI's media criticism shows, anti-communists viewed audiences made up of anyone but white men as gullible and undiscriminating masses, a view the television industry came to share. Persuaded by anti-communism that white male audiences alone had value, the industry pitched prime-time programming and content to them, using the bottom line to justify this.[85]

Because they were members of audiences considered less valuable and thus less intelligent, many progressives approached their own audiences very differently from studio heads and executives. They knew that audiences enjoyed progressive ideas from their work in theater and music and were much less likely to accept on faith what anti-communists and industry moguls said about mass media audiences. Disparaged by industry moguls and anti-communists as both producers and audience members themselves, they took umbrage at this treatment, creating content that reflected a more respectful view of audiences and an awareness of media as tools for educational and intellectual advancement.

The Broadcast 41 openly expressed frustration with the industry's bigoted attitudes toward audiences. Lillian Hellman complained of her work at MGM that "you had to write the kind of idiot-simple report that Louis Mayer's professional lady storyteller could make even more simple when she told it to Mr. Mayer."[86] Hellman knew that the "idiot-simple" intelligence attributed to audiences often reflected executives' own tastes and attitudes toward the people for whom they were producing mass culture. Many of the Broadcast 41 suspected, like Hellman, that these "lady storytellers" were really pandering to Mayer's own tastes, tastes projected onto audiences that had no means other than fan letters locked up in corporate archives to register their actual feelings about content. The stories the industry told, that is, had to be stupid enough so Mayer would not feel threatened by them, a point that speaks volumes about executives' investment in the idea of stupid audiences rather than the realities of audiences.[87]

In this, Hellman shared Vera Caspary's belief that audiences were more intelligent than Hollywood "big shots." "I have sat in movie houses in Bridgeport, Connecticut, Marshalltown, Iowa, Milwaukee, Wisconsin, and Encinitas, California," Caspary wrote, "and I have never found any audience as dull as the big shots who attend story conferences solemnly believe."[88] Hellman contrasted theater's and film's attitude toward audiences and found the latter wanting. Where theater offered the "ability to present an idea for the consideration of intelligent audiences," in film, executives "wouldn't know an idea if they saw it ... and if by any chance they should recognize it the film people would be frightened right out of their suede shoes."[89] Anne Revere similarly thought audiences were made up of intelligent and educable citizens, capable of interpretation and independent thought. Unlike anti-communists, who thought audiences needed to be protected from subversion and controversy, Revere maintained "that the American people are not easily gulled."[90]

Progressive women producers, directors, writers, and performers assumed their audiences and fans to be active and intelligent interpreters of culture. Lisa Sergio spoke to news listeners she considered her intellectual equal, people who shared her interest in global politics and the histories of international political struggles. Popular radio show host Mary Margaret McBride; soap opera writers and producers like Irna Phillips and Elaine Sterne Carrington; and sitcom giants like Gertrude Berg were not members of the Broadcast 41, but their successes in the industry confirm that progressive women spoke to their audiences differently than did the industry as a whole. Historian Susan Ware says that McBride—whose work in radio began in 1934 and spanned a period of nearly forty years—was unique in her respect for her female listeners. According to Ware, this characteristic "endeared her to female listeners tired of being patronized by radio personalities and advertising executives who assumed that all they were interested in was recipes and curtains."[91]

Like McBride, Gertrude Berg and radio and television writer and actress Peg Lynch listened carefully to their fans, reading and responding to the many thousands of letters they received over decades of work in broadcasting. For them, audiences and fans were not abstract, faceless multitudes, but people—often women—who wrote them thoughtful, intelligent letters. In these letters, viewers and listeners took exception to the industry's definition of what was popular and complained, as one fan did to Peg Lynch, that "not all us housewives dropped everything to listen to [Arthur] Godfrey. Occasionally he had interesting guests. Then the program was worth taking the time to watch. But, our time is too valuable to waste on programs featuring pop-tune singers, quiz shows, animated soap operas and off-color quips."[92] Berg and Lynch relied in turn on their audiences for support, mobilizing them in letter-writing and telephone campaigns when networks threatened to cancel their popular programs. The relationships between these stars and their listeners and viewers—relationships that remain to be studied and documented—were intimate and meaningful.

Shirley Graham's work in developing a national television system in Ghana shows just how radical progressive women's ideas about audiences could have been, unfettered by the collusion between anti-communism and the industry's own sexism and racism. After years of state surveillance and harassment—in 1954, Graham wrote to a friend, "McCarthy's hound dogs snarl at our heels, prowl about our doors and sniff at our windows"—Graham and Du Bois sought refuge in Ghana, where President Kwame Nkrumah asked her to help establish the country's first national television system.[93] Eager to reach underserved and unrepresented audiences with new media, Graham envisioned a non-commercial television system that served the educational and public health needs of Ghanaian culture rather than those of Western, corporate elites. Drawing on her own experiences of an educational system that denied histories to people of color, Graham planned to build an infrastructure for indigenous television production, establishing programs to train writers for the new medium.[94] In order to generate content for television news, she wanted to "send reporters into every part of Ghana," so that "the inhabitants of seldom-visited villages of the interior will know, seeing themselves on the screen, that they are not forgotten."[95]

Like Graham, other members of the Broadcast 41 knew it was important for people to see themselves represented on screen and to understand they were not forgotten. And despite anti-communists' assertion of some mass audience that hated progressives so much that they would boycott shows that featured them or the themes they were associated with, the Broadcast 41 had much evidence that suggested otherwise. In their haste to demonstrate their loyalty to anti-communism, media industries elected to overlook this evidence. For example, when stage director and actress Margaret Webster first began discussing a production of *Othello* starring African American actor Paul Robeson in the late 1930s, she was told that it would be a box office disaster. In the end, she financed the production largely on her own. She produced the play in 1943, with José Ferrer and Uta Hagen cast alongside Robeson. As Webster recalled, "in the teeth of every possible hostility and prediction of doom," when the curtain fell on the first performance of *Othello* at the Shubert Theater in Manhattan on October 19, 1943, the standing ovation lasted for a full twenty minutes.[96] Webster's *Othello* ran for 296 performances, a record for a Shakespeare play on Broadway that stands today.[97]

Even within the more restrictive environment of broadcast media, evidence of interest in stories told from perspectives other than those sanctioned by G-Men was abundant. Gertrude Berg successfully spoke to audiences across the U.S. about Judaism, opting not to concede to the beliefs of the anti-Semites conjured by network and film executives to justify the industry's anti-Semitism. Although advertisers repeatedly expressed surprise about *The Goldbergs*' popularity among Jewish and non-Jewish listeners and viewers alike, over the course of the show's long run, Berg often received more than a thousand letters a week. These letters, she later recalled, "came from all over the country, and, contrary to everyone's belief, the majority of the mail didn't come from the Jewish population."[98] In fact, Berg argued that the show's successes showed how wrong the industry's governing ideas about audiences really were:

> The audience refused to be typed and from the mail I learned a great lesson: There is no way for anyone to predict what the American public is going to like, going to do, or going to say. I've gotten letters from priests, ministers, and rabbis, and from millionaires and paupers.... The reactions of the people who listened only showed that we all respond

to human situations and human emotions—and that dividing people into rigid racial, economic, social, or religious categories is a lot of nonsense.[99]

The fan letters *The Goldbergs* received conveyed a portrait of a listening public inspired not by the desire to see only their own images on television screens, but by what they saw as shared American values of curiosity, education, and inclusion.[100]

As these examples suggest, even within the constraints of capitalist media systems, a wider range of representational fare for far more diverse audiences could have been possible. But by threatening that so-called controversial programs would result in boycotts and plunging revenues, the blacklist allowed the industry to use the fiction of a purely economic rationale to eliminate progressive ideas. According to social scientist Marie Jahoda, who conducted a landmark study of the impact of blacklisting on the industry:

Apparently many sponsors, producers, directors, casting officers, and others in the industry go along with the blacklisting of accused individuals even though they consider the practice to be foolish or wrong. What induces them to go along with the demands of the blacklists is the argument that an objectively small, but economically important portion of the audience might take offense and refrain from buying an advertised article if the industry did not go along.[101]

It did not matter that there was little evidence that audiences would boycott any of the limited content on the new medium's three networks: anti-communists brandished fear of boycotts as if these were inevitable.

Because control of what appeared on television lay in the hands of network oligarchs, there was no feedback loop for fans, many thousands of whom wrote letters to networks, sponsors, and advertisers when programs like *The Goldbergs* were cancelled. Progressive audiences' objections went unheard and, like the Broadcast 41 themselves, have largely been forgotten. As for the popularity of progressive theater, it was dismissed as elitist East Coast fare that would not play in Peoria, as an old adage from American theater went, much less on the conservative landscape of television. Aided by the blacklist, the industry's concern with white audiences and silent majorities created representational redlining in television and then institutionalized it.

Decades after the publication of *Red Channels*, television writer and producer John Markus described the "Network's oversensitivity to special interest groups" as emerging during the 1950s.[102] But the vagueness of Markus' claim is deceptive. The audiences anti-communists cared most about were those whose views could be used to channel their own political interests.

The audience that television was most concerned with was an audience that lived down to anti-communist expectations, best represented as people with immoveable attitudes toward people of color, women, immigrants, and those less fortunate than them. This lack of belief in people's better natures meant that television worried about offending silent majorities of audience members who affirmed anti-communist beliefs and thus white supremacy, misogyny, and xenophobia.

In fact, the blacklist institutionalized oversensitivity to anti-communist groups, whose threats to picket and boycott television programs employing black- or gray-listed progressives were incorporated into the common-sense thinking of the industry. Long after the era of direct sponsorship was over, producers and writers self-censored to avoid any hint of controversy—to avoid "anything that might bother people," in Gertrude Berg's words.[103] Anti-communists justified this censorship in the name of an audience they had in large part created, helping to ensure that until the late 1980s, women and African American, Asian American, Native American, and Latinx writers, directors, and actors would continue to "struggle for drama," as journalist Kristal Brent Zook puts it, in order to create and star in roles in which they could be represented as multidimensional human beings.[104]

It was, of course, perfectly acceptable to abuse women and working-class people, through humiliating stereotypes that persist today; to insult people of color, through images that represented them as lazy, licentious, and inherently criminal; to disappear immigrants from the representational spectrum; and to offend thoughtful people as a whole. The blacklist caused the industry to affirm intolerance under the guise of fighting East Coast liberalism, a geography of politics it considered, after all, only a transfer or two away from Red Square.

❖ ❖ ❖

When I saw you [Ruth Gordon] in "Years Ago" it gave me the courage to really try and see if I too couldn't do as you have done.

Cynthia Allen (actress)[105]

And then I went to Chicago where I was sort of drawn into the Federal Theatre as Supervisor of the Negro Unit of the Chicago Federal Theatre. Now this was purely sort of accidental when I got to Chicago they were getting ready to dismiss and throw out all the people of the … Negro Unit because they hadn't been able to do anything. And in a burst of indignation, I went down and talked to the director of the Chicago Federal Theatre and told them they didn't know what they were doing.

That these people were the most talented and most gifted of anybody that they could possibly have in the Federal Theatre and they evidently just didn't know how to handle the situation. Well he acknowledged they never had anybody but whites over this group, and when I left, getting ready to go back to my own job in the south just as I was about to leave, I got this telephone call and he offered me the job—"Okay," he said, "so you know so much about it, well you just do it."

Shirley Graham (musician, writer, civil rights activist)[106]

In addition to denying generations of producers the means to create and share stories about the diverse perspectives of the people who live in the Americas, past and present, the blacklist also eliminated a generation of industry leaders, teachers, and mentors who might have transformed the climate within media industries. Media studies scholar Kristen Warner reminds us that "creativity is not a mystical, inspirational act." Within media industries, she observes, creativity "is a learned and socialized behavior."[107] After the blacklist, writers, directors, producers, and performers were socialized within a work culture whose organizational hierarchies not surprisingly looked a lot like the world reflected on television screens, with white men firmly in charge, white women in supporting roles, and people of color—when they appeared at all—as servants, subordinates, or deviants. The work cultures that resulted from the blacklist reenergized practices of discrimination against women and people of color that had been subject to increasing scrutiny during World War II. Those most likely to oppose discrimination were either fired or silenced. The blacklist eliminated the few women who had advanced to leadership positions within the industry, thereby also wiping out opportunities to learn from a generation of talented progressive women. The events of the blacklist era taught women, as one FBI informant put it, "that to be good citizens they should stick to their knitting and keep their noses out of politics."[108]

Forms of alliance and mutual support were vital to women's advancement and survival in media industries like television, as well as to nurturing progressive attitudes toward women and people of color among newcomers and socializing them in ways that countered media industries' racism and sexism. Many progressive women got their breaks in media industries because of these networks. Vera Caspary's screenwriting break came about because of a chance encounter at the Algonquin Hotel with Laura Wilck, a story editor for Paramount Pictures, who gave the jobless and nearly broke Caspary a $2,000 advance to write the script for the film *The Night of June 13th*.[109] A generation of talented progressive writers and actors passed through the doors of *The Goldbergs*, including Abraham Polonsky, Garson Kanin, Louise Beavers, Fredi Washington, and Joe Julien. Ruth Gordon's papers at the Library of Congress are full of thank-you notes from aspiring actors who turned to the star for advice and support. Mary Margaret McBride got Stella Karn her first job in radio as business manager for her show; Karn's "first act" was to get McBride the salary increase she deserved.[110] Actress Donna Keath worked with others to found Stage for Action (SFA) in 1944, a theater company providing community for progressive cultural workers.

Horne and Scott found comfort and sustenance in the company of other black singers and musicians, many of them women, such as Mary Williams, Billie Holliday, and Lil Hardin Armstrong. When Lena Horne decided that she wanted to resume her career after having two children, Fredi Washington set up an audition for her and the Negro Actors Guild of America paid for Horne to travel from Pittsburgh to New York City.[111]

In 1950, many of the Broadcast 41 were well established in media and creative industries. They were trailblazers, with their own networks of sustenance and survival. Wartime labor shortages had given them significant experience in their unions. They were leaders as well in industry and community-based philanthropic efforts. Actress Selena Royle formed the Actors Dinner Club, which provided free dinners to needy actors. She was a sponsor of the Stage Door Canteen, which offered food and entertainment for military personnel during World War II in New York City. A journalist described Marsha Hunt as "one of Hollywood's first celebrity activists."[112] In 1938, Hunt founded the Valley Mayors' Fund for the Homeless to advocate for shelters and services in the Los Angeles area. After the blacklist, she became involved in humanitarian issues, opening the first United Nations Association offices in Southern California and working closely with the World Health Organization and UNICEF. Hunt served as a board member of the Community Relations Conference of Southern California and founded the Southern California Freedom from Hunger Committee, remaining an advocate for progressive social change into the twenty-first century.[113]

Members of the Broadcast 41 also founded and led organizations providing support for immigrants and people of color across media industries. Pianist Ray Lev told the FBI when they questioned her that "as a member of a minority group she believes her responsibility is to aid minority groups and foreign born."[114] She fulfilled this responsibility through hundreds of fundraising performances on behalf of groups working on civil rights for African Americans and the foreign-born.

When the intransigent racism of the industry and the blacklist prevented them from contributing meaningful content to media, the Broadcast 41 became leaders in creating alternative venues for education and celebration of cultures excluded from anti-communist versions of Americanism.

illustration of the work that this capable generation of women was prevented from doing in the U.S. Although she was not one of the Broadcast 41, Weinstein played an important role in the history of the blacklist and, indeed, in the history of progressive media production. A former advertising executive and supporter of Henry Wallace's failed 1948 presidential campaign, Weinstein left the U.S. before the Hollywood Ten were jailed and moved to London, where she founded the television studio Sapphire Films.[45] Norma Barzman credited Weinstein with saving "many exiled blacklisted Americans," over the course of a decade employing at least twenty-two American writers living in Europe and the United States who could no longer find work in the U.S. because of the blacklist.[46]

Although Weinstein's Sapphire Studios is perhaps best known for inaugurating a costume-drama craze in England, with *The Adventures of Robin Hood* and *Lancelot*, she is also credited with producing an innovative crime series written by blacklisted writers Walter Bernstein and Abraham Polonsky. *Colonel March of Scotland Yard*, as scholar Dave Mann documents, featured "the celebration of professional and resourceful women," including "murderesses," a "plucky female undercover insurance investigator who corners the villain singlehanded," and an anthropologist and documentary maker who joins an Everest expedition.[47]

Under Weinstein's direction, *Robin Hood* in particular proved a powerful vehicle for progressive political views. In this show, blacklisted authors like Ring Lardner, Jr. and Adrian and Joan LaCour Scott explored themes of betrayal and social justice that were very much on their minds. In an episode written by the Scotts, for example, titled "The Cathedral," the mason in charge of building the structure is falsely accused of "being a tool of an international conspiracy, anti-Church and anti-Christ."[48] In "The Charter," also written by the Scotts, Robin located a lost document that protected the rights of progressive nobles who wanted to reform the aristocracy and redistribute land and other forms of wealth.[49]

Such themes were, of course, too subversive for anti-communists. Adrian Scott told a friend that the climate in the U.S. had become such that, "Today, when you characterize the rich as stingy, this is subversive."[50] Ilana Girard Singer, whose activist father was blacklisted in northern California, recalled that her "beloved *Robin Hood* had been banished from some school libraries because Senator Joe McCarthy called it 'communist doctrine.'"[51] *Robin Hood*'s considerable success in England allowed it to breach the blacklist in America in 1955: the show was broadcast on CBS from 1955 to 1960.[52] Still, Rod Erickson, who handled television spots for Young & Rubicam at the time, said that when he bought the show for American sponsor Johnson & Johnson,

Margo—Mexican-American dancer Maria Margarita Guadalupe Teresa Estella Castilla Bolado y O'Donnell Albert—founded Plaza de la Raza in 1970 with trade union activist Frank Lopez in East Los Angeles. A cultural center that provided arts education programs to children, adolescents, and adults, Plaza de la Raza continues to operate today, more than thirty years after Margo's death in 1985, its mission even more urgent in light of continued defunding of arts education throughout the U.S.

In addition to using their stardom to draw attention to progressive causes and modeling forms of citizenship for those aspiring to work in the industry, progressive women and men served as mentors for those who, often like them, were disenfranchised and marginalized within media industries, especially African Americans, who were barred from most unions until the 1950s. In 1937, along with Bill Robinson, Noble Sissle, Duke Ellington, and W.C. Handy, Fredi Washington co-founded the Negro Actors Guild of America (NAGA), a benevolent association that provided support for performers during the Depression. Washington served as executive director and secretary, overseeing NAGA's day-to-day operations.[115] Graham's Chicago Negro Unit supported work by other writers of color, often gambling on plays by black writers dismissed as too risky by white producers. Graham's was the first unit to stage a production of Theodore Ward's *Big White Fog* (1938), a play about political tensions between reform and revolution in the life of one black family and a play that white critics predicted would cause a race riot.

Existing networks had been torn apart by the blacklist in the 1950s. Anti-communists had always been clear in their intent—to dismantle networks of those critical of them, thereby eliminating dissent of all kinds. "All those people in their 40s, 50s, and 60s," blacklisted actress Lee Grant remembered, who "had made names for themselves were crushed and never came back."[116] The destruction of this pipeline prevented the transmission of experience and information from one generation of progressives to the next. The American Business Consultants' and the FBI's attacks on progressive networks in broadcasting show that anti-communists understood the power of networks of mutual respect and support among women, people of color, and other progressives and took deliberate steps to destroy them.

Buoyed by the civil rights movement and the easing of the blacklist in film, in the late 1960s, blacklisted producer Hannah Weinstein joined a group of black and Puerto Rican directors, producers, actors, and writers that included Ossie Davis, James Earl Jones, and Rita Moreno to found the Third World Cinema Corporation, a minority-controlled independent company that planned "to produce feature films and train minority group members in the film and television fields."[117] Third World Cinema went on to produce *Greased*

Lightning (1977)—about the first black stock car racer in the U.S.—and *Stir Crazy* (1980)—a buddy film with a multiracial cast and a gay character. Both films starred comedian Richard Pryor and were directed by African American directors (Michael Schultz and Sidney Poitier).

The redaction of these women and the generations who might have followed created a persistent silence in television around race, nation, gender, and other aspects of people's lives considered controversial by anti-communists. Notwithstanding the popularity of Berg's *The Goldbergs* in the 1930s and 1940s, and even the popularity of less progressive representations of immigrants like *Life with Luigi* (1952), immigrant life seldom appeared on television after 1950, because anti-communists understood these representations to be as subversive as representations of black lives. In fact, after the 1950s, immigrants reemerged on entertainment programming only by way of the metaphoric aliens of *ALF* (1986–90), *Mork and Mindy* (1978–82), and *Alien Nation* (1989–90), and immigrants from fictitious countries, like Balki from *Perfect Strangers* (1986–83). Even in the first decades of the twenty-first century, stories about immigrants and their families remain broadly confined to sitcoms like gay Iranian American television writer and producer writer Nahnatchka Khan's *Fresh Off the Boat* (2015–), with prime-time dramas still dominated by the native-born.

Representations of race that dared to question white supremacy—even if only by virtue of featuring non-stereotypical black characters—also disappeared from prime-time line-ups as a result of the blacklist. Progressive stars like Gertrude Berg, Milton Berle, and Eddie Cantor had challenged the color line in television before 1950 and showed every intention of continuing to do so, while writers and producers like Shirley Graham and Hannah Weinstein demonstrated their ability and desire to create and support the work of people of color in media industries. But after Hazel Scott's show was cancelled in 1950, television did not feature another African American as host of a variety show until *The Flip Wilson Show* premiered on NBC in 1970, twenty years to the day that Hazel Scott had given her defiant speech to the HUAC. Today, Scott's groundbreaking show remains largely forgotten: the National Museum of African American History and Culture in Washington, DC identifies *The Flip Wilson Show* as the first variety show to star an African American.

Female characters who defied the formula approved by anti-communists appeared only sporadically, mainly, as television historian Elana Levine observes, on soap operas and only occasionally in sitcoms like *Maude* (1972–78), *One Day at a Time* (1975–84), and *Alice* (1976–85), and dramas like *Family* (1976–80) and *St. Elsewhere* (1982–88). Although African American women featured prominently in anti-communist-inspired news stories about welfare and poverty that blamed them for all manner of social woes for the last twenty-five years of the twentieth century, entertainment programming all but ignored their presence, save for short-lived programs like *Frank's Place* (1987–88) and *South Central* (1992) until powerful women like Oprah Winfrey and Shonda Rhimes began to change the face of American television.[118]

Because media industries are so risk-averse, the suppression of stories about immigrants, people of color, women, and working-class people in the 1950s had longer-term consequences for American culture. As television and film became ever more concerned about the bottom line, even as their profits increased, these industries mined their own limited archives for ideas. As Adrian Scott put it, even in its infancy television was particularly dependent on adapting "something that has been done before."[119]

The industry reproduced the constraints of the blacklist in programs that revived a history the medium had itself created, presenting the 1950s as an era full of blissful cultural and social harmony, recycling its past in remakes and spin-offs. These constraints were most visible in the main tenets of anti-communist culture: the sanctity of the nuclear family and the need for white men to protect the family from the procession of racialized public enemies presented in police procedurals and crime news. "Numerous topics had become dangerous" because of the blacklist, television historian Eric Barnouw observed: "But one subject was always safe: law and order."[120] This remains broadly true today, as prime-time programming continues to reproduce tried and true tropes of law-and-order programming that routinely feature the violent deaths of women and people of color and the valorization of the repressive power of the security state.

While the blacklist does not bear sole responsibility for what ultimately appeared on American television, it was instrumental in policing limits that became foundational to the industry's common-sense thinking about content and audiences. In her statement to the House Un-American Activities Committee in 1950, Hazel Scott warned that the "vicious slanders" of anti-communists would kill "the years of preparation, sacrifice, and devotion" of American entertainers. As a result, she concluded, "Instead of a loyal troupe of patriotic, energetic citizens, ready to give their all for America, you will demoralize them and end up with a dejected, wronged group whose creative value has been destroyed."[121] Writer and television producer Rod Serling later confirmed Scott's prediction. By the mid-1950s, he told talk show host Mike Wallace that he had stopped writing "anything important" for television because "I don't want to battle sponsors and agencies. I don't want to fight for something I want and have to settle for second best. I don't want to have to compromise all the time, which is in essence what a television writer does if he wants to take on controversial themes."[122]

The political repression that followed the broadcast blacklist may not have been aimed at women *per se*, but the impact on the small group of women working in the industry was devastating. By eliminating a generation of their critics, anti-communists made sure climates in media industries hostile to the work and presence of women and people of color would persist for decades. The ongoing procession of revelations about racism and sexism in media and technology industries illustrates that the forms of oppression the Broadcast 41 had fought against in the 1930s and 1940s remain very much alive well into the twenty-first century.[123] Hollywood's disregard for the work of actors of color, media industries' refusal to hire people of color in positions of industrial power, reports by generations of women who have experienced sexual violence at the hands of Hollywood producers and directors, television producers, executives, and many others caused women to take to social media. Using hashtags like #MeToo and #TimesUp they described the impact of a culture that has historically excluded them and whose representations continue to degrade them. These revelations have been greeted with hypocritical shock by journalistic establishments that have long helped suppress criticisms of media industries' sexism and racism. The Broadcast 41 knew that industries that represented women and people of color as subordinate and subhuman could hardly be expected to treat women and people of color accurately either on screen or in the workplace.

The work of the Broadcast 41 shows us what might have been on television, how television themes and genres might have evolved, and how the medium might have addressed audiences outside the now familiar clichés of paternalistic and treacherous white protection. The content that the blacklist denied to viewers also troubles anti-communists' use of television audiences as evidence of a consensus held by a silent majority to justify racism and misogyny. And the courage of so many of the Broadcast 41 in the face of a culture war that sought to permanently still their voices shows us that criticism of mass media industries' sexism, racism, and xenophobia is as old as these media themselves. These criticisms came from people like the Broadcast 41, who were brave and idealistic enough to believe that change was possible. "My own belief," Lillian Hellman said at Hannah Weinstein's memorial in 1984, "is that she was the only person in the world Joe McCarthy was frightened of."[124]

But the cultural and political cost of the blacklist cannot be measured in terms of individual resistance, agency, or resilience. Instead, it must be assessed in terms of its impact on a generation of cultural producers whose often divergent perspectives (from the pluralistic liberalism of people like

Margo, Jean Muir, and Ireene Wicker to the communist beliefs of Caspary, Graham, and producer Betty Todd), experiences, and networks might have allowed them to collectively impact the future of American television. Because of the loss of groups of people like these, who drew inspiration and support from one another's work and presence, the new medium could only represent, theorize, and grapple with social change across the twentieth century through restrictive lenses ground into being by anti-communism.

Conclusion

I remember as a kid living in Southern California and every TV show was set in that typical East Coast high school. And I remember seeing a high school near me that looked like that and thinking, "Oh, a real high school!" That's not feeling marginalized. Now, if I thought about the way my school looked, imagine being a Filipino person who's like "I'm not a real American because I'm not on TV." We're a nation of immigrants. That's what being an American is.

Rachel Bloom (producer, director, writer)[1]

There is an antagonistic context toward images of women by women, images by black people, brown people, indigenous people, that are outside of dominant culture. And the way that things are—they're run by men, there's a comfort level there.

Ava Duvernay (director)[2]

Fast forward to 2016. Writer, director, producer, actor, and web series creator Issa Rae's *Insecure*, about the experiences of an African American woman living in contemporary Los Angeles, premiered on HBO, five years after her web series, *The Misadventures of Awkward Black Girl*, underlined the existence of what media scholar Aymar Christian described as an "untapped market."[3] Media producers and critics understood the show's revolutionary role in creating "art—from television and film to paint canvases—[that] is giving platforms to Black women to tell their honest stories."[4] "Rae," one journalist observed, "is proud of *Insecure*'s diverse writers' room."[5]

Also in 2016, Rachel Bloom, writer, producer, and actor in a feminist-inspired television show with the unlikely name *Crazy Ex-Girlfriend*, won a Golden Globe award for best actress. The show's multiracial cast of recurring characters grew out of Bloom's sense that she had "never seen a show that took place in Southern California and portrayed people the way it *is* in Southern California. The prom king in my high school was Chinese and the prom queen was Japanese." The romantic lead was a Filipino American man. *Crazy Ex-Girlfriend* had little patience with television's tired conventions of gender and race. Not surprisingly, the networks' responses to it were reminiscent of the industry's longstanding discomfort over programs suspected of being subversive. In an interview, Bloom described the frustration she experienced shopping the show to networks. "All of the rejections," she recalled, "were different," ranging from "it's not edgy enough" to "Oh, we wish you were younger."[6]

It has taken decades for shows like *Insecure* and *Crazy Ex-Girlfriend* to appear on American television. Opportunities like those provided by *Insecure*—for black women to create and perform in their honest stories—were what Lena Horne, Fredi Washington, and other progressives had been fighting for in the 1930s and 1940s. *Crazy Ex-Girlfriend* satirized romance in ways that would have made Vera Caspary and Dorothy Parker proud. Both shows defied old genres: comedy became warmedy and dramedy, and the romantic comedy was upended and then blended with the musical.[7]

Despite decades of pressure by fans and organizations representing people of color, women, and children, network television resisted changing its representational practices and patterns. The stories that television has told about America, Americans, and American "values that nothing could change," as *Leave It to Beaver* once put it, shaped how American culture thinks about past, present, and future based on a vision of the past purified of all those elements that rightwing ideologues identified as subversive and un-American.[8] The so-called traditional family is still most frequently depicted by reference to images from television: "the Ozzie and Harriet family with a breadwinner father and a homemaker mother."[9] In 2014, more than sixty years after the publication of *Red Channels*, a journalist referred to "The iconic 1950s family of the breadwinner father going off to work and caregiving mother taking care of the homefront" as if this was a reality all (or even most) Americans had shared, adding that this family continues to be "described by economists as the most efficient family structure."[10]

More recently, fights over history and the memorialization of white supremacy in popular culture and everyday life alike have intensified under the toxic tutelage of G-Man masculinity's current disciples. As communities try to undo the institutionalization of white supremacy that took place in the American South after Reconstruction, by removing monuments to the "Lost Cause" of the Confederacy, a backlash not dissimilar to the one described in the pages of this book has been unfolding. When a white supremacist protest against the removal of a statue of Confederate general Robert E. Lee in Charlottesville, Virginia in 2017 turned violent, resulting in a counter-protestor's death, U.S. President Donald Trump refused to hold racist protestors accountable, telling reporters, "I think there is blame on both sides."[11] White House Chief of Staff John Kelly backed his boss up, telling an interviewer, "You know, 500 years later [sic], it's inconceivable to me that you would take what we think now and apply it back then. I think it's just very,

very dangerous. I think it shows you just how much of a lack of appreciation of history and what history is." [12]

Kelly's assertion, *"that you would take what we think now and apply it back then,"* is the boilerplate response of institutionalized white power, one that assumes that there was consensus about slavery "back then" and that resistance is not something that had been there all along, for those white people who chose to acknowledge it, but a contemporary breakthrough. Kelly's sloppy and inconsistent historical thinking not only gets tradition off the hook, it sanitizes the past by suggesting a historical consensus in which historical figures simply did not have access to the ideas and information we have in the present.

Suppressing the Broadcast 41's efforts to change media representations and industries allows for a similarly depoliticized view of the present, a view whose refrains typically appear as "those were different times," "everybody did it," or "that's just how things were back then." And it minimizes injustice in the present by suggesting that we have come so far from the past. Insofar as American culture suppresses the presence of people who fought for a democracy of images even when the cost of doing so was high, it denies a historical place to women who fought against racist stereotypes, sexual violence, and other forms of discrimination in media industries, dismissing the virulent misogyny of Hollywood's studio system, to take a stark example, as being just part of the way business was conducted back then.

As much as anti-communists persuaded themselves and their followers that the Broadcast 41 were totalitarians of the airwaves, intent on installing a monolithic version of reality on screens in homes around the nation, historical evidence shows they were not. Constitutionally critical of anti-communism and its insistence on a narrow, overarching narrative about an American past, present, and future, the Broadcast 41 valued the power of diverse and conflicting traditions. They wanted to transform popular culture to reflect the heterogeneous experiences of many Americans and not just a few, and to confront the trauma that underlay many Americans' experiences. As writers, musicians, performers, and artists, the Broadcast 41 insisted understanding could be encouraged by a plurality of voices rather than the fearfulness promoted by their anti-communist adversaries.

The *radical distance* described in the previous chapter between what progressives imagined for the future of television as a medium and what appeared on television screens after 1952 hints at the sweeping impact of the broadcast blacklist. Before the blacklist, the Broadcast 41 worked to remedy their exclusion—as women, people of color, immigrants, and queer people—from the narratives that dominated American culture. Anticipating the rise of a new medium that, like the internet, promised to forever alter the global nature of culture and communication, they challenged traditions that either excluded them or narrowed their visibility to a swath of stereotypes that made their continued subordination seem natural and eternal. Against the grain of traditions invented by white men, Shirley Graham and other progressive women uncovered traditions that valued the perspectives and contributions of heterogeneous communities. Graham wrote operas, plays, and novels to show "the contributions of our people to American history and development, because I knew not only didn't *our* young people know anything about it but the whites *certainly* knew nothing about it."[13]

In order to create a lineage of struggles in which they participated, progressive women were drawn to stories about those like them who previously had defied restrictive definitions of Americanism. For Gertrude Berg, Vera Caspary, Lena Horne, Dorothy Parker, Lisa Sergio, and many others, movements for women's liberation had made their independence and careers possible in the first place. They wanted to know, document, and share the lives of those who had preceded them in struggle. Lisa Sergio wrote one of the first biographies of Anita Garibaldi, partner and comrade-in-arms of Italian revolutionary Giuseppe Garibaldi. After she was blacklisted, Sergio completed a biography of Lena Madesin Phillips, a twentieth-century American feminist and early critic of the gender gap in wage equality.[14] Sergio continued to give speeches around the country, invoking tradition in the service of social change. "If we can't live equality, we'll lose," she told an audience at Madison College. "If we don't really believe that all men are created equal we should strike that phrase from our Declaration of Independence."[15]

Vera Caspary, whose career spanned advertising, journalism, film, and fiction writing, looked to the history of vaudeville for forerunners, proposing a dramatization of vaudevillian Texas Guinan's life for British television. Like the Broadcast 41, Guinan had defied norms of gender and sexuality. She was the first female emcee in a New York City club and the first silent-era movie cowgirl, known as the "Queen of the West."[16] During the Depression, Guinan built a reputation for scandal, claiming to have been turned away at every port of entry because of her uncensored representations of female sexuality. Undeterred, Guinan created a hugely popular revue based on her experiences, titled *Too Hot for Paris*. Guinan was a touchstone for female power, a reminder that earlier women had also asserted agency in the face of patriarchal sexual norms. A Guinan fan herself, actress Mae West's first screen appearance was in *Night After Night* (1932), in a role based on Guinan. Frank Butler directed a 1945 musical biography of Guinan's life—*Incendiary*

Blonde—starring Betty Hutton as Guinan.[17] Comedian Martha Raye toured in a 1969 musical based on Guinan's life named after Guinan's signature line, "Hello, Sucker!" In the late 1980s, the character Guinan (played by actress Whoopi Goldberg) on the television series *Star Trek: The Next Generation* paid tribute to this predecessor.

The Broadcast 41's efforts to document the lives of people of color and women who had preceded them—to represent them with dignity and complexity—were acts of political resistance. As Shirley Graham put it, "Men have written the great historical chronicles and they turn out to be records of the deeds of men." But, Graham continued, "we, too, live in crucial times, we, too, are privileged to make stirring history ... we have Mrs. Ingram, and the legacy left by Ethel Rosenberg and the memory of how the mother of Emmett Till faced that courtroom of savages in Mississippi."[18]

Like Graham, the Broadcast 41 knew all too well the cost of being misrepresented in the memory of a culture. Marginalized by whiteness and masculinity, rendered inferior, such misrepresentations normalized bigotry by suppressing resistance to it. The Broadcast 41 valued being able to see the presence and accomplishments of people who looked like them in history because they realized how histories of struggle against oppression fueled futures of resistance. By creating traditions documenting the historical presence of those who had fought for democracy before them, they honored those struggles and created foundations for criticism and political struggle in the present.

The work of progressives like the Broadcast 41 shows how the themes of recent television programs about immigrants, people of color, and queer people—including *Atlanta* (2016–), *Black-ish* (2014–), *Empire* (2015–), *Fresh Off the Boat* (2015–), *The Get Down* (2016); *How to Get Away with Murder* (2014–), *Insecure* (2016–), *The Mindy Project* (2012–17), *Queen Sugar* (2016–), *She's Got to Have It* (2017–), *Transparent* (2014–), and *Underground* (2016–17)—were very much on the minds of progressives long years before these were finally able to make their way onto screens.[19] The work of the Broadcast 41 seems so contemporary in its attention to gender, race, sexuality, and nation because the blacklist suppressed alternative forms of storytelling that showcased Americans in all their historicity and heterogeneity. In 2015, journalist James Hibberd wrote that "networks struck gold when they started letting those actors play characters who authentically capture the experiences of a diverse America."[20] Progressives knew that this might also have been possible in 1950.

Progressives and anti-communists also knew that the new medium of television had the potential to allow people to identify with characters and topics outside their personal frames of reference. Where progressives perceived in this potential hope for democracy, anti-communists saw only a threat to the strain of Americanism they were dead set on protecting. Controlling televisual forms of storytelling was something that anti-communists in the FBI dedicated decades to, realizing that when given options, significant numbers of people might choose compassion over fear.

The dogmatic belief that 1950s televisual representations of the social world resulted from "a consensus ideology"—the desires of a newly massive audience—remains a powerfully racialized and gendered one, driven by the television industry's own penchant for anchoring its accounts of history in images it had created in the first place.[21] These images, as this book has shown, resulted from what feminist theorist Rosemary Ndubuizu powerfully describes as the "curation of the illusion" of consent, one in which the voices of a few were in her words, "lifted up," while voices of criticism and dissent were elided or actively suppressed.[22]

In the case of television, the voices of anti-communist white supremacy were lifted up, while those of progressives were marginalized and then suppressed. Television critic David Zurawik identified this process, observing of Gertrude Berg and the blacklist, "I think the founders of the networks were uncomfortable with that history," as well as "their role in it and so she sort of became a story they didn't want to tell because it brought up the narrative of the blacklist."[23] A version of Berg's *The Goldbergs* appeared on ABC in 2013, but Berg and the work of so many of the Broadcast 41 remain—in the words Graham chose to describe the historical figures she wrote about—"outside of history." As Graham went on to put it, "It is not only the Negro, it is not only the Indian, who is dropped out of history—it is also the dissenter, the person who didn't go along with the majority!"[24] That Graham's many groundbreaking achievements—from her early work in the Federal Theatre Project to her fictionalized accounts of the lives of prominent people of color—are scarcely mentioned in any of the overlapping media fields to which she contributed is powerful evidence of the continuing effects of this silencing.[25] In the face of the suppression of the diverse perspectives that attended television's birth, documenting the lives of the Broadcast 41 and other progressives remains a crucial political task.

Fighting against the redaction of these women also highlights the heterogeneity of progressive women's political views. The Broadcast 41 were rebellious and opinionated people. However much they may have shared views on the social issues of the era, as well as the belief that art and culture had a responsibility to help inform and educate audiences about these issues, their work did not add up to some feminist consensus. Instead, they disagreed—vehemently and sometimes acrimoniously—about art and politics. Like later generations, the Broadcast 41 had principled and divergent views of gender's primacy in people's lives. Caspary, Lillian Hellman, Horne, Madeline Lee, Dorothy Parker, and others described themselves as feminists, but they heatedly disagreed about the nature of women's oppression. White women's attitudes toward race were not consistently self-reflexive and they struggled, with varying degrees of success, to be effectively anti-racist.

Class was uppermost in many progressive women's minds, moreover, in ways that would disappear from white women's consciousness as the twentieth century wore on. Lillian Hellman, for example, acknowledged that it is "very hard for women, hard to get along, to support themselves, to live with some self-respect," but she saw women's liberation as "diversionary" insofar as it took people's eyes "off the problems in our capitalist society."[26] Shirley Graham convincingly criticized capitalism in plays like *It's Morning* and *Coal Dust*, while at the same time maintaining that race was inseparable from class and, to a lesser degree, gender. While debates like these remained alive in black left feminist circles, they were denied the broader audiences Graham once dreamed of for them. The Broadcast 41 had principled and important disagreements about the limits of gender, race, and class as isolated categories of analysis. This chorus of dissent shows just how wrongheaded were anti-communists' portrayals of progressives as thought police, intent on imposing a monolithic party line.

The breakdown of the network system and the concomitant rise of cable and the internet over the past twenty years have undermined some of the blacklist's dogmatic beliefs about audiences. But with the exception of television production taking place outside domains of traditional power, even so-called quality television remains unrepentant about its representations of women and people of color and extraordinarily resistant to transforming work cultures that might encourage diversity in media industries.[27] At the time of this writing, much of what's deemed quality television continues to rely on tired plot lines that begin with the sexualized murders of young white women or feminized men (*True Detective*, *American Crime Story*, *The Night Of*, *The Killing*, to name only a handful). These pathetic, bloodied victims are a far cry from Caspary's savvy career girls—with their talk of sexual agency, their progressive racial politics, and their status as live agents; a reflection of the continued legacies of a G-Man social world in which white men alone are powerful and safe.

The Broadcast 41 and other progressives longed for a postwar world where generosity and compassion were virtues and not signs of subversion, where the rights of women and men of all colors and political affiliations were respected, and where the government served the interests of people and not corporations, to paraphrase blacklisted actress Rose Hobart.[28] What was once said of blacklisted screenwriter and producer Adrian Scott—"He was one of the most decent men I have ever met"—was not a statement that applied to anti-communists, past or present.[29] Instead, these titans of intolerance continue to whip modern day G-Men into a frenzy with chants of "lock her up" at rallies (a reference to political rival Hillary Clinton), in scenes of misogyny and white supremacy that look chillingly like the dystopian future of Margaret Atwood's novel, *The Handmaid's Tale.*[30]

In this vein, playwright and theater historian Loften Mitchell wrote of Paul Robeson that he "was a devastating challenge to a society built on hypocrisy, greed and profit-seeking at the expense of common humanity. A curtain of silence had to be brought down on him. He had to be kept off TV, maligned and omitted from the history books."[31] Sexism and racism feed on historical amnesia like this. Just as white supremacists created and tended the hideous gardens of white supremacy in the monuments that littered the landscape of the American South, so the anti-communist blacklist in television generated representations of race, gender, and nation that fueled nostalgia for an era in which they controlled the images that would be broadcast to millions.

The invisibility of people like the Broadcast 41 from historical view ensures that successive generations of producers, critics, and viewers approach social justice struggles without the benefit of a history that emphasizes how intransigent media industries have been in terms of addressing the white supremacist and sexist practices that the blacklist helped institutionalize in the new medium. By eradicating progressive voices and ideas from television and thus from history, the blacklist denied the existence of persistent and principled opposition to racial and sexual violence, suggesting that no alternatives to what appeared on screens ever existed before protests suddenly erupted in a contemporary moment rendered unexpectedly progressive by the barbarism of the past. The work of the Broadcast 41 provides a rich testament to the creativity American television lost because of the alliance between anti-communists and the FBI and, at the same time, a bracing reminder of just how far media industries need to go to address their bigotry.

Restoring the Broadcast 41 to television history reminds us that people of conviction and principle fought against racism and sexism from the beginnings of this mass medium. Blacklisted actresses Jean Muir and Fredi Washington, for example, would recognize their concerns about racist roles in Hollywood in early twenty-first-century controversies over films like *The Butler* (2013) and *The Help* (2011), as well as the continuing dearth of roles for people of color in film reflected in the 2016 Twitter hashtag campaign

#OscarsSoWhite. If she had lived to see them, blacklisted writer Vera Caspary would have applauded series like *Broad City* (2014) and *Girls* (2012–17), insofar as they focused on the lives of young women who worked, even though she probably would have preferred Issa Rae's more nuanced understanding of race and gender in *Awkward Black Girl* and *Insecure*. Remembering the Broadcast 41 helps us to think differently about the history of women's resistance across the twentieth century, not as some mythic post-Cold War awakening to a white, suburban problem that had no name, but as a persistent dimension of the lives of a diverse group of progressive women, who found themselves politically and professionally abandoned in 1950.[32]

At a moment when powerful forms of collective storytelling on social media have been challenging the G-Man's old monopoly over America and Americanism, recalling that this is not the first time progressives have challenged repressive representations and practices in media allows us to understand the aggressive misogyny and racism of traditional media and online cultures alike in historical context. Current controversies about social justice warriors' alleged stifling of free speech and feminists' efforts at "mind control" and imposing a "matriarchy" are reviving anti-communist tropes used to marginalize and demonize people like the Broadcast 41. Inheritors of G-Man masculinity have been increasingly strident as resistance in the shape of alliances between activists and powerful actors, athletes, producers, and politicians begin to demand the social transformations progressives like the Broadcast 41 dreamt of in the long-ago summer of 1950.

These fears crystallized around Oprah Winfrey's 2018 acceptance speech for the Cecil B. DeMille Award for lifetime achievement at the Golden Globes. Winfrey told the audience what it meant for her as a young black girl, seeing Sidney Poitier—a black man—celebrated on television. She spoke about the power of the women's movement that had emerged in the wake of G-Man Donald Trump's victory in 2016, emphasizing "that speaking your truth is the most powerful tool we all have." Recognizing that for too long American media have deprived publics of the stories reflective of realities G-Man masculinity repressed, Winfrey took this opportunity to tell a different kind of story about what the movement against sexual violence in Hollywood meant:

In 1944, Recy Taylor was a young wife and mother walking home from a church service she'd attended in Abbeville, Alabama, when she was abducted by six armed white men, raped, and left blindfolded by the side of the road coming home from church. They threatened to kill her if she ever told anyone, but her story was reported to the NAACP where a young worker by the name of Rosa Parks became the lead investigator on her case and together they sought justice. But justice wasn't an option in the era of

Jim Crow. The men who tried to destroy her were never prosecuted. Recy Taylor died ten days ago, just shy of her 98th birthday. She lived as we all have lived, too many years in a culture broken by brutally powerful men. For too long, women have not been heard or believed if they dare speak the truth to the power of those men. But their time is up. Their time is up.[33]

Winfrey's speech located activists at the end of a long line of oppositional storytellers—Taylor herself; Rosa Parks, who investigated and documented the crime for the NAACP; historian Danielle McGuire, who in 2011 published a history of black women, rape, and resistance in which Taylor's story was centered; Nancy Buirski, who directed a 2017 documentary about Taylor.[34]

The response to this speech from prominent Republican strategist, Breitbart News founder, and contemporary G-Man Stephen Bannon was swift. Bannon called Winfrey's speech "a definitional moment in the culture," warning that a puritanical "anti-patriarchy movement is going to undo ten thousand years of recorded history."[35] In the late 1940s, anti-communists found themselves similarly threatened by a rising tide of anti-racist sentiment and incipient feminism. Today, white supremacists invested in traditions of exclusion are desperate to reestablish their dominance over American culture, in opposition to the force of social movements against racial and gender-based violence that are taking advantage of the new affordances of social media to speak their truths.

The moment a person leaves an abusive relationship is the most dangerous moment of all: it's when abusers turn desperate to restore control, violent in their attempts to cling to previous forms of power and privilege. The Americanism the G-Man reimposed on American television in the middle of the twentieth century was the product of abusive relationships in which demeaning portrayals of women, people of color, and immigrants helped normalize bigotry and discrimination. Creating a tradition that includes the stories of the Broadcast 41 helps us understand what happens when these narratives of abuse are institutionalized, as well as what the world might look like freed from representations of repression and disrespect and viewed from wide-ranging perspectives. Remembering the lives of women whose political beliefs and convictions were at odds with the forms of Americanism the blacklist institutionalized reminds us of the persistence of these struggles, our own position within a broader chain of resistance, and the still urgent need to reimagine more radical possibilities for media in our own eras.

Notes

Prologue

1 Shirley Graham, "Letter to Mr. Joseph Goldstein," Box 17, Folder 5, December 22, 1951, 2, Shirley Graham Du Bois Papers, Schlesinger Library, Radcliffe Institute for Advanced Study, Harvard University, Cambridge, MA.
2 Jean Muir, "Autobiography," n.d., 2–3, Jean Muir Papers, University of Oregon Special Collections and Archives, Eugene, OR.
3 Ibid., 5.
4 Ibid., 6.
5 Graham, "Letter to Mr. Joseph Goldstein," 2.
6 Gertrude Berg, "The Goldbergs," Box 39, February 27, 1950, 24, Gertrude Berg Papers, Nightingale Library, Syracuse University, Syracuse, NY. Bob Schiller and Bob Weiskopf, "Lucy Wants a Career," The Lucy-Desi Comedy Hour, directed by Jerry Thorpe, aired April 13, 1959, https://www.youtube.com/watch?v=s9waRE001Vs.
7 Bob Schiller and Bob Weiskopf, "Lucy Wants a Career," *The Lucy-Desi Comedy Hour,* directed by Jerry Thorpe, aired April 13, 1959, https://www.youtube.com/watch?v=s9waRE001Vs.
8 Richard Sanville (Adrian Scott), "Ellie," Box 13, File Folder 6, n.d., 49, Adrian and Joan Scott Papers, American Heritage Center, University of Wyoming, Laramie, WY.
9 Ibid., 51.
10 Ibid., 99.
11 Adrian Scott, "Letter to Joseph Losey," Box 5, Folder 19, "Correspondence," August 1, 1960, Adrian and Joan Scott Papers, American Heritage Center, University of Wyoming, Laramie, WY. The gray list referred to those who were not included on public blacklists, but who found themselves subject to forms of retaliation and joblessness similar to those whose names appeared in *Red Channels* and *CounterAttack.*
12 Some important examples to the contrary include: Steven D. Classen, *Watching Jim Crow: The Struggles over Mississippi TV, 1955–1969* (Durham, NC: Duke University Press, 2004); Anna McCarthy, *Ambient Television: Visual Culture and Public Space* (Durham, NC: Duke University Press, 2001); Susan Murray, *Hitch Your Antenna to the Stars: Early Television and Broadcast Stardom* (New York, NY: Routledge, 2005).
13 Alan Nadel, *Containment Culture: American Narratives, Postmodernism, and the Atomic Age* (Durham, NC: Duke University Press, 1995).
14 Ronald Reagan, "Address Before a Joint Session of the Congress Reporting on the State of the Union," February 4, 1986, 135–36, reagan2020.us/speeches/state_of_the_union_1986.asp.
15 *Morning Edition,* National Public Radio, September 17, 1992.
16 Kathleen Madigan, "You Want 'Family Values'? They'll Cost Billions," *Business Week,* September 28, 1992.
17 Charles Osgood, "Survey Shows the Nuclear Family Is Making a Comeback," *The Osgood File,* CBS, May 2, 1996.

18 Charles Bethea, "What a White Supremacist Told Me After Donald Trump Was Elected," *New Yorker*, August 17, 2017, www.newyorker.com/news/news-desk/what-a-white-supremacist-told-me-after-donald-trump-was-elected.

19 Jane Mayer, *Dark Money: The Hidden History of the Billionaires Behind the Rise of the Radical Right* (Garden City, NY: Doubleday, 2016); Nancy MacLean, *Democracy in Chains: The Deep History of the Radical Right's Stealth Plan for America* (New York, NY: Viking, 2017).

20 Jana Winter and Sharon Weinberger, "The FBI's New U.S. Terrorist Threat: 'Black Identity Extremists,'" *Foreign Policy*, October 16, 2017, https://foreignpolicy.com/2017/10/06/the-fbi-has-identified-a-new-domestic-terrorist-threat-and-its-black-identity-extremists/.

Chapter 1 Redacted Women

1 Patricia Hill Collins, *Black Feminist Thought: Knowledge, Consciousness, and the Politics of Empowerment* (New York, NY: Routledge, 2008), 3.

2 William Bruce Johnson, *Miracles and Sacrilege: Roberto Rossellini, the Church and Film Censorship in Hollywood* (Toronto: University of Toronto Press, 2008), 182.

3 Joe Connelly and Bob Mosher, "Beaver Gets Spelled," *Leave It to Beaver*, CBS, directed by Norman Tokar, aired October 4, 1957 (Burbank, CA: Universal Studios Home Entertainment, 2005), DVD.

4 The American Business Consultants, *Red Channels: The Report of Communist Influence in Radio and Television* (New York, NY: The author, 1950), 1.

5 Lillian Hellman and Wendy Wasserstein, *An Unfinished Woman: A Memoir* (Boston, MA: Back Bay Books, 1999), 119.

6 Herman Gray, *Watching Race: Television and the Struggle for "Blackness"* (Minneapolis, MN: University of Minnesota Press, 1995), 74.

7 Angela Y. Davis, "Black Nationalism: The Sixties and the Nineties," in *Black Popular Culture*, ed. Gina Dent (Seattle, WA: Bay, 1992), 317–24.

8 Albert Abramson, *The History of Television, 1942 to 2000* (Jefferson, NC: McFarland, 2007); Rick Marschall, *The Golden Age of Television* (New York, NY: Smithmark Publications, 1995); Robert St. John, *Encyclopedia of Radio and Television: The Man Behind the Microphone*, Milwaukee, WI: Cathedral Square Publishing Company, 1967; Harvey Sheldon, *The History of the Golden Age of Television* (n.p.: The author, 2013).

9 Matthew Desmond, *Evicted: Poverty and Profit in the American City* (New York, NY: Crown, 2016), 325–26.

10 Lillian Hellman, *Conversations with Lillian Hellman*, Literary Conversations Series (Jackson, MS: University Press of Mississippi, 1986), 149.

11 Kate Mostel, *170 Years of Show Business* (New York, NY: Random House, 1978), 96–97.

12 Lillian Hellman, *Pentimento* (Boston, MA: Little, Brown & Company, 1973), 102.

13 Lena Horne, "Lena Horne—From Me to You," *The People's Voice*, January 10, 1948.

14 Rose Hobart, *A Steady Digression to a Fixed Point* (Metuchen, NJ: Scarecrow Press, 1994), 50.

15 Mostel, *170 Years of Show Business*, 96–97.

16 *Lena Horne: The Lady and Her Music*, Harold Wheeler, musical director, New York, NY, 1981, www.youtube.com/watch?v=6rpIfQQv_T0.

17 James Haskins, *Lena: A Personal and Professional Biography of Lena Horne* (New York, NY: Stein and Day, 1984), 158.
18 Gary Carey, *Judy Holliday: An Intimate Life Story* (New York, NY: Putnam Adult, 1984), 35.
19 "Artists' Play to Aid War," *New York Times*, October 14, 1942.
20 Pierre Bourdieu and Loïc J.D. Wacquant, *An Invitation to Reflexive Sociology* (Chicago, IL: University of Chicago Press, 1992), 88.
21 Michael Denning, *The Cultural Front: The Laboring of American Culture in the Twentieth Century* (London: Verso, 2011), 4.
22 Alan M. Wald, *Trinity of Passion: The Literary Left and the Antifascist Crusade* (Chapel Hill, NC: University of North Carolina Press, 2007), 118.
23 Karen Sue Foley, *The Political Blacklist in the Broadcast Industry: The Decade of the 1950s* (New York, NY: Arno Press, 1972), 109.
24 Pierre Bourdieu et al., *The Weight of the World: Social Suffering in Contemporary Society*, trans. Priscilla Parkhurst Ferguson (Stanford, CA: Stanford University Press, 2000), 3.
25 Betty Millard, "Woman Against Myth," Box 6, Folder 18, 1948, 21, American Left Ephemera Collection, 1894–2008, University of Pittsburgh, Pittsburgh, PA.
26 Alice R. Sheldon, "The Women-Haters," James Tiptree, Jr. Papers, 1947, 11, University of Oregon Special Collections and University Archives, Eugene, OR.
27 Stephanie Coontz, *The Way We Never Were: American Families and the Nostalgia Trap* (New York, NY: Basic Books, 1992), 92.
28 Michael Stewart Foley, ed., *Home Fronts: A Wartime America Reader* (New York, NY: New Press, 2008), 210.
29 Elizabeth Dilling, "Dear Friends," *Patriotic Research Bureau for the Defense of Christianity and Americanism*, October 1943, 5.
30 Cynthia Enloe, *Maneuvers: The International Politics of Militarizing Women's Lives* (Berkeley, CA: University of California Press, 2000).
31 Kathleen Belew, "Veterans and White Supremacy," *New York Times*, April 15, 2014, www.nytimes.com/2014/04/16/opinion/veterans-and-white-supremacy.html.
32 The FBI refused to hire African Americans as special agents until forced to do so in the 1960s; with segregated churches in the South and a long history of fighting against civil rights, the Catholic Church deeply opposed progressive social change; and the American Legion, the Veterans of Foreign Wars, and Catholic War Veterans prohibited black membership until the 1960s.
33 Elizabeth Valentine, "The Girls They Didn't Leave Behind Them," *New York Times Magazine*, February 10, 1946.
34 Saul K. Padover, "Why Americans Like German Women," *American Mercury*, September 1946, 356.
35 Philip Wylie, *Generation of Vipers* (New York, NY: Rinehart, 1955), 199.
36 Ralph S. Banay, "Statement," in *Hearings before the Senate Subcommittee to Investigate Juvenile Delinquency* (Washington, DC: U.S. Government Printing Office, 1955), http://archive.org/stream/juveniledelinque951unit/juveniledelinque951unit_djvu.txt.
37 Ralph S. Banay, "Is Modern Woman a Failure?," *Milwaukee Journal*, December 7, 1946.
38 American Legion, "Summary of Trends and Developments Exposing the Communist Conspiracy," *Spotlight*, February 1950, 18, https://ia601706.us.archive.org/26/items/foia_American_Legion-NAC-18/American_Legion-NAC-18.pdf; The American Business Consultants, "Letter No. 120," *CounterAttack*, September 9, 1949, 2–3.

39 Alice Dunbar Nelson, "As in a Looking Glass," *Washington-Eagle*, February 1, 1929.
40 Denning, *The Cultural Front*, 34.
41 Mostel, *170 Years of Show Business*, 123.
42 Lena Horne and Richard Schickel, *Lena* (Garden City, NY: Doubleday, 1965), 82.
43 Gertrude Berg, *Molly and Me: A Memoir* (New York, NY: McGraw-Hill, 1961), 10.
44 Farah Jasmine Griffin, *Harlem Nocturne: Women Artists and Progressive Politics during World War II* (New York, NY: Basic Civitas Books, 2013), xi.
45 Dorothy Parker, *The Portable Dorothy Parker*, ed. Marion Meade (New York, NY: Penguin Classics, 2006), 460.
46 Carey, *Judy Holliday*, 112.
47 "Madeline Lee's Statement to the Witchhunters," *Daily Worker*, August 22, 1955, FBI #100-39-3334-A, National Archives and Records Administration, College Park, MD.
48 Jeff Kisseloff, *The Box: An Oral History of Television 1920–1961* (n.p.: ReAnimus Press, 2013), 423.
49 Albert Maltz, "General Information about the Investigation of Hollywood by the Congressional Committee on Un-American Activities," Albert Maltz Papers, Box 48, "Blacklist," n.d., 1, American Heritage Center, University of Wyoming, Laramie, WY.
50 According to Steven D. Stark, prime-time television's representations of lawyers, police, and the legal system dramatically shaped public perceptions of police, policing, and justice ("Perry Mason Meets Sonny Crockett: The History of Lawyers and the Police as Television Heroes," *University of Miami Law Review*, 42, no. 229, 1987: 229–283).
51 See FBI #100-350512-899 for information about the final issues of *CounterAttack* in spring 1971.
52 The American Business Consultants, *Red Channels*, 4.
53 Ibid., 2.
54 Betty Medsger, *The Burglary: The Discovery of J. Edgar Hoover's Secret FBI* (New York, NY: Knopf, 2014), 353.
55 The American Business Consultants, *Red Channels*, 1.
56 U.S. Congress, House of Representatives. Committee on Un-American Activities, *100 Things You Should Know About Communism* (Washington, DC: U.S. Government Printing Office, 1949), 15, https://archive.org/stream/100thingsyoushou1949unit/100thingsyoushou1949unit_djvu.txt.
57 In 1948, actor Fredric March and his wife, Florence Eldridge, brought a successful libel suit against *CounterAttack*; Larry Adler and Paul Draper's libel suit against Hester McCullough ended in a hung jury in May 1950; journalist Quentin Reynolds won his 1955 libel case against conservative Hearst columnist and FBI informant Westbrook Pegler; and in 1962, John Henry Faulk won his landmark libel case against AWARE, Inc.
58 J. Edgar Hoover, *Masters of Deceit: The Story of Communism in America and How to Fight It* (New York, NY: Henry Holt, 1958).
59 Medsger, *The Burglary*, 246.
60 Marie Jahoda, "Anti-Communism and Employment Policies in Radio and Television," in *Report on Blacklisting: II Radio – Television*, ed. John Cogley (New York, NY: Fund for the Republic, 1956), 255.
61 Ibid., 241.
62 Julia L. Mickenberg, *Learning from the Left: Children's Literature, the Cold War, and Radical Politics in the United States* (New York, NY: Oxford University Press, 2005); Denning, *The Cultural Front*.

63 Alan Filreis, *Counter-Revolution of the Word: The Conservative Attack on Modern Poetry, 1945–1960* (Chapel Hill, NC: University of North Carolina Press, 2008).
64 Bill Mullen and James Edward Smethurst, eds., *Left of the Color Line: Race, Radicalism, and Twentieth-Century Literature of the United States* (Chapel Hill, NC: University of North Carolina Press, 2003); James Edward Smethurst, *The New Red Negro: The Literary Left and African American Poetry, 1930–1946* (New York, NY: Oxford University Press, 1999); Mary Helen Washington, *The Other Blacklist: The African American Literary and Cultural Left of the 1950s* (New York, NY: Columbia University Press, 2014).
65 William J. Maxwell, *F.B. Eyes: How J. Edgar Hoover's Ghostreaders Framed African American Literature* (Princeton, NJ: Princeton University Press, 2015).
66 Hoover, *Masters of Deceit*, 228.
67 Edward S. Herman and Noam Chomsky, *Manufacturing Consent: The Political Economy of the Mass Media* (New York, NY: Pantheon, 2002), 29.
68 The American Business Consultants, "Letter No. 120," 3.
69 Elizabeth Dilling, *Red Revolution: Do We Want It Here?* (Kenilworth, IL: Wilmette Announcements, 1932), 5.
70 Herman and Chomsky, *Manufacturing Consent.*
71 Kisseloff, *The Box*, 203.
72 Milly S. Barranger, *Unfriendly Witnesses: Gender, Theater, and Film in the McCarthy Era* (Carbondale, IL: Southern Illinois University Press, 2008), 125.
73 Quoted in Jean Stein, *West of Eden: An American Place* (New York, NY: Random House, 2016), 76.
74 See Barnouw (1968, 1970). William Boddy, Michele Hilmes, Jason Mittell, and Lynn Spigel, for example, focus on issues as varied as political economy, genre, and ideology, but do not include the blacklist as a pivotal event in television history. George Lipsitz's *Time Passages* and David Zurawik's *The Jews of Prime Time* are notable exceptions as far as they acknowledge the repressive force of anti-communism and the Red Scare's enduring effects on cultural memory, but neither address the blacklist's impact on representations of gender, sexualities, race, and nation. See William Boddy, *Fifties Television: The Industry and Its Critics* (Urbana, IL: University of Illinois Press, 1990); George Lipsitz, *Time Passages: Collective Memory and American Popular Culture* (Minneapolis, MN: University of Minnesota Press, 1990); Anna McCarthy, *The Citizen Machine: Governing by Television in 1950s America* (New York, NY: New Press, 2010); Jason Mittell, *Genre and Television: From Cop Shows to Cartoons in American Culture* (New York, NY: Routledge, 2004); Spigel, *Make Room for TV*; David Zurawik, *The Jews of Prime Time* (Waltham, MA: Brandeis University Press, 2003).
75 Eric Bentley, *Are You Now or Have You Ever Been: The Investigation of Show Business by the Un-American Activities Committee, 1947–1958* (New York, NY: Harper & Row, 1972); Paul Buhle and Dave Wagner, *Hide in Plain Sight: The Hollywood Blacklistees in Film and Television, 1950–2002* (New York, NY: Palgrave Macmillan, 2005); Patrick McGilligan and Paul Buhle, *Tender Comrades: A Backstory of the Hollywood Blacklist* (New York, NY: St. Martin's Press, 1997); Victor S. Navasky, *Naming Names*, rev. edn. (New York, NY: Hill and Wang, 2003); Robert Vaughn, *Only Victims: A Study of Show Business Blacklisting* (New York, NY: Limelight Editions, 1972).
76 Thomas Doherty, *Cold War, Cool Medium: Television, McCarthyism, and American Culture* (New York, NY: Columbia University Press, 2003), 2.

77 David Everitt, *A Shadow of Red: Communism and the Blacklist in Radio and Television* (Chicago, IL: Ivan R. Dee, 2007). Everitt was also co-author of *The Manly Handbook*, a trade paperback that "humorously" preached the gospel of Cold War masculinity against the encroachments of "the Feminist Movement ... and the hysterical assaults of these vicious lesbian propagandists," David Everitt and Harold Schechter, *The Manly Handbook* (New York, NY: Berkley Trade, 1982), 2.
78 Ben H. Bagdikian, *The Media Monopoly* (Boston, MA: Beacon Press, 1997); Herman and Chomsky, *Manufacturing Consent*; Michael Schudson, *The Power of News* (Cambridge, MA: Harvard University Press, 1996).
79 Schudson, *The Power of News*.
80 Jeff Kisseloff, "Another Award, Other Memories of McCarthyism," *New York Times*, May 30, 1999.
81 Washington, *The Other Blacklist*, 240.
82 Berg, *Molly and Me*, 190–91.
83 Ruth Gordon, *My Side: The Autobiography of Ruth Gordon* (New York, NY: Harper & Row, 1976), 8.
84 Athan G. Theoharis, *The FBI: A Comprehensive Reference Guide* (Westport, CT: Greenwood Publishing Group, 1999), 271.
85 Medsger, *The Burglary*, 259.
86 Seth Rosenfeld, *Subversives: The FBI's War on Student Radicals, and Reagan's Rise to Power* (New York, NY: Picador, 2013), 511.
87 So far, I have received nineteen of the forty-one files of the women listed in *Red Channels*. In some cases, women who had been married and changed their name proved difficult to locate, since the FBI had no systematic way of indexing people who had what they described as multiple "aliases." Stella Adler's file had been destroyed. In a number of cases, I challenged the Bureau's redaction of information. The results of some of those appeals are still pending at the time of this writing. One such a challenge afforded me access to thousands of pages of FBI files on anti-communist author Elizabeth Dilling.
88 Ellen W. Schrecker, *The Age of McCarthyism: A Brief History with Documents* (Boston, MA: Bedford/St. Martin's, 2001), 92.
89 Collins, *Black Feminist Thought*, 3.
90 The leadership provided by black women in efforts to consider how race, gender, class, ethnicity, and national identity combined in structures of oppression in the United States and to fight against these is the subject of vital scholarship, as recent work on Alice Childress, Septima Poinsette Clark, Shirley Graham, and Claudia Jones illustrates. See Katherine Mellen Charron, *Freedom's Teacher: The Life of Septima Clark* (Chapel Hill, NC: University of North Carolina Press, 2012); Barbara Ransby, *Ella Baker and the Black Freedom Movement: A Radical Democratic Vision* (Chapel Hill, NC: University of North Carolina Press, 2005); Carole Boyce Davies, *Left of Karl Marx: The Political Life of Black Communist Claudia Jones* (Durham, NC: Duke University Press, 2008); Mary Helen Washington, "Alice Childress, Lorraine Hansberry, and Claudia Jones: Black Women Write the Popular Front," in Mullen and Smethurst, *Left of the Color Line*, 183–204; Griffin, *Harlem Nocturne*; Danielle L. McGuire, *At the Dark End of the Street: Black Women, Rape, and Resistance. A New History of the Civil Rights Movement from Rosa Parks to the Rise of Black Power* (New York, NY: Vintage, 2011); Ruth Feldstein, *How It Feels to Be Free: Black Women Entertainers and the Civil Rights Movement* (New York, NY: Oxford University Press, 2013).

91 Kristen Warner, *The Cultural Politics of Colorblind TV Casting* (New York, NY/ London: Routledge, 2015), 126.

92 Susan J. Douglas, *Listening In: Radio and the American Imagination* (Minneapolis, MN: University of Minnesota Press, 2004); Michele Hilmes, *Radio Voices: American Broadcasting, 1922–1952* (Minneapolis, MN: University of Minnesota Press, 1997); Michele Hilmes, ed., *NBC: America's Network* (Berkeley, CA: University of California Press, 2007); Susan Smulyan, *Selling Radio: The Commercialization of American Broadcasting 1920–1934* (Washington, DC: Smithsonian Institution Press, 1996).

Chapter 2 A Field of Many Perspectives

1 Garson Kanin, *Hollywood: A Memoir* (New York, NY: Viking Press, 1974), 219–20.

2 Gale Sondergaard, "We Speak of Peace," *Jewish Life*, August 1951, 6.

3 See Barbara Neely, *Blanche on the Lam* (New York, NY: Penguin, 1993) for a wonderful example of how telling the mystery from the point of view of the African American domestic worker changes what the mystery has to tell readers. See also Robin R. Means Coleman's *African American Viewers and the Black Situation Comedy: Situating Racial Humor* (New York, NY: Routledge, 2000) for a historical overview of representations of African Americans in sitcoms and responses to those representations.

4 Lena Horne, "Lena Horne—From Me to You," *The People's Voice*, September 20, 1947.

5 Lloyd Lewis, "Frederick Douglass, the Abolitionist Who Began as a Slave," *New York Times Book Review*, April 6, 1947.

6 Vera Caspary, *The Secrets of Grown-Ups* (New York, NY: McGraw-Hill, 1979), 281.

7 Gertrude Berg, *Molly and Me: A Memoir* (New York, NY: McGraw-Hill, 1961), 47–48.

8 Kate Mostel, *170 Years of Show Business* (New York, NY: Random House, 1978), 59–60.

9 Eva Le Gallienne, *With a Quiet Heart: An Autobiography* (New York, NY: Viking Press, 1953), 111.

10 Ruth Gordon, *Ruth Gordon: An Open Book* (Garden City, NY: Doubleday, 1980), 339.

11 Christopher Hitchens, "Rebel in Evening Clothes," *Vanity Fair*, October 1999, www.vanityfair.com/magazine/1999/10/hitchens199910.

12 Caspary, *The Secrets of Grown-Ups*, 17.

13 Vera Caspary, *Thelma* (Boston, MA: Little, Brown, 1952), 331.

14 Mel Gussow, "Uta Hagen, Tony-Winning Broadway Star and Teacher of Actors, Dies at 84," *New York Times*, January 15, 2004, sec. Theater, www.nytimes.com/2004/01/15/theater/uta-hagen-tony-winning-broadway-star-and-teacher-of-actors-dies-at-84.html.

15 Bruce Lambert, "Aline L. MacMahon, 92, Actress Over 50 Years and in 43 Movies," *New York Times*, October 31, 1991, www.nytimes.com/1991/10/13/nyregion/aline-l-macmahon-92-actress-over-50-years-and-in-43-movies.html.

16 Rita Morley Harvey, *Those Wonderful, Terrible Years: George Heller and the American Federation of Television and Radio Artists* (Carbondale, IL: Southern Illinois University Press, 1996), 57.

17 Shirley Graham Du Bois, "As a Man Thinketh in His Heart, So Is He," *Parish News: Church of the Holy Trinity*, February 1954, vol. 57, no. 4, Box 27, Folder 3, Shirley Graham Du Bois Papers, Schlesinger Library, Radcliffe Institute for Advanced Study, Harvard University, Cambridge, MA.

18 Gail Buckley, *The Hornes: An American Family* (New York, NY: Knopf, 1986), 60.

19 Megan E. Williams, "*The Crisis* Cover Girl: Lena Horne, the NAACP, and Representations of African American Femininity," *American Periodicals* 16, no. 2 (2006): 200.
20 Buckley, *The Hornes*, 60.
21 According to Vera Caspary, her father Paul was among a group of white residents who resisted the racist backlash directed at the Barnetts, although as she later observed, they never interacted socially with their black neighbors. See Caspary, *The Secrets of Grown-Ups*, 19.
22 Lena Horne and Richard Schickel, *Lena* (Garden City, NY: Doubleday, 1965), 42.
23 Vera Caspary, *The Rosecrest Cell* (London: W.H. Allen, 1968), 39–40.
24 "Leopardess Takes the Hilda Vaughn," *New York Times*, November 29, 1924; Milly S. Barranger, *Unfriendly Witnesses: Gender, Theater, and Film in the McCarthy Era* (Carbondale, IL: Southern Illinois University Press, 2008), 132.
25 Judy Kaplan and Linn Shapiro, eds., *Red Diapers: Growing Up in the Communist Left* (Urbana, IL: University of Illinois Press, 1998), 285.
26 George Chauncey, *Gay New York: Gender, Urban Culture, and the Making of the Gay Male World, 1890–1940* (New York, NY: Basic Books, 1995), 358.
27 Lillian Hellman, *Pentimento* (Boston, MA: Little, Brown & Company, 1973), 154.
28 Vera Caspary, *Bedelia* (London: Eyre and Spottiswoode, 1945), 92.
29 Milly S. Barranger, *Margaret Webster: A Life in the Theater* (Ann Arbor, MI: University of Michigan Press, 2004), 87.
30 Gary Carey, *Judy Holliday: An Intimate Life Story* (New York, NY: Putnam Adult, 1984), 44.
31 Lisa E. Davis, "The FBI's Lesbian, Eleanor Roosevelt and Other Tales from the Red Scare," *Rethinking Marxism* 21, no. 4 (2009): 628–29.
32 Stacy L. Spaulding, "Lisa Sergio: How Mussolini's 'Golden Voice' of Propaganda Created an American Mass Communication Career" (Ph.D. dissertation, University of Maryland, 2005), 87, 128.
33 Koa Beck, "How Marriage Inequality Prompts Gay Partners to Adopt One Another," *The Atlantic*, November 27, 2013, www.theatlantic.com/national/archive/2013/11/how-marriage-inequality-prompts-gay-partners-to-adopt-one-another/281546/.
34 Barranger, *Margaret Webster*, 87.
35 Norma Jean Darden, "Oh, Sister! Fredi and Isabel Washington Relive '30s Razzmatazz," *Essence Magazine*, September 1978, 100; Carole Boyce Davies, *Left of Karl Marx: The Political Life of Black Communist Claudia Jones* (Durham, NC: Duke University Press, 2008); Gerald Horne, *Race Woman: The Lives of Shirley Graham Du Bois* (New York, NY: New York University Press, 2002).
36 Davies, *Left of Karl Marx*; Dayo F. Gore, *Radicalism at the Crossroads: African American Women Activists in the Cold War* (New York, NY: New York University Press, 2011).
37 "Lena Horne Tells How Paul Robeson Changed Her Life," *Daily Worker*, October 7, 1947, FBI #100-353031, National Archives and Records Administration, College Park, MD.
38 Horne and Schickel, *Lena*, 116–17.
39 Megan E. Williams, "'Meet the Real Lena Horne'': Representations of Lena Horne in *Ebony* Magazine, 1945–1949," *Journal of American Studies* 43, no. 1 (2009): 119.
40 Shane Vogel, "Lena Horne's Impersona," *Camera Obscura* 23, no. 1 (67) (2008): 14.
41 Donald Bogle, *Toms, Coons, Mulattoes, Mammies, and Bucks: An Interpretive History of Blacks in American Films* (New York, NY: Continuum, 2001); "Part in 'Imitation' Is Not Real Me,' Says Fredi," *Chicago Defender*, January 19, 1935, National edition;

Charlene B. Regester, *African American Actresses: The Struggle for Visibility, 1900–1960* (Bloomington, IN: Indiana University Press, 2010).

42 Mary Margaret McBride, "Marriage on a Fifty-Fifty Basis," *Scribner's Magazine*, December 1929, 662.

43 Dorothy Parker, *The Portable Dorothy Parker*, ed. Marion Meade (New York, NY: Penguin Classics, 2006), 613.

44 Lisa Yaszek, *Galactic Suburbia: Recovering Women's Science Fiction* (Columbus, OH: Ohio State University Press, 2008), 35.

45 Carlyle M. Bass and Grace F. Johnson, "Summary of File References," October 19, 1950, 15, FBI #100-371261, Federal Bureau of Investigation, New York, NY.

46 Ruth Gordon, *My Side: The Autobiography of Ruth Gordon* (New York, NY: Harper & Row, 1976), 75.

47 Sol Siegel, "Letter to Vera Caspary," May 19, 1947, Vera Caspary Papers, Wisconsin Historical Society, Madison, WI.

48 Caspary, *Bedelia*, 52.

49 Gordon, *Ruth Gordon*, 241.

50 James Haskins, *Lena: A Personal and Professional Biography of Lena Horne* (New York, NY: Stein and Day, 1984), 16.

51 Jeremiah Favara and Carol Stabile, "Hollywood, the Sexual Violence Factory," *Ms. Magazine Blog* (blog), November 23, 2015, http://msmagazine.com/blog/2015/11/23/hollywood-the-sexual-violence-factory/.

52 Gordon, *My Side*, 16.

53 Jean Muir, "Autobiography," n.d., 152, Jean Muir Papers, University of Oregon Special Collections and Archives, Eugene, OR.

54 Carey, *Judy Holliday*, 59.

55 Myrna Oliver, "Rose Hobart; SAG Official, Blacklisted Actress," *Los Angeles Times*, August 31, 2000, 36, http://articles.latimes.com/2000/aug/31/local/me-13393.

56 Sherrie Tucker, *Swing Shift: "All-Girl" Bands of the 1940s* (Durham, NC: Duke University Press, 2001), 138–39; Barbara Y. Welke, "Where All the Women Were White, and All the Blacks Were Men: Gender, Class, Race, and the Road to Plessy, 1855–1914," *Law and History Review* 13, no. 2 (1995): 261–316.

57 Le Gallienne, *With a Quiet Heart*, 188–89.

58 Gordon, *My Side*, 136.

59 Barbara Leaming, *Marilyn Monroe*, repr. edn. (New York, NY: Three Rivers Press, 2000), 15.

60 The extent to which below-the-line personnel participated in these cultures of misogyny remains to be documented. *Born Yesterday*'s costume designer, Jean-Louis, later recalled that he designed Judy Holliday's dresses so as to punish her for gaining weight: he "cinched in the waists of her dresses and fitted the bodices with a tightly boned inner structure. 'If she was even an ounce overweight,' he recalled, 'she would have gasped with pain every time she sat down.' " Carey, *Judy Holliday*, 108.

61 Sylvia Jarrico, "Evil Heroines of 1953," *Hollywood Review* 1, no. 3 (July 1953): 4.

62 Bogle, *Toms, Coons, Mulattoes*; Richard Dyer, *White* (New York, NY: Psychology Press, 1997); Stuart Hall, "The Whites of Their Eyes: Racist Ideologies and the Media," in *The Media Reader*, ed. Manuel Alvarado and John O. Thompson (London: BFI, 1990), 7–23; Eric Lott, *Love and Theft: Blackface Minstrelsy and the American Working Class* (New York, NY: Oxford University Press, 1993).

63 Anne Helen Petersen, *Scandals of Classic Hollywood: Sex, Deviance, and Drama from the Golden Age of American Cinema* (New York, NY: Plume, 2014), 196.
64 Horne and Schickel, *Lena*, 134–35.
65 Karen Chilton, *Hazel Scott: The Pioneering Journey of a Jazz Pianist, from Café Society to Hollywood to HUAC* (Ann Arbor, MI: University of Michigan Press, 2010), 72.
66 Kanin, *Hollywood*, 214.
67 John Szwed, *Billie Holiday: The Musician and the Myth* (New York, NY: Viking, 2015), 58.
68 Adam Bernstein, "Lena Horne Dies at 92; Performer Altered Hollywood's Image of Black Women," *Washington Post*, May 11, 2010.
69 This was the case with one of Horne's scenes in the film *Panama Hattie* (1942). See Horne and Schickel, *Lena*, 139–40.
70 Lena Horne, "Lena Horne—From Me to You," *The People's Voice*, January 10, 1948.
71 As Buhle and Wagner point out, some women writers succeeded because of collaborations with husbands or romantic partners, like Jean Rouverol Butler and Hugo Butler; Dorothy and DuBose Heyward; Helen Slote Levitt and Alfred Lewis Levitt (who wrote under the pseudonyms Tom and Helen August); and Faith and John Hubley. Paul Buhle and David Wagner, *Hide in Plain Sight: The Hollywood Blacklistees in Film and Television, 1950–2002* (New York, NY: Palgrave Macmillan, 2005).
72 Caspary, *The Secrets of Grown-Ups*, 209. Preminger had a child with Gypsy Rose Lee, another member of the Broadcast 41, and later a highly publicized and disastrous affair with Dorothy Dandridge.
73 Quoted in Ann L. Warren, "Word Play: The Lives and Work of Four Women Writers in Hollywood's Golden Age" (Ph.D. dissertation, University of Southern California, 1988), 73, original emphases.
74 Cohn's sexism was notorious. He balked at casting Judy Holliday in the film version of *Born Yesterday* because she appeared to his eyes to be too Jewish and fat (he had wanted Rita Hayworth to play the role). Even after she was cast, he was heard bemoaning this choice: "If only that cunt Hayworth ... hadn't married that fucking Moslem playboy!" (Carey, Judy Holliday, 102).
75 Jeff Kisseloff, *The Box: An Oral History of Television, 1929–1961* (New York, NY: Viking Adult, 1995), 268.
76 "Ethel Waters in Rehearsal," *Chicago Defender*, December 17, 1938; David W. Kellum, "Ethel Waters Is Superb in 'Mamba's Daughters,'" *Chicago Defender*, October 7, 1939.
77 Laurie Avant Woodard, "Performing Artists of the Harlem Renaissance: Resistance, Identity, and Meaning in the Life and Work of Fredi Washington from 1920 to 1950" (Ph.D. dissertation, Yale University, 2007), 302.
78 Muir, "Autobiography," 144–45.
79 Lillian Hellman, *Conversations with Lillian Hellman*, Literary Conversations Series (Jackson, MS: University Press of Mississippi, 1986), 5.
80 Rhonda S. Pettit, ed., *The Critical Waltz: Essays on the Work of Dorothy Parker* (Madison, NJ: Fairleigh Dickinson University Press, 2005), 362.
81 Parker, *The Portable Dorothy Parker*, 201. The extent to which fashion and the fashion industry has been the source of so much misery to women in media deserves a book all its own. Jill Soloway, the producer/writer of *Transparent*, wrote in one of her own essays that, "Pointy shoes make me want to cry. Anything [actress] Sarah Jessica Parker ever wore makes me cry" (quoted in Ariel Levy, "Dolls and Feelings," *New Yorker*, December 14, 2015, 42).

82 Anna Everett, *Returning the Gaze: A Genealogy of Black Film Criticism, 1909–1949* (Durham, NC: Duke University Press, 2001), 222.
83 Hellman, *Conversations with Lillian Hellman*, 109.
84 Vera Caspary, "Letter to Monica McCall," Personal (June 26, 1968), Box 28, Folder 1, General Correspondence, Vera Caspary Papers, Wisconsin Historical Society, Madison, WI.
85 Susan Lydon, "The Faa-Bu-Lous Long Run of Gordon and Kanin," *New York Times*, October 5, 1969, 70.
86 Dennis McLellan and Valerie J. Nelson, "Lena Horne Dies at 92," *Los Angeles Times*, May 10, 2010.
87 Horne and Schickel, *Lena*, 274.
88 Muir, "Autobiography," 197.
89 New York Field Office Special Agent in Charge, "Uta Hagen Berghof, Was SM-C," August 22, 1956, FBI #100371261, National Archives and Records Administration, College, MD.
90 Noralee Frankel, *Stripping Gypsy: The Life of Gypsy Rose Lee* (New York, NY: Oxford University Press, 2009), 174; June Havoc, *Early Havoc* (n.p.: Literary Licensing, LLC, 2011).
91 Ronald Bergan, "Obituary: Rose Hobart," *Guardian*, September 14, 2000, 42, www.theguardian.com/news/2000/sep/14/guardianobituaries3.
92 Muir, "Autobiography," 179.
93 "Megger Draws Up Slate for Ballot," *Billboard*, May 21, 1949.
94 "Editorial," *Hollywood Review*, October 1953.
95 "Bill Robinson Named Guild Honorary Head," *Chicago Defender*, February 18, 1939.
96 "Norman Granz to Receive a New Award for His Campaign on Discrimination," *Chicago Defender*, May 17, 1947, National edition.
97 Chilton, *Hazel Scott*, 138.
98 Bernstein, "Lena Horne Dies at 92."
99 "Hazel Scott Attorneys Score in Initial Round," *Spokane Daily Chronicle*, April 17, 1950.
100 Dwayne Mack, "Hazel Scott: A Career Curtailed," *Journal of African American History* 91, no. 2 (April 1, 2006): 160.
101 Langston Hughes, "From Here to Yonder," *Chicago Defender*, June 10, 1944, National edition, 12.
102 Harvey, *Those Wonderful, Terrible Years*, 53.
103 Robert E. Russell, Los Angeles, CA: April 7, 1951, 5, FBI #100-33176.
104 Federal Bureau of Investigation, "Correlation Summary," June 18, 1956, 14, FBI #100-420699-3, National Archives and Records Administration, College Park, MD.
105 John J. Manning, "Lena Horne, Was, Lina Horne, Helena Horne," Washington, DC: February 12, 1948, Federal Bureau of Investigation, FBI #100-88027, National Archives and Records Administration, College Park, MD.
106 Founded by the American Civil Liberties Union in 1933, the American Committee for the Protection of the Foreign Born assisted people facing deportation, protected the rights of immigrant workers, and opposed anti-immigrant legislation. See Rachel Ida Buff, *Against the Deportation Terror: Organizing for Immigrant Rights in the Twentieth Century* (Philadelphia, PA: Temple University Press, 2017) for an account of the American Committee for the Protection of the Foreign Born.

107 Horne, "Lena Horne—From Me to You."
108 Horne and Schickel, *Lena*, 156–57.
109 Barranger, *Unfriendly Witnesses*, 63.
110 Vera Caspary, "What Price Martyrdom?" *Chicago Defender*, January 9, 1932.
111 Caspary, *The Rosecrest Cell*, 179, 57.
112 Aaron D. Purcell, *White Collar Radicals: TVA's Knoxville Fifteen, the New Deal, and the McCarthy Era* (Knoxville, TN: University of Tennessee Press, 2009).
113 Gary May, *Un-American Activities: The Trials of William Remington* (New York, NY: Oxford University Press, 1994).
114 Horne, *Race woman*, 26.
115 Shirley Graham, "Letter to Mr. T.O. Thackrey, Publisher, *The Daily Compass*," September 11, 1952, Box 17, Folder 8, Shirley Graham Du Bois Papers, Schlesinger Library, Radcliffe Institute for Advanced Study, Harvard University, Cambridge, MA.
116 Eric Bentley, *Are You Now or Have You Ever Been: The Investigation of Show Business by the Un-American Activities Committee, 1947-1958* (New York, NY: Harper & Row, 1972), 154.
117 Robert Vaughn, *Only Victims: A Study of Show Business Blacklisting* (New York, NY: Limelight Editions, 1972), 31.
118 Vera Caspary, "Letter to Don Fine (Editor in Chief, Dell Publishing Company)," July 6, 1971, Box 1, Folder 6, General Correspondence 1961–63, Vera Caspary Papers, Wisconsin Historical Society, Madison, WI.
119 Darryl Zanuck, "Inter-Office Memo to Sol Siegel," May 19, 1947, 1, Vera Caspary Papers, Wisconsin Historical Society, Madison, WI.
120 Shirley Graham, "Address to Kwame Nkrumah Ideological Institute," Accra, Ghana, May 26, 1964, Box 44, Folder 9, Shirley Graham Du Bois Papers, Schlesinger Library, Radcliffe Institute for Advanced Study, Harvard University, Cambridge, MA.
121 Muir, "Autobiography," 213.
122 "Is Television New to Our Entertainers?" *Chicago Defender*, July 1, 1939, National edition.
123 Griffin, *Harlem Nocturne*, 8.
124 Michelle Stephens, "The First Negro Matinee Idol: Harry Belafonte and American Culture in the 1950s," in *Left of the Color Line: Race, Radicalism, and Twentieth-Century Literature of the United States*, ed. Bill V. Mullen and James Smethurst (Chapel Hill, NC: University of North Carolina Press, 2004), 225.
125 Erik Barnouw, *The Image Empire: A History of Broadcasting in the United States*, vol. 3: *From 1953* (New York, NY: Oxford University Press, 1970), 25.
126 Berg, *Molly and Me*, 209.
127 Sondergaard, "We Speak of Peace," 7–8.
128 Horne and Schickel, *Lena*, 195. Anti-communists believed that relationships like those of Hayton and Horne should be forbidden, understanding them to have crossed the racialized dividing line between Americans and un-Americans.
129 Shirley Graham, "Letter Sent to the *New York Post* and *New York Star*," Letter to the editor, June 25, 1948, Box 17, Folder 1, Shirley Graham Du Bois Papers, Schlesinger Library, Radcliffe Institute for Advanced Study, Harvard University, Cambridge, MA.
130 Muir, "Autobiography," 170.
131 Gertrude Berg, *The Rise of the Goldbergs* (New York, NY: Barse and Company, 1931), 247.

Chapter 3 G-Man Nation

1 Adrian Scott, "Blacklist: The Liberal's Straightjacket and Its Effect on Content," *Hollywood Review*, October 1955, Adrian and Joan Scott Papers, #3238, American Heritage Center, University of Wyoming, Laramie, WY.
2 Dalton Trumbo, *The Time of the Toad: A Study of Inquisition in America* (New York, NY: Perennial Library, 1972), 145.
3 Denis D. O'Sullivan, "Madeline Lee, Was Madeline Fein," October 18, 1955, FBI #100-1393334-10, National Archives and Records Administration, College Park, MD.
4 Stephen Miller, "Madeline Lee Gilford, 84, Actress and Activist," *New York Sun*, April 18, 2008, www.nysun.com/obituaries/madeline-lee-gilford-84-actress-and-activist/74950/.
5 O'Sullivan, "Madeline Lee, Was Madeline Fein."
6 Special Agent in Charge, New York, "Madeleine Lee Gellman, Was: Madeline Lee, Madeline Rosaline Laderman, Madeline Rosalind Letterman, Madeline Gilford, Madeline Guilford, Mrs. Jacob Gellman, Mrs. Jack Guilford, Mrs. Jack Gilford, Madeline Fein, Mrs. Mitchell Fein," Office Memorandum, New York, NY: December 16, 1955, FBI #100-393334, National Archives and Records Administration, College Park, MD.
7 Robert Simonson, "Madeline Lee Gilford, Actress, Producer and Widow of Jack Gilford, Is Dead," *Playbill*, April 15, 2008, www.playbill.com/article/madeline-lee-gilford-actress-producer-and-widow-of-jack-gilford-is-dead-com-149241.
8 Special Agent in Charge, New York, "Madeline Lee, Was SM-C," New York, NY: April 23, 1954, FBI #100-39334-6, National Archives and Records Administration, College Park, MD.
9 David Pratt, "Actress Charges Probe Sought False Testimony," *Daily Worker*, May 11, 1955, FBI #100-393334-A, National Archives and Records Administration, College Park, MD.
10 "Miss Lee Accuses Red Inquiry Aide," *New York Times*, August 18, 1955.
11 "Agents Pressured Actress to Become 'False Witness,'" *Daily Worker*, August 21, 1955, FBI #100-393334, National Archives and Records Administration, College Park, MD.
12 Pratt, "Actress Charges."
13 Robert Vaughn, *Only Victims: A Study of Show Business Blacklisting* (New York, NY: Limelight Editions, 1972), 24.
14 Robyn Muncy, *Relentless Reformer: Josephine Roche and Progressivism in Twentieth-Century America* (Princeton, NJ: Princeton University Press, 2014), 29.
15 Lillian Hellman and Wendy Wasserstein, *An Unfinished Woman: A Memoir* (Boston, MA: Back Bay Books, 1999), 119.
16 Eric Bentley, *Are You Now or Have You Ever Been: The Investigation of Show Business by the Un-American Activities Committee, 1947–1958* (New York, NY: Harper & Row, 1972), 147.
17 William C. Sullivan, *The Bureau: My Thirty Years in Hoover's FBI* (New York, NY: Norton, 1979), 16.
18 Richard Gid Powers, *G-Men: Hoover's FBI in American Popular Culture* (Carbondale, IL: Southern Illinois University Press, 1983), 55.
19 Ibid., viii.

20 J. Edgar Hoover, "Unmasking the Communist Masquerader," *Educational Forum*, May 1950, 401.
21 Elizabeth Dilling, *The Roosevelt Red Record and Its Background* (Kenilworth, IL: The author, 1936), 144.
22 J. Edgar Hoover, "Communist 'New Look': A Study in Duplicity," *Elks Magazine*, August 1956, 5.
23 U.S. Congress, House of Representatives. Committee on Un-American Activities, "Report on the Congress of American Women" (Washington, DC: U.S. Government Printing Office, October 23, 1949 [1950]).
24 American Legion, "Special Report," April 4, 1950, FBI #100-368669, Federal Bureau of Investigation, National Archives and Records Administration, College Park, MD.
25 Troy Duster, *Backdoor to Eugenics* (New York, NY: Routledge, 2003); Kelly E. Happe, *The Material Gene: Gender, Race, and Heredity after the Human Genome Project* (New York, NY: New York University Press, 2013).
26 Quoted in John Sbardellati, *J. Edgar Hoover Goes to the Movies: The FBI and the Origins of Hollywood's Cold War* (Ithaca, NY: Cornell University Press, 2012), 171.
27 Ferdinand Lundberg and Marynia F. Farnham, *Modern Woman: The Lost Sex* (New York, NY: Harper & Brothers, 1947), 303.
28 Edward F. Cline, *My Little Chickadee*, comedy (Universal Pictures, 1940).
29 Elizabeth Dilling, *The Red Network: A "Who's Who" and Handbook of Radicalism for Patriots* (Chicago, IL: The author, 1934), 22.
30 Vincent Hartnett, "Red Fronts in Radio," *The Sign*, October 1949, 12.
31 Bentley, *Are You Now or Have You Ever Been*, 115.
32 Angela Calomiris, *Red Masquerade: Undercover for the F.B.I.* (Philadelphia, PA: Lippincott, 1950).
33 M.A. Jones, "Office Memorandum to Mr. Nichols," April 11, 1952, 2, Federal Bureau of Investigation, FBI #67-334296-3, National Archives and Records Administration, College Park, MD.
34 Special Agent in Charge, Los Angeles, "Judy Holliday Aka Judy Tuvim, Security Matter-C," Special Report, Los Angeles, CA: June 14, 1950, 2, FBI #100-368669, National Archives and Records Administration, College Park, MD.
35 John J. Manning, "Lena Horne, Was, Lina Horne, Helena Horne," New York, NY: February 12, 1948, 14, FBI #100-88027, National Archives and Records Administration, College Park, MD.
36 David K. Johnson, *The Lavender Scare: The Cold War Persecution of Gays and Lesbians in the Federal Government* (Chicago, IL: University of Chicago Press, 2004), 13.
37 Richard Gid Powers, "One G-Man's Family: Popular Entertainment Formulas and J. Edgar Hoover's F.B.I.," *American Quarterly* 30, no. 4 (Autumn 1978): 480.
38 E.J. Kahn, Jr., "The Greenwich Tea Party," *New Yorker*, April 15, 1968, 113.
39 Tim Weiner, *Enemies: A History of the FBI* (New York, NY: Random House, 2012), 178.
40 Matthew Cecil, *Branding Hoover's FBI: How the Boss's PR Men Sold the Bureau to America* (Lawrence, KS: University Press of Kansas, 2016), 25.
41 Athan G. Theoharis and John Stuart Cox, *The Boss: J. Edgar Hoover and the Great American Inquisition* (New York, NY: Bantam, 1990), 204.
42 "Application for Employment, Theodore Cooper Kirkpatrick," May 14, 1942, 1, Federal Bureau of Investigation, FBI #67-334296-3, National Archives and Records Administration, College Park, MD; "Application for Appointment, John Gorman

Keenan," Washington, DC: April 1, 1941, FBI #1308733-0, FBI #67E-HQ-198001, National Archives and Records Administration, College Park, MD.

43 W.S. Tavel, "To Mr. Mohr," March 30, 1959, FBI #67-198001-130, National Archives and Records Administration, College Park, MD; J.P. Mohr, "Theodore Cooper Kirkpatrick," January 25, 1945, FBI #67-334296-2, National Archives and Records Administration, College Park, MD; W.S. Tavel, "John G. Keenan, Former Special Agent," March 30, 1959, FBI #1308733-0, FBI #67E-HQ-198001, National Archives and Records Administration, College Park, MD.

44 Thomas Borstelmann, *The Cold War and the Color Line: American Race Relations in the Global Arena* (Cambridge, MA: Harvard University Press, 2003), 54.

45 Interview with Former Special Agent James R. Healy (1948–80), by Sandra Robinette, May 3, 2007, 37, www.nleomf.org/assets/pdfs/nlem/oral-histories/FBI_Healy_interview.pdf.

46 Ibid., 32–33.

47 Ibid., 40.

48 Cecil, *Branding Hoover's FBI*, 50.

49 Vera Caspary, "To Jo Stewart," Personal, December 31, 1960, Box 1, Folder 5, General Correspondence 1955–60, Vera Caspary Papers, Wisconsin Historical Society, Madison, WI.

50 Hoover, "Communist 'New Look.'"

51 Cecil, *Branding Hoover's FBI*, 24.

52 Ibid., 34–35.

53 Powers, "One G-Man's Family," 475.

54 See Cecil, *Branding Hoover's FBI*, 34–5.

55 Interview with Former Special Agent James R. Healy (1948–80).

56 Athan G. Theoharis, *The FBI: A Comprehensive Reference Guide* (Westport, CT: Greenwood Publishing Group, 1999), 227.

57 Sbardellati, *J. Edgar Hoover Goes to the Movies*, 167.

58 See Jennifer Frost, "Hollywood Gossip as Public Sphere: Hedda Hopper, Reader-Respondents, and the Red Scare, 1947–1965," *Cinema Journal* 50, no. 2 (2011): 84–103.

59 Louis B. Nichols, "To Mr. Tolson," August 11, 1949, 5, FBI #1308733-0 - 67E-HQ-198001, National Archives and Records Administration; Tavel, "To Mr. Mohr," 5.

60 Powers, "One G-Man's Family," 473.

61 Sullivan, *The Bureau*, 14.

62 Quoted in Powers, *G-Men*, 6.

63 Claire Bond Potter, *War on Crime: Bandits, G-Men, and the Politics of Mass Culture* (New Brunswick, NJ: Rutgers University Press, 1998), 126.

64 Powers, *G-Men*, 134.

65 Jean Owens Hayworth and Vinton J. Hayworth, "Mr. J. Edgar Hoover, Director," Personal, November 16, 1953, FBI #62-100575-1, National Archives and Records Administration, College Park, MD, 2.

66 Cecil, *Branding Hoover's FBI*, 29.

67 The American Business Consultants, "Letter No. 84," *CounterAttack*, December 31, 1948, 2.

68 Powers, "One G-Man's Family," 471.

69 William J. Maxwell, “F.B. Eyes: The Bureau Reads Claude McKay,” in *Left of the Color Line: Race, Radicalism, and Twentieth-Century Literature of the United States*, ed. Bill V. Mullen and James Smethurst (Chapel Hill, NC: University of North Carolina Press, 2003), 44.
70 See Farah Jasmine Griffin, *Harlem Nocturne: Women Artists and Progressive Politics during World War II* (New York, NY: Basic Civitas Books, 2013); William J. Maxwell, *F.B. Eyes: How J. Edgar Hoover's Ghostreaders Framed African American Literature* (Princeton, NJ: Princeton University Press, 2015); James Edward Smethurst, *The New Red Negro: The Literary Left and African American Poetry, 1930–1946* (New York, NY: Oxford University Press, 1999); Mary Helen Washington, *The Other Blacklist: The African American Literary and Cultural Left of the 1950s* (New York, NY: Columbia University Press, 2014).
71 Jeremiah F. Buckley, “John Quincy Adams Associates, Inc.,” #100-HQ-350512, National Archives and Records Administration, College Park, MD.
72 Hoover, “Unmasking the Communist Masquerader,” 401.
73 Interview with Former Special Agent James R. Healy (1948–80), 25.
74 Special Agent in Charge, New York, “To Director, FBI,” September 27, 1950, FBI #67-334296-3, National Archives and Records Administration, College Park, MD.
75 The American Business Consultants, “So Help Me Citadel,” *CounterAttack*, July 27, 1956, 121.
76 Interview with Former Special Agent James R. Healy (1948–80), 28.
77 J. Edgar Hoover, “Could Your Child Become a Red?” *Parade Magazine*, May 13, 1952.
78 J. Edgar Hoover, “The American Way of Life,” *The Militant*, May 19, 1952, 2.
79 Cecil, *Branding Hoover's FBI*, 46.
80 Maxwell, *F.B. Eyes*, 17.
81 AWARE, Inc., “AWARE: Statement of Principles,” 13, AWARE, Inc., n.d., FBI #62-100575, National Archives and Records Administration, College Park, MD.
82 Dilling, *The Roosevelt Red Record*, 226.
83 Marcus Bright, “Changed Anne Revere Rosen, Nee Anne Revere, Alias Mrs. Sam Rosen,” Los Angeles, CA: January 29, 1951, 18, FBI #100-22606, National Archives and Records Administration, College Park, MD.
84 The American Business Consultants, “CounterAttack's Ten-Point Program,” 1–2, p. 76, The American Business Consultants, n.d., https://archive.org/stream/foia_Kirkpatrick_Theodore_2/Kirkpatrick_Theodore_2_djvu.txt.
85 “Testimony of J. Edgar Hoover, Director Federal Bureau of Investigation.” Investigation of Un-American Propaganda Activities in the United States. Washington, DC: U.S. Congress, House of Representatives, Committee on Un-American Activities. March 26, 1947. https://archive.org/stream/investigationofu194702unit/investigationofu194702unit_djvu.txt.
86 *The American Negro in the Communist Party*, The Committee on Un-American Activities, U.S. House of Representatives, Washington, DC: Government Printing Office, December 22, 1954, 3.
87 The American Business Consultants, *CounterAttack*, January 11, 1952, 11.
88 Ibid. History proved their assertion untrue. The FBI was called in to investigate the crime. No one was ever indicted for the murders, which happened in Sims, Florida, less than thirty miles from where Trayvon Martin would be murdered by George Zimmerman some sixty years later.

89 J.Y. Smith, "William C. Sullivan, Once High FBI Aide, Killed by Hunter," *Washington Post*, November 10, 1977, www.washingtonpost.com/archive/local/1977/11/10/william-c-sullivan-once-high-fbi-aide-killed-by-hunter/9d6295ad-cf1b-461c-a110-4d1db4ef6613/.

90 M. Wesley Swearingen and Ward Churchill, *FBI Secrets: An Agent's Exposé* (Boston, MA: South End Press, 1995), 24.

91 Ellen Schrecker, *Many Are the Crimes*, pbk. edn. (Princeton, NJ: Princeton University Press, 1999), 221.

92 L.B. Nichols, "To Mr. Tolson," December 11, 1951, FBI #67-334296-3, National Archives and Records Administration, College Park, MD.

93 Kenneth O'Reilly, *Hoover and the Un-Americans* (Philadelphia, PA: Temple University Press, 1983); Athan G. Theoharis, *Spying on Americans: Political Surveillance from Hoover to the Huston Plan* (Philadelphia, PA: Temple University Press, 1978); see Cecil, *Branding Hoover's FBI*, ch. 3, for an account of the FBI's formal relationship with the American Legion.

94 Larry Ceplair, *Anti-Communism in Twentieth-Century America: A Critical History* (Santa Barbara, CA: ABC-CLIO, 2011), 85.

95 See Anne Revere, FBI #100-HQ-336762, National Archives and Records Administration, College Park, MD.

96 J. Edgar Hoover, "Memorandum for the Attorney General," May 26, 1945, FBI #100-339626, National Archives and Records Administration, College Park, MD.

97 "Lillian Hellman, Alias Lillian Hellman Kober," Anchorage, Alaska: November 28, 1944, 3, Federal Bureau of Investigation, https://vault.fbi.gov/Lillian%20%28Lily%29%20Hellman/Lillian%20%28Lily%29%20Hellman%20Part%201%20of%204/view#document/p1.

98 Shirley Graham, Oral History Interview with Mrs. Shirley Graham Du Bois, January 7, 1971, 1, Box 1, Folder 1, Shirley Graham Du Bois Papers, Schlesinger Library, Radcliffe Institute for Advanced Study, Harvard University, Cambridge, MA.

99 "Elizabeth Dilling Spreads Negro Hate Theories," *Chicago Defender*, March 4, 1944, National edition.

100 Gerald Horne, *Race Woman: The Lives of Shirley Graham Du Bois* (New York, NY: New York University Press, 2000), 96.

101 For analyses of the FBI's racism, see Claire Bond Potter, *War on Crime: Bandits, G-Men, and the Politics of Mass Culture* (New Brunswick, NJ: Rutgers University Press, 1998); Johnson, *The Lavender Scare*; Natalie Robins, *Alien Ink: The FBI's War on Freedom of Expression* (New Brunswick, NJ: Rutgers University Press, 1993); Theoharis, *Spying on Americans*; Maxwell, *F.B. Eyes*.

102 Jean Stein, *West of Eden: An American Place*, New York, NY: Random House, 2017, 85.

103 Bright, "Changed Anne Revere Rosen," 3.

104 Special Agent in Charge, New York, "Anne Revere Rosen, Nee Anne Revere, Aka.," New York, NY: April 24, 1958, FBI #100-101399, National Archives and Records Administration, College Park, MD.

105 Special Agent in Charge, New York, "To Director, FBI," New York, NY: February 17, 1958, FBI #100-336762-27, National Archives and Records Administration, College Park, MD.

106 Frank J. Keeney, "Vera Caspary," Los Angeles, CA: March 31, 1945, 1, FBI #100-22897, National Archives and Records Administration, College Park, MD.

107 Ibid., 3.

108 J. Edgar Hoover, "Vera Caspary, Internal Security-R," To Special Agent in Charge, Los Angeles, CA: January 18, 1945, FBI #101-6700, National Archives and Records Administration, College Park, MD.

109 Nichols, "To Mr. Tolson," December 11, 1951.

110 John R. Vicars, "Mrs. Herbert Joseph (Gale) Biberman, with Aliases, Gale Sondergaard Biberman, Gale Sondergaard, Gail Sondergaard, Nee Edith Sondergaard," Report, Los Angeles, CA: May 11, 1945, 13, FBI #100-100757-33, National Archives and Records Administration, College Park, MD.

111 J. Edgar Hoover, "Madeline Lee Security Matter-C," New York, NY: November 3, 1955, FBI #100-106821, National Archives and Records Administration, College Park, MD.

112 Walt H. Sirene, "Gale Biberman," Report, New York, NY: July 28, 1966, 2, FBI #199-370749, National Archives and Records Administration, College Park, MD.

113 J. Edgar Hoover, "Re: Lillian Hellman, Internal Security-C," To Special Agent in Charge, New York, NY: October 20, 1943, https://vault.fbi.gov/Lillian%20%28Lily%29%20Hellman/Lillian%20%28Lily%29%20Hellman%20Part%201%20of%204/view#document/p1.

114 William P. Mullaly, "Madeleine Lee Gellman, Aka," Report, New York City: October 21, 1959, FBI #100-106821, National Archives and Records Administration, College Park, MD.

115 Donald W. White, "Anne Revere Rosen, Aka," New York, NY: April 20, 1959, FBI #100-336762-34, National Archives and Records Administration, College Park, MD.

116 Federal Bureau of Investigation, "Lola Graham Du Bois, Aka," Case Report, New York, NY: June 19, 1961, FBI #100-87531, National Archives and Records Administration, College Park, MD.

117 Milly S. Barranger, *Unfriendly Witnesses: Gender, Theater, and Film in the McCarthy Era* (Carbondale, IL: Southern Illinois University Press, 2008), 70, 63.

118 "Howard Rushmore Kills Wife and Slays Himself in Cab Here," *New York Times*, January 4, 1958.

119 "Socialite, Escort to Face Judge," *The Chicago American*, May 6, 1949.

120 Glen Jeansonne, *Women of the Far Right: The Mother's Movement and World War II*, Chicago, IL: University of Chicago Press, 1996, 9

121 Gary Carey, *Judy Holliday: An Intimate Life Story* (New York, NY: Putnam Adult, 1984), 149.

122 U.S. Congress, House of Representatives. Committee on Un-American Activities, *100 Things You Should Know About Communism* (Washington, DC: U.S. Government Printing Office, 2008), 16.

123 Ibid., 15. National Film Preservation Foundation, Robert Cannon, *The Brotherhood of Man*, animated (United Productions of America, 1945).

124 John G. Keenan, "To J. Edgar Hoover," Personal, March 24, 1958, John Keenan File, National Archives and Records Administration, College Park, MD; M.A. Jones, "John G. Keenan," to Mr. DeLoach, March 27, 1959, FBI #1308733-0, National Archives and Records Administration, College Park, MD; M.A. Jones, "To Mr. DeLoach," March 27, 1959, FBI #67-198001-130, National Archives and Records Administration, College Park, MD.

Chapter 4 Cashing In on the Cold War

1 "Testimony of J. Edgar Hoover, Director Federal Bureau of Investigation." Investigation of Un-American Propaganda Activities in the United States. Washington, DC: U.S. Congress, House of Representatives, Committee on Un-American Activities. March 26, 1947. https://archive.org/stream/investigationofu194702unit/investigationofu194702unit_djvu.txt.
2 William C. Sullivan, *The Bureau: My Thirty Years in Hoover's FBI* (New York, NY: Norton, 1979), 14–15.
3 Kate Mostel, *170 Years of Show Business* (New York, NY: Random House, 1978), 118.
4 John Crosby, "Miss Muir Loses Her Job," *Herald Tribune*, September 7, 1950.
5 T.C. Kirkpatrick, "Letter to FBI," May 14, 1942, FBI #67-334296-2, National Archives and Records Administration, College Park, MD.
6 W.S. Tavel, "To Mr. Mohr," March 30, 1959, FBI #67-198001-130, National Archives and Records Administration, College Park, MD.
7 L.B. Nichols, "To Mr. Tolson," Washington, DC: March 10, 1948, FBI #100-340922, National Archives and Records Administration, College Park, MD; Erik Barnouw, *Tube of Plenty: The Evolution of American Television* (New York, NY: Oxford University Press, 1990), 122.
8 Marie Jahoda, "Anti-Communism and Employment Policies in Radio and Television," in *Report on Blacklisting: II Radio - Television*, ed. John Cogley (New York, NY: Fund for the Republic, 1956), 225.
9 Edward Scheidt, "Letter to Director, FBI," Personal and Confidential, October 22, 1946, 5, https://archive.org/stream/foia_Kirkpatrick_Theodore_2/Kirkpatrick_Theodore_2_djvu.txt. Nichols described Kirkpatrick as being "persona non grata" in the eyes of the FBI (see Nichols, Letter to Mr. Tolson, March 10, 1948, FBI #100-350512).
10 In doing so, they were joined for a time by a fourth former agent: Jeremiah F. Buckley. Jeremiah F. Buckley, "John Quincey Adams Associates, Inc.: Dedicated to Lead, Direct and Unify the Fight Against Un-American Activities," n.d.
11 David Everitt, *A Shadow of Red: Communism and the Blacklist in Radio and Television* (Chicago, IL: Ivan R. Dee, 2007), 16–17.
12 Edwin A. Tamm, "Father John F. Cronin," Letter to Director, April 18, 1946, 2, FBI #67-334296-5, National Archives and Records Administration, College Park, MD.
13 "Blacklisting," *AdAge*, September 15, 2003, http://adage.com/article/adage-encyclopedia/blacklisting/98350/.
14 Buckley, "John Quincy Adams Associates, Inc.," 8. See also the Ernie Lazar FBI Freedom of Information Act Files on Anti-Communism and Rightwing Movements for information about John Quincy Adams Associates: http://dlib.nyu.edu/findingaids/html/tamwag/tam_576/dscref3.html.
15 Bill Cunningham, "Ex-FBI Men Expose Reds," *Boston Herald*, August 1950.
16 Edward Scheidt, "To Director, FBI," Personal and Confidential, February 3, 1947, 1, https://archive.org/stream/foia_Kirkpatrick_Theodore_2/Kirkpatrick_Theodore_2_djvu.txt.
17 John G. Keenan, "Dear Mr. Hoover," July 28, 1950, FBI #100-350512-344, National Archives and Records Administration, College Park, MD.
18 Alex Rosen, "To Mr. Ladd," August 2, 1949, https://ia801708.us.archive.org/14/items/foia_Kirkpatrick_Theodore_2/Kirkpatrick_Theodore_2_text.pdf.

19 E.E. Conroy, "Letter to Director, FBI," August 19, 1946, 3, https://archive.org/stream/foia_Kirkpatrick_Theodore_2/Kirkpatrick_Theodore_2_djvu.txt.

20 Bierly had been known for his ability "to find and enlist citizens who make good plants," citizens willing to "join the Communist Party and observe it for the F.B.I." (Angela Calomiris, *Red Masquerade: Undercover for the F.B.I.* [Philadelphia, PA: Lippincott, 1950], 36, 15). After his resignation from the Bureau, Bierly capitalized on his previous relationships with these spies, paying them "for information concerning activities" regarded as subversive. The American Business Consultants then used "knowledge obtained in their employment with the Bureau to their personal advantage" and in the financial interests of the American Business Consultants by selling it to businesses. See also J.P. Coyne, "Activity of Ex-Agents of the New York Field Division Proselyting Our Confidential Informants," Washington, DC: October 3, 1947, Federal Bureau of Investigation, FBI #67-198001-92, National Archives and Records Administration, College Park, MD; Rosen, "To Mr. Ladd," 1; M.A. Jones, "Office Memorandum to Gordon A. Nease," FBI, November 3, 1958, 1, https://ia801708.us.archive.org/14/items/foia_Kirkpatrick_Theodore_2/Kirkpatrick_Theodore_2_text.pdf.

21 Tavel, "To Mr. Mohr," 2.

22 The American Business Consultants, "CounterAttack's Ten-Point Program," The American Business Consultants, n.d., p. 76, https://archive.org/stream/foia_Kirkpatrick_Theodore_2/Kirkpatrick_Theodore_2_djvu.txt.

23 New York City Field Office, "To Director," July 21, 1949, 1, FBI #100-350512, National Archives and Records Administration, College Park, MD.

24 Ibid., 3.

25 Louis B. Nichols, "Letter to Clyde Tolson," February 15, 1949, FBI #67-334296-1, https://archive.org/details/TheodoreKirkpatrick.

26 Coyne, "Activity of Ex-Agents."

27 Special Agent in Charge, New York, "Confidential Letter to Director, FBI," May 12, 1947, 1, FBI #67-334296-88, National Archives and Records Administration, College Park, MD; Benjamin Mandel, "Memorandum for Mr. Louis J. Russell," October 30, 1950, https://archive.org/stream/foia_Kirkpatrick_Theodore_2/Kirkpatrick_Theodore_2_djvu.txt. Edward Scheidt, "To Director, FBI," May 12, 1947, FBI #100-35881-5, National Archives and Records Administration, College Park, MD; Edward Scheidt, "To FBI Director," Letter, July 31, 1947, 2–3, FBI #100-350512, National Archives and Records Administration, College Park, MD; Edward Scheidt, "Director, FBI," Personal and Confidential, October 22, 1946, 4, https://archive.org/stream/foia_Kirkpatrick_Theodore_2/Kirkpatrick_Theodore_2_djvu.txt.

28 Scheidt, "To FBI Director," 2–3.

29 Coyne, "Activity of Ex-Agents," 9.

30 J.P. Coyne, "Memorandum for Mr. E.A. Tamm," October 25, 1946, https://archive.org/stream/foia_Kirkpatrick_Theodore_2/Kirkpatrick_Theodore_2_djvu.txt.

31 A.H. Belmont, "Re: Apparently Missing Serials from Communist Infiltration into Labor Union Cases," Personal and Confidential, September 6, 1946, 9, https://archive.org/stream/foia_Kirkpatrick_Theodore_2/Kirkpatrick_Theodore_2_djvu.txt.

32 Edward Scheidt, "To Mr. Hoover," September 8, 1950, FBI #100-350512, National Archives and Records Administration, College Park, MD.

33 M.R. Bonnell, "To Milton Ladd," Personal, October 22, 1951, FBI #67-198001-130, National Archives and Records Administration, College Park, MD.
34 M.A. Jones, "To Mr. Nichols," April 11, 1952, 3, https://ia801708.us.archive.org/14/items/foia_Kirkpatrick_Theodore_2/Kirkpatrick_Theodore_2_text.pdf. Hoover harbored a particular hatred for Miller. In 1952, he wrote to Keenan, "I have always refused to dignify with a denial anything which he has said or written" (see letter from J. Edgar Hoover to John Keenan, February 11, 1971, FBI #100-350512-896, National Archives and Records Administration, College Park. MD).
35 A.H. Belmont, "To D. Milton Ladd," June 21, 1952, 4, https://ia801708.us.archive.org/14/items/foia_Kirkpatrick_Theodore_2/Kirkpatrick_Theodore_2_text.pdf.
36 Edward Scheidt, "American Business Consultants, Inc., 'CounterAttack,' Information Concerning," July 21, 1949, 4, FBI #67-334296-1, National Archives and Records Administration, College Park, MD.
37 The American Business Consultants, "Letter No. 84," *CounterAttack*, December 31, 1948, 2.
38 D.M. Ladd, "To The Director," March 10, 1948, FBI #67-334296-110, National Archives and Records Administration, College Park, MD.
39 Jeff Kisseloff, *The Box: An Oral History of Television 1920–1961* (n.p.: ReAnimus Press, 2013), 410.
40 George Seldes, "'CounterAttack' Prints Sequel to Liz Dilling's 'Red Network,' Sets Self Up as Radio Censor," *In Fact*, July 17, 1950, 1.
41 The American Business Consultants, "Letter No. 84," 3.
42 Ibid.
43 Jeremiah F. Buckley, "John Quincy Adams Associates, Inc.," FBI #100-HQ-350512, National Archives and Records Administration, College Park, MD.
44 The American Business Consultants, "CounterAttack's Ten-Point Program," 76.
45 The American Business Consultants, "Letter No. 184," *CounterAttack*, December 1, 1950, 4.
46 The American Business Consultants, "Letter No. 186," *CounterAttack*, December 15, 1950, FBI #67-334296-1.
47 M.A. Jones, "Office Memorandum to Gordon A. Nease," FBI, November 3, 1958, 1, https://ia801708.us.archive.org/14/items/foia_Kirkpatrick_Theodore_2/Kirkpatrick_Theodore_2_text.pdf.
48 The American Business Consultants, "Letter No. 172," *CounterAttack*, September 13, 1950, 3.
49 Ibid.
50 The American Business Consultants, "Letter No. 81," *CounterAttack*, December 10, 1948, 4.
51 E.J. Kahn, Jr., "The Greenwich Tea Party," *New Yorker*, April 15, 1968, 109.
52 Ibid.; Chris Drake, *You Gotta' Stand Up: The Life and High Times of John Henry Faulk*, Newcastle upon Tyne, England: Cambridge Scholars Publishing, 2009.
53 *Draper* v. *Commissioner*, No. 51111 (United States Tax Court April 30, 1956).
54 "Special Supplement," *CounterAttack*, March 18, 1949, 2.
55 J. Edgar Hoover, "Could Your Child Become a Red?" *Parade Magazine*, May 13, 1952, 24.
56 The American Business Consultants, "Letter No. 88," *CounterAttack*, January 28, 1949, 4.
57 Kahn, "The Greenwich Tea Party," 110.
58 The American Business Consultants, "Letter No. 107," *CounterAttack*, June 10, 1949, 4.

59 Kahn, "The Greenwich Tea Party."
60 Warren Weaver, Jr., "Adler-Draper Suit Ends in a Deadlock," *New York Times*, May 28, 1950.
61 Erik Barnouw, *The Golden Web: A History of Broadcasting in the United States*, vol. 2: *1933 to 1953* (New York, NY: Oxford University Press, 1968), 263.
62 Denise-Marie Santiago, "Hester R. McCullough, Former Township Leader," *Philadelphia Inquirer*, March 21, 1988, http://articles.philly.com/1988-03-21/news/26277960_1_entertainers-communist-front-organizations-larry-adler.
63 Charles C. Nast was heir to the Condé Nast publishing empire; the lawyer who represented McCullough in court was another Greenwich neighbor.
64 The American Business Consultants, "Letter No. 184," 4.
65 Merle Miller, *The Judges and the Judged: The Report on Blacklisting in Radio and Television* (New York, NY: Doubleday & Company, 1952), 151.
66 "Hung Jury," *Time Magazine*, June 5, 1950.
67 In a curious coda, MI5 investigated Adler. Determining that he was not a security risk, they disagreed with the FBI that he was a member of the Communist Party. See Phillip Deery, "Larry Adler and the Cold War," *Labour History*, no. 101 (November 2011): 195–204.
68 Barnouw, *The Golden Web*, 264.
69 The American Federation of Radio Artists (AFRA) merged with the Television Authority in 1952 to become AFTRA.
70 AWARE, Inc., "AWARE: Statement of Principles," 15, AWARE, Inc., n.d., FBI #62-100575, National Archives and Records Administration, College Park, MD.
71 Everitt, *A Shadow of Red*, 162.
72 In August 1949, for example, Allen Dibble of *Time* magazine called assistant FBI director Nichols. They were going to write a story on Sweets "who was recently dropped by the Phillips Lord outfit for 'political reasons' " and *Time* "wanted to know the character of these three Agents and as to whether they left under normal circumstances and if they had any special category while in the Bureau." See L.B. Nichols, "To Clyde Tolson," August 11, 1949, https://archive.org/stream/foia_Kirkpatrick_Theodore_2/Kirkpatrick_Theodore_2_djvu.txt.
73 Jones, "To Mr. Nichols," 4–5.
74 "Radio: Who's Blacklisted?" *Time*, August 22, 1949, http://content.time.com/time/magazine/article/0,9171,800646,00.html.
75 Miller, *The Judges and the Judged*, 24.
76 "Radio: Who's Blacklisted?"
77 John Cogley and Merle Miller, *Blacklisting: Two Key Documents* (New York, NY: Arno Press and the New York Times, 1971), 92–93. Hartnett told the *New York Times*' Jack Gould that he did not accept money from artists who wanted their names cleared and in his "Confidential Notebook" (File 13), Hartnett denied receiving payment for his activities. In testimony before the HUAC, he later claimed that "his talent consultant business" was distinct from his work for AWARE, Inc., a spin-off of *CounterAttack* he founded with support from Syracuse grocery-store owner Laurence Johnson in 1952 ("Investigations of So-Called 'Blacklisting' in Entertainment Industry: Hearings before the Committee on Un-American Activities," 84th Congress 5248 [July 12, 1956]). These statements were untrue: when radio personality John Henry Faulk sued Hartnett and Johnson for libel in 1957 it became evident that Hartnett had been

paid by NBC and other networks, advertisers, and sponsors for work as a clearance officer. See Cogley, *Report on Blacklisting*; Everitt, *A Shadow of Red*; Miller, *The Judges and the Judged*; Robert M. Lichtman and Ronald Cohen, *Deadly Farce: Harvey Matusow and the Informer System in the McCarthy Era* (Urbana, IL: University of Illinois Press, 2008).

78 The American Business Consultants, "Letter No. 119," *CounterAttack*, September 2, 1949.
79 Miller, *The Judges and the Judged*, 29.
80 Barnouw, *The Golden Web*, 265.
81 Quoted in Miller, *The Judges and the Judged*.
82 Margaret Webster, "To the Drama Editor," *New York Times*, October 1950.
83 "Gypsy, Scott & Wicker in Red Denials," *Billboard*, September 23, 1950.
84 J.F. Bland, "Infiltration of Communists in the Entertainment Field, Information Concerning," Letter, New York, NY: n.d., FBI #100-336762, National Archives and Records Administration, College Park, MD.
85 The American Business Consultants, "Letter No. 172," 3.

Chapter 5 Cleaning the House of Broadcasting

1 Lillian Hellman, "The Judas Goats," *The Screenwriter* 3, no. 7 (December 1947), 7.
2 Jean Muir, "Autobiography," n.d., 224, Jean Muir Papers, University of Oregon Special Collections and Archives, Eugene, OR.
3 "Gypsy Claims Past Bare of Red Tint," *Pittsburgh Free Press*, September 12, 1950.
4 Nat King Cole's equally short-lived variety show did not appear until 1956.
5 Marie Jahoda, "Anti-Communism and Employment Policies in Radio and Television," in *Report on Blacklisting: II Radio - Television*, ed. John Cogley (New York, NY: Fund for the Republic, 1956), 225. The American Business Consultants, "Letter No. 167," CounterAttack, August 4, 1950, 2.
6 The American Business Consultants, *Red Channels: The Report of Communist Influence in Radio and Television* (New York, NY: The author, 1950), 2.
7 Rob Roy, "Meet Hazel Scott, That Mystery Magnet Who Worries the Nation," *Chicago Defender*, June 16, 1945, National edition.
8 Eric Bentley, *Are You Now or Have You Ever Been: The Investigation of Show Business by the Un-American Activities Committee, 1947–1958* (New York, NY: Harper & Row, 1972).
9 "Gypsy Rose Lee, Hazel Scott, Ireene Wicker in Red Spotlight," *Billboard*, September 23, 1950.
10 Special Agent in Charge, Philadelphia, "Dorothy Rothschild Parker, Security Matter-C," July 19, 1950, FBI #100-56075-5, National Archives and Records Administration, College Park, MD.
11 David Caute, *The Great Fear: The Anti-Communist Purge Under Truman and Eisenhower* (New York, NY: Simon & Schuster, 1978), 531; "Gypsy, Scott & Wicker in Red Denials," *Billboard*, September 23, 1950, 16.
12 The partnership between the American Business Consultants and the American Legion continued throughout the 1950s: as late as 1956, the Legion used *Red Channels* to try to prevent Broadcast 41 actress Gale Sondergaard from appearing on stage in Philadelphia. See "Philly in Uproar on 'Blacklisting' Attempt Against Gale Sondergaard," *Variety*, July

4, 1956, 1; William G. Weart, "Quakers Defend 'Christian' Hiring," *New York Times*, July 18, 1956; "Invoking of 5th Hampered Her Career, Actress Asserts," *New York Herald Tribune*, July 18, 1956; "Actress Again Takes '5th' at Red-Link Quiz," *New York Mirror*, July 18, 1956; "Shelved for Red Clam Up, Gale Says," *New York News*, July 18, 1956; "No 'Official' Picketing Vs. Gale Sondergaard, Philly, But 'Unofficially' Maybe," *Variety*, July 11, 1956.

13 Merle Miller, *The Judges and the Judged: The Report on Blacklisting in Radio and Television* (New York, NY: Doubleday & Company, 1952), 112.

14 John Cogley, "The First Cases," in *Report on Blacklisting*, 30; Bill Cunningham, "Ex-FBI Men Expose Reds," *Boston Herald*, August 1950. The campaign against Muir was also enabled by the victory of anti-communists within AFRA. Less than two weeks before Muir was fired, the anti-blacklist resolution introduced in the NY local of AFRA was beaten by a vote of 472 to 270. See the American Business Consultants, "Letter No. 169," *CounterAttack*, August 18, 1950, 3.

15 Jeff Kisseloff, *The Box: An Oral History of Television 1920–1961* (n.p.: ReAnimus Press, 2013), 408.

16 Jack Gould, "'Aldrich Show' Drops Jean Muir; TV Actress Denies Communist Ties," *New York Times*, August 29, 1950; David Everitt, *A Shadow of Red: Communism and the Blacklist in Radio and Television* (Chicago, IL: Ivan R. Dee, 2007), 60.

17 Miller, *The Judges and the Judged*, 157.

18 "Hysteria and Civil Liberties," *The Survey*, October 1950, 458–59.

19 In fact, a few years later, the FBI reported in the pages of its classified correspondence that Muir had been the victim of a transcription error by the HUAC. Informant John Leech had said he had not seen her name on a Communist Party card, but the HUAC reported that he had. Neither the FBI nor the HUAC ever retracted the error.

20 Marlow Stern, "When Congress Slut-Shamed Ingrid Bergman," *Daily Beast*, November 21, 2015, www.thedailybeast.com/articles/2015/11/21/when-congress-slut-shamed-ingrid-bergman.html.

21 Hazel Scott, "Testimony of Hazel Scott," U.S. Congress, House of Representatives, Committee on Un-American Activities, Eighty-First Congress, September 22, 1950, 3619–20.

22 Jay Nelson Tuck, "Unholy Alliance: AFTRA and the Blacklist," *The Nation*, September 3, 1955.

23 Noralee Frankel, *Stripping Gypsy: The Life of Gypsy Rose Lee* (New York, NY: Oxford University Press, 2009), 174.

24 Glenn D. Smith Jr, "'The Guiding Spirit': Philip Loeb, The Battle for Television Jurisdiction, and the Broadcasting Industry Blacklist," *American Journalism* 26, no. 3 (2009): 104.

25 Rita Morley Harvey, *Those Wonderful, Terrible Years: George Heller and the American Federation of Television and Radio Artists* (Carbondale, IL: Southern Illinois University Press, 1996), 59–60.

26 "Mrs. FDR Speaks at Testimonial for Walter White," *Chicago Defender*, June 3, 1944, National edition.

27 Smith, "'The Guiding Spirit.'"

28 "Report Truman to Probe Ban Against Hazel Scott," *Chicago Defender*, October 13, 1945, Washington Bureau edition.

29 Venice T. Spraggs, "Hazel Scott Won't Play for Lily-White Press Club," *Chicago Defender*, November 17, 1945, National edition.

30 Burt A. Folkart, "Ireene Wicker Hammer, 86; Radio's 'Singing Lady,'" *Los Angeles Times*, November 19, 1987, http://articles.latimes.com/1987-11-19/news/mn-22331_1_ireene-wicker-hammer.

31 Angela Calomiris, *Red Masquerade: Undercover for the F.B.I.* (Philadelphia, PA: Lippincott, 1950), 14; Lisa E. Davis, "The FBI's Lesbian, Eleanor Roosevelt and Other Tales from the Red Scare," *Rethinking Marxism* 21, no. 4 (2009): 621–33.

32 L.B. Nichols, "To Mr. Tolson", March 4, 1952, 1, FBI #100-390769, National Archives and Records Administration, College Park, MD.

33 FBI Director, "Judy Holliday," Confidential, June 15, 1951, FBI #100-368669, National Archives and Records Administration, College Park, MD.

34 L.B. Nichols, "To Mr. Tolson"; Louis B. Nichols, "This Is Your FBI," March 4, 1952, FBI #100-390769, National Archives and Records Administration, College Park, MD.

35 Joanne Rapf, "In Focus: Children of the Blacklist," *Cinema Journal* 44, no. 4 (Summer 2005): 77; Griffin Fariello, *Red Scare: Memories of the American Inquisition* (New York, NY: Norton, 2008); Patrick McGilligan and Paul Buhle, *Tender Comrades: A Backstory of the Hollywood Blacklist* (New York, NY: St. Martin's Press, 1997).

36 Special Agent in Charge, New York, to Director, FBI, "Uta Hagen Berghof, Was SM-C," August 22, 1956, 2, FBI #100-371261, National Archives and Records Administration, College Park, MD.

37 Milly S. Barranger, *Unfriendly Witnesses: Gender, Theater, and Film in the McCarthy Era* (Carbondale, IL: Southern Illinois University Press, 2008), 31.

38 AWARE, Inc., *The Road Back* (New York, NY: The author, 1955), 1.

39 Marcus Bright, "Changed Anne Revere Rosen, Nee Anne Revere, Alias Mrs. Sam Rosen" January 29, 1951, 22, FBI #100-22606, National Archives and Records Administration, College Park, MD.

40 Fitch was not the only progressive woman who named names. Actress Tallulah Bankhead informed on Lillian Hellman (H.J. Bobbitt, "To Director," San Francisco, CA: March 11, 1941, 1, FBI #64-2226, National Archives and Records Administration, College Park, MD). Actress, director, and writer Winifred Lenihan also provided the FBI with names and publicly accused other actresses, including Eva Le Gallienne, of being members of the Communist Party.

41 Barranger, *Unfriendly Witnesses*, 95.

42 Letter from Vera Caspary to Allan A. Mussehl, July 7, 1979, General Correspondence, Box 28, Folder 1, Vera Caspary Papers, Wisconsin Historical Society, Madison, WI.

43 Barranger, *Unfriendly Witnesses*, 95.

44 Kisseloff, *The Box*, 413.

45 Jack Gould, "Legion Won't Back Lee Case Charges: Says 'Red Channels' Must Prove," *New York Times*, September 14, 1950.

46 "CounterAttack Gives Denials of 3 Listed," *New York Times*, October 28, 1950.

47 "Gypsy, Scott & Wicker in Red Denials."

48 L.B. Nichols, "Ella Logan, Bureau File No. 100-339626," September 28, 1950, 2, FBI #100-339626-31, National Archives and Records Administration, College Park, MD.

49 Special Agent in Charge, New York, to Director, FBI, July 28, 1956, FBI #105-18873, National Archives and Records Administration, College Park, MD.

50 "CounterAttack Gives Denials of 3 Listed."

51 Barranger, *Unfriendly Witnesses*, 36.

52 "Letter to Director," July 26, 1956, 3, FBI #105-18873-1A, National Archives and Records Administration; The American Business Consultants, "Letter No. 183," *CounterAttack*, November 24, 1950, 2.

53 John Roddy, "Lena Horne's Manager Says Counterattack Clears Her," *New York City Compass*, October 9, 1951.

54 John Roddy, "Attempt to Bar Lena Horne from TV Show Rebuffed," *New York City Compass*, September 25, 1951.

55 Kenneth Bierly to Columbia Pictures Corp., June 8, 1951, 2, FBI #100-368669, National Archives and Records Administration, College Park, MD. See also Lisa E. Davis, *Undercover Girl: The Lesbian Informant Who Helped the FBI Bring Down the Communist Party*, New York, NY: Imagine, 2017.

56 Barranger, *Unfriendly Witnesses*, 31.

57 "Gypsy, Scott & Wicker in Red Denials," 16.

58 Benjamin Mandel, research director for HUAC, was well acquainted with the compilers of *Red Channels*, having participated in the meetings with Bierly, Kirkpatrick, Keenan, and financier Alfred Kohlberg that resulted in the founding of the American Business Consultants in 1947. See also "Dixie Leader Says Ike Nominee a Klansman," *Jet*, March 24, 1955; "High-Low Democracy," *Chicago Defender*, September 23, 1950, National edition.

59 "Testimony of Hazel Scott," 3620.

60 Donald E. Waller, "Dorothy Rothschild Parker, Was," May 26, 1951, 1, 13, FBI #100-32635, National Archives and Records Administration, College Park, MD.

61 John R. Vicars, "Federal Bureau of Investigation Report," Security Matter-C, May 11, 1945, 2, FBI #100-370749, National Archives and Records Administration, College Park, MD.

62 In fact, Ernst closely corresponded with J. Edgar Hoover for over twenty-five years. Harrison E. Salisbury, "The Strange Correspondence of Morris Ernst and J. Edgar Hoover," *The Nation*, January 25, 2007, www.thenation.com/article/strange-correspondence-morris-ernst-and-j-edgar-hoover/.

63 "Committee to Get TV 'Red' Problem," *New York Times*, October 3, 1950.

64 Untouched by the smear that ruined his wife's career, Jaffe became a successful television producer, whose shows included *The Dinah Shore Show* and *Goodyear Playhouse*. See "Henry Jaffe Is Dead; TV Producer Was 85," *New York Times*, September 30, 1992, www.nytimes.com/1992/09/30/obituaries/henry-jaffe-is-dead-tv-producer-was-85.html.

65 "Ballot for National Referendum," AFTRA, May 1, 1955, Box 4, "Blacklisting: 1945–1955," Margaret Webster Papers, Washington, DC: Library of Congress.

66 Lewis L. Gould, ed., *Watching Television Come of Age: The New York Times Reviews by Jack Gould* (Austin, TX: University of Texas Press, 2002).

67 "No More 'Muir Incidents,'" *Business Week*, September 16, 1950.

68 Sigurd S. Larmon, *A Primer for Americans* (n.p.: The author, 1950), 16.

69 Kisseloff, *The Box*, 415.

70 Ibid., 413.

71 Miller, *The Judges and the Judged*, 149.

72 Ibid.

73 Cynthia B. Meyers, "Inside a Broadcasting Blacklist: *Kraft Television Theatre*, 1951–1955," *Journal of American History*, December 2018, 3.

74 Jack Gould, "Network Rejects Protest by Legion: A.B.C. Refuses to Cancel New Gypsy Rose Lee Program," *New York Times*, September 13, 1950.

75 Gould, "Legion Won't Back Lee Case."
76 "FBI Monograph: Pretext and Cover Techniques," unpublished manuscript, May 1956, https://archive.org/details/FBI-Monograph-Pretexts-and-Cover-Techniques-nsia.
77 The American Business Consultants, "Letter No. 110," *CounterAttack*, July 1, 1949, 110.
78 The American Business Consultants, "Letter No. 185," *CounterAttack*, December 8, 1950, 4.
79 E.M. Torrens, "Office Memorandum to F.J. Baumgardner," April 21, 1949, https://ia801708.us.archive.org/14/items/foia_Kirkpatrick_Theodore_2/Kirkpatrick_Theodore_2_text.pdf.
80 Louis B. Nichols, "Office Memorandum to Clyde Tolson," February 18, 1949, FBI #67-334296-1, National Archives and Records Administration, College Park, MD.
81 Louis B. Nichols, "Letter to Clyde Tolson," November 5, 1951, FBI #100-350512-435, National Archives and Records Administration, College Park, MD.
82 Nichols was the head of the FBI's public relations operation, the Crime Records Division. See Athan G. Theoharis and John Stuart Cox, *The Boss: J. Edgar Hoover and the Great American Inquisition* (New York, NY: Bantam, 1990), 145.
83 It seems likely that Few was exercised because of a letter-writing campaign initiated by *CounterAttack*. See The American Business Consultants, "Letter No. 224," *CounterAttack*, September 7, 1951.
84 This was not the only occasion upon which Ellis complained to Nichols. Later that year, Ellis forwarded a copy of *Sponsor* magazine's critique of *Red Channels* and *CounterAttack*. See L.B. Nichols, "To Mr. Tolson." December 6, 1951, FBI #100-350512-435, National Archives and Records Administration, College Park, MD.
85 Neither Tolson nor Nichols considered that inserting a "message on Americanism" into a television show mirrored the very practice for which they were vilifying communists and fellow-travelers: using television as a "transmission belt" for conveying propaganda. Nor did they question the inference that the appearance of a leftwing singer (as it turned out, this was a case of mistaken identity—Doodles Weaver was not the leftist folk-singing group the Weavers) on a show that sold cigarettes was in any way a threat to domestic security.
86 M.A. Jones, "To Mr. Nichols," April 11, 1952, 14, https://ia801708.us.archive.org/14/items/foia_Kirkpatrick_Theodore_2/Kirkpatrick_Theodore_2_text.pdf.
87 As further evidence of the close ties between the American Business Consultants and the HUAC, one of the HUAC's researchers, J.B. Matthews, had also been present at the meeting with Alfred Kohlberg that resulted in the founding of the American Business Consultants. See note 58, above.
88 M.A. Jones, "To Mr. DeLoach," March 27, 1959, 2, FBI #67-198001-130, National Archives and Records Administration, College Park, MD.
89 See Cynthia B. Meyer, "Advertising, the Red Scare, and the Blacklist: BBDO, US Steel, and Theatre Guild on the Air," *Cinema Journal* 55, no. 4 (Fall 2016): 55–83.
90 L.B. Nichols "To Mr. Tolson," April 7, 1951, FBI #100-368669, National Archives and Records Administration, College Park, MD.
91 John B. Oakes, "To Stay Out of Trouble," *New York Times Book Review*, April 13, 1952, B6.
92 Miller, *The Judges and the Judged*, 31.
93 Miller, *The Judges and the Judged*, 31.

94 “Manners and Morals: By Appointment,” *Time*, September 11, 1950, www.time.com/time/magazine/article/0,9171,813149,00.html; Margaret Bauer, Interview by Carol A. Stabile, Phoenix, AZ, May 26, 2012.
95 Cogley, “The First Cases,” 30–31.
96 The American Business Consultants, “Letter No. 189,” *CounterAttack*, January 5, 1951, 189.
97 Special Agent in Charge, New York, “To Director, FBI,” September 27, 1950, https://archive.org/stream/foia_Kirkpatrick_Theodore_2/Kirkpatrick_Theodore_2_djvu.txt.
98 Kisseloff, *The Box*, 421.
99 Meyers, “Inside a Broadcasting Blacklist,” 24.
100 John G. Keenan, “To J. Edgar Hoover,” February 11, 1971, FBI #67-198001-130, National Archives and Records Administration, College Park, MD.
101 “Faulk Wins Round Against AWARE,” *New York Herald Tribune*, November 22, 1955; “AWARE Denies Charges in $500,000 Libel Suit,” *New York Herald Tribune*, November 22, 1955; Leon Racht, “AWARE Will Keep Fighting,” *New York Journal-American*, July 9, 1955.
102 Oliver Pilat, “Blacklist: The Panic in TV-Radio,” *New York Post*, January 26, 1953.
103 Cogley, “The First Cases,” 42.
104 The American Business Consultants, “Letter No. 167,” *CounterAttack*, August 4, 1950, 2.
105 Margaret Webster, “Letter to the Editor” (unpublished), *New York Times*, September 29, 1958, Box 4, “Blacklisting: 1945–55,” Margaret Webster Papers, Library of Congress, Washington, DC.
106 J. Edgar Hoover, “SAC Letter No. 60-30,” June 21, 1960, https://archive.org/stream/SACLetter6030ReserveIndex/SAC%20Letter%2060-30%20-%20Reserve%20Index_djvu.txt; Tim Weiner, “Hoover Planned Mass Jailing in 1950,” *New York Times*, December 23, 2007, www.nytimes.com/2007/12/23/washington/23habeas.html.
107 Special Agent in Charge, Los Angeles, “To Director, FBI,” April 11, 1951, FBI #100-56075-2, National Archives and Records Administration, College Park, MD.
108 “Blacklist: Memories of a Word That Marks an Era,” *New York Times*, July 31, 1994, 17.
109 Barranger, *Unfriendly Witnesses*, 46.
110 Karen Chilton, *Hazel Scott: The Pioneering Journey of a Jazz Pianist, from Café Society to Hollywood to HUAC* (Ann Arbor, MI: University of Michigan Press, 2010), 158, 176.
111 “Letter to Mr. Joseph Goldstein,” December 22, 1951, Box 17, Folder 5, 1, Shirley Graham Du Bois Papers, Schlesinger Library, Radcliffe Institute for Advanced Study, Harvard University, Cambridge, MA.
112 That Graham continued to publish as long as she did is owed to another woman who opposed McCarthyism: publisher Messner’s editor Gertrude Blumenthal. See Julia L. Mickenberg, *Learning from the Left: Children’s Literature, the Cold War, and Radical Politics in the United States* (New York, NY: Oxford University Press, 2006), 151.
113 “Letter to Mr. Joseph Goldstein,” 2. Original emphases.
114 “Subpoena from HUAC (signed by McCarthy),” June 25, 1953, Box 17, Folder 10, Shirley Graham Du Bois Papers, Schlesinger Library, Radcliffe Institute for Advanced Study, Harvard University, Cambridge, MA.
115 Special Agent in Charge, New York, “Ray Lev, Aka SM-C,” July 5, 1968, 2, FBI #100-370898-81, National Archives and Records Administration, College Park, MD.

116 "Writing for Television: Television and the Blacklist," panel discussion, Museum of Television and Radio Seminar Series, Los Angeles, CA, September 17, 1997.

117 Erik Barnouw, *The Image Empire: A History of Broadcasting in the United States from 1953* (New York, NY: Oxford University Press, 1970), 35 (see also ch. 2, n. 118)

118 Ibid., 34.

119 Lillian Ross, "Come In, Lassie!" *New Yorker*, February 21, 1948, 19, www.newyorker.com/magazine/1948/02/21/come-in-lassie.

120 Vincent Brook, "The Americanization of Molly: How Mid-Fifties TV Homogenized 'The Goldbergs' (And Got 'Berg-Iarized' in the Process)," *Cinema Journal* 38, no. 4 (Summer 1999): 45–67.

121 Leonard Feather, "Lena at 60 Still a Horne of Plenty," *Los Angeles Times*, April 16, 1979.

122 Ellen Schrecker, *Many Are the Crimes* (Princeton, NJ: Princeton University Press, 1999), 400.

123 Jerry D. Lee (Louise Fitch) Lewis, "Statement from Mrs. Jerry D. Lewis to the FBI," March 13, 1952, FBI #100-390769, National Archives and Records Administration, College Park, MD; L.B. Nichols, "Letter to Mr. Tolson," FBI #100-390769, National Archives and Records Administration, College Park, MD; M.A. Jones, "Jerry D. Lewis and Louise Fitch," January 18, 1952, 3, FBI #100-390769, National Archives and Records Administration, College Park, MD.

124 Jack Gould, "C.B.S Demanding Loyalty Oath from Its 2,500 Regular Employees," *New York Times*, December 21, 1950.

125 Gertrude Berg, *Molly and Me: A Memoir* (New York, NY: McGraw-Hill, 1961), 10.

126 Stefan Kanfer, *A Journal of the Plague Years* (New York, NY: Athenaeum, 1973), 23.

127 William F. Buckley, "Rabble-Rouser," *New Yorker*, March 1, 2004, www.newyorker.com/magazine/2004/03/01/rabble-rouser.

128 Westbrook Pegler, "Fair Enough," *Washington Times-Herald*, September 22, 1953.

129 Jack Gould, "A.B.C. Puts Off Jean Muir Blacklist Interview," *New York Times*, December 25, 1965.

Chapter 6 Red *Lassie*: A Counterfactual History of Television

1 Ellen W. Schrecker, *The Age of McCarthyism: A Brief History with Documents* (Boston, MA: Bedford/St. Martin's, 2001), 398.

2 Rodney Stewart, "Mrs. Herbert Joseph (Gale) Biberman," Los Angeles, CA: June 15, 1950, 6, FBI #100-22800, National Archives and Records Administration, College Park, MD.

3 Peter Noble, *Negro in Films* (New York, NY: Arno Press, 1949), 158.

4 Gary Carey, *Judy Holliday: An Intimate Life Story* (New York, NY: Putnam Adult, 1984), 130.

5 Donald Bogle, *Toms, Coons, Mulattoes, Mammies, and Bucks: An Interpretive History of Blacks in American Films* (New York, NY: Continuum, 2001), 127.

6 Courtney Thorsson, *Women's Work: Nationalism and Contemporary African American Women's Novels* (Charlottesville, VA: University of Virginia Press, 2013), 27.

7 Polina Kroik, "Producing Modern Girls: Gender and Work in American Literature and Film, 1910–1960," Ph.D. dissertation, University of California, Irvine, 2011;

Alesia Elaine McFadden, "The Artistry and Activism of Shirley Graham Du Bois: A Twentieth Century African American Torchbearer," Ph.D. dissertation, University of Massachusetts, Amherst, 2009, http://scholarworks.umass.edu/cgi/viewcontent.cgi?article=1076&context=open_access_dissertations; Alison McKee, "To Speak of Love: Female Desire and Lost Narrative in Women's Films," Ph.D. dissertation, UCLA, 1993; Clementine Pirlot, "Working Women in 1940s Hollywood," Ph.D. dissertation, California State University, 2011, http://clementinepirlot.fr/images/Memoire_working_women_M1.pdf; Stacy L. Spaulding, "Lisa Sergio: How Mussolini's 'Golden Voice' of Propaganda Created an American Mass Communication Career," Ph.D. dissertation, University of Maryland, 2005; Ann L. Warren, "Word Play: The Lives and Work of Four Women Writers in Hollywood's Golden Age," Ph.D. dissertation, University of Southern California, 1988; Laurie Avant Woodard, "Performing Artists of the Harlem Renaissance: Resistance, Identity, and Meaning in the Life and Work of Fredi Washington from 1920 to 1950," Ph.D. dissertation, Yale University, 2007.

8 Jeffrey M. Elliot, ed., *Conversations with Maya Angelou* (Jackson, MS: University Press of Mississippi, 1989), 175.

9 Shirley Graham Du Bois, "As a Man Thinketh in His Heart, So Is He," *Parish News: Church of the Holy Trinity*, February 1954, vol. 57, no. 4, 5, Box 27, Folder 3, Shirley Graham Du Bois Papers, Schlesinger Library, Radcliffe Institute for Advanced Study, Harvard University, Cambridge, MA.

10 Bob Lauter, "Around the Dial: Radio Launches Fight Against Discrimination," *Daily Worker*, July 12, 1949, 11.

11 Lena Horne and Richard Schickel, *Lena* (Garden City, NY: Doubleday, 1965), 187.

12 " 'Lysistrata' Quits After 4 Days," *Chicago Defender*, November 2, 1946, National edition.

13 Kathlene McDonald, *Feminism, the Left, and Postwar Literary Culture* (Jackson, MI: University Press of Mississippi, 2012), 55.

14 " 'Tom,' Big Opera, Scores Success," *Chicago Defender* (July 9, 1932), 2.

15 See Eric Lott, *Love and Theft: Blackface Minstrelsy and the American Working Class* (New York, NY: Oxford University Press, 1995) for more on minstrelsy and white audiences. Graham drew upon the book's own contentious production history in her adaptation. Scottish author Helen Bannerman's original story, first published in 1899, was set in India. In it, Sambo appears as a very dark-skinned Southern Indian or Tamil child. The U.S. edition of the book, illustrated by John O'Neill (best known for his illustrations for *The Wizard of Oz* series), drew heavily upon racist representations of black children and women. Further situating the story within a racist American context was the inclusion of an unsigned story about Topsy, a character from *Uncle Tom's Cabin* and "the most woebegone little darkey ever seen." Production notes and photographs from the Chicago production confirm that Graham's version was the only one to feature a black cast and Pan-African images rather than depictions drawn from minstrelsy.

16 Charles Stewart, "Sambo, Director's Notes," 1938, Container 1032, Box 47, Federal Theatre Project Collection, Library of Congress, Washington, DC; "Little Black Sambo," n.d., Containers 1032 and 1179, Federal Theatre Project Collection, Library of Congress, Washington, DC.

17 "WMEX Boston Interview," Box 27, Folder 3, February 18, 1950, Shirley Graham Du Bois Papers, Schlesinger Library, Radcliffe Institute for Advanced Study, Harvard University, Cambridge, MA.

18 Barbara Smith, "Toward a Black Feminist Criticism," *Conditions: Two* 1, no. 2 (1977): 25–44.
19 Pauline Tish, "Remembering Helen Tamiris," *Dance Chronicle* 17, no. 3 (January 1, 1994): 328.
20 Ibid., 350.
21 Dorothy Parker, *The Portable Dorothy Parker*, ed. Marion Meade (New York, NY: Penguin Classics, 2006).
22 Ben Urwand, *The Collaboration: Hollywood's Pact with Hitler*, repr. edn. (Cambridge, MA: Belknap Press of Harvard University Press, 2015); David Weinstein, "Why Sarnoff Slept: NBC and the Holocaust," in *NBC: America's Network*, ed. Michele Hilmes (Berkeley, CA: University of California Press, 2007), 98–116.
23 Gertrude Berg, "The Real Story Behind 'The House of Glass,'" *Radio Mirror*, General Scrapbook 12, July 1935, 22, Gertrude Berg Papers, Nightingale Library, Syracuse University, Syracuse, NY.
24 Gertrude Berg, *Molly and Me: A Memoir* (New York, NY: McGraw-Hill, 1961), 167.
25 Ibid., 168.
26 Ayn Rand, "Screen Guide for Americans," in *Plain Talk: An Anthology from the Leading Anti-Communist Magazine of the 40s*, ed. Isaac Don Levine (New Rochelle, NY: Arlington House, 1947), 392.
27 Berg, *Molly and Me*, 177.
28 Lina Mainiero, ed., *American Women Writers: A Critical Reference Guide from Colonial Times to the Present* (New York, NY: Ungar, 1979), 313.
29 See Laurie Ouellette, "Inventing the Cosmo Girl: Class Identity and Girl-Style American Dreams," *Media, Culture and Society* 21, no. 3 (1999): 359–83. When Paramount Pictures hired writer Zoe Akins to write the screenplay for Caspary's *Three Blind Mice* (1930), Caspary objected to Akins' acting "as if working girls were dirt. I have them as running around having dates, a good time, but getting into trouble, but she wrote them with a snobbish look down" (in Warren, "Word Play," 69).
30 Vera Caspary, *Laura* (Boston, MA: Houghton Mifflin, 1943), 102.
31 Vera Caspary, *Thelma* (Boston, MA: Little, Brown, 1952), 90.
32 Vera Caspary, "Letter to Don Fine (Editor in Chief, Dell Publishing Company)," July 6, 1971, Box 1, Folder 6, General Correspondence 1961–63, Vera Caspary Papers, Wisconsin Historical Society, Madison, WI.
33 Glenn D. Smith, Jr., *Something on My Own: Gertrude Berg and American Broadcasting, 1929–1956* (Syracuse, NY: Syracuse University Press, 2007), 29.
34 Ibid.
35 Donna L. Halper, *Invisible Stars: A Social History of Women in American Broadcasting* (New York, NY: M.E. Sharpe, 2001), 67.
36 Stacy Spaulding, "Off the Blacklist, But Still a Target: The Anti-Communist Attacks on Lisa Sergio," *Journalism Studies* 10, no. 6 (2009): 792.
37 Phillips would also mentor an even more famous soap opera writer: Agnes Nixon.
38 Judith E. Smith, "Judy Holliday's Urban Working Girl Characters in 1950s Hollywood Film," *American Studies Faculty Publication Series* Paper 6 (2010): 7, http://scholarworks.umb.edu/amst_faculty_pubs/6.
39 Even so, critics and reviewers assumed that these successful scripts were actually written by men. When Gordon wrote a play, "some people say her husband wrote it for her and everyone says Kaufman put in the funny lines." See Ruth Gordon, *Ruth Gordon: An Open Book* (Garden City, NY: Doubleday, 1980), 129.

40 Joanne Court, "The Bandit," *Have Gun—Will Travel*, Box 29, Folder, 1961, 18-a. Adrian and Joan Scott Papers, American Heritage Center, University of Wyoming, Laramie, WY.
41 "Blacklist: Memories of a Word That Marks an Era," *New York Times*, July 31, 1994, 17.
42 Quoted in Milly S. Barranger, *Unfriendly Witnesses: Gender, Theater, and Film in the McCarthy Era* (Carbondale, IL: Southern Illinois University Press, 2008), 90.
43 "Last 8 Times," *New York Times*, May 21, 1950.
44 Kate Mostel, *170 Years of Show Business* (New York, NY: Random House, 1978), 139.
45 Patrick McGilligan and Paul Buhle, *Tender Comrades: A Backstory of the Hollywood Blacklist* (New York, NY: St. Martin's Press, 1997), 260–61.
46 Ibid.; Tom Dewe Matthews, "The Outlaws," *Guardian*, October 7, 2006, www.guardian.co.uk/film/2006/oct/07/books.featuresreviews1.
47 Dave Mann, *Britain's First TV/Film Crime Series and the Industrialisation of Its Film Industry, 1946–1964* (Lewiston, NY: Edwin Mellen Press, 2009), 152–53.
48 "Robin Hood Episodes: The Cathedral," File Folder 2, 1957–58, 4, Adrian and Joan Scott Papers, American Heritage Center, University of Wyoming, Laramie, WY. From 1955 to 1958, the series was broadcast during the 7.30–8 p.m. time slot on CBS. CBS later ran reruns on Saturday mornings, from 1958 to 1959.
49 "Robin Hood Episodes: The Charter," File Folder 2, 1957–58, 1, Adrian and Joan Scott Papers, American Heritage Center, University of Wyoming, Laramie, WY.
50 Adrian Scott, "Letter to Harry Miller," Box 5, "Correspondence," November 12, 1947, Adrian and Joan Scott Papers, American Heritage Center, University of Wyoming, Laramie, WY.
51 Judy Kaplan and Linn Shapiro, eds., *Red Diapers: Growing Up in the Communist Left* (Urbana, IL: University of Illinois Press, 1998), 197.
52 See Steve Neale, "Transatlantic Ventures and Robin Hood," in *ITV Cultures: Independent Television over Fifty Years*, ed. Catherine Johnson and Rob Turnock (Maidenhead: Open University Press, 2005).
53 Jeff Kisseloff, *The Box: An Oral History of Television 1920–1961* (n.p.: ReAnimus Press, 2013), 414.
54 Although women continued to find it difficult to find jobs as writers on prime-time television programs, a number of women (Florence Britton, *Studio One*; Jane Arthur and Ethel Frank, *The Hallmark Playhouse*) found work as story editors. See Kisseloff, *The Box*, 245, 266. Other women wrote for prime-time shows as the 1950s wore on, such as Katherine Albert, who wrote for *Leave It to Beaver* (1957–63); Dorothy Cooper Foote, who wrote for *Father Knows Best* (1954–60), *My Three Sons* (1960–72), and *The Flying Nun* (1967–70); and Madelyn Davis, who wrote for *I Love Lucy* (1951–57). But they did so within the narrow, formulaic grooves of gender and family ideologies established during the blacklist era.
55 Adrian Scott, "Letter to Allan Scott," Box 6, File Folder 13, September 11, 1966, 2, Adrian and Joan Scott Papers, American Heritage Center, University of Wyoming, Laramie, WY.
56 Lisa Yaszek, *Galactic Suburbia: Recovering Women's Science Fiction* (Columbus, OH: Ohio State University Press, 2008), 3.
57 The Broadcast 41 were the most visible, in many ways, of the women working in broadcasting in the 1930s and 1940s. Others were less so. Anne and Frank Hummert, for example, were one of the most successful husband-and-wife teams in radio drama in the 1930s and 1940s. Their casting director, Frances von Bernhardi, was broadly

acknowledged as being an extraordinarily influential figure in radio as well. See Joseph Julian, *This Was Radio* (New York, NY: Viking Press, 1975), 33–34.

58 Joan Scott wrote under her name, as well as a pseudonym she used in the 1950s: Joanne Court.

59 Scott, "Letter to Allan Scott," 2.

60 Joan LaCour Scott, "Adrian's Wife" n.d., 2, Patrick McGilligan Papers, Wisconsin Center for Film and Theater Research, Wisconsin Historical Society, Madison, WI.

61 Joanne Court, "A Girl and a Boy, Part I," Box 19, File Folder 2, n.d., 19A, Adrian and Joan Scott Papers, American Heritage Center, University of Wyoming, Laramie, WY.

62 Joan Scott, "The New Refrigerator," CBS, September 6, 1959.

63 Joanne Court, "Golden Eagle," Box 29, Folder 5, June 21, 1972, 10, Adrian and Joan Scott Papers, American Heritage Center, University of Wyoming, Laramie, WY.

64 "Letter to Cerf Bennett," Box 4, "Correspondence," Folder 23, n.d., 19, Adrian and Joan Scott Papers, American Heritage Center, University of Wyoming, Laramie, WY.

65 Kisseloff, *The Box*, 259.

66 Adrian Scott, "Letter to Hannah Weinstein," Box 2, Folder 13, June 19, 1957, 1, Adrian and Joan Scott Papers, American Heritage Center, University of Wyoming, Laramie, WY.

67 Norma Jean Darden, "Oh, Sister! Fredi and Isabel Washington Relive '30s Razzmatazz," *Essence Magazine*, September 1978, 105.

68 Shirley Graham, "Naïveté, the Story of Anne Royale," Box 38, Folder 1, *c.* 1947, 13, Shirley Graham Du Bois Papers, Schlesinger Library, Radcliffe Institute for Advanced Study, Harvard University, Cambridge, MA.

69 Drafts of the novel appear under two different titles: "The Woman on the Case" and "Naïveté, the Story of Anne Royale." Graham used two different spellings for Royall's name. Royall is also the most sexual of Graham's depictions, a person who enjoyed her sexuality and eschewed both monogamy and chastity, her whiteness perhaps allowing Graham room to explore issues of sexuality absent the constraints of racism.

70 Vera Caspary, Untitled proposal for "The Private World of the Morleys," Box 30, Folder 7, 5, Vera Caspary Papers, Wisconsin Historical Society, Madison, WI.

71 *June Jordan*'s cast and crew featured several of those who would go on to be blacklisted in the 1950s: writer Joe Julian and actresses Betty Winkler and Ann Shepherd. Brown also wrote *Hilda Hope, MD*, starring another of the blacklisted: Serena Royle. Brown was uniquely aware of the groundbreaking nature of these representations. "I always believed in women in the professions," he said, "without women's lib, without anyone prodding me, and not chauvinistically, I had women in the professions where women were not really ... lawyers, educators, doctors" (Ira Skutch, *Five Directors: The Golden Years of Radio: Based on Interviews with Himan Brown, Axel Gruenberg, Fletcher Markle, Arch Oboler, Robert Lewis Shayon* [Metuchen, NJ: Scarecrow Press, 1998], 22).

72 Megan E. Williams, "'Meet the Real Lena Horne': Representations of Lena Horne in *Ebony* Magazine, 1945–1949," *Journal of American Studies* 43, no. 1 (2009): 122.

73 Both of these scripts had originally been produced for theater—*Set My People Free* and *Nat Turner*. Neither of the film scripts Washington received was ever made into a film.

74 Shane Vogel, "Lena Horne's Impersona," *Camera Obscura* 23, no. 1 (2008): 19.

75 Darden, "Oh, Sister!," 105; Woodard, "Performing Artists of the Harlem Renaissance," 249.

76 Eva Le Gallienne, *With a Quiet Heart: An Autobiography* (New York, NY: Viking Press, 1953), 245.

77 Robert St. John, *Encyclopedia of Radio and Television: The Man Behind the Microphone*, Milwaukee, WI: Cathedral Square Publishing Company, 1967, 304.

78 Farah Jasmine Griffin, "That the Mothers May Soar and the Daughters May Know Their Names: A Retrospective of Black Feminist Literary Criticism," *Signs* 32 (2007): 483–507.

79 Fredi Washington, "Fredi Says," *The People's Voice*, February 12, 1944.

80 Lena Horne, "Lena Horne—From Me to You," *The People's Voice*, January 10, 1948.

81 David J. Krajicek, "Journalist Went out in Front-Page Fashion with Murder-Suicide," *New York Daily News*, April 23, 2016, www.nydailynews.com/news/crime/journalist-front-page-fashion-murder-suicide-article-1.2612301; Tara McPherson, *Reconstructing Dixie: Race, Gender, and Nostalgia in the Imagined South* (Durham, NC: Duke University Press, 2003).

82 Graham Du Bois, "As a Man Thinketh."

83 Marcus Bright, "Changed Anne Revere Rosen, Nee Anne Revere, Alias Mrs. Sam Rosen," Los Angeles, CA: January 29, 1951, 22, FBI #100-22606, National Archives and Records Administration, College Park, MD.

84 "Letter from Susan Welch (7th grader), Long Beach, CA," Box 17, Folder 14, May 23, 1954, 2, Shirley Graham Du Bois Papers, Schlesinger Library, Radcliffe Institute for Advanced Study, Harvard University, Cambridge, MA.

85 See Eileen Meehan, "Heads of Household and Ladies of the House: Gender, Genre, and Broadcast Ratings, 1929–1990," in *Ruthless Criticism: New Perspectives in U.S. Communication History*, ed. William S. Solomon and Robert W. McChesney (Minneapolis, MN: University of Minnesota Press, 1993), 204–22; Robert Weems, *Desegregating the Dollar: African American Consumerism in the Twentieth Century* (New York, NY: New York University Press, 1998).

86 Lillian Hellman and Wendy Wasserstein, *An Unfinished Woman: A Memoir* (Boston, MA: Back Bay Books, 1999), 57.

87 See Sahar Khamis, "Multiple Meanings, Identities, and Resistances: Egyptian Rural Women's Readings of Televised Family Planning Campaigns," *International Journal of Communication* 3 (2009): 433–90, for a relevant discussion of what she describes as "the insensitivity" of televised family planning campaigns produced by Europeans and the inability of educated elites to communicate with women they considered inferior to them in nearly every way.

88 William Lorenz [Vera Caspary], "The Movie Original," *New Theatre*, August 1936, 21.

89 Lillian Hellman, *Conversations with Lillian Hellman*, Literary Conversations Series (Jackson, MS: University Press of Mississippi, 1986), 4.

90 Marcus Bright, "Changed Anne Revere Rosen, Nee Anne Revere, Alias Mrs. Sam Rosen," Los Angeles, CA: January 29, 1951, FBI #100-22606, National Archives and Records Administration, College Park, MD.

91 Susan Ware, *It's One O'Clock and Here Is Mary Margaret McBride: A Radio Biography* (New York, NY: New York University Press, 2005), 7.

92 Jean C. Anderson, "To Peg Lynch," May 20, 1959, 1, Peg Lynch Collection, Special Collections and University Archives, University of Oregon, Eugene, OR.

93 Shirley Graham, "Letter to Martin Anderson Nexo," June 5, 1954, Box 17, Folder 14, Shirley Graham Du Bois Papers, Schlesinger Library, Radcliffe Institute for Advanced Study, Harvard University, Cambridge, MA.

94 "African Editors Round-Table Report," Box 44, Folder 9, April 26, 1965, 1, Shirley Graham Du Bois Papers, Schlesinger Library, Radcliffe Institute for Advanced Study, Harvard University, Cambridge, MA.
95 "This is Ghana Television" (pamphlet), Tema, Ghana: The State Publishing Corporation, Box 44, Folder 6, 22, Shirley Graham Du Bois Papers, Schlesinger Library, Radcliffe Institute for Advanced Study, Harvard University, Cambridge, MA.
96 Margaret Webster, *Don't Put Your Daughter on the Stage* (New York, NY: Knopf, 1972), 106.
97 Ibid., 107.
98 "Meet the Goldbergs, All Rolled Up in One," *Brooklyn Daily Eagle*, March 29, 1936, Sunday edition; Berg, *Molly and Me*, 190; Lord & Thomas Advertising Agency, "Telegram to Gertrude Berg," January 9, 1933, General Correspondence, Volume 1, Gertrude Berg Papers, Gertrude Berg Papers, Nightingale Library, Syracuse University, Syracuse, NY.
99 Berg, *Molly and Me*, 190–91.
100 Anna McCarthy's *The Citizen Machine: Governing by Television in 1950s America* (New York, NY: New Press, 2010) recounts similar stories about some rare broadcasts involving race. When *DuPont Cavalcade Theater* aired a piece on Ralph Bunche, the Nobel Prize winner, in 1955, "Thirty viewers wrote letters to DuPont praising the company for sponsoring the broadcast" (64) and requesting that the network feature more programs like it (67).
101 Marie Jahoda, "Psychological Issues in Civil Liberties," *American Psychologist* 11, no. 5 (May 1956), 239.
102 John Markus, "From the Goldbergs to 2005: The Evolution of the Sitcom," Museum of Television and Radio Satellite Seminar Series, Los Angeles, CA, 2005.
103 David Zurawik, *The Jews of Prime Time* (Waltham, MA: Brandeis University Press, 2003), 45.
104 Kristal Brent Zook, *Color by Fox: The Fox Network and the Revolution in Black Television* (New York, NY: Oxford University Press, 1999), 9.
105 Cynthia Allen, "To Ruth Gordon," June 1949, Container 1, Correspondence, General Correspondence File A, Ruth Gordon Papers, Library of Congress, Washington, DC.
106 Shirley Graham, "Oral History Interview with Mrs. Shirley Graham Du Bois," January 7, 1971, 1, Box 1, Folder 1, Shirley Graham Du Bois Papers, Schlesinger Library, Radcliffe Institute for Advanced Study, Harvard University, Cambridge, MA.
107 Kristen Warner, *The Cultural Politics of Colorblind TV Casting* (New York, NY/London: Routledge, 2015), 35.
108 Robert E. Russell, April 7, 1951, 5, Federal Bureau of Investigation, Los Angeles Field Office.
109 Quoted in Warren, "Word Play," 68.
110 Mary Margaret McBride, "My Most Unforgettable Character," *Reader's Digest*, January 1962, 98–102.
111 Darden, "Oh, Sister!," 106; Woodard, "Performing Artists of the Harlem Renaissance," 294.
112 Sandra Barrera, "At 98, Actress Marsha Hunt Is Grateful for a Life Helping Others," *Los Angeles Daily*, December 11, 2015, www.dailynews.com/arts-and-entertainment/20151211/at-98-actress-marsha-hunt-is-grateful-for-a-life-helping-others.
113 Ibid.

114 Robert J. Wilkison, "Changed: Ray Lev, Was: Mrs. George P. Edgar," New York, NY: December 28, 1953, FBI #100-370898-10, National Archives and Records Administration, College Park, MD.
115 Woodard, "Performing Artists of the Harlem Renaissance," 282.
116 Kisseloff, *The Box*, 427.
117 A.H. Weiler, "Third World Cinema to Make Films to Get Minorities Jobs," *New York Times*, February 23, 1971, sec. Archives, www.nytimes.com/1971/02/23/archives/third-world-cinema-to-make-films-to-get-minorities-jobs.html.
118 References to economic inequalities were so obviously indications of the presence of communist thought as to make it all but impossible to create content that represented working-class and poor people as anything but victims of their own inability to seize the American dream or victims of each other. The commercial nature of American television meant that it was already difficult to create content that in any way diverged from the consumerist norm. The blacklist made it impossible.
119 Adrian Scott, "Letter to John Briley," Box 4, "Correspondence," October 2, 1969, Adrian and Joan Scott Papers, American Heritage Center, University of Wyoming, Laramie, WY.
120 Erik Barnouw, *Tube of Plenty: The Evolution of American Television* (New York, NY: Oxford University Press, 1990), 130.
121 Hazel Scott, "Testimony of Hazel Scott," U.S. Congress, House of Representatives, Committee on Un-American Activities, Eighty-First Congress, September 22, 1950, 3617.
122 Novotny Lawrence, "Reflections of a Nation's Angst; or, How I Learned to Stop Worrying and Love *The Twilight Zone*," in *Space and Time: Essays on Visions of History in Science Fiction and Fantasy Television*, ed. David C. Wright and Allan W. Austin (New York, NY: McFarlane, 2010), 11.
123 That these forms of sexist violence are frequently accompanied by racism and homophobia has been the subject of much less media attention, despite activists' efforts to ensure that credit for the #MeToo hashtag go to the women of color who created it and continue to be ignored. See Tarana Burke, "#MeToo Was Started for Black and Brown Women and Girls," *Washington Post*, November 9, 2017, www.washingtonpost.com/news/post-nation/wp/2017/11/09/the-waitress-who-works-in-the-diner-needs-to-know-that-the-issue-of-sexual-harassment-is-about-her-too/. Fox's Roger Ailes' sexism was accompanied by both racist and homophobic slurs: he reportedly called NBC executive David Zaslav "a little fucking Jew prick" and referred to Media Matters for America founder David Brock as a "faggot" (Neal Broverman, "More Reason to Despise Him: Fired Fox Exec Roger Ailes Loved the F Word," *The Advocate*, July 10, 2016, www.advocate.com/media/2016/7/29/more-reason-despise-him-fired-fox-exec-roger-ailes-loved-f-word).
124 Dale Pollock, "Tribute Paid to Memory of Pioneer Woman Studio Chief," *Los Angeles Times*, April 14, 1984.

Conclusion

1 Samantha Allen, "'Crazy Ex-Girlfriend' Star Rachel Bloom on Why TV Needs More Asian Bros," *Daily Beast*, January 25, 2016, www.thedailybeast.com/articles/2016/01/25/crazy-ex-girlfriend-star-rachel-bloom-on-why-tv-needs-more-asian-bros.
2 Jessica P. Ogilvie, "How Hollywood Keeps Out Women," *LA Weekly*, April 29, 2015, www.laweekly.com/news/how-hollywood-keeps-out-women-5525034.

3 Albert Martin, "Awkward Black Girl: Too Black for TV," *In Media Res* (blog), May 1, 2013, http://mediacommons.futureofthebook.org/imr/2013/05/01/awkward-black-girl-too-black-tv; Aymar Jean Christian, *Open TV: Innovation beyond Hollywood and the Rise of Web Television* (New York, NY: New York University Press, 2018).
4 Danielle Kwateng-Clark, "Issa Rae Was Still Rooting for Black People at Her First Art Basel Experience," *Essence.com*, December 11, 2017, www.essence.com/news/issa-rae-art-basel-2017.
5 Brittany Spanos, "Issa Rae: Why 'Insecure' Is Not Made 'for Dudes' or 'White People,'" *Rolling Stone*, September 1, 2017, www.rollingstone.com/tv/features/insecure-issa-rae-on-hbo-show-not-made-for-dudes-w500665.
6 Allen, "'Crazy Ex-Girlfriend' Star."
7 See also Ariel Levy on American television creator, showrunner, director, and producer Jill Soloway's work ("Dolls and Feelings," *New Yorker*, December 14, 2015, 40–45).
8 "Beaver Gets Spelled," *Leave It to Beaver* (CBS, October 4, 1957).
9 Gregory Curtis, "Leave Ozzie and Harriet Alone," *New York Times*, January 19, 1997, sec. Magazine, www.nytimes.com/1997/01/19/magazine/leave-ozzie-and-harriet-alone.html.
10 Brigid Schulte, "Unlike in the 1950s, There is No 'Typical' U.S. Family Today," *Washington Post*, September 4, 2014, www.washingtonpost.com/news/local/wp/2014/09/04/for-the-first-time-since-the-1950s-there-is-no-typical-u-s-family/.
11 Dan Merica, "Trump: 'Both Sides' to Blame for Charlottesville," *CNN Politics*, August 16, 2017, www.cnn.com/2017/08/15/politics/trump-charlottesville-delay/index.html.
12 Alex Johnson, "White House Chief of Staff John Kelly Defends Confederate Monuments," *NBC News*, October 31, 2017, www.nbcnews.com/news/us-news/trump-chief-staff-john-kelly-defends-confederate-monuments-n815886.
13 Shirley Graham, "Oral History Interview with Mrs. Shirley Graham Du Bois," January 7, 1971, 1, Box 1, Folder 1, 2–3, Shirley Graham Du Bois Papers, Schlesinger Library, Radcliffe Institute for Advanced Study, Harvard University, Cambridge, MA.
14 Lisa Sergio, *I Am My Beloved: The Life of Anita Garibaldi* (New York, NY: Weybright and Talley, 1969), ix; Lisa Sergio, *A Measure Filled: The Life of Lena Madesin Phillips Drawn from Her Autobiography* (New York, NY: R.B. Luce, 1972).
15 "Says America 'Losing World' with Racial Politics," *Jet*, January 4, 1962.
16 Vera Caspary, "Letter to Hal Stanley," Box 1, Folder 4, Correspondence 1957–1958, 1, Vera Caspary Papers, Wisconsin Historical Society, Madison, WI.
17 Butler's son was blacklisted screenwriter Hugo Butler, who left the U.S. in 1951 with his writer wife Jean Rouverol because of government surveillance and harassment.
18 Shirley Graham, "Women: Then and Now," Box 29, Folder 2, n.d., 3, Shirley Graham Du Bois Papers, Schlesinger Library, Radcliffe Institute for Advanced Study, Harvard University, Cambridge, MA.
19 Both *The Get Down* and *Underground* were cancelled after Netflix and WGN America determined that they were, respectively, not connecting with audiences and not in line with their brand. See Daniel Holloway, "'The Get Down' Cancelled by Netflix," *Variety*, May 24, 2017, http://variety.com/2017/tv/news/the-get-down-canceled-1202443885/ and Bethonie Butler, "'Underground' was a Hit for WGN America. Here's Why it was Canceled," *Washington Post*, May 31, 2017, www.washingtonpost.com/news/arts-and-entertainment/wp/2017/05/31/underground-was-a-hit-for-wgn-america-heres-why-it-got-canceled/?utm_term=.52b7cb9cda82.
20 James Hibberd, "Can Empire Change TV?," *Entertainment Weekly*, March 6, 2015.

21 Lynn Spigel, *Make Room for TV: Television and the Family Ideal in Postwar America* (Chicago, IL: University of Chicago Press, 1992), 2.
22 Rosemary Ndubuizu, "Faux Heads of Households: The Racialized and Gendered Politics of Housing Reform," paper presented at the National Women's Studies Association Conference, Baltimore, MD, November 2017.
23 David Zurawik, "From the Goldbergs to 2005: The Evolution of the Sitcom," Museum of Television and Radio Satellite Seminar Series, Los Angeles, CA, 2005.
24 Shirley Graham Du Bois, "As a Man Thinketh in His Heart, So Is He," *Parish News: Church of the Holy Trinity*, February 1954, vol. 57, no. 4, Box 27, Folder 3, Shirley Graham Du Bois Papers, Schlesinger Library, Radcliffe Institute for Advanced Study, Harvard University, Cambridge, MA.
25 Quoted in Rena Fraden, *Blueprints for a Black Federal Theatre* (New York, NY: Cambridge University Press, 1996); Milly S. Barranger, *Unfriendly Witnesses: Gender, Theater, and Film in the McCarthy Era* (Carbondale, IL: Southern Illinois University Press, 2008); E. Quita Craig, *Black Drama of the Federal Theatre Era: Beyond the Formal Horizons* (Amherst, MA: University of Massachusetts Press, 1980).
26 Lillian Hellman, *Conversations with Lillian Hellman*, Literary Conversations Series (Jackson, MS: University Press of Mississippi, 1986), 136.
27 Christian, *Open TV*.
28 Ronald Bergan, "Obituary: Rose Hobart," *Guardian*, September 14, 2000, www.theguardian.com/news/2000/sep/14/guardianobituaries3.
29 Bernard F. Dick, *Radical Innocence: A Critical Study of the Hollywood Ten* (Lexington. KY: University Press of Kentucky, 2015), 124.
30 Indeed, in a further example of the symbiosis between cultural production and political activism, in the summer of 2017, defenders of reproductive rights donned red robes and white bonnets to protest proposed cuts to Planned Parenthood. See Christine Hauser, "A Handmaid's Tale of Protest," *New York Times*, June 30, 2017, www.nytimes.com/2017/06/30/us/handmaids-protests-abortion.html.
31 Loften Mitchell, "Time to Break the Silence Surrounding Paul Robeson?," in *Paul Robeson: The Great Forerunner*, ed. Editors of *Freedomways* (New York, NY: Dodd, Mead & Company, 1978), 71.
32 Betty Friedan, *The Feminine Mystique* (New York, NY: Norton, 1963).
33 "Oprah Winfrey's Full Golden Globes Speech," CNN, January 10, 2018, www.cnn.com/2018/01/08/entertainment/oprah-globes-speech-transcript/index.html.
34 Danielle L. McGuire, *At the Dark End of the Street: Black Women, Rape, and Resistance: A New History of the Civil Rights Movement from Rosa Parks to the Rise of Black Power* (New York, NY: Vintage, 2011); Nancy Buirski, *The Rape of Recy Taylor*, documentary, 2017.
35 Rebecca Savransky, "Bannon Worried Oprah Could Be 'Existential Threat' to Trump Presidency," *The Hill*, February 12, 2018, http://thehill.com/homenews/administration/373386-bannon-worried-oprah-could-be-existential-threat-to-trump-presidency.

Figures

Bibliography

Abramson, Albert. *The History of Television, 1942 to 2000*. Jefferson, NC: McFarland, 2007.

"Actress Again Takes '5th' at Red-Link Quiz." *New York Mirror*. July 18, 1956.

"Blacklisting." *AdAge*. September 15, 2003. adage.com/article/adage-encyclopedia/blacklisting/98350/.

"African Editors Round-Table Report," April 26, 1965. Box 44, Folder 9. Shirley Graham Du Bois Papers, Schlesinger Library, Radcliffe Institute for Advanced Study, Harvard University, Cambridge, MA.

"Agents Pressured Actress to Become 'False Witness.'" *Daily Worker*. August 21, 1955. FBI #100-393334. National Archives and Records Administration, College Park, MD.

Allen, Cynthia. "To Ruth Gordon." June 1949. Container 1, Correspondence, General Correspondence File A. Ruth Gordon Papers, Library of Congress, Washington, DC.

Allen, Samantha. "'Crazy Ex-Girlfriend' Star Rachel Bloom on Why TV Needs More Asian Bros." *Daily Beast*. January 25, 2016. www.thedailybeast.com/articles/2016/01/25/crazy-ex-girlfriend-star-rachel-bloom-on-why-tv-needs-more-asian-bros.

The American Business Consultants. "CounterAttack's Ten-Point Program." n.d. https://archive.org/stream/foia_Kirkpatrick_Theodore_2/Kirkpatrick_Theodore_2_djvu.txt.

——. "Jan. 11, 1952." *CounterAttack*, January 11, 1952.

——. "Letter." *CounterAttack*. May 16, 1947.

——. "Letter." *CounterAttack*. August 11, 1950.

——. "Letter No. 81." *CounterAttack*. December 10, 1948.

——. "Letter No. 84." *CounterAttack*. December 31, 1948.

——. "Letter No. 88." *CounterAttack*. January 28, 1949.

——. "Letter No. 107." *CounterAttack*. June 10, 1949.

——. "Letter No. 110." *CounterAttack*. July 1, 1949.

——. "Letter No. 119." *CounterAttack*. September 2, 1949.

——. "Letter No. 120." *CounterAttack*. September 9, 1949.

——. "Letter No. 167." *CounterAttack*. August 4, 1950.

——. "Letter No. 169." *CounterAttack*. August 18, 1950.

——. "Letter No. 172." *CounterAttack*. September 13, 1950.

——. "Letter No. 178." *CounterAttack*. October 20, 1950.

——. "Letter No. 183." *CounterAttack*. November 24, 1950.

——. "Letter No. 184." *CounterAttack*. December 1, 1950.

——. "Letter No. 185." *CounterAttack*. December 8, 1950.

——. "Letter No. 186." *CounterAttack*. December 15, 1950.

——. "Letter No. 189." *CounterAttack*. January 5, 1951.

——. "Letter No. 224." *CounterAttack*. September 7, 1951.

——. "Letter to Subscribers." *CounterAttack*. September 4, 1959.

——. *Red Channels: The Report of Communist Influence in Radio and Television*. New York, NY: The authors, 1950.

——. "So Help Me Citadel," *CounterAttack*, July 27, 1956.

"American Civil Liberties Union Boosts Legion." *Firing Line: Facts for Fighting Communism*. July 1, 1952. https://archive.org/stream/foia_American_Legion-Firing_Line-1/American_Legion-Firing_Line-1#page/n25/mode/2up.

American Legion. "Special Report," April 4, 1950. FBI #100-368669 Sub A. Federal Bureau of Investigation.

——. "Summary of Trends and Developments Exposing the Communist Conspiracy." *Spotlight*, February 1950. https://ia601706.us.archive.org/26/items/foia_American_Legion-NAC-18/American_Legion-NAC-18.pdf.

The American Negro in the Communist Party. The Committee on Un-American Activities. U.S. House of Representatives, Washington, DC: Government Printing Office. December 22, 1954, 3.

Anderson, Jean C. "To Peg Lynch." May 20, 1959, 1. Special Collections and University Archives, University of Oregon, Eugene, OR.

"Application for Employment, Theodore Cooper Kirkpatrick." Federal Bureau of Investigation, May 14, 1942. https://archive.org/stream/foia_Kirkpatrick_Theodore_2/Kirkpatrick_Theodore_2_djvu.txt.

"Artists' Play to Aid War." *New York Times*. October 14, 1942.

Atwood, Margaret. *Alias Grace: A Novel*. New York, NY: Knopf Doubleday Publishing Group, 2011.

AWARE, Inc. "AWARE: Statement of Principles." AWARE, Inc., n.d. FBI #62-100575. National Archives and Records Administration, College Park, MD.

——. *The Road Back (Self-Clearance)*. New York, NY: AWARE, Inc., 1950. Alan Hewitt Archive, Dartmouth University, Hanover, NH.

Bagdikian, Ben H. *The Media Monopoly*. Boston, MA: Beacon Press, 1997.

"Ballot for National Referendum." AFTRA. May 1, 1955. Box 4, "Blacklisting: 1945–1955," Margaret Webster Papers. Washington, DC: Library of Congress.

Banay, Ralph S. "Is Modern Woman a Failure?" *Milwaukee Journal*. December 7, 1946.

——. "Statement," in *Hearings before the Senate Subcommittee to Investigate Juvenile Delinquency ... Pursuant to Investigation of Juvenile Delinquency in the United States*. Washington, DC: U.S. Government Printing Office, 1955. http://archive.org/stream/juveniledelinque951unit/juveniledelinque951unit_djvu.txt.

——. "The Trouble with Women." *Collier's Weekly*. December 7, 1946.

Bannerman, Helen. *Little Black Sambo*. Racine, WI: Whitman Publishing Company, 1953.

Barnouw, Erik. *The Golden Web: A History of Broadcasting in the United States*, vol. 2: *1933 to 1953*. New York, NY: Oxford University Press, 1968.

——. *The Image Empire: A History of Broadcasting in the United States*, vol. 3: *From 1953*. New York, NY: Oxford University Press, 1970.

——. *Tube of Plenty: The Evolution of American Television*. New York, NY: Oxford University Press, 1990.

Barranger, Milly S. *Margaret Webster: A Life in the Theater*. Ann Arbor, MI: University of Michigan Press, 2004.

——. *Unfriendly Witnesses: Gender, Theater, and Film in the McCarthy Era*. Carbondale, IL: Southern Illinois University Press, 2008.

Barrera, Sandra. "At 98, Actress Marsha Hunt Is Grateful for a Life Helping Others," *Los Angeles Daily News*. December 11, 2015. www.dailynews.com/arts-and-entertainment/20151211/at-98-actress-marsha-hunt-is-grateful-for-a-life-helping-other.

Barzman, Norma. *The Red and the Blacklist: The Intimate Memoir of a Hollywood Expatriate*. New York, NY: Nation Books, 2004.

Bauer, Margaret. "Interview by Carol A. Stabile." Phoenix, AZ: May 26, 2012.

"Beaver Gets Spelled." *Leave It to Beaver*. CBS, October 4, 1957.

Beck, Koa. "How Marriage Inequality Prompts Gay Partners to Adopt One Another." *The Atlantic*, November 27, 2013. www.theatlantic.com/national/archive/2013/11/how-marriage-inequality-prompts-gay-partners-to-adopt-one-another/281546/.

Belafonte, Harry, and Michael Shnayerson. *My Song: A Memoir*. New York, NY: Knopf, 2011.

Belew, Kathleen. "Veterans and White Supremacy." *New York Times*. April 15, 2014. www.nytimes.com/2014/04/16/opinion/veterans-and-white-supremacy.html.

Belmont, A.H. "Office Memorandum to D. Milton Ladd." June 21, 1952. Federal Bureau of Investigation. https://ia801708.us.archive.org/14/items/foia_Kirkpatrick_Theodore_2/Kirkpatrick_Theodore_2_text.pdf.

——."Re: Apparently Missing Serials from Communist Infiltration into Labor Union Cases." September 6, 1946. https://archive.org/stream/foia_Kirkpatrick_Theodore_2/Kirkpatrick_Theodore_2_djvu.txt.

Bentley, Eric. *Are You Now or Have You Ever Been: The Investigation of Show Business by the Un-American Activities Committee, 1947–1958*. New York, NY: Harper & Row, 1972.

Berg, Gertrude. "The Goldbergs." TV Script, February 27, 1950. Box 39. Gertrude Berg Papers, Nightingale Library, Syracuse University, Syracuse, NY.

——. *Molly and Me: A Memoir*. New York, NY: McGraw-Hill, 1961.

——. "The Real Story Behind 'The House of Glass.'" *Radio Mirror*. July 1935. General Scrapbook 12. Gertrude Berg Papers, Nightingale Library, Syracuse University, Syracuse, NY.

——. *The Rise of The Goldbergs*. New York, NY/Newark, NJ: Barse and Company, 1931.

Bergan, Ronald. "Obituary: Rose Hobart." *Guardian*. September 14, 2000. www.theguardian.com/news/2000/sep/14/guardianobituaries3.

Bernstein, Adam. "Lena Horne Dies at 92; Performer Altered Hollywood's Image of Black Women." *Washington Post*. May 11, 2010.

Bernstein, Walter. "To the Radio-Television Editor." *New York Times*. January 25, 1953.

Bethea, Charles. "What a White Supremacist Told Me After Donald Trump Was Elected." *New Yorker*. August 17, 2017.

Bierly, Kenneth. "Letter to Columbia Picture Corps." FBI #100-368669. National Archives and Records Administration, College Park, MD.

"Bill Robinson Named Guild Honorary Head." *Chicago Defender*. February 18, 1939.

"Blacklist: Memories of a Word That Marks an Era." *New York Times*. July 31, 1994.

Bland, J.F. "Infiltration of Communists in the Entertainment Field, Information Concerning." Letter. New York, NY: Federal Bureau of Investigation, n.d. FBI #100-336762. National Archives and Records Administration, College Park, MD.

Blee, Kathleen M. "Troubling Women's History: Women in Right-Wing and Colonial Politics." *Journal of Women's History* 15, no. 2 (2003): 214–21.

——. *Women of the Klan: Racism and Gender in the 1920s*. University of California Press, 1991.

Bobbitt, H.J. "To Director." San Francisco, CA: March 11, 1941. FBI #64-2226. National Archives and Records Administration, College Park, MD.

Bobo, Jacqueline. *Black Women as Cultural Readers*. New York, NY: Columbia University Press, 1995.

Boddy, William. *Fifties Television: The Industry and Its Critics*. Urbana, IL: University of Illinois Press, 1990.

Bogle, Donald. *Toms, Coons, Mulattoes, Mammies, and Bucks: An Interpretive History of Blacks in American Films*. New York, NY: Continuum, 2001.

Bonnell, M.R. "To Milton Ladd." October 22, 1951. FBI #67-198001-130. National Archives and Records Administration, College Park, MD.

Borstelmann, Thomas. *The Cold War and the Color Line: American Race Relations in the Global Arena*. Cambridge, MA: Harvard University Press, 2003.

Bourdieu, Pierre. *The Field of Cultural Production*. Edited by Randal Johnson. New York, NY: Columbia University Press, 1993.

Bourdieu, Pierre, and Loïc J.D. Wacquant. *An Invitation to Reflexive Sociology*. Chicago, IL: University of Chicago Press, 1992.

Bourdieu, Pierre, et al. *The Weight of the World: Social Suffering in Contemporary Society*. Translated by Priscilla Parkhurst Ferguson. Stanford, CA: Stanford University Press, 2000.

Brennan, Mary C. *Wives, Mothers, and the Red Menace: Conservative Women and the Crusade Against Communism*. Louisville, CO: University Press of Colorado, 2008.

Bright, Marcus. "Changed Anne Revere Rosen, Nee Anne Revere, Alias Mrs. Sam Rosen." Los Angeles, CA: January 29, 1951. FBI #100-22606. National Archives and Records Administration, College Park, MD.

Brook, Vincent. "The Americanization of Molly: How Mid-Fifties TV Homogenized 'The Goldbergs' (And Got 'Berg-Iarized' in the Process)." *Cinema Journal* 38, no. 4 (Summer 1999): 45–67.

Broverman, Neal. "More Reason to Despise Him: Fired Fox Exec Roger Ailes Loved the F Word," *The Advocate*. July 10, 2016. www.advocate.com/media/2016/7/29/more-reason-despise-him-fired-fox-exec-roger-ailes-loved-f-word.

Buckley, Gail. *The Hornes: An American Family*. New York, NY: Knopf, 1986.

Buckley, Jeremiah F. "John Quincy Adams Associates, Inc." Self-published, n.d. FBI #100-HQ-350512. National Archives and Records Administration, College Park, MD.

Buff, Rachel Ida. *Against the Deportation Terror: Organizing for Immigrant Rights in the Twentieth Century*. Philadelphia, PA: Temple University Press, 2017.

Buhle, Paul, and Dave Wagner. *Hide in Plain Sight: The Hollywood Blacklistees in Film and Television, 1950–2002*. New York, NY: Palgrave Macmillan, 2005.

Buirski, Nancy. *The Rape of Recy Taylor*. Documentary, 2017.

Burke, Tarana. "#MeToo Was Started for Black and Brown Women and Girls." *Washington Post*. November 9, 2017. www.washingtonpost.com/news/post-nation/wp/2017/11/09/the-waitress-who-works-in-the-diner-needs-to-know-that-the-issue-of-sexual-harassment-is-about-her-too/.

Burrough, Bryan. *Public Enemies: America's Greatest Crime Wave and the Birth of the FBI, 1933–34*. New York, NY: Penguin Books, 2009.

Butler, Bethonie. "'Underground' was a Hit for WGN America. Here's Why it was Canceled." *Washington Post.* May 31, 2017. www.washingtonpost.com/news/arts-and-entertainment/wp/2017/05/31/underground-was-a-hit-for-wgn-america-heres-why-it-got-canceled/?utm_term=.52b7cb9cda82.

Calomiris, Angela. *Red Masquerade: Undercover for the F.B.I.* Philadelphia, PA: Lippincott, 1950.

Cannon, Robert. *The Brotherhood of Man.* United Productions of America, 1945.

Carey, Gary. *Judy Holliday: An Intimate Life Story.* New York, NY: Putnam Adult, 1984.

Carini, Susan M. "Love's Labors Almost Lost: Managing Crisis during the Reign of *I Love Lucy.*" *Cinema Journal* 43, no. 1 (2003): 44–62.

Caspary, Vera. *Bedelia.* London: Eyre and Spottiswoode, 1945.

——. *Laura.* Boston, MA: Houghton Mifflin, 1943.

——. *Laura.* Screenplay. Twentieth Century Fox Film Corporation, 1944.

——. "Letter to Alfred Black," September 8, 1954. Box 1, Folder 1, General Correspondence 1942–52. Vera Caspary Papers, Wisconsin Historical Society, Madison, WI.

——. "Letter to Allan A. Mussehl," July 17, 1979. Box 28, Folder 1, General Correspondence. Vera Caspary Papers, Wisconsin Historical Society, Madison, WI.

——. "Letter to Don Fine (Editor in Chief, Dell Publishing Company)," July 6, 1971. Box 1, Folder 6, General Correspondence 1961–63. Vera Caspary Papers, Wisconsin Historical Society, Madison, WI.

——. "Letter to Jo Stewart," December 31, 1960, Box 1, Folder 5, General Correspondence 1955–60. Vera Caspary Papers, Wisconsin Historical Society, Madison, WI.

——. "Letter to Miss Schwartz," October 16, 1977. Box 28, Folder 1, General Correspondence. Vera Caspary Papers, Wisconsin Historical Society, Madison, WI.

——. "Letter to Monica McCall." June 26, 1968. Box 28, Folder 1, General Correspondence. Vera Caspary Papers, Wisconsin Historical Society, Madison, WI.

——. "The Private Life of the Morleys," n.d. Box 30, Folder 7, General Correspondence. Vera Caspary Papers, Wisconsin Historical Society, Madison, WI.

——. *The Rosecrest Cell.* London: W.H. Allen, 1968.

——. *The Secrets of Grown-Ups.* New York, NY: McGraw-Hill, 1979.

——. *Thelma.* Boston, MA: Little, Brown & Company, 1952.

——. *Thicker than Water.* New York, NY: Liveright, 1932.

——. "What Price Martyrdom?" *Chicago Defender.* January 9, 1932, 14.

——. *The White Girl.* New York, NY: J.H. Sears, 1929.

Caspary, Vera [William Lorenz]. "The Movie Original." *New Theatre*. August 1936, 21.

Caute, David. *The Great Fear: The Anti-Communist Purge Under Truman and Eisenhower*. New York, NY: Simon & Schuster, 1978.

Cecil, Matthew. *Branding Hoover's FBI: How the Boss's PR Men Sold the Bureau to America*. Lawrence, KS: University of Kansas Press, 2016.

——. "'Whoa, Edgar': *The Des Moines Register and Tribune*, Cowles Publications, and J. Edgar Hoover's FBI." *Annals of Iowa* 71, no. 2 (Spring 2012): 111–36.

Ceplair, Larry. *Anti-Communism in Twentieth-Century America: A Critical History*. Santa Barbara, CA: ABC-CLIO, 2011.

Chambers, Jason. *Madison Avenue and the Color Line: African Americans in the Advertising Industry*. Philadelphia, PA: University of Pennsylvania Press, 2007.

Charron, Katherine Mellen. *Freedom's Teacher: The Life of Septima Clark*. Chapel Hill, NC: University of North Carolina Press, 2012.

Chauncey, George. *Gay New York: Gender, Urban Culture, and the Making of the Gay Male World, 1890–1940*. New York, NY: Basic Books, 1995.

Chilton, Karen. *Hazel Scott: The Pioneering Journey of a Jazz Pianist, from Café Society to Hollywood to HUAC*. Ann Arbor, MI: University of Michigan Press, 2010.

Christian, Aymar Jean. *Open TV: Innovation beyond Hollywood and the Rise of Web Television*. New York, NY: NYU Press, 2018.

Classen, Steven D. *Watching Jim Crow: The Struggles over Mississippi TV, 1955–1969*. Durham, NC: Duke University Press, 2004.

Cline, Edward F. *My Little Chickadee*. Universal Pictures. 1940.

Cogley, John, ed. *Report on Blacklisting: II Radio - Television*. New York, NY: Fund for the Republic, 1956.

Cogley, John, and Merle Miller. *Blacklisting: Two Key Documents*. New York, NY: Arno Press and the New York Times, 1971.

Cohn, David L. "Do American Men Like Women?" *Atlantic Monthly*. August 1946.

Coleman, Robin R. Means. *African American Viewers and the Black Situation Comedy: Situating Racial Humor*. New York, NY: Routledge, 2000.

——. *Horror Noire: Blacks in American Horror Films from the 1890s to Present*. New York, NY: Routledge, 2011.

Collins, Patricia Hill. *Black Feminist Thought: Knowledge, Consciousness, and the Politics of Empowerment*. New York, NY: Routledge, 2008.

"Committee to Get TV 'Red' Problem." *New York Times*. October 3, 1950.

Conroy, E.E. "Letter to Director, FBI." August 19, 1946. https://archive.org/stream/foia_Kirkpatrick_Theodore_2/Kirkpatrick_Theodore_2_djvu.txt.

Cook, Jim, and Kingsley Canham. "Interview with Abraham Polonsky." *Screen* 11, no. 3 (June 20, 1970): 57–73.

Coontz, Stephanie. *The Way We Never Were: American Families and the Nostalgia Trap*. New York, NY: Basic Books, 1992.

Cooper, Courtney Ryley. *Ten Thousand Public Enemies*. Boston, MA: Little, Brown & Company, 1935.

"CounterAttack Gives Denials of 3 Listed." *New York Times*. October 28, 1950.

Court, Joanne. "The Bandit." *Have Gun—Will Travel*, 1961. Box 29. Adrian and Joan Scott Papers, American Heritage Center, University of Wyoming, Laramie, WY.

——. "A Girl and a Boy, Part I," n.d. Box 19, File Folder 2. Adrian and Joan Scott Papers, American Heritage Center, University of Wyoming, Laramie, WY.

——. "Golden Eagle," June 21, 1972. Box 29, Folder 5. Adrian and Joan Scott Papers, American Heritage Center, University of Wyoming, Laramie, WY.

Coyne, J.P. "Activity of Ex-Agents of the New York Field Division Proselyting Our Confidential Informants." Washington, DC: October 3, 1947. FBI #67-198001-92. National Archives and Records Administration, College Park, MD.

——. "Memorandum for Mr. E.A. Tamm." October 25, 1946. https://archive.org/stream/foia_Kirkpatrick_Theodore_2/Kirkpatrick_Theodore_2_djvu.txt.

Craig, E. Quita. *Black Drama of the Federal Theatre Era: Beyond the Formal Horizons*. Amherst, MA: University of Massachusetts Press, 1980.

Crosby, John. "Miss Muir Loses Her Job." *Herald Tribune*. September 7, 1950.

Cunningham, Bill. "Ex-FBI Men Expose Reds." *Boston Herald*. August 1950.

Curtis, Gregory. "Leave Ozzie and Harriet Alone." *New York Times*. January 19, 1997, sec. Magazine. www.nytimes.com/1997/01/19/magazine/leave-ozzie-and-harriet-alone.html.

Darden, Norma Jean. "Oh, Sister! Fredi and Isabel Washington Relive '30s Razzmatazz." *Essence Magazine*. September 1978.

Davies, Carole Boyce. *Left of Karl Marx: The Political Life of Black Communist Claudia Jones*. Durham, NC: Duke University Press, 2008.

Davis, Angela Y. "Black Nationalism: The Sixties and the Nineties." In *Black Popular Culture*, edited by Gina Dent, 317–24. Seattle, WA: Bay, 1992.

Davis, Lisa E. "The FBI's Lesbian, Eleanor Roosevelt and Other Tales from the Red Scare." *Rethinking Marxism* 21, no. 4 (2009): 621–33.

——. *Undercover Girl: The Lesbian Informant Who Helped the FBI Bring Down the Communist Party*. New York, NY: Imagine, 2017.

Deery, Phillip. "Larry Adler and the Cold War." *Labour History*, no. 101 (November 2011): 195–204.

Denning, Michael. *The Cultural Front: The Laboring of American Culture in the Twentieth Century*. London: Verso, 2011.

Desmond, Matthew. *Evicted: Poverty and Profit in the American City*. New York, NY: Crown, 2016.

Dick, Bernard F. *Radical Innocence: A Critical Study of the Hollywood Ten*. Lexington, KY: University Press of Kentucky, 2015.

Dilling, Elizabeth. "Dear Friends." *Patriotic Research Bureau for the Defense of Christianity and Americanism*. October 1943.

——. *The Octopus*. Metairie, LA: Sons of Liberty, 1985.

——. *The Red Network: A "Who's Who" and Handbook of Radicalism for Patriots*. Chicago, IL: The author, 1934.

——. *Red Revolution: Do We Want It Here?* Kenilworth, IL: Wilmette Announcements, 1932.

——. *The Roosevelt Red Record and Its Background*. Kenilworth, IL: The author, 1936.

"Dixie Leader Says Ike Nominee a Klansman." *Jet*. March 24, 1955.

Doherty, Thomas. *Cold War, Cool Medium: Television, McCarthyism, and American Culture*. New York, NY: Columbia University Press, 2003.

Douglas, Susan J. *Listening In: Radio and the American Imagination*. Minneapolis, MN: University of Minnesota Press, 2004.

Douglass, Frederick. *The Essential Douglass: Selected Writings and Speeches*. Indianapolis, IN: Hackett Publishing, 2016.

Drake, Chris. *You Gotta' Stand Up: The Life and High Times of John Henry Faulk*. Newcastle Upon Tyne, England: Cambridge Scholars Publishing, 2009.

Draper v. *Commissioner*, No. 51111. United States Tax Court. April 30, 1956.

Duster, Troy. *Backdoor to Eugenics*. New York, NY: Routledge, 2003.

Dyer, Richard. *White*. New York, NY: Psychology Press, 1997.

"Editorial." *Hollywood Review*. October 1953. Adrian and Joan Scott Papers, #3238. American Heritage Center, University of Wyoming, Laramie, WY.

"Elizabeth Dilling Spreads Negro Hate Theories." *Chicago Defender*. March 4, 1944, National edition.

Elliot, Jeffrey M., ed. *Conversations with Maya Angelou*. Jackson, MS: University Press of Mississippi, 1989.

Enloe, Cynthia. *Maneuvers: The International Politics of Militarizing Women's Lives*. Berkeley, CA: University of California Press, 2000.

"Ethel Waters in Rehearsal." *Chicago Defender*. December 17, 1938.

Everett, Anna. *Returning the Gaze: A Genealogy of Black Film Criticism, 1909–1949.* Durham, NC: Duke University Press, 2001.

Everitt, David. *A Shadow of Red: Communism and the Blacklist in Radio and Television.* Chicago, IL: Ivan R. Dee, 2007.

Everitt, David, and Harold Schechter. *The Manly Handbook.* New York, NY: Berkley Trade, 1982.

Fariello, Griffin. *Red Scare: Memories of the American Inquisition.* New York, NY: Norton, 2008.

Faulk, John Henry. *Fear on Trial.* Austin, TX: University of Texas Press, 1983.

"Faulk Wins Round Against AWARE." *New York Herald Tribune.* November 22, 1955.

Favara, Jeremiah, and Carol Stabile. "Hollywood, the Sexual Violence Factory." *Ms. Magazine Blog.* November 23, 2015. http://msmagazine.com/blog/2015/11/23/hollywood-the-sexual-violence-factory/.

Feather, Leonard. "Lena at 60 Still a Horne of Plenty." *Los Angeles Times.* April 16, 1979.

Federal Bureau of Investigation. "Correlation Summary." June 18, 1956. FBI #100-420699-3. National Archives and Records Administration, College Park, MD.

——. "FBI Monograph: Pretext and Cover Techniques." Federal Bureau of Investigation, May 1956. https://archive.org/stream/FBI-Monograph-Pretexts-and-Cover-Techniques-nsia/FBI%20Monograph-Pretexts%20and%20Cover%20Techniques_djvu.txt.

——. "Lola Graham Du Bois, Aka." New York: FBI, June 19, 1961. FBI #100-87531. National Archives and Records Administration, College Park, MD.

Federal Bureau of Investigation Director. "Judy Holliday." June 15, 1951. FBI #100-368669. National Archives and Records Administration, College Park, MD.

Feldstein, Ruth. *How It Feels to Be Free: Black Women Entertainers and the Civil Rights Movement.* New York, NY: Oxford University Press, 2013.

Feuer, Jane, Paul Kerr, and Tise Vahimagi. *MTM: "Quality Television."* London: BFI Publishing, 1984.

Filreis, Alan. *Counter-Revolution of the Word: The Conservative Attack on Modern Poetry, 1945–1960.* Chapel Hill, NC: University of North Carolina Press, 2007.

Fisher, Heather Elise. "Mythologizing Charles Van Doren: The 1950s, the Media, and the Making of Cultural Memory." Ph.D. dissertation. University of Pittsburgh, 2011. http://gradworks.umi.com/34/85/3485635.html.

Foley, Karen Sue. *The Political Blacklist in the Broadcast Industry: The Decade of the 1950s.* New York, NY: Arno Press, 1972.

Foley, Michael Stewart, ed. *Home Fronts: A Wartime America Reader.* New York, NY: New Press, 2008.

Folkart, Burt A. "Ireene Wicker Hammer, 86; Radio's 'Singing Lady.'" *Los Angeles Times*. November 19, 1987. http://articles.latimes.com/1987-11-19/news/mn-22331_1_ireene-wicker-hammer.

Fraden, Rena. *Blueprints for a Black Federal Theatre*. New York, NY: Cambridge University Press, 1996.

Frankel, Noralee. *Stripping Gypsy: The Life of Gypsy Rose Lee*. New York, NY: Oxford University Press, 2009.

Friedan, Betty. *The Feminine Mystique*. New York, NY: Norton, 1963.

"From the Goldbergs to 2005: The Evolution of the Sitcom." Museum of Television and Radio Satellite Seminar Series. Los Angeles, CA, 2005.

Frost, Jennifer. "Hollywood Gossip as Public Sphere: Hedda Hopper, Reader-Respondents, and the Red Scare, 1947–1965." *Cinema Journal* 50, no. 2 (2011): 84–103.

Gamman, Lorraine, and Margaret Marshment. *The Female Gaze*. London: Women's Press, 1988.

Gordon, Ruth. *My Side: The Autobiography of Ruth Gordon*. New York, NY: Harper & Row, 1976.

——. *Ruth Gordon: An Open Book*. Garden City, NY: Doubleday, 1980.

Gordon, Ruth, and Garson Kanin. *Adam's Rib*. Metro-Goldwyn-Mayer, 1949.

——. *Pat and Mike*. Metro-Goldwyn-Mayer, 1952.

Gore, Dayo F. *Radicalism at the Crossroads: African American Women Activists in the Cold War*. New York, NY: New York University Press, 2011.

Gould, Jack. "A.B.C. Puts Off Jean Muir Blacklist Interview." *New York Times*. December 25, 1965.

——. "'Aldrich Show' Drops Jean Muir; TV Actress Denies Communist Ties." *New York Times*. August 29, 1950.

——. "C.B.S. Demanding Loyalty Oaths from its 2,500 Regular Employees." *New York Times*. December 21, 1950.

——. "Legion Won't Back Lee Case Charges: Says 'Red Channels' Must Prove." *New York Times*. September 14, 1950.

——. "Network Rejects Protest by Legion: A.B.C. Refuses to Cancel New Gypsy Rose Lee Program." *New York Times*. September 13, 1950.

——. "'Red Purge' for Radio, Television Seen in Wake of Jean Muir Ouster." *New York Times*. August 30, 1950.

Gould, Jay. "Globe News and Gossip." *Chicago Defender*. July 22, 1939.

Gould, Lewis L., ed. *Watching Television Come of Age: The New York Times Reviews by Jack Gould*. Austin, TX: University of Texas Press, 2002.

Graham (Du Bois), Shirley. "5 Days That Made History." *Drum*. September 1963.

——. "Address to Kwame Nkrumah Ideological Institute." Accra, Ghana, May 26, 1964. Box 44, Folder 9. Shirley Graham Du Bois Papers, Schlesinger Library, Radcliffe Institute for Advanced Study, Harvard University, Cambridge, MA.

——. "As a Man Thinketh in His Heart, So Is He." *Parish News: Church of the Holy Trinity* 57, no. 4 (February 1954). Box 27, Folder 3. Shirley Graham Du Bois Papers, Schlesinger Library, Radcliffe Institute for Advanced Study, Harvard University, Cambridge, MA.

——. "Autobiographical Sketch," n.d. Box 1, Folder 1. Shirley Graham Du Bois Papers, Schlesinger Library, Radcliffe Institute for Advanced Study, Harvard University, Cambridge, MA.

——. "The Bannekers." Radio script, 1945. Box 41, Folder 7. Shirley Graham Du Bois Papers, Schlesinger Library, Radcliffe Institute for Advanced Study, Harvard University, Cambridge, MA.

——. "Coal Dust." Play, 1938. Box 41, Folders 8–11, Shirley Graham Du Bois Papers, Schlesinger Library, Radcliffe Institute for Advanced Study, Harvard University, Cambridge, MA.

——. *Dr. George Washington Carver, Scientist*. New York, NY: Julian Messner, 1944.

——. "Dust to Earth." Play, 1940. Box 41, Folders 20–24, Shirley Graham Du Bois Papers, Schlesinger Library, Radcliffe Institute for Advanced Study, Harvard University, Cambridge, MA.

——. "Elijah's Ravens: A Comedy in Three Acts." Play, 1939. Box 42, Folders 1–3. Shirley Graham Du Bois Papers, Schlesinger Library, Radcliffe Institute for Advanced Study, Harvard University, Cambridge, MA.

——. "It's Morning: A One-Act Play." In *Plays by American Women: 1930–1960*, edited by Judith E. Barlow, 235–62. New York, NY: Applause Books, 2001.

——. *Jean Baptiste Pointe de Sable, Founder of Chicago*. New York, NY: Julian Messner, 1953.

——. "Letter Sent to the New York Post and New York Star." June 25, 1948. Box 17, Folder 1. Shirley Graham Du Bois Papers, Schlesinger Library, Radcliffe Institute for Advanced Study, Harvard University, Cambridge, MA.

——. "Letter to Ben Davis," December 15, 1957. Box 17, Folder 20. Shirley Graham Du Bois Papers, Schlesinger Library, Radcliffe Institute for Advanced Study, Harvard University, Cambridge, MA.

——. "Letter to Elmer Rice," January 30, 1952. Box 17, Folder 9. Shirley Graham Du Bois Papers, Schlesinger Library, Radcliffe Institute for Advanced Study, Harvard University, Cambridge, MA.

——. “Letter to Martin Anderson Nexo.” June 5, 1954. Box 17, Folder 14. Shirley Graham Du Bois Papers, Schlesinger Library, Radcliffe Institute for Advanced Study, Harvard University, Cambridge, MA.

——. “Letter to Mr. Joseph Goldstein,” December 22, 1951. Box 17, Folder 5. Shirley Graham Du Bois Papers, Schlesinger Library, Radcliffe Institute for Advanced Study, Harvard University, Cambridge, MA.

——. “Little Black Sambo.” Musical Score, 1938. Box 22, Folders 19–21. Shirley Graham Du Bois Papers, Schlesinger Library, Radcliffe Institute for Advanced Study, Harvard University, Cambridge, MA.

——. “Naïveté, the Story of Anne Royale,” 1947. Box 38, Folder 1. Shirley Graham Du Bois Papers, Schlesinger Library, Radcliffe Institute for Advanced Study, Harvard University, Cambridge, MA.

——. “Oral History Interview with Mrs. Shirley Graham DuBois,” January 7, 1971, Fisk University Library, Nashville, TN (Schlesinger Library, Box 1, Folder 1, SGD Oral History Transcript). Shirley Graham Du Bois Papers, Schlesinger Library, Radcliffe Institute for Advanced Study, Harvard University, Cambridge, MA.

——. *Paul Robeson, Citizen of the World.* New York, NY: Julian Messner, 1946.

——. “Sambo, Director’s Notes,” n.d. Container 1032, Box 47. Federal Theatre Project Collection, Library of Congress, Washington, DC.

——. “The Shadow of Olive Trees.” Script, n.d. Box 42, Folder 18. Shirley Graham Du Bois Papers, Schlesinger Library, Radcliffe Institute for Advanced Study, Harvard University, Cambridge, MA.

——. *The Story of Phillis Wheatley.* New York, NY: Julian Messner, 1969.

——. *The Story of Pocahontas.* New York, NY: Grosset & Dunlap, 1953.

——. *There Was Once a Slave: The Heroic Story of Frederick Douglass.* New York, NY: Julian Messner, 1947.

——. “To Mr. T.O. Thackrey, Publisher, *The Daily Compass*,” September 11, 1952. Box 17, Folder 8. Shirley Graham Du Bois Papers, Schlesinger Library, Radcliffe Institute for Advanced Study, Harvard University, Cambridge, MA.

——. “Tom-Tom.” Libretto, 1932. Box 23, Folder 3, Shirley Graham Du Bois Papers, Schlesinger Library, Radcliffe Institute for Advanced Study, Harvard University, Cambridge, MA.

——. *Your Most Humble Servant.* New York, NY: Simon & Schuster Trade, 1949.

Gray, Herman. *Watching Race: Television and the Struggle for “Blackness.”* Minneapolis, MN: University of Minnesota Press, 1995.

Griffin, Farah Jasmine. *Harlem Nocturne: Women Artists and Progressive Politics during World War II.* New York, NY: Basic Civitas Books, 2013.

——. "That the Mothers May Soar and the Daughters May Know Their Names: A Retrospective of Black Feminist Literary Criticism." *Signs* 32 (2007): 483–507.

Gussow, Mel. "Uta Hagen, Tony-Winning Broadway Star and Teacher of Actors, Dies at 84." *New York Times*. January 15, 2004, sec. Theater. www.nytimes.com/2004/01/15/theater/uta-hagen-tony-winning-broadway-star-and-teacher-of-actors-dies-at-84.html.

"Gypsy Claims Past Bare of Red Tint." *Pittsburgh Free Press*. September 12, 1950.

"Gypsy, Scott & Wicker in Red Denials." *Billboard*. September 23, 1950.

Hall, Stuart. "The Whites of Their Eyes: Racist Ideologies and the Media." In *The Media Reader*, edited by Manuel Alvarado and John O. Thompson, 7–23. London: BFI Publishing, 1990.

Halper, Donna L. *Invisible Stars: A Social History of Women in American Broadcasting*. New York, NY: M.E. Sharpe, 2001.

Happe, Kelly E. *The Material Gene: Gender, Race, and Heredity after the Human Genome Project*. New York, NY: New York University Press, 2013.

Haralovich, Mary Beth, and Lauren Rabinovitz, eds. *Television, History, and American Culture: Feminist Critical Essays*. Durham, NC: Duke University Press, 1999.

Hartnett, Vincent. "Red Fronts in Radio." *The Sign*. October 1949.

Harvey, Rita Morley. *Those Wonderful, Terrible Years: George Heller and the American Federation of Television and Radio Artists*. Carbondale, IL: Southern Illinois University Press, 1996.

Haskins, James. *Lena: A Personal and Professional Biography of Lena Horne*. New York, NY: Stein and Day, 1984.

Hauser, Christine. "A Handmaid's Tale of Protest." *New York Times*. June 30, 2017. www.nytimes.com/2017/06/30/us/handmaids-protests-abortion.html.

Havoc, June. *Early Havoc*. N.p.: Literary Licensing, LLC, 2011.

Hayworth, Jean Owens, and Vinton J. Hayworth. "Mr. J. Edgar Hoover, Director." November 16, 1953. FBI #62-100575-1. National Archives and Records Administration, College Park, MD.

"Hazel Scott Attorneys Score in Initial Round." *Spokane Daily Chronicle*. April 17, 1950.

Hellman, Lillian. *Conversations with Lillian Hellman*. Literary Conversations Series. Jackson, MS: University Press of Mississippi, 1986.

——. "The Judas Goats." *The Screenwriter* 3, no. 7 (December 1947).

——. *Pentimento*. Boston, MA: Little, Brown & Company, 1973.

Hellman, Lillian, and Wendy Wasserstein. *An Unfinished Woman: A Memoir*. Boston, MA: Back Bay Books, 1999.

Hendershot, Heather. *What's Fair on the Air? Cold War Right-Wing Broadcasting and the Public Interest.* Chicago, IL: University of Chicago Press, 2011.

"Henry Jaffe Is Dead; TV Producer Was 85." *New York Times*. September 30, 1992. www.nytimes.com/1992/09/30/obituaries/henry-jaffe-is-dead-tv-producer-was-85.html.

Herman, Edward S., and Noam Chomsky. *Manufacturing Consent: The Political Economy of the Mass Media.* New York, NY: Pantheon, 2002.

Hibberd, James. "Can *Empire* Change TV?" *Entertainment Weekly*. March 15, 2016.

"High-Low Democracy." *Chicago Defender*. September 23, 1950, National edition.

Hilmes, Michele, ed. *NBC: America's Network*. Berkeley, CA: University of California Press, 2007.

——. *Radio Voices: American Broadcasting, 1922–1952*. Minneapolis, MN: University of Minnesota Press, 1997.

Hitchens, Christopher. "Rebel in Evening Clothes." *Vanity Fair*. October 1999. www.vanityfair.com/magazine/1999/10/hitchens199910.

Hobart, Rose. *A Steady Digression to a Fixed Point*. Metuchen, NJ: Scarecrow Press, 1994.

Holloway, Daniel. "'The Get Down' Cancelled by Netflix." *Variety*. May 24, 2017. http://variety.com/2017/tv/news/the-get-down-canceled-1202443885/.

Hoover, J. Edgar. "The American Way of Life." *The Militant*. May 19, 1952, 2.

——. "Communist 'New Look': A Study in Duplicity." *Elks* Magazine. August 1956, 5.

——. "Could Your Child Become a Red?" *Parade*. May 13, 1952.

——. "Madeline Lee Security Matter-C." November 3, 1955. FBI #100-106821. National Archives and Records Administration, College Park, MD.

——. *Masters of Deceit: The Story of Communism in America and How to Fight It*. New York, NY: Henry Holt, 1958.

——. "Memorandum for the Attorney General." May 26, 1945. FBI #100-339626. National Archives and Records Administration, College Park, MD.

——. "Re: Lillian Hellman, Internal Security-C." To Special Agent in Charge, New York, NY, October 20, 1943. https://vault.fbi.gov/Lillian%20%28Lily%29%20Hellman/Lillian%20%28Lily%29%20Hellman%20Part%201%20of%204/view#document/p1.

——. "SAC Letter No. 60-30," June 21, 1960. https://archive.org/stream/SACLetter6030ReserveIndex/SAC%20Letter%2060-30%20-%20Reserve%20Index_djvu.txt.

——. "Testimony of J. Edgar Hoover, Director Federal Bureau of Investigation." *Investigation of Un-American Propaganda Activities in the United States*. Washington, DC: U.S. Congress, House of Representatives, Committee on Un-American Activities. March 26, 1947. https://archive.org/stream/investigationofu194702unit/investigationofu194702unit_djvu.txt.

——. "Unmasking the Communist Masquerader." *Educational Forum*. May 1950, 399-401.

——. "Vera Caspary, Internal Security - R." To Special Agent in Charge. Los Angeles, CA: January 18, 1945. FBI #101-6700. National Archives and Records Administration, College Park, MD.

Hopper, Hedda. "Happy to Have Cleared up Rumors, Lucy Tells Columnist Hedda Hopper." *Los Angeles Times*. September 12, 1953.

——. "Letter from Hedda Hopper to J. Edgar Hoover," April 7, 1949. Federal Bureau of Investigation. National Archives and Records Administration, College Park, MD. www.webharvest.gov/peth04/20041019025808/http://foia.fbi.gov/hopper_heda/hoper_heda_part01.pdf.

Horne, Gerald. *Race Woman: The Lives of Shirley Graham Du Bois*. New York, NY: New York University Press, 2002.

Horne, Lena. "Lena Horne—From Me to You." *The People's Voice*. January 10, 1948.

Horne, Lena, and Richard Schickel. *Lena*. Garden City, NY: Doubleday, 1965.

"Howard Rushmore Kills Wife and Slays Himself in Cab Here." *New York Times*. January 4, 1958.

Hughes, Langston. "From Here to Yonder." *Chicago Defender*. June 10, 1944, National edition.

"Hung Jury." *Time*. June 5, 1950.

"Hysteria and Civil Liberties." *The Survey*. October 1950, 458-59.

Interview with Former Special Agent James R. Healy (1948-80). Interview by Sandra Robinette, May 3, 2007, for the FBI Oral History Project. www.nleomf.org/assets/pdfs/nlem/oral-histories/FBI_Healy_interview.pdf.

"Invoking of 5th Hampered Her Career, Actress Asserts." *New York Herald Tribune*. July 18, 1956.

"Is Television New to Our Entertainers?" *Chicago Defender*. July 1, 1939, National edition.

Jahoda, Marie. "Anti-Communism and Employment Policies in Radio and Television." In *Report on Blacklisting: II Radio - Television*, edited by John Cogley, 221-81. New York, NY: Fund for the Republic, 1956.

——. "Psychological Issues in Civil Liberties." *American Psychologist* 11, no. 5 (May 1956): 234-40.

Jarrico, Sylvia. "Evil Heroines of 1953." *Hollywood Review* 1, no. 3 (July 1953): 3-4.

Jeansonne, Glen. *Women of the Far Right: The Mother's Movement and World War II*. Chicago, IL: University of Chicago Press, 1996.

Johnson, David K. *The Lavender Scare: The Cold War Persecution of Gays and Lesbians in the Federal Government*. Chicago, IL: University Of Chicago Press, 2004.

Johnson, William Bruce. *Miracles and Sacrilege: Roberto Rossellini, the Church and Film Censorship in Hollywood*. Toronto, Canada: University of Toronto Press, 2008.

Jones, M.A. "Jerry D. Lewis and Louise Fitch." Los Angeles, CA: Federal Bureau of Investigation, January 18, 1952. FBI #100-390769. National Archives and Records Administration, College Park, MD.

——. "Office Memorandum to Gordon A. Nease." November 3, 1958. Federal Bureau of Investigation. https://ia801708.us.archive.org/14/items/foia_Kirkpatrick_Theodore_2/Kirkpatrick_Theodore_2_text.pdf.

——. "Office Memorandum to Mr. Nichols," April 11, 1952. Federal Bureau of Investigation. https://ia801708.us.archive.org/14/items/foia_Kirkpatrick_Theodore_2/Kirkpatrick_Theodore_2_text.pdf.

——. "To Mr. DeLoach." March 27, 1959. FBI #67-198001-130. National Archives and Records Administration, College Park, MD.

——. "To Mr. Nichols." April 11, 1952. https://ia801708.us.archive.org/14/items/foia_Kirkpatrick_Theodore_2/Kirkpatrick_Theodore_2_text.pdf.

Julian, Joseph. *This Was Radio*. New York, NY: Viking Press, 1975.

Kahn, E.J. Jr. "The Greenwich Tea Party." *New Yorker*. April 15, 1968.

Kanfer, Stefan. *A Journal of the Plague Years*. New York, NY: Athenaeum, 1973.

Kanin, Garson. *Hollywood: A Memoir*. New York, NY: Viking Press, 1974.

Kaplan, Judy, and Linn Shapiro, eds. *Red Diapers: Growing Up in the Communist Left*. Urbana, IL: University of Illinois Press, 1998.

Kaufman, Sarah. " 'Brethren's' Time, If It Ever Really Ended, Comes Again." *Washington Post*. November 25, 2007. www.washingtonpost.com/wp-dyn/content/article/2007/11/23/AR2007112301058.html.

Keenan, John G. "Dear Mr. Hoover," July 28, 1950. FBI #100-350512-344. National Archives and Records Administration, College Park, MD.

——. "To J. Edgar Hoover," February 11, 1971. FBI #67-198001-130. National Archives and Records Administration, College Park, MD.

——. "To J. Edgar Hoover," March 24, 1958. FBI #1308733-0. National Archives and Records Administration, College Park, MD.

Keeney, Frank J. "Vera Caspary." Los Angeles, CA: March 31, 1945. FBI #100-22897. National Archives and Records Administration, College Park, MD.

Kellum, David W. "Ethel Waters Is Superb in 'Mamba's Daughters.' " *Chicago Defender*. October 7, 1939.

Khamis, Sahar. "Multiple Meanings, Identities, and Resistances: Egyptian Rural Women's Readings of Televised Family Planning Campaigns." *International Journal of Communication* 3 (2009): 443–90.

Kimball, Harry M. "To Director, FBI." July 27, 1949. https://archive.org/stream/foia_Kirkpatrick_Theodore_2/Kirkpatrick_Theodore_2_djvu.txt.

Kisseloff, Jeff. "Another Award, Other Memories of McCarthyism." *New York Times.* May 30, 1999.

——. *The Box: An Oral History of Television 1920–1961.* N.p.: ReAnimus Press, 2013.

Krajicek, David J. "Journalist Went Out in Front-Page Fashion with Murder-Suicide." *New York Daily News.* April 23, 2016. www.nydailynews.com/news/crime/journalist-front-page-fashion-murder-suicide-article-1.2612301.

Kroik, Polina. "Producing Modern Girls: Gender and Work in American Literature and Film, 1910–1960." Ph.D. dissertation. University of California, Irvine, 2011.

Kwateng-Clark, Danielle. "Issa Rae Was Still Rooting for Black People At Her First Art Basel Experience." *Essence.com.* December 11, 2017. www.essence.com/news/issa-rae-art-basel-2017.

Ladd, D.M. "To The Director." March 10, 1948. FBI #67-334296-110. National Archives and Records Administration, College Park, MD.

Lambert, Bruce. "Aline L. MacMahon, 92, Actress Over 50 Years and in 43 Movies." *New York Times.* October 31, 1991. www.nytimes.com/1991/10/13/nyregion/aline-l-macmahon-92-actress-over-50-years-and-in-43-movies.html.

Larmon, Sigurd S. *A Primer for Americans.* N.p.: The author, 1950.

"Last 8 Times." *New York Times.* May 21, 1950.

Lauter, Bob. "Around the Dial: Radio Launches Fight Against Discrimination." *Daily Worker.* July 12, 1949.

Lawrence, Novotny. "Reflections of a Nation's Angst; or, How I Learned to Stop Worrying and Love *The Twilight Zone.*" In *Space and Time: Essays on Visions of History in Science Fiction and Fantasy Television*, edited by David C. Wright, Jr. and Allan W. Austin, 9–28. New York, NY: McFarland, 2010.

Le Gallienne, Eva. *With a Quiet Heart: An Autobiography.* New York, NY: Viking Press, 1953.

Leaming, Barbara. *Marilyn Monroe*, New York, NY: Three Rivers Press, 2000.

Ledbetter, Les. "Hazel Scott, 61, Jazz Pianist, Acted in Films, on Broadway." *New York Times.* October 3, 1981.

Lee, Gypsy Rose. *The G-String Murders.* New York, NY: The Feminist Press, 1941/2005.

Le Guin, Ursula K. *The Wild Girls.* Oakland, CA: PM Press, 2011.

Leibman, Nina C. *Living Room Lectures: The Fifties Family in Film and Television.* Austin, TX: University of Texas Press, 1995.

Lena Horne: The Lady and Her Music. Harold Wheeler, musical director, New York, NY, 1981. www.youtube.com/watch?v=6rpIfQQv_T0.

"Lena Horne Tells How Paul Robeson Changed Her Life." *Daily Worker.* October 7, 1947. FBI # 100-353031. National Archives and Records Administration, College Park, MD.

"Leopardess Takes the Hilda Vaughn." *New York Times.* November 29, 1924.

"Letter from Susan Welch (7th Grader), Long Beach, CA," May 23, 1954. Box 17, Folder 14. Shirley Graham Du Bois Papers, Schlesinger Library, Radcliffe Institute for Advanced Study, Harvard University, Cambridge, MA.

"Letter to Director," July 26, 1956. FBI #105-18873-1A. National Archives and Records Administration, College Park, MD.

Levine, Elana. *Wallowing in Sex: The New Sexual Culture of 1970s American Television.* Durham, NC: Duke University Press, 2006.

Levine, Isaac Don. *Plain Talk: An Anthology from the Leading Anti-Communist Magazine of the 40s.* New Rochelle, NY: Arlington House, 1976.

Levy, Ariel. "Dolls and Feelings." *New Yorker.* December 14, 2015.

Lewis, Jerry D. Lee [Louise Fitch]. "Statement from Mrs. Jerry D. Lewis to the FBI." Signed statement, March 13, 1952. Letter to Mr. Tolson from L.B. Nichols. FBI #100-390769. National Archives and Records Administration, College Park, MD.

Lewis, Lloyd. "Frederick Douglass, the Abolitionist Who Began as a Slave." *New York Times Book Review.* April 6, 1947.

Lichtman, Robert M., and Ronald Cohen. *Deadly Farce: Harvey Matusow and the Informer System in the McCarthy Era.* Urbana, IL: University of Illinois Press, 2008.

"Lillian Hellman, Alias Lillian Hellman Krober." Anchorage, AK: Federal Bureau of Investigation, November 28, 1944. https://vault.fbi.gov/Lillian%20%28Lily%29%20Hellman/Lillian%20%28Lily%29%20Hellman%20Part%201%20of%204/view#document/p1.

Lipsitz, George. *Time Passages: Collective Memory and American Popular Culture.* Minneapolis, MN: University of Minnesota Press, 1990.

Lord & Thomas Advertising Agency. "Telegram to Gertrude Berg," January 9, 1933. General Correspondence, Volume 1. Gertrude Berg Papers, Nightingale Library, Syracuse University, Syracuse, NY.

Lott, Eric. *Love and Theft: Blackface Minstrelsy and the American Working Class.* New York, NY: Oxford University Press, 1993.

Lundberg, Ferdinand, and Marynia F. Farnham. *Modern Woman: The Lost Sex.* New York, NY: Harper & Brothers, 1947.

Lydon, Susan. "The Faa-Bu-Lous Long Run of Gordon and Kanin." *New York Times.* October 5, 1969.

“ ‘Lysistrata’ Quits After 4 Days.” *Chicago Defender*. November 2, 1946, National edition.

Mack, Dwayne. “Hazel Scott: A Career Curtailed.” *Journal of African American History* 91, no. 2 (April 1, 2006): 153–70.

MacLean, Nancy. *Democracy in Chains: The Deep History of the Radical Right’s Stealth Plan for America*. New York, NY: Viking, 2017.

“Madeline Lee’s Statement to the Witchhunters.” *Daily Worker*. August 22, 1955. FBI #100-39-3334-A. National Archives and Records Administration, College Park, MD.

Madigan, Kathleen. “You Want ‘Family Values’? They’ll Cost Billions.” *Business Week*. September 28, 1992.

Mainiero, Lina, ed. *American Women Writers: A Critical Reference Guide from Colonial Times to the Present*. New York, NY: Ungar, 1979.

Maltz, Albert. “General Information about the Investigation of Hollywood by the Congressional Committee on Un-American Activities,” n.d. Albert Maltz Papers, Box 48, “Blacklist.” American Heritage Center, University of Wyoming, Laramie, WY.

Mandel, Benjamin. “Memorandum for Mr. Louis J. Russell.” October 30, 1950. https://archive.org/stream/foia_Kirkpatrick_Theodore_2/Kirkpatrick_Theodore_2_djvu.txt.

Mann, Dave. *Britain’s First TV/Film Crime Series and the Industrialisation of its Film Industry, 1946–1964*. Lewiston, NY: Edwin Mellen Press, 2009.

“Manners and Morals: By Appointment.” *Time*. September 11, 1950. www.time.com/time/magazine/article/0,9171,813149,00.html.

Manning, John J. “Lena Horne, Was, Lina Horne, Helena Horne.” Washington, DC: February 12, 1948. FBI #100-88027. National Archives and Records Administration, College Park, MD.

Marschall, Rick. *The Golden Age of Television*. New York, NY: Smithmark Publications, 1995.

Martin, Albert. “Awkward Black Girl: Too Black for TV.” *In Media Res*. May 1, 2013. http://mediacommons.futureofthebook.org/imr/2013/05/01/awkward-black-girl-too-black-tv.

Matthews, Tom Dewe. “The Outlaws.” *Guardian*. October 7, 2006. www.guardian.co.uk/film/2006/oct/07/books.featuresreviews1.

Matusow, Harvey. *False Witness*. New York, NY: Cameron & Kahn, 1955.

Maxwell, William J. *F.B. Eyes: How J. Edgar Hoover’s Ghostreaders Framed African American Literature*. Princeton, NJ: Princeton University Press, 2015.

May, Elaine Tyler. *Homeward Bound: American Families in the Cold War Era*. New York, NY: Basic Books, 2008.

May, Gary. *Un-American Activities: The Trials of William Remington*. New York, NY: Oxford University Press, 1994.

Mayer, Jane. *Dark Money: The Hidden History of the Billionaires Behind the Rise of the Radical Right.* New York, NY: Doubleday, 2016.

McBride, Mary Margaret. "Marriage on a Fifty-Fifty Basis." *Scribner's Magazine.* December 1929, 656–61.

——. "My Most Unforgettable Character." *Reader's Digest.* January 1962, 98–102.

McCarthy, Anna. *Ambient Television: Visual Culture and Public Space.* Durham, NC: Duke University Press, 2001.

——. *The Citizen Machine: Governing by Television in 1950s America.* New York, NY: New Press, 2010.

McCarthy, Joseph. "Subpoena from HUAC," June 25, 1953. Box 17, Folder 10. Shirley Graham Du Bois Papers, Schlesinger Library, Radcliffe Institute for Advanced Study, Harvard University, Cambridge, MA.

McDonald, Kathlene. *Feminism, the Left, and Postwar Literary Culture.* Jackson, MI: University Press of Mississippi, 2012.

McDuffie, Erik S. "A 'New Freedom Movement of Negro Women': Sojourning for Truth, Justice, and Human Rights during the Early Cold War." *Radical History Review* 2008, no. 101: 81–106.

McFadden, Alesia Elaine. "The Artistry and Activism of Shirley Graham Du Bois: A Twentieth Century African American Torchbearer." Ph.D. Dissertation, University of Massachusetts, Amherst, 2009.

McGilligan, Patrick, and Paul Buhle. *Tender Comrades: A Backstory of the Hollywood Blacklist.* New York, NY: St. Martin's Press, 1997.

McGuire, Danielle L. *At the Dark End of the Street: Black Women, Rape, and Resistance – A New History of the Civil Rights Movement from Rosa Parks to the Rise of Black Power.* New York, NY: Vintage, 2011.

McKee, Alison. "To Speak of Love: Female Desire and Lost Narrative in Women's Films." Ph.D. dissertation. UCLA, 1993.

McLellan, Dennis, and Valerie J. Nelson. "Lena Horne Dies at 92." *Los Angeles Times.* May 10, 2010.

McPherson, Tara. *Reconstructing Dixie: Race, Gender, and Nostalgia in the Imagined South.* Durham, NC: Duke University Press, 2003.

Medsger, Betty. *The Burglary: The Discovery of J. Edgar Hoover's Secret FBI.* New York, NY: Knopf, 2014.

Meehan, Eileen. "Heads of Household and Ladies of the House: Gender, Genre, and Broadcast Ratings, 1929–1990." In *Ruthless Criticism: New Perspectives in U.S. Communication History,* edited by William S. Solomon and Robert W. McChesney, 204–22. Minneapolis, MN: University of Minnesota Press, 1993.

"Meet the Goldbergs, All Rolled Up in One." *Brooklyn Daily Eagle*. March 29, 1936, Sunday edition.

"Megger Draws Up Slate for Ballot." *Billboard*. May 21, 1949.

Merica, Dan. "Trump: 'Both Sides' to Blame for Charlottesville." *CNN Politics*. August 16, 2017. www.cnn.com/2017/08/15/politics/trump-charlottesville-delay/index.html.

Meyer, Cynthia B. "Advertising, the Red Scare, and the Blacklist: BBDO, US Steel, and Theatre Guild on the Air." *Cinema Journal* 55, no. 4 (Fall 2016): 55–83.

——. "BBDO and US Steel on Radio and Television, 1948–53: The Problems of Sponsorship, New Media, and the Communist Threat," 2010. http://mountsaintvincent.academia.edu/CynthiaMeyers/Papers/723259/BBDO_and_US_Steel_on_Radio_and_Television_1948-53_The_Problems_of_Sponsorship_New_Media_and_the_Communist_Threat.

——. "Inside a Broadcasting Blacklist: *Kraft Television Theatre*, 1951–1955." *Journal of American History*. Forthcoming, December 2018.

Meyerowitz, Joanne. *Not June Cleaver: Women and Gender in Postwar America, 1945–1960*. Philadelphia, PA: Temple University Press, 1994.

Mickenberg, Julia L. *Learning from the Left: Children's Literature, the Cold War, and Radical Politics in the United States*. New York, NY: Oxford University Press, 2005.

Millard, Betty. "Woman Against Myth." Box 6, Folder 18, 1948, 21. American Left Ephemera Collection, 1894-2008, University of Pittsburgh, Pittsburgh, PA.

Miller, Merle. *The Judges and the Judged: The Report on Blacklisting in Radio and Television*. New York, NY: Doubleday & Company, 1952.

Miller, Stephen. "Madeline Lee Gilford, 84, Actress and Activist." *New York Sun*. New York, NY: April 18, 2008. www.nysun.com/obituaries/madeline-lee-gilford-84-actress-and-activist/74950/.

Mishkin, Leo. "What's with 'Molly'? And Sam Levenson?" *New York City Telegraph*. February 2, 1952. General Scrapbook 38. Gertrude Berg Papers, Nightingale Library, Syracuse University, Syracuse, NY.

"Miss Lee Accuses Red Inquiry Aide." *New York Times*. August 18, 1955.

Mitchell, Loften. "Time to Break the Silence Surrounding Paul Robeson?" In *Paul Robeson: The Great Forerunner*, edited by Editors of *Freedomways*, 68–86. New York, NY: Dodd, Mead & Company, 1978.

Mitchell, Margaret. "On *Gone with the Wind*." In *Plain Talk: An Anthology from the Leading Anti-Communist Magazine of the 40s*, edited by Isaac Don Levine, 398–99. New Rochelle, NY: Arlington House, 1949.

Mittell, Jason. *Genre and Television: From Cop Shows to Cartoons in American Culture*. New York, NY: Routledge, 2004.

Mohr, J.P. "Theodore Cooper Kirkpatrick." January 25, 1945, Federal Bureau of Investigation, Washington, DC. https://archive.org/stream/foia_Kirkpatrick_Theodore_2/Kirkpatrick_Theodore_2_djvu.txt.

——. "To Mr. Mohr." March 30, 1959. FBI #67-198001-130. National Archives and Records Administration, College Park, MD.

"Morning Edition." *National Public Radio*. September 17, 1992.

Mostel, Kate. *170 Years of Show Business*. New York, NY: Random House, 1978.

"Mrs. FDR Speaks at Testimonial for Walter White." *Chicago Defender*. June 3, 1944, National edition.

Muir, Jean. "Autobiography," n.d. Jean Muir Papers, University of Oregon Special Collections and Archives, Eugene, OR.

Mullaly, William P. "Madeleine Lee Gellman, Aka." New York City: October 21, 1959. FBI #100-106821. National Archives and Records Administration, College Park, MD.

Mullen, Bill, and James Edward Smethurst, eds. *Left of the Color Line: Race, Radicalism, and Twentieth-Century Literature of the United States*. Chapel Hill, NC: University of North Carolina Press, 2003.

Muncy, Robyn. *Relentless Reformer: Josephine Roche and Progressivism in Twentieth-Century America*. Princeton, NJ: Princeton University Press, 2014.

Murray, Susan. *Hitch Your Antenna to the Stars: Early Television and Broadcast Stardom*. New York, NY: Routledge, 2005.

Nadel, Alan. *Containment Culture: American Narratives, Postmodernism, and the Atomic Age*. Durham, NC: Duke University Press, 1995.

Navasky, Victor S. *Naming Names*. New York, NY: Hill and Wang, 2003.

Ndubuizu, Rosemary. "Faux Heads of Households: The Racialized and Gendered Politics of Housing Reform." Paper presented at National Women's Studies Association Conference, Baltimore, MD, November 2017.

Neale, Steve. "Pseudonyms, Sapphire and Salt: 'Un-American' Contributions to Television Costume Adventure Series in the 1950s." *Historical Journal of Film, Radio and Television* 23, no. 3 (2003): 245–57.

——. "Transatlantic Ventures and Robin Hood." In *ITV Cultures: Independent Television over Fifty Years*, edited by Catherine Johnson and Rob Turnock. Maidenhead: Open University Press, 2005.

Neely, Barbara. *Blanche on the Lam*. New York, NY: Penguin, 1992.

Nelson, Alice Dunbar. "As in a Looking Glass." *Washington-Eagle*. February 1, 1929.

"New *Hazel Scott Show* Is Set for the Video." *Chicago Defender*. July 8, 1950, National edition.

Nichols, L.B. "Ella Logan, Bureau File No. 100-339626." September 28, 1950. FBI #100-339626-31. National Archives and Records Administration, College Park, MD.

——. "Letter to Clyde Tolson." November 5, 1951. FBI #100-350512-435. National Archives and Records Administration, College Park, MD.

——. "Letter to Clyde Tolson." February 15, 1949. FBI #67-334296-1. https://archive.org/details/TheodoreKirkpatrick.

——. "Letter to Mr. Tolson." March 10, 1948. FBI #100-350512. National Archives and Records Administration, College Park, MD.

——. "Office Memorandum to Clyde Tolson." February 18, 1949. FBI #100-350512-435. National Archives and Records Administration, College Park, MD.

——. "This Is Your FBI." Washington, DC: Federal Bureau of Investigation. March 4, 1952. FBI #100-390769. National Archives and Records Administration, College Park, MD.

——. "To Clyde Tolson." August 11, 1949. https://archive.org/stream/foia_Kirkpatrick_Theodore_2/Kirkpatrick_Theodore_2_djvu.txt.

——. "To Mr. Tolson." April 11, 1952. FBI #100-350512-435. National Archives and Records Administration, College Park, MD.

——. "To Mr. Tolson." December 6, 1951. FBI #100-350512-435. National Archives and Records Administration, College Park, MD.

——. "To Mr. Tolson." December 11, 1951. https://archive.org/stream/foia_Kirkpatrick_Theodore_2/Kirkpatrick_Theodore_2_djvu.txt.

——. "To Mr. Tolson." March 4, 1952. FBI #100-390769. National Archives and Records Administration, College Park, MD.

——. "To Mr. Tolson." Washington, DC: March 10, 1948. FBI #100-340922. National Archives and Records Administration, College Park, MD.

Nizer, Louis. *My Life in Court.* New York, NY: Doubleday, 1961.

Noble, Peter. *Negro in Films.* New York, NY: Arno Press, 1949.

"No More 'Muir Incidents.' " *Business Week.* September 16, 1950.

"No 'Official' Picketing vs. Gale Sondergaard, Philly, But 'Unofficially' Maybe." *Variety.* July 11, 1956.

"Norman Granz to Receive a New Award for His Campaign on Discrimination." *Chicago Defender.* May 17, 1947, National edition.

"Notes from Narrative Reports of U.S.O. Worker in Fort Huachuca Area," n.d. Box 43, Folder 10. Shirley Graham Du Bois Papers, Schlesinger Library, Radcliffe Institute for Advanced Study, Harvard University, Cambridge, MA.

Ogilvie, Jessica P. "How Hollywood Keeps Out Women." *LA Weekly.* April 29, 2015. www.laweekly.com/news/how-hollywood-keeps-out-women-5525034.

Oliver, Myrna. "Rose Hobart; SAG Official, Blacklisted Actress." *Los Angeles Times*. August 31, 2000. http://articles.latimes.com/2000/aug/31/local/me-13393.

"Oprah Winfrey's Full Golden Globes Speech." CNN. January 10, 2018. www.cnn.com/2018/01/08/entertainment/oprah-globes-speech-transcript/index.html.

O'Reilly, Kenneth. *Hoover and the Un-Americans*. Philadelphia, PA: Temple University Press, 1983.

Osgood, Charles. "Survey Shows the Nuclear Family Is Making a Comeback." *The Osgood File*. CBS. May 2, 1996.

O'Sullivan, Denis D. "Madeline Lee, Was Madeline Fein." Federal Bureau of Investigation, October 18, 1955. FBI #100-1393334-10. National Archives and Records Administration, College Park, MD.

Ouellette, Laurie. "Inventing the Cosmo Girl: Class Identity and Girl-Style American Dreams." *Media, Culture and Society* 21, no. 3 (1999): 359–83.

Padover, Saul K. "Why Americans Like German Women." *American Mercury*. September 1946.

Parker, Dorothy. "Arrangement in Black and White." *New Yorker*. October 8, 1927.

——. *The Portable Dorothy Parker*. Ed. Marion Meade. New York, NY: Penguin Classics, 2006.

Pegler, Westbrook. "Fair Enough." *Washington Times-Herald*. September 22, 1953.

Petersen, Anne Helen. *Scandals of Classic Hollywood: Sex, Deviance, and Drama from the Golden Age of American Cinema*. New York, NY: Plume, 2014.

Pettit, Rhonda S., ed. *The Critical Waltz: Essays on the Work of Dorothy Parker*. Madison, NJ: Fairleigh Dickinson University Press, 2005.

Phillips, Julie. *James Tiptree, Jr.: The Double Life of Alice B. Sheldon*. New York, NY: Picador, 2007.

"Philly in Uproar on 'Blacklisting' Attempt Against Gale Sondergaard." *Variety*. July 4, 1956.

Pilat, Oliver. "Blacklist Series." *New York Post*. January 26, 1963.

——. "Blacklist: The Panic in TV-Radio." *New York Post*. January 26, 1953.

Pirlot, Clementine. "Working Women in 1940s Hollywood." MA Thesis. California State University, 2011.

Pollock, Dale. "Tribute Paid to Memory of Pioneer Woman Studio Chief." *Los Angeles Times*. April 14, 1984.

Potter, Claire Bond. *War on Crime: Bandits, G-Men, and the Politics of Mass Culture*. New Brunswick, NJ: Rutgers University Press, 1998.

Powers, Richard Gid. *G-Men: Hoover's FBI in American Popular Culture*. Carbondale, IL: Southern Illinois University Press, 1983.

——. "One G-Man's Family: Popular Entertainment Formulas and J. Edgar Hoover's F.B.I." *American Quarterly* 30, no. 4 (Autumn 1978): 471–92.

Pratt, David. "Actress Charges Probe Sought False Testimony." *Daily Worker*. May 11, 1955. FBI #100-393334-A. National Archives and Records Administration, College Park, MD.

Price, David H. *Threatening Anthropology: McCarthyism and the FBI's Surveillance of Activist Anthropologists*. Durham, NC: Duke University Press, 2004.

Purcell, Aaron D. *White Collar Radicals: TVA's Knoxville Fifteen, the New Deal, and the McCarthy Era*. Knoxville, TN: University of Tennessee Press, 2009.

"Rachel Bloom Upends Romantic Comedy Tropes on 'Crazy Ex-Girlfriend.'" *NPR.org*. January 17, 2017. www.npr.org/2017/01/17/510259862/rachel-bloom-upends-romantic-comedy-tropes-on-crazy-ex-girlfriend.

"Radio: Who's Blacklisted?" *Time*, August 22, 1949. http://content.time.com/time/magazine/article/0,9171,800646,00.html.

Rand, Ayn. "Screen Guide for Americans." In *Plain Talk: An Anthology from the Leading Anti-Communist Magazine of the 40s*, edited by Isaac Don Levine, 386–93. New Rochelle, NY: Arlington House, 1947.

Ransby, Barbara. *Ella Baker and the Black Freedom Movement: A Radical Democratic Vision*. Chapel Hill, NC: University of North Carolina Press, 2005.

Rapf, Joanne. "In Focus: Children of the Blacklist." *Cinema Journal* 44, no. 4 (Summer 2005): 75–115.

Reagan, Ronald. "Address Before a Joint Session of the Congress Reporting on the State of the Union." February 4, 1986. reagan2020.us/speeches/state_of_the_union_1986.asp.

Regester, Charlene B. *African American Actresses: The Struggle for Visibility, 1900–1960*. Bloomington, IN: Indiana University Press, 2010.

"Report Truman to Probe Ban Against Hazel Scott." *Chicago Defender*. October 13, 1945, Washington Bureau edition.

Robins, Natalie. *Alien Ink: The FBI's War on Freedom of Expression*. New Brunswick, NJ: Rutgers University Press, 1993.

Roddy, John. "Attempt to Bar Lena Horne from TV Show Rebuffed." *New York City Compass*. September 25, 1951, 3.

——. "Lena Horne's Manager Says Counterattack Clears Her." *New York City Compass*. October 9, 1951, 3.

Rosen, Alex. "Office Memorandum to Mr. Ladd." FBI, August 2, 1949. https://ia801708.us.archive.org/14/items/foia_Kirkpatrick_Theodore_2/Kirkpatrick_Theodore_2_text.pdf.

Rosenfeld, Seth. *Subversives: The FBI's War on Student Radicals, and Reagan's Rise to Power*. New York, NY: Picador, 2013.

Ross, Lillian. "Come In, Lassie!" *New Yorker*. February 21, 1948. www.newyorker.com/magazine/1948/02/21/come-in-lassie.

Roy, Rob. "Meet Hazel Scott, That Mystery Magnet Who Worries the Nation." *Chicago Defender*. June 16, 1945, National edition.

Russell, Robert E. "FBI Report." Los Angeles Field Office: Federal Bureau of Investigation, April 7, 1951. FBI #1308733-0. National Archives and Records Administration, College Park, MD.

Salisbury, Harrison E. "The Strange Correspondence of Morris Ernst and J. Edgar Hoover." *The Nation*. January 25, 2007. www.thenation.com/article/strange-correspondence-morris-ernst-and-j-edgar-hoover/.

St. John, Robert. *Encyclopedia of Radio and Television: The Man Behind the Microphone*. Milwaukee, WI: Cathedral Square Publishing Company, 1967.

Santiago, Denise-Marie. "Hester R. McCullough, Former Township Leader." *Philadelphia Inquirer*. March 21, 1988. http://articles.philly.com/1988-03-21/news/26277960_1_entertainers-communist-front-organizations-larry-adler.

Sanville, Richard. "Ellie," n.d. Box 13, File Folder 6. Adrian and Joan Scott Papers, American Heritage Center, University of Wyoming, Laramie, WY.

——. "Ellie Teleplay Script," n.d. Box 13, File Folder 6. Adrian and Joan Scott Papers, American Heritage Center, University of Wyoming, Laramie, WY.

"Says America 'Losing World' with Racial Politics." *Jet* 21, no. 11 (January 4, 1962): 6.

Savransky, Rebecca. "Bannon Worried Oprah Could Be 'Existential Threat' to Trump Presidency." *The Hill*. February 12, 2018. http://thehill.com/homenews/administration/373386-bannon-worried-oprah-could-be-existential-threat-to-trump-presidency.

Sbardellati, John. *J. Edgar Hoover Goes to the Movies: The FBI and the Origins of Hollywood's Cold War*. Ithaca, NY: Cornell University Press, 2012.

Scheidt, Edward. "American Business Consultants, Inc., 'CounterAttack,' Information Concerning," July 21, 1949. FBI #67-334296-1. National Archives and Records Administration, College Park, MD.

——. "Letter to Director, FBI." October 22, 1946. https://archive.org/stream/foia_Kirkpatrick_Theodore_2/Kirkpatrick_Theodore_2_djvu.txt.

——. "Letter to FBI Director." July 31, 1947. FBI #100-350512. National Archives and Records Administration, College Park, MD.

——. "To Director, FBI." February 3, 1947. https://archive.org/stream/foia_Kirkpatrick_Theodore_2/Kirkpatrick_Theodore_2_djvu.txt.

——. "To J. Edgar Hoover." September 8, 1950. FBI #67-334296-1. National Archives and Records Administration, College Park, MD.

Schiller, Bob and Bob Weiskopf. "Lucy Wants a Career." *The Lucy-Desi Comedy Hour*. Directed by Jerry Thorpe. Aired April 13, 1959, https://www.youtube.com/watch?.v=s9waRE001Vs.

Schrecker, Ellen. *The Age of McCarthyism: A Brief History with Documents.* Boston, MA: Bedford/St. Martin's, 2001.

——. *Many Are the Crimes.* Princeton, NJ: Princeton University Press, 1999.

Schudson, Michael. *The Power of News.* Boston, MA: Harvard University Press, 1996.

Schulte, Brigid. "Unlike in the 1950s, There Is No 'Typical' U.S. Family Today." *Washington Post.* September 4, 2014. www.washingtonpost.com/news/local/wp/2014/09/04/for-the-first-time-since-the-1950s-there-is-no-typical-u-s-family/.

Scott, Adrian. "Blacklist: The Liberal's Straightjacket and Its Effects on Content." *Hollywood Review* 2, no. 2 (October 1955): 1–6.

——. "Letter to Allan Scott," September 11, 1966. Box 6, File Folder 13. Adrian and Joan Scott Papers, American Heritage Center, University of Wyoming, Laramie, WY.

——. "Letter to Cerf Bennett," n.d. Box 4, "Correspondence," Folder 23, n.d. Adrian and Joan Scott Papers, American Heritage Center, University of Wyoming, Laramie, WY.

——. "Letter to Hannah Weinstein," June 19, 1957. Box 2, Folder 13. Adrian and Joan Scott Papers, American Heritage Center, University of Wyoming, Laramie, WY.

——. "Letter to Harry Miller," November 12, 1947. Box 5, "Correspondence". Adrian and Joan Scott Papers, American Heritage Center, University of Wyoming, Laramie, WY.

——. "Letter to John Briley," October 2, 1969. Box 4, "Correspondence." Adrian and Joan Scott Papers, American Heritage Center, University of Wyoming, Laramie, WY.

——. "Letter to Joseph Losey," August 1, 1960. Box 5, Folder 19, "Correspondence". Adrian and Joan Scott Papers, American Heritage Center, University of Wyoming, Laramie, WY.

——. "Robin Hood Episodes: The Cathedral," n.d. File Folder 2, 1957–58. Adrian and Joan Scott Papers, American Heritage Center, University of Wyoming, Laramie, WY.

——. "Robin Hood Episodes: The Charter," n.d. File Folder 2, 1957–58. Adrian and Joan Scott Papers, American Heritage Center, University of Wyoming, Laramie, WY.

Scott, Hazel, "Testimony of Hazel Scott." U.S. Congress, House of Representatives. Committee on Un-American Activities, Eighty-First Congress, September 22, 1950.

Scott, Joan LaCour. "Adrian's Wife," n.d. Patrick McGilligan Papers. Wisconsin Center for Film and Theater Research, Wisconsin Historical Society, Madison, WI.

Scott, Joan LaCour, and Scott, Adrian. "The Cathedral," 1957. Folder 2, 1957–58 Robin Hood Episodes. Adrian and Joan Scott Papers, American Heritage Center, University of Wyoming, Laramie, WY.

Seldes, George. "'CounterAttack' Prints Sequel to Liz Dilling's 'Red Network,' Sets Self up as Radio Censor." *In Fact.* July 17, 1950.

Sergio, Lisa. *I Am My Beloved: The Life of Anita Garibaldi.* New York, NY: Weybright and Talley, 1969.

——. *A Measure Filled: The Life of Lena Madesin Phillips Drawn from Her Autobiography.* New York, NY: R.B. Luce, 1972.

Sheldon, Alice R. "The Women-Haters," 1947. James Tiptree, Jr. Papers. University of Oregon Special Collections and University Archives, Eugene, OR.

Sheldon, Harvey. *The History of the Golden Age of Television.* N.p.: Author, 2013.

"Shelved for Red Clam Up, Gale Says." *New York News.* July 18, 1956.

Siegel, Sol. "Letter to Vera Caspary," May 19, 1947. Vera Caspary Papers, Wisconsin Historical Society, Madison, WI.

Simonson, Robert. "Madeline Lee Gilford, Actress, Producer and Widow of Jack Gilford, Is Dead." *Playbill.* April 15, 2008. www.playbill.com/article/madeline-lee-gilford-actress-producer-and-widow-of-jack-gilford-is-dead-com-149241.

Sirene, Walt H. "Gale Biberman." New York, NY: July 28, 1966. FBI #199-370749. National Archives and Records Administration, College Park, MD.

Sklaroff, Lauren Rebecca. *Black Culture and the New Deal: The Quest for Civil Rights in the Roosevelt Era.* Chapel Hill, NC: University of North Carolina Press, 2009.

Skutch, Ira. *Five Directors: The Golden Years of Radio: Based on Interviews with Himan Brown, Axel Gruenberg, Fletcher Markle, Arch Oboler, Robert Lewis Shayon.* Metuchen, NJ: Scarecrow Press, 1998.

Smethurst, James. *The New Red Negro: The Literary Left and African American Poetry, 1930–1946.* New York, NY: Oxford University Press, 1999.

Smith, Barbara. "Toward a Black Feminist Criticism." *Conditions* 1, no. 2 (October 1977): 25–44.

Smith, Glenn D., Jr. " 'The Guiding Spirit': Philip Loeb, The Battle for Television Jurisdiction, and the Broadcasting Industry Blacklist," *American Journalism* 26, no. 3 (2009): 93–126.

——. " 'It's Your America': Gertrude Berg and American Broadcasting, 1929–1956." Ph.D. dissertation, University of Southern Mississippi, 2005.

——. *Something on My Own: Gertrude Berg and American Broadcasting, 1929–1956.* Syracuse, NY: Syracuse University Press, 2007.

Smith, J.Y. "William C. Sullivan, Once High FBI Aide, Killed by Hunter." *Washington Post.* November 10, 1977. www.washingtonpost.com/archive/local/1977/11/10/william-c-sullivan-once-high-fbi-aide-killed-by-hunter/9d6295ad-cf1b-461c-a110-4d1db4ef6613/.

Smith, Judith E. "Judy Holliday's Urban Working Girl Characters in 1950s Hollywood Film." *American Studies Faculty Publication Series* Paper 6 (2010). http://scholarworks.umb.edu/amst_faculty_pubs/6.

Smulyan, Susan. *Selling Radio: The Commercialization of American Broadcasting 1920–1934.* Washington, DC: Smithsonian Institution Press, 1996.

"Socialite, Escort to Face Judge." *The Chicago American.* May 6, 1949.

Sondergaard, Gale. "We Speak of Peace." *Jewish Life*. August 1951, 6–8.

Spanos, Brittany. "Issa Rae: Why 'Insecure' Is Not Made 'for Dudes' or 'White People.'" *Rolling Stone*. www.rollingstone.com/tv/features/insecure-issa-rae-on-hbo-show-not-made-for-dudes-w500665.

Spaulding, Stacy. "Lisa Sergio: How Mussolini's 'Golden Voice' of Propaganda Created an American Mass Communication Career." Ph.D. dissertation. University of Maryland, 2005.

——. "Off the Blacklist, But Still a Target: The Anti-Communist Attacks on Lisa Sergio." *Journalism Studies* 10, no. 6 (2009): 789–804.

Special Agent in Charge, Los Angeles. "Judy Holliday Aka Judy Tuvim, Security Matter—C." Los Angeles, CA: June 14, 1950. FBI #100-368669. National Archives and Records Administration, College Park, MD.

Special Agent in Charge, New York City Field Office. "Anne Revere Rosen." New York, NY: March 21, 1962. FBI #100-336762. National Archives and Records Administration, College Park, MD.

——. "Anne Revere Rosen, Nee Anne Revere, Aka." April 24, 1958. FBI #100-101399. National Archives and Records Administration, College Park, MD.

——. "Confidential Letter to Director, FBI," May 12, 1947. FBI #100-350512-554. National Archives and Records Administration, College Park, MD.

——. "Jean Muir: Security Matter-C." October 27, 1955. FBI #100-100140. National Archives and Records Administration, College Park, MD.

——. "Madeleine Lee." New York, NY: April 23, 1954.FBI #100-393334-6. National Archives and Records Administration, College Park, MD.

——. "Madeleine Lee, Was: Madeline Lee, Madeline Rosaline Laderman, Madeline Rosalind Letterman, Madeline Gilford, Madeline Guilford, Mrs. Jacob Gellman, Mrs. Jack Guilford, Mrs. Jack Gilford, Madeline Fein, Mrs. Mitchell Fein." New York, NY: December 16, 1955. FBI #100-393334. National Archives and Records Administration, College Park, MD.

——. "Madeline Lee, Was SM-C." April 23, 1954. FBI #100-39334-6. National Archives and Records Administration, College Park, MD.

——. "Memorandum to Director, FBI," July 28, 1956. FBI #105–18873. National Archives and Records Administration, College Park, MD.

——. "To Director." July 21, 1949. FBI #100-350512. National Archives and Records Administration, College Park, MD.

——. "To Director, FBI." June 22, 1949. FBI #62-9189. National Archives and Records Administration, College Park, MD.

——. "To Director, FBI." New York, NY: February 17, 1958. FBI #100-336762-27. National Archives and Records Administration, College Park, MD.

——. “To Director, FBI.” September 27, 1950. https://archive.org/stream/foia_Kirkpatrick_Theodore_2/Kirkpatrick_Theodore_2_djvu.txt.

——. “Uta Hagen Berghof, Was SM-C.” August 22, 1956. FBI #100371261. National Archives and Records Administration, College Park, MD.

——. “Washington, Fredi.” New York, NY: November 30, 1943. FBI #100-HQ-330380. National Archives and Records Administration, College Park, MD.

Special Agent in Charge, Philadelphia. “Dorothy Rothschild Parker, Security Matter-C.” July 19, 1950. FBI #100-56075-5. National Records and Archive Administration, College, MD.

Spigel, Lynn. *Make Room for TV: Television and the Family Ideal in Postwar America.* Chicago, IL: University of Chicago Press, 1992.

Spraggs, Venice T. “Hazel Scott Won’t Play for Lily-White Press Club.” *Chicago Defender.* November 17, 1945, National edition.

Stark, Steven D. “Perry Mason Meets Sonny Crockett: The History of Lawyers and the Police as Television Heroes.” *University of Miami Law Review* 42, no. 229 (1987): 229–83.

Stein, Jean. *West of Eden: An American Place.* New York, NY: Random House, 2017.

Stern, Marlow. “When Congress Slut-Shamed Ingrid Bergman.” *Daily Beast.* November 21, 2015. www.thedailybeast.com/articles/2015/11/21/when-congress-slut-shamed-ingrid-bergman.html.

Stewart, Charles. “Sambo, Director’s Notes.” 1938. Container 1032, Box 47. Federal Theatre Project Collection, Library of Congress, Washington, DC.

Stewart, Rodney. “Mrs. Herbert Joseph (Gale) Biberman.” Los Angeles, CA: June 15, 1950. FBI #100-22800. National Archives and Records Administration, College Park, MD.

Sullivan, William C. *The Bureau: My Thirty Years in Hoover’s FBI.* New York, NY: Norton, 1979.

Swearingen, M. Wesley, and Ward Churchill. *FBI Secrets: An Agent’s Exposé.* Boston, MA: South End Press, 1995.

Szwed, John. *Billie Holiday: The Musician and the Myth.* New York, NY: Viking, 2015.

Tamm, Edwin A. “Father John F. Cronin.” April 18, 1946, 2. FBI #67-334296-5. National Archives and Records Administration, College Park, MD.

Tavel, W.S. “John G. Keenan, Former Special Agent.” FBI #1308733-0 and FBI #67E-HQ-198001. National Archives and Records Administration, College Park, MD.

——. “To Mr. Mohr.” March 30, 1959. FBI #67-198001-130. National Archives and Records Administration, College Park, MD.

Taylor, Ella. *Prime-Time Families: Television Culture in Post-War America.* Berkeley, CA: University of California Press, 1989.

Theoharis, Athan. *J. Edgar Hoover, Sex, and Crime: An Historical Antidote*. Chicago, IL: Ivan R. Dee, 1995.

Theoharis, Athan G. *The FBI: A Comprehensive Reference Guide*. Westport, CT: Greenwood Publishing Group, 1999.

——. *Spying on Americans: Political Surveillance from Hoover to the Huston Plan*. Philadelphia, PA: Temple University Press, 1978.

Theoharis, Athan G., and John Stuart Cox. *The Boss: J. Edgar Hoover and the Great American Inquisition*. New York, NY: Bantam, 1990.

"This Is Ghana Television." Tema, Ghana: The State Publishing Corporation, n.d. Box 44, Folder 6. Shirley Graham Du Bois Papers, Schlesinger Library, Radcliffe Institute for Advanced Study, Harvard University, Cambridge, MA.

Thorsson, Courtney. *Women's Work: Nationalism and Contemporary African American Women's Novels*. Charlottesville, VA: University of Virginia Press, 2013.

Tish, Pauline. "Remembering Helen Tamiris." *Dance Chronicle* 17, no. 3 (January 1, 1994): 327–60.

" 'Tom,' Big Opera, Scores Success." *Chicago Defender*. July 9, 1932.

Torrens, E.M. "Office Memorandum to F.J. Baumgardner," April 21, 1949. https://ia801708.us.archive.org/14/items/foia_Kirkpatrick_Theodore_2/Kirkpatrick_Theodore_2_text.pdf.

Trumbo, Dalton. *The Time of the Toad: A Study of Inquisition in America*. New York, NY: Perennial Library, 1972.

Tuck, Jay Nelson. "Unholy Alliance: AFTRA and the Blacklist." *The Nation*. September 3, 1955, 187–9.

Tucker, Sherrie. *Swing Shift: "All-Girl" Bands of the 1940s*. Durham, NC: Duke University Press, 2001.

Urwand, Ben. *The Collaboration: Hollywood's Pact with Hitler*. Cambridge, MA: Belknap Press, 2015.

U.S. Congress, House of Representatives. House Committee on Un-American Activities. *100 Things You Should Know About Communism*. Washington, DC: U.S. Government Printing Office, 2008.

——. *Investigation of So-Called "Blacklisting" in Entertainment Industry, House Un-American Activities Committee*. Washington, DC: U.S. Government Printing Office, 1956. http://hdl.handle.net/2027/uiug.30112102050074.

——. "Report on the Congress of American Women." Washington, DC: U.S. Government Printing Office, October 23, 1949 [1950]. http://archive.org/stream/reportoncongress1949unit/reportoncongress1949unit_djvu.txt.

Valentine, Elizabeth. "The Girls They Didn't Leave Behind Them." *New York Times Magazine*. February 10, 1946.

Van Der Horn-Gibson, Jodi. "Dismantling Americana: Sambo, Shirley Graham, and African Nationalism." *Americana: The Journal of American Popular Culture* 7, no. 1 (Spring 2008): n.p.

Vaughn, Robert. *Only Victims: A Study of Show Business Blacklisting*. New York, NY: Limelight Editions, 1972.

Vicars, John R. "Security Matter-C." Los Angeles, CA: May 11, 1945. FBI #100-370749. National Archives and Records Administration, College Park, MD.

——. "Mrs. Herbert Joseph (Gale) Biberman, with Aliases, Gale Sondergaard Biberman, Gale Sondergaard, Gail Sondergaard, Nee Edith Sondergaard." Los Angeles: May 11, 1945. FBI #100-100757-33. National Archives and Records Administration, College Park, MD.

Vogel, Shane. "Lena Horne's Impersona." *Camera Obscura* 23, no. 1 (67) (2008): 11–45.

Wald, Alan M. *Trinity of Passion: The Literary Left and the Antifascist Crusade*. Chapel Hill, NC: University of North Carolina Press, 2007.

"Walter White at Writers Meeting." *Chicago Defender*. October 9, 1943.

Wanzo, Rebecca. *The Suffering Will Not Be Televised: African American Women and Sentimental Political Storytelling*. Albany, NY: State University of New York Press, 2009.

Ward, Theodore. *The Big White Fog*. New York, NY: Nick Hern Books, 2008.

Ware, Susan. *It's One O'Clock and Here Is Mary Margaret McBride: A Radio Biography*. New York, NY: New York University Press, 2005.

Warner, Kristen. *The Cultural Politics of Colorblind TV Casting*. New York, NY/London: Routledge, 2015.

Warren, Ann L. "Word Play: The Lives and Work of Four Women Writers in Hollywood's Golden Age." Ph.D. dissertation. University of Southern California, 1988.

Washington, Fredi. "Fredi Says." *The People's Voice*. February 12, 1944.

——. "Headlines and Footlights." *The People's Voice*. May 27, 1944.

Washington, Mary Helen. "Alice Childress, Lorraine Hansberry, and Claudia Jones: Black Women Write the Popular Front." In *Left of the Color Line: Race, Radicalism, and Twentieth-Century Literature of the United States*, edited by Bill V. Mullen and James Smethurst 183–204. Chapel Hill, NC: University of North Carolina Press, 2003.

——. *The Other Blacklist: The African American Literary and Cultural Left of the 1950s*. New York, NY: Columbia University Press, 2014.

Waters, Ethel, and Charles Samuels. *His Eye is on The Sparrow: An Autobiography*. New York, NY: Da Capo Press, 1992.

Weart, William G. "Quakers Defend 'Christian' Hiring." *New York Times*. July 18, 1956.

Weaver, Warren, Jr. "Adler-Draper Suit Ends in a Deadlock." *New York Times*. May 28, 1950.

Webster, Margaret. *Don't Put Your Daughter on the Stage*. New York, NY: Knopf, 1972.

——. "Letter to the Editor" (unpublished). *New York Times*. September 29, 1958. Box 4, "Blacklisting: 1945–55. Margaret Webster Papers, Library of Congress, Washington, DC.

——. "To the Drama Editor." *New York Times*. October 1950.

Weems, Robert. *Desegregating the Dollar: African American Consumerism in the Twentieth Century*. New York, NY: New York University Press, 1998.

Weigand, Kate. *Red Feminism: American Communism and the Making of Women's Liberation*. Baltimore, MD: Johns Hopkins University Press, 2000.

Weiler, A.H. "Third World Cinema to Make Films to Get Minorities Jobs." *New York Times*. February 23, 1971. www.nytimes.com/1971/02/23/archives/third-world-cinema-to-make-films-to-get-minorities-jobs.html.

Weiner, Tim. *Enemies: A History of the FBI*. New York, NY: Random House, 2012.

——. "Hoover Planned Mass Jailing in 1950." *New York Times*. December 23, 2007, sec. Washington. www.nytimes.com/2007/12/23/washington/23habeas.html.

Weinstein, David. "Why Sarnoff Slept: NBC and the Holocaust." In *NBC: America's Network*, edited by Michele Hilmes, 98–116. Berkeley, CA: University of California Press, 2007.

Welke, Barbara Y. "Where All the Women Were White, and All the Blacks Were Men: Gender, Class, Race, and the Road to Plessy, 1855–1914." *Law and History Review* 13, no. 2 (1995): 261–316.

White, Donald W. "Anne Revere Rosen, Aka." New York, NY: April 20, 1959. FBI #100-336762-34. National Archives and Records Administration, College Park, MD.

Wilkison, Robert J. "Changed: Ray Lev, Was: Mrs. George P. Edgar." New York, NY: December 28, 1953. FBI #100-370898-10. National Archives and Records Administration, College Park, MD.

Williams, Megan E. "'Meet the Real Lena Horne': Representations of Lena Horne in *Ebony* Magazine, 1945–1949." *Journal of American Studies* 43, no. 1 (2009): 117–30.

Winter, Jana, and Sharon Weinberger. "The FBI's New U.S. Terrorist Threat: 'Black Identity Extremists.'" *Foreign Policy*. October 16, 2017. https://foreignpolicy.com/2017/10/06/the-fbi-has-identified-a-new-domestic-terrorist-threat-and-its-black-identity-extremists/.

"WMEX Radio Interview: Negro History Month." Boston, MA, February 18, 1950. Box 27, Folder 3. Shirley Graham Du Bois Papers, Schlesinger Library, Radcliffe Institute for Advanced Study, Harvard University, Cambridge, MA.

Woodard, Laurie Avant. "Performing Artists of the Harlem Renaissance: Resistance, Identity, and Meaning in the Life and Work of Fredi Washington from 1920 to 1950." Ph.D. Dissertation. Yale University, 2007.

"Writing for Television: Television and the Blacklist." Panel discussion presented at the Museum of Television and Radio Seminar Series, Los Angeles, CA. September 17, 1997.

Wylie, Philip. *Generation of Vipers*. New York, NY: Rinehart, 1955.

Yaszek, Lisa. *Galactic Suburbia: Recovering Women's Science Fiction*. Columbus, OH: Ohio State University Press, 2008.

Young, Iris Marion. "The Logic of Masculinist Protection: Reflections on the Current Security State." *Signs* 29, no. 1 (2003): 1–25.

Zanuck, Darryl. "Inter-Office Correspondence to Sol Siegel," February 14, 1949. Box 1, Folder 2, General Correspondence 1942–52. Vera Caspary Papers, Wisconsin Historical Society, Madison, WI.

——. "Inter-Office Memo to Sol Siegel," May 19, 1947. Vera Caspary Papers, Wisconsin Historical Society, Madison, WI.

Zook, Kristal Brent. *Color by Fox: The Fox Network and the Revolution in Black Television*. New York, NY: Oxford University Press, 1999.

Zurawik, David. *The Jews of Prime Time*. Waltham, MA: Brandeis University Press, 2003.

Index